Explorations in
Transactional Psychology

CONTRIBUTORS

✠ADELBERT AMES, JR.

HADLEY CANTRIL

EDWARD ENGEL

MAREA GRACE

ALBERT H. HASTORF

WILLIAM H. ITTELSON

FRANKLIN P. KILPATRICK

KEITH B. RADCLIFFE, JR.

HANS H. TOCH

WARREN J. WITTREICH

Explorations in Transactional Psychology

EDITED BY

Franklin P. Kilpatrick

NEW YORK UNIVERSITY PRESS

1961

Second Printing, 1970

© 1961 by The Institute for International Social Research
Library of Congress Catalog Card Number: 60-14321
MANUFACTURED IN THE UNITED STATES OF AMERICA

Foreword

For the past dozen years a small and informally organized group of us have been engaged in investigating problems of perception and systematically elaborating the theoretical framework which best seems to account for the many phenomena studied. Since perception, as we use the term and as we feel it must be used if it is to be meaningful, is so central a process in human experience, our work has led us into a wide variety of fields concerned with the study of human behavior.

The Ames demonstrations in perception which have provided a concrete take-off for much of our theoretical considerations and our experimentation were initially set up in Hanover, N.H. These were later transferred to Princeton University, where over seven thousand people from many nations experienced them. Recently the demonstrations were transferred to Brooklyn College to form a perceptual demonstration center under the direction of Professor W. H. Ittelson. Some of the demonstrations have been reproduced in over 150 research centers in 21 different countries and excellent research in a number of fields of inquiry is proceeding in many lands.

[v]

Effective communication with all the persons interested has become a major problem. In 1952, Dr. Kilpatrick prepared a litho-printed handbook *Human Behavior from the Transactional Point of View,* which was brought out under the auspices of the Office of Naval Research, Neuropsychiatric Branch of the Bureau of Medicine and Surgery for communication to interested colleagues. The first printing was quickly exhausted as was a second printing made in 1953.

For this reason, among others, there is a need for this revised volume which brings together a representative sample of theoretical statements and of investigations which give some idea of the sweep of the point of view expressed and of its implications for many fields of inquiry. Although a number of papers appear here as they were in the 1952 handbook, many others have been either drastically edited or deleted in the interest of making room for some important articles published since 1952 and for three papers not previously published.

Dr. Kilpatrick joins me in expressing, in behalf of our group, our special indebtedness to three people whose help and skill made so much of our work possible in its early years. John Pearson, Managing Trustee of the Institute for Associated Research during its existence, was a model as an administrator of scientific research: always trying to find ways that would make it easy or possible for investigators to do what they wanted to do and not, as are so many administrators, looking for reasons that made particular investigations difficult or well-nigh impossible. Kimball Whipple not only built all the perceptual apparatus but was ingenious and creative in its design. Alice Weymouth acted as general secretary to Mr. Ames for many years and often translated books or articles for our information. We are not here expressing our debt to the late Mr. Ames, because he is regarded as an active participant in this volume.

The major source of financial support for the work came from grants made by the Rockefeller Foundation to Princeton University. For several years the Office of Naval Research had contracts both with the Institute for Associated Research and with Princeton University. Generous support also came from both the Quaker Hill Foundation and from Mr. E. K. Hall, Jr. More recently, the Rockefeller Brothers Fund through its endowment of the Institute for International Social Research has made it possible for us to continue our systematic inqury in broader fields of social behavior.

In this volume Dr. Kilpatrick presents a systematic point of view that has stemmed from and stimulated a number of laboratory experiments. Drawing upon this same background of theory and experimentation, to which he has contributed so much, W. H. Ittelson has written a book on visual space perception, to be published soon by the Springer

Press, under the title *Visual Space Perception*. Also, the transactional view has been discussed recently with reference to the observations and writings of novelists, poets, and other observers of the human scene in *Reflections on the Human Venture* (H. Cantril and C. H. Bumstead), New York University Press, 1959.

HADLEY CANTRIL

Princeton, N.J.

Contents

[*ix*]

Contents [*xi*

Preface

It is tempting to enumerate all the papers I wanted to put into this volume, but couldn't because of practical limitations of size. A glance at the bibliography (Appendix B) shows that much more is left out than is included. My aim in making the selections has been to give the reader a broad introduction to transactional psychology, an exposure to the Ames demonstrations and to representative examples of research, and to carry the theme from simple visual perception through to social behavior.

Although specific acknowledgments to authors, journals, and publishers are made at appropriate places in the text, I wish to express here my sincere thanks to the participants in this volume. My debts to Adelbert Ames, Jr., Marea Grace, Albert Hastorf, William Ittelson, Keith Radcliffe, Jr., Hans Toch, and Warren Wittreich, whose works are reprinted, and to Hadley Cantril and Edward Engel, who wrote material especially for this book, are obvious and are gratefully acknowledged.

Reprint permissions were kindly extended by the *American Journal of Psychology,* the American Psychological Association, the *Journal of Individual Psychology,* the Journal Press, the Rutgers University Press,

Science, the Society for Applied Anthropology, and the William Alanson White Psychiatric Foundation.

Mrs. Pauline Smith not only typed a major share of the manuscript but handled patiently and efficiently innumerable details of illustrations, captions, references, and footnotes. Miss Amy Reeves aided greatly in the final stages of manuscript preparation. To them both, my thanks.

FRANKLIN P. KILPATRICK

Washington, D.C.
April, 1960

Dedicated to the memory of
Hadley Cantril

Introduction

W HAT DO WE mean by "transactional psychology"? While the
burden of this volume is to clarify what this particular abstraction refers to, it may be helpful here if we briefly describe the theme
song running through the various chapters.

The fact that we see a chair, and then are able to go to the place at
which we localize it and rest our bodies on a substantial object, does not
at first glance appear to present a psychological problem. However, the
problem is there, and it is not a superficial one. In any philosophy or
comprehensive theory of psychology, of science, or of knowledge in general, some answer to this problem is implicit. In our present age the
statement that we can never be aware of the world as such, but only of
the nervous impulses arising from the impingement of physical forces
on the sensory receptors, meets with rather easy acceptance. Once this
is accepted, however, one immediately faces the necessity of explaining
the correspondence between what is perceived and what is there.

An extremely logical, unbeatable, and scientifically useless answer is
simply to say that there is no externality; that everything exists in the

mind, and there is thus no problem of correspondence. The second, and more fruitful, approach, whose limitations are not quite so obvious, is to postulate the existence of an external world, to grant that there is some general correspondence between that world and what we perceive, and to seek some understandable and useful explanation of why that should be.

Most of the prominent perceptual theories have grown out of this latter approach. In general, they have agreed that, even though much of this correspondence may be due to learning, at some basic level there exists without learning an absolute correspondence between what is "out there" and what is in the "mind." Disagreement has, for the most part, been confined to notions concerning the level at which such natively determined correspondence occurs. At one extreme are theorists such as Titchener, for whom it occurs at the level of simple sensations or attributes (e.g., color, brightness, etc.) available to introspection, out of which more complex awarenesses are somehow compounded; at the other extreme are those Gestalt psychologists who feel that such complex perceptions as form and depth are the result of an inherent relationship between the properties of the thing perceived and the properties of the brain. Regardless, then, of the differences of opinion as to the kind of observation it must be, theorists seem to agree that there is some perceptual level at which there exists a one-to-one correspondence between experience and reality.

This belief in the possibility of reducing observation to absolute objectivity is basic to much of our current thinking. It leads to dichotomies, such as fact versus value, organism versus environment, subjective versus objective, etc. It underlies most theorizing concerning the nature of science. In psychology one is hard put to find an approach to human behavior which departs from this basic premise. Stimuli or stimulus patterns are treated as though they exist apart from the perceiving organism. Mechanical or interactional relationship between the organism and an "objectively defined" environment are sought, and purposes and values are often ruled out as not belonging in a strictly scientific psychology. A growing awareness of the false nature of such dichotomies, and the acute contrast between the theoretical possibility and the practical impossibility of leaving values and purposes out of scientific observation, has pointed up the necessity for re-examining the basic formulations from which these problems stem.

Historically, these formulations stem from experimentation which reasoned from *object* to *organism*. If one begins, thus, with an external object, an invariant correspondence between object and stimulus pattern is demonstrable. For example, it is simple geometry to show that, in standardized illumination, a specific object at a specific location relative to the eye will always yield the same stimulus pattern on the retina. Once this invariance is *in the organism* (on the retina), it is completely logical to propose that what is seen basically corresponds to what is there. This sort of analysis depends upon introducing the object at the beginning; having been introduced, it is always present.

But what happens when one turns matters around and attempts, instead, to reason from a given physiological stimulus pattern to a uniquely related external configuration? It becomes apparent that the treasured invariant relationship disappears. For example, in visual perception one is faced with the fact that any given visual stimulus-pattern can be produced by an infinity of different external conditions, and this holds true for both monocular and binocular vision. But we never see an infinity of configurations; we see just one. This means, of course, that perception cannot be "due to" the physiological stimulus pattern; some physiological stimulus probably is necessary, but it is not sufficient. There must be, in addition, some basis for the organism's "choosing" one from among the infinity of external conditions to which the pattern might be related. Thus, any notion concerning a unique correspondence between percept and object must be abandoned, and a discovery of the factors involved in the "choosing" activity of the organism becomes the key problem in perceptual theory.

Our work has been aimed at a systematic examination of such problems, and out of this examination there has been developed a basic formulation concerning the nature of knowing and of observation, which is neither a solipsistic denial of reality nor a postulation of its independent existence. This basic theory is one which has elsewhere been called "transactional." According to this view, living is an enormously complex evolving process which includes space and time and environment, as well as the organism, in an indissoluble whole. A segment in time of this process may be labeled a "transaction" (Dewey) or "occasion" (Whitehead) in which all aspects of the process are contained, including purposes, past experience in the form of assumptions, and the future in the form of expectancies. Cantril explains this position in the following way: "Each transaction of living involves numerous capacities and aspects of man's nature which operate together. Each occasion of life can occur only through an environment; is imbued with some purpose; requires action of some kind, and the registration of the consequences of action. Every action is based upon some awareness or perception, which in turn is determined by the assumptions brought to the occasion. All of these processes are interdependent. No one process could function without the others." [1]

Evidence for the necessity for such an approach is to be found in the

[1] Cantril, Hadley. *The "Why" of Man's Experience.* New York: Macmillan, 1950, p. 59

demonstrations and experiments reported in this volume, which suggest strongly that the search for absolute objectivity is a vain one. Apparently, the correspondence between percept and object is never absolute. Instead, perception is of functional probabilities, of constructs which emerge from the consequences of past action and serve as directives for furthering the purposes of the organism through action. "Percept" and "object" are but two abstracted aspects of this total process and correspondence between the two is simply a function of their being part and parcel of the same thing.

At a somewhat higher conceptual level, it would appear that the perceptual process itself is but an abstraction from a total evolving process which includes space and time and environment, as well as the organism in an indissoluble whole. Perception is that phase of the total process which is an implicit awareness of the probable consequences of purposive action with respect to some object. Man never can know more of the external world than those aspects which are directly relevant to the carrying out of his purposes. Each man's perceptions are therefore his own, unique and personal; common perceptions become possible in so far as common experiences and common strivings are shared among individuals. This approach places perceiving squarely within the context of human striving, the "thing perceived" being inseparably a part of the "process of perceiving" and both reflecting "reality" only by virtue of the active participation of the perceiver in the full-bodied, ongoing process of living.

By perception, then, is meant that part of the transactional process which is an implicit awareness of the probable significance for action of present impingements from the environment, based on assumptions related to the same or similar impingements from the environment. By assumption is meant that generally unconscious aspect of the transactional process which may be described as a weighted average of past experience in dealing with those portions of the impingements from the environment to which it is related. Assumptions function as probabilities which are built up by action, checked by action, and modified by action as the consequences of these actions are registered in relation to purposes. Taken altogether, our assumptions form our "assumptive world" which we bring to every occasion and on which our perceptions are based; therefore, the only world we know is determined by our assumptions. The assumptive world is conceptualized as that complex set of internalized, interrelated generalizations or standards which are not dependent for their effectiveness on any given reference point in space or in time. It thus provides whatever constancy there is in our environment and whatever continuity there is in our experience.

From this description the perceptual process emerges as a dynamic fusion involving cues from the environment, assumptions, and action. The process is one in which cues from the environment are related to assumptions, giving rise to perceptions which are "prognostic directives" for action. Action based on perception not only results in different cues being received from the environment, but its consequences in relation to purposes are reflected in the modification of assumptions and/or the bringing into play of different assumptions. Of course, it should not be supposed that the perceptual process proceeds in the step-by-step fashion necessitated by verbal description; it is a process involving at any one moment a complex integration of at least those factors mentioned.

Psychology and Scientific Research[1]

Hadley Cantril, Adelbert Ames, Jr., Albert H. Hastorf & William H. Ittelson

---

I. THE NATURE OF SCIENTIFIC INQUIRY

THE TRADITIONAL code of science—that is, the objectives sought and the methods of investigation—cannot satisfy the requirements of our critical times, and this is why science has failed to measure up to the opportunities and obligations before it. The generally accepted ideas of what natural science is and what it is for are out of date and need radical revision.—C. J. HERRICK (21)

A feeling of urgency for a more adequate understanding of man and his social relations can be sensed in today's intellectual atmosphere. People are becoming more and more anxious about the ability of psychologists and social scientists to help solve the problems arising from

[1] Reprinted in slightly modified form from *Science*, 1949, *110*, Nos. 2862, 2863, and 2864, pp. 461–64, 491–97, 517–22, by permission of the authors and publisher.

our technological advances and from the swift social transitions they leave in their wake. But, unfortunately, what Herrick has said about the natural sciences applies especially to those sciences which deal with man—psychology and the social sciences in general. Moreover, in these sciences, in contrast to the physical sciences, there seems to be less agreement as to what constitutes significant research.

Obviously, an increase in our understanding of man can come about only as we extend our empirical knowledge and improve our formulations through research of demonstrated significance. Before that is possible we must increase our understanding of the scientific process through which discoveries are made. But sometimes the scientist's interest in building up the content of his discipline sidetracks him from a consideration of the scientific process itself and creates a lag in the understanding and improvement of scientific tools. What follows is an attempt to clarify our thinking about the nature of scientific research in those fields which take upon themselves the primary responsibility of accounting for man's thoughts and behavior. Only then will such research accomplish what we have a right to expect of it.

We shall first consider the nature of scientific inquiry, trying to find out why man pursues scientific inquiry, anyway—what function it serves him and what steps seem to be involved. We shall then distinguish between scientific inquiry and scientific method—a distinction which seems necessary to avoid certain pitfalls and to assure a scientific progress. Then we shall try to point out some of the specific implications to be derived for psychology from a better understanding of the nature of scientific inquiry and the role of scientific method, and we shall indicate to what degree science can be "objective." Finally, some suggestions will be made which might accelerate the kind of scientific research that will increase our understanding of man.

The apparent reason for scientific inquiry is essentially the reason for any inquiry—to solve a problem. Scientific inquiry can never be understood if it is somehow put on a pedestal and viewed as something remote and apart from man's everyday activities. "Science," says Conant, "emerges from the other progressive activities of man to the extent that new concepts arise from experiments and observations" (7, p. 24).

These activities of life are carried through in an environment which includes people, artifacts, the phenomena of nature. Man's only contact with this environment is through his senses, and the impressions man's senses give him are cryptograms in the sense that they have no meaning unless and until they become functionally related to man's purposive activities. The world man creates for himself through what Einstein has called the "rabble of the senses" is one that takes on a degree of order, system, and meaning as man builds up through tested experience a pattern of assumptions and expectancies on which he can base action.

What man brings to any concrete event is an accumulation of assumptions, of awarenesses, and of knowledge concerning the relatively determined aspects of his environment as derived from his past experiences. But since the environment through which man carries out his life transactions is constantly changing, any person is constantly running into hitches and trying to do away with them. The assumptive world a person brings to the "now" of a concrete situation cannot disclose to him the undetermined significances continually emerging; and so we run into hitches in everyday life because of our inadequate understanding of the conditions giving rise to a phenomenon, and our ability to act effectively for a purpose becomes inadequate.

When we try to grasp this inadequacy intellectually and get at the "why" of the ineffectiveness of our purposeful action we are adopting the attitude of scientific inquiry. Man as scientist tries to understand what aspect of his environment is responsible for a hitch and then calls upon what knowledge he has that is relevant to an understanding of the determined, predictable nature of the particular phenomenon in question. Modern man uses the scientific method as a tool because he has found empirically that he can increase his understanding and act more effectively if his pursuits are guided by some knowledge concerning the determined aspects of the phenomenal world. G. H. Mead pointed out (24, p. 41) that

> . . . Every discovery as such begins with experiences which have to be stated in terms of the biography of the discoverer. The man can note exceptions and implications which other people do not see and can only record them in terms of his own experience. He puts them in that form in order that other persons may get a like experience, and then he undertakes to find out what the explanation of these strange facts is.

Since the scientist's acquired purpose is to increase his understanding of a certain range of phenomena, when he experiences a hitch in his understanding of such phenomena he tries to bring to conscious awareness the reason for the hitch; that is, he tries to formulate intellectual concepts that will explain away the hitch. He does this by examining the probable conditional relationships except for which he, as an experiencing individual in a concrete situation, would not be faced with the hitch. He abstracts out of the hitch situation those aspects he believes are probably necessary to his understanding of the original hitch. In his inquiry the scientist arbitrarily treats these abstracted aspects of a phenomenon as if they existed in their own right. He does not do this simply because he wants to but because he has to, in order to recall and manipulate the phenomenon intellectually. The abstractions man is able to form have on him what Dewey and Bentley characterize as a tremendous "liberative effect," making possible the voluntary, controlled, conceptual thinking necessary for scientific inquiry and for the use of scientific method.

From this point of view, we might say in general that science is an activity designed by man to increase the reliability and verifiability of his assumptive world. For it would appear that in the last analysis any scientific pursuit—no matter how abstruse it seems—is carried on because it is somehow of concern to man. Science is the human effort to understand more about nature and human nature in verifiable, determined terms. The word "determined" is used here in the scientific sense as meaning high in prognostic reliability. From this it is clear that real progress in any science involves an awareness of our assumptive worlds, a consciousness of their inadequacy, and a constant, self-conscious attempt to change them so that the intellectual abstractions they contain will achieve increasing breadth and usefulness. Real progress in science means much more than merely adding to existing knowledge.

The processes involved in scientific inquiry would seem to be somewhat as follows: (1) sensing the inadequacy of the conceptual aspects of our assumptive world, thereby being faced with a problem for which we must seek an answer; (2) deciding on all those aspects of a phenomenon that might have a significant bearing on the problem: deciding on those aspects except for which the functional activities in question would not exist; (3) picking out from the various aspects assumed to be involved those that seem most important in terms of the original hitch we faced and that will serve as bases for standards we can think about and manipulate; (4) working out some method of changing those aspects we have chosen as variables or bases for standards and conducting our empirical investigations accordingly; (5) modifying our assumptive world on the basis of the empirical evidence concerning the validity of formulations that have resolved an immediate problem.

The solving of the immediate problem will automatically give rise to new hitches and the above process constantly repeats itself.[2]

---

[2] There seems to be a striking similarity between the processes used in scientific inquiry and the processes man makes use of in building up the assumptive world. Both science and common sense can be regarded as functional activities man uses in carrying out his life transactions. The method of scientific inquiry seems in many ways to be an unconscious imitation of those age-old processess man has employed in his common-sense solutions of problems. In common-sense activity, the assumptions and awarenesses on which man depends for effective action are the hypotheses he has built up from his many experiences; weighted averages he unconsciously uses to give him a high prognosis for effective action.

Specifically, it seems that scientific inquiry has two major functions for man. First, it provides man with a bundle of what are called "scientific facts." This bundle is composed of his up-to-the-now understandings of the determined, predictable aspects of nature and is used by him for purposes of prediction and control. There are essentially two varieties of these scientific facts: general statements of relationships of determined aspects of nature which we refer to as "scientific laws" and which, in the physical sciences, tend to be expressed in mathematical formulas; second, applications of these general laws to concrete situations for purposes of verification, specific prediction, or control. The characteristic of all these generalized scientific laws is that they disclose predictable aspects of types of phenomena no matter where or when they occur, irrespective of actual concrete situations.

A second function of science is that it provides a conceptual reorganization of the knowledge man has already acquired of the determined aspects of nature. Here we are trying to increase our range of understanding, or, as Dewey and Bentley phrase it, to improve our "specification"; that is, our accuracy in naming (13, 14). Here, for example, the specifications involved in relativity are more accurate namings of phenomena than are Newton's concepts and, in this sense, Newton's concepts are not to be regarded as "wrong." This function of science includes that of increasing the range of man's conceptual knowledge through the discovery of more and more predictable aspects of nature that up to the present time remain undetermined.

UNDERSTANDING AND PREDICTION. The aim of science is often defined as the attempt to increase the accuracy of our predictions. While the accuracy of predictions is clearly a most important criterion of progress in scientific formulation, emphasis on prediction alone can easily obscure the more fundamental aim of science covered by the word "understanding." When we use the word "understanding" we are giving emphasis to the importance of increasing the range of our conceptual knowledge. Increased accuracy of prediction will be an inevitable co-product of increased understanding in this sense. Any increase in understanding is

---

There are, however, certain important differences between the steps involved in pursuing scientific inquiry and the apparent processes that constitute common sense. A most important difference is the fact that, in using scientific inquiry, man is the operator who decides what he is going to operate on and how. In an everyday life situation, however, man is not only the operator but is also being operated on and must carry out his activities in the midst of the situation itself. When we meet hitches in everyday life and try to overcome them with hunches for effective action we test these hunches by the action itself in a more or less insightful, more or less conscious way. In scientific inquiry, on the other hand, hunches are tested by controlled experiments and a deliberate attempt is made to intellectualize the processes involved (cf. 12).

also inevitably accompanied, sooner or later, by an increased ability to control variables and to apply our knowledge. Understanding also avoids the implication of a rigid determinism which seems, among other things, to be inconsistent with the fundamental indeterminism of modern physics.

Every scientific investigator must bear in mind that it is impossible for scientific research to disclose the unique specificity involved in any one actual occasion—e.g., the student of modern physics knows that there is no law governing the behavior of an individual atom. The investigator must also remember that it is impossible to predict with any complete accuracy the specific nature of growth and emergence, which are themselves undetermined. While it is impossible to determine the undetermined nature of emergence, it is still possible to increase our scientific knowledge about emergence through understanding more about the relatively determined phenomena immediately related to these undetermined emergent aspects. For example, we may hope to understand more about the extent of the undetermined field; to understand more about the conditions which make it possible for the undetermined aspects to emerge. In other words, our understanding of emergence can improve only in so far as we become more and more aware of the boundaries of our determined world.

It is here that many of those who equate science with prediction or who use a narrow working definition of operationism are also those who will say they want nothing to do with the speculations of philosophy. Yet it is only by taking the philosopher's point of view, by bringing in freely all factors that might conceivably be involved in a single situation, that we can become aware of the boundaries of our up-to-now determined scientific world. In discussing the role of philosophy, Conant writes that "there must be constant critical appraisal of the progress of science and in particular of scientific concepts and operation" (7, p. 13f). In their book on *The Evolution of Physics,* Einstein and Infeld repeatedly emphasize the new philosophic views which have both helped to evolve and have evolved from physical research. Any scientific investigator who pushes his field of inquiry beyond the realm of the determinable and the repeatable out into the no man's land of emergence will inevitably become entangled with metaphysical problems. In so doing he can hope that what is metaphysical for him today can tomorrow be part of the understood, physically determined, repeatable, and verifiable.

TRANSACTIONAL OBSERVATION. Our own philosophical basis for our thinking concerning the nature and function of scientific inquiry and scientific method should be made explicit. We are using as our take-off point what Dewey and Bentley have referred to in a series of articles as a "transactional approach." [3] What they mean by the term *transactional* can best be gathered by their own words. "Observation of this general (transactional) type sees man-in-action not as something radically set over against an environing world, nor yet as merely action 'in' a world, but as action *of* and *by* the world in which the man belongs as an integral constituent" (13, p. 228). Under this procedure all of man's behavings, "including his most advanced knowings," are treated as "activities not of himself alone, nor even as primarily his, but as processes of the full situation of organism-environment" (15, p. 506). "From birth to death every human being is a *Party,* so that neither he nor anything done or suffered can possibly be understood when it is separated from the fact of participation in an extensive body of transactions—to which a given human being may contribute and which he modifies, but only in virtue of being a partaker in them" (12, p. 198).

Dewey and Bentley distinguish this transactional procedure from two other procedures which they feel have largely dominated the history of science up till now. First is what they call the antique view of "self-action, where things are viewed as acting under their own powers." Second is the interaction view of classical mechanics, "where thing is balanced against thing in causal interconnection." In transactional observation, "systems of description and naming are employed to deal with aspects and phases of action, without final attribution to 'elements' or other presumptively detachable or independent 'entities,' 'essences,' or 'realities,' and without isolation of presumptively detachable 'relations' from such detachable 'elements' " (15, p. 509).[4]

While it is easy enough to understand this point of view intellectually, it is not nearly so easy to put it into operation in pursuing actual scientific inquiry. It tends to go against the grain of the psychologist's working procedures to regard any formulation merely as a certain "connection of conditions" (11, p. 217). It is perhaps particularly difficult for psychologists to understand the full implications of the transactional

---

[3] Since this article was written, Dewey and Bentley have brought together in a single volume, *Knowing and the Known* (Boston: Beacon Press, 1949), references 12, 13, 14, 15 and 16 cited here, together with other articles previously published by them.

[4] In citing these distinctions made by Dewey and Bentley we are not implying (and they may not be) that in our own view either self-action or interaction can by any means be completely ruled out in any adequate explanation. Self-action is seen in the behavior of the simplest bodily cell, in the uniqueness of individual behavior, in the behavior of "nations," etc., while interactional assumptions appear to be essential first steps in providing an intellectual grasp of the form for the flow of transactional processes. The role of self-action and interaction in an inclusive transactional view must be left open as a problem, and cannot be considered here in detail.

point of view, because, as Dewey and Bentley have pointed out, "The interactional treatment, as everyone is aware, entered psychological inquiry just about the time it was being removed from basic position by the physical sciences from which it was copied" (16, p. 546). But we must remember that psychology, by comparison, is still in its infancy, that the transactional approach, which Dewey and Bentley trace to the preface of Clerk Maxwell's *Matter and Motion,* dated 1876, antedated the first psychological laboratory.[5]

II. SCIENTIFIC INQUIRY AND SCIENTIFIC METHOD

WE HAVE HAD to discuss the nature of, and the apparent reason for, scientific inquiry because "scientific research" has so often been thought of merely as a technique or method of investigation. What we know as the scientific method is a means for pursuing scientific inquiry. If we do not bear this in mind, real progress in scientific research is liable to be thwarted. For the implicit equating of scientific inquiry and scientific method to a technique of investigation leaves out an all-important consideration: the problem of formulating a problem for scientific investigation. For the formulation of the problem for investigation must contain within itself the possibility of going beyond what is now scientifically established if it is to satisfy the definition of scientific research. If the formulation of the problem does not do this, then succeeding steps in investigation are futile.

Although there is likely to be little argument here, some "research" in psychology seems to reflect only a lip service to this fundamental tenet. It may be appropriate to underscore the point here in the words of modern scientists. Whitehead has pointed out that "no systematic thought has made progress apart from some adequately general working hypothesis, adapted to its special topic. Such an hypothesis directs observation and decides upon the mutual relevance of various types of evidence. In short, it prescribes method" (30, p. 286). Einstein and Infeld have written that "the formulation of a problem is often more essential than its solution, which may be merely a matter of mathematical or experimental skill. To raise new questions, new possibilities, to

[5] Since this was written we have found in Arnold J. Toynbee's *Greek Historical Thought* (A Mentor Book published by arrangement with Beacon Press, May, 1952) reference to a much earlier use of transactionalism by the Greek historian Polybius (201–120 B.C.). Apparently he employed the Greek equivalent of the word with essentially the same meaning. We are sure that Dewey, Bentley, and Ames, all of whom died before we happened to run across this information, would have been as fascinated by it as we were.

regard old problems from a new angle, requires creative imagination and makes a real advance in science" (17, p. 95). Oppenheimer indicates that the experimental techniques of science enable us to define and detect our "errors of conception" (26, p. 22).

It should be emphasized that, if an hypothesis is to be regarded as adequate, it must be more than a statement or description of current data and more than a prediction that data will reproduce themselves. An hypothesis must be tested, in terms of both its ability to predict immediate events and its promise of leading to further, more adequate hypotheses. For in scientific procedure there is a never-ending process of hypothesizing, a constant flow of one hypothesis from another, with each hypothesis trying to go beyond established formulations in its inclusiveness.[6]

It is the way in which the investigator poses his problem that determines where he will come out—what functional activities he will feel have a bearing on the problem, which of these he will use as the bases for standards in empirical investigation, and what methodological procedures he will follow or try to devise. In this connection it is relevant to note that the popular conception of what makes a scientist "great" is that he has solved problems that have long baffled others.

While this may be true enough, a review of the history of science will show that, in general, the solution of a problem is relatively easy once the problem has been posed; and that the real scientific contribution of those scientists we now regard as outstanding is due to the way in which they have formulated problems which they or others have solved. The tremendous advances in the physical sciences since the seventeenth century, for example, are due more to improved formulations than to changes in methodology. In the seventeenth century and continuing into the twentieth, science sought all-inclusive "laws" and felt that reality was firmly in hand. But today both all-inclusive laws and reality seem more elusive than ever. Contemporary physics is seeing its ultimate particle disappear, physiology is realizing that it is not dealing with the classical closed energy system. The need for a basic conceptual reformulation to bring about newer and greater understanding is apparent on all sides. In his history of science, Dampier-Whetham has noted that

---

[6] In a memorandum concerning the conceptualization of novel problems, Horace Fries has called attention to the necessity of making a distinction between an increase in our understanding and the solution of an immediate problem. He points out that "the degree of success in the resolution of the difficulty is always relative; i.e., better or worse relative to the interests or desires affected. But the *solution* of a problem brings about an adequate *resolution* of the difficulty in proportion to the adequacy in which the difficulty is organized into a problem; i.e., the adequacy of the problemization of the difficulty" (20).

"insight, imagination, and perhaps genius are required firstly to pick out the best fundamental concepts" (8, p. 457).

SEARCH VERSUS RESEARCH. Much that now passes for scientific research, not only in psychology but in many fields, has precious little to do with what may be honestly called scientific pursuit. But the surface similarity between much current work and real scientific investigation may be sufficient to deceive the investigator himself. If investigators are not to hoodwink themselves and each other and pervert scientific inquiry for some end that has little if anything to do with increasing our understanding of man, it is clearly imperative that they be concerned as consciously as possible with research that will bring about major reformulations. Otherwise, they are forced to close their eyes to important problems that face them or to devote themselves only to methodological problems, rationalizing these activities as research.

One variety of this perversion is represented in the shotgun approach, in which the idea seems to be that, if one only gathers enough data, possibly with the use of new gadgets or apparatus, one must sooner or later come out with some sort of scientific result. A precedent for this type of activity was set by Francis Bacon, who held that "by recording and tabulating all possible observations and experiments, the relations would emerge almost automatically" (9, p. 58). In the three hundred years since Bacon's time, many investigators have proceeded either without any clear hypothesis or with what they call "limited hypotheses," often so limited that they cannot possibly provide a springboard for further emergence. Much of such data today is concerned with correlational relationships. The situation is such that to an outside observer reviewing the history of modern thought psychology seems to be merely "trying correlation after correlation in the hope of stumbling on something significant" (29, p. 495).

Another perversion of scientific method is found in the tendency in some areas of psychology to work out elaborate classifications, with the implication that, if the behavior of an individual can only be properly pigeonholed in some static system, then further analysis of a functional nature is relatively unimportant for understanding. Karl Pearson's emphasis on classification as a major pursuit of science undoubtedly did a great deal to establish this misconception. One needs only to review the literature in the field of personality or to watch many clinicians diagnose psychiatric patients to see how some men in these areas are struggling to free themselves from older classificatory systems.

Scientific inquiry and scientific method are also not to be confused with investigations limited solely to a so-called "quantitative approach." An overconcentration on problems of measurement as such can easily sidetrack the investigator from the more important concentration on what data are significant to gather and can blind him completely to the problem of problemization, with its concurrent problem of selecting the standards worth measuring. Furthermore, those who are wedded solely to a quantitative approach are all too frequently unwilling to tackle problems for which there are no available quantitative techniques, thus limiting themselves to research impressive only in the elaborate quantitative treatment of data. Current attempts to refine sampling techniques in the field of public opinion research, for example, while indispensable, run the danger of making investigators myopic to certain areas of inquiry that would seem much more important for an understanding or prediction of public behavior—for example, the problem of asking the right questions, of determining the surety of opinion under different circumstances, or the effect of different interviewing situations on response. The current vogue of factor analysis in the study of personality, while most significant as a means of testing a theory as Eysenck's report shows (18), frequently reflects insufficient consideration of the relevance or adequacy of the variables thrown into the hopper for analysis.

THE FUNCTION OF EXPERIMENTATION AND MEASUREMENT. In saying that what now passes for research (scientific inquiry instrumented by scientific method) is often only scientific pretension, we do not mean to imply at all that reasonable problems for scientific research can be formulated or operated on without including empirical investigation. Experimentation is clearly indispensable as a test of formulation. An hypothesis can be tested only if one is able to do something with it. But it is often forgotten that the value of an experiment is directly proportional to the degree to which it aids the investigator in formulating better problems. While a single experiment may solve a problem, it can never give us complete understanding. If an investigator believes that by solving a problem he has achieved complete understanding, it only shows that his problem has been defined inadequately and is not a step in the constant, never-ending scientific search for more and more comprehensive formulations.

The importance of any scientific experiment in which relevant variables are manipulated must be in terms of the breadth of the formulation it has a bearing on. It should be borne in mind that the first and most significant step in experimentation is to determine *if* the variation of one abstracted phenomenon affects other abstracted phenomena at all. The next most disclosing step is to determine *how* the variation of one abstracted phenomenon affects other abstracted phenomena. We confirm or deny the validity of an hypothesis by determining if and how the manipulation of one variable affects another variable or the total group of phenomena in which we are interested. In the process of using the scientific method of relevant variables, the investigator can discover if and how variables are affected only with reference to some inclusive, higher-order formulation. Otherwise, relevant variables could be manipulated forever without making any scientific advance at all. It is also imperative to bear in mind that *how much* a change in one variable affects another variable does not give us new insight on the "if" and "how" relationship. We determine how much one variable affects another in order to increase our prediction and control, not to increase our range of understanding.

In the process of experimentation, the investigator must be ready to use whatever procedures appear most relevant to an understanding of the problem at hand. These procedures will be both quantitative and nonquantitative. Obviously, if we select some phenomenon or characteristic as a variable for experimentation, we can do so only because it exists in some degree, some amount, some quantity in relation to the abstracted standard upon which it is based. In scientific research quantitative and nonquantitative procedures are interdependent, and highly refined quantitative investigation may be necessary before one can establish a nonquantitative formulation as, for example, the relationship between the Michelson-Morley experiment and Einstein's formulation. Thus, the establishment of any dichotomy between quantitative and nonquantitative procedure is an artificial barrier to scientific progress, separating and taking apart what really belong together in scientific method. Scientific inquiry will be strapped if the investigator feels that he cannot be scientific without being one hundred per cent quantitative.

Because scientific methodology is now so often equated solely with quantitative procedures, it may be useful here to distinguish what seems to us to be the function of quantitative procedures in scientific method.

First is the design of controlled experiments or other systematic investigations which involve measurement for the specific purpose of checking a hunch, validating an hypothesis, or testing a general law in a specific concrete situation. As we have already emphasized, the verification of this hypothesis is itself to be regarded only as a steppingstone to further, more inclusive hypotheses. In the fields of psychology and the social sciences, this general function usually translates itself into the purpose of checking some experienced relationships and causalities in an effort to intellectualize and systematize hunches that seem significant.

A second role played by quantitative measurement is the systematic recording of data. But it must be emphasized again in this connection that the accumulation of quantitative results is profitable only to the extent that some previous intellectual excursions have led to an hypothesis which is subjectively held with some degree of surety. Recording without an hypothesis in mind, if it is indeed possible at all, has no place in scientific method.[7]

A third function of quantitative research is to establish norms for the purpose of studying single cases in psychology, for example, individual or group variations. As any experimental, clinical, or social psychologist knows, quantitative standards are of the utmost importance in predicting how specific individuals or groups of individuals will react in specific situations. But again it must be borne in mind that one undertakes measurement for such purposes only after the formulation of some hunch which may itself be based on nonquantitative evidence. We must furthermore remember that we can only measure something relative to an arbitrarily established norm.

Whereas most investigators would undoubtedly give a nod of approval to the thesis that quantitative and nonquantitative procedures are interdependent in scientific method, much current work in psychology and the social sciences indicates that in practice this kind of thinking and research planning is not followed, and that, on the contrary, there is often a conscious or unconscious attempt to imitate the physical scientists, in the false belief that their success has been due chiefly to the quantitative techniques they have designed. It may, therefore, be worth a brief historical glance at Isaac Newton's procedure to gain some perspective

[7] Occasionally, Charles Darwin's work has been used as an illustration of the way in which an hypothesis suddenly appears if one can only accumulate sufficient data. But in the famous first paragraph of his introduction to the *Origin of Species* (1859), Darwin clearly belies any such contention:

"When on board H.M.S. 'Beagle' as naturalist, I was much struck with certain facts in the distribution of the organic beings inhabiting South America, and in the geological relations of the present to the past inhabitants of that continent. These facts, as will be seen in the latter chapters of this volume, seemed to throw some light on the origin of species—that mystery of mysteries, as it has been called by one of our greatest philosophers. On my return home, it occurred to me, in 1837, that something might perhaps be made out of this question by patiently accumulating and reflecting on all sorts of facts which could possibly have any bearing on it. After five years' work I allowed myself to speculate on the subject, and drew up some short notes; these I enlarged in 1844 into a sketch of the conclusions, which then seemed to me probable. From that period to the present day I have steadily pursued the same object. I hope that I may be excused for entering on these personal details, as I give them to show that I have not been hasty in coming to a decision."

We find in Darwin's letter this further statement (10, p. 183):

"In October, 1838; that is, fifteen months after I had begun my systematic inquiry, I happened to read for amusement Malthus on population, and, being well prepared to appreciate the struggle for existence which everywhere goes on from long-continued observation of the habits of animals and plants, it at once struck me that under these circumstances favorable variations would tend to be preserved, and unfavorable ones to be destroyed. The result of this would be the formation of new species. Here, then, I had at last got a theory by which to work."

on the role of quantitative experimentation in verifying and extending nonquantitative observations.

Although Newtonian concepts have been superseded, the Newtonian method remains essentially unchanged and still provides the framework for most of modern science. While Newton's aim was to find absolute mathematical "laws of nature," his method clearly consisted of (1) simplification and isolation of fundamental concepts, (2) formulation of relevant hypotheses on the basis of these essentially nonquantitative concepts, and (3) intensive quantitative verification and amplification of these hypotheses. Although the concepts of mass and the mutual attraction of gravitation are inherent in a falling apple, it is doubtful if they would ever emerge from a statistical study of *all* falling objects on the face of the globe. As Newton expressed it, "Our purpose is only . . . to apply what we discover in some simple cases, as principles, by which . . . we may estimate the effects thereof in more involved cases." The inverse of this, the attempt to find the "principles" in the welter of "involved cases," would have seemed senseless to Newton.

In developing his methodology, which he nowhere explicity defines, Newton was in effect systematizing what had become over the centuries the *de facto* method of the "natural philosophers." Nineteen hundred years before Newton there was sufficient evidence for Aristarchus to advance his heliocentric concept of the universe. This significant concept was, of course, lost until Copernicus, reading the ancients, discovered that some philosophers had "thought the earth was moved." "When for this reason, therefore, I had conceived its possibility, I myself also began to meditate upon the mobility of the earth." The immediate result of this fruitful hypothesis was, of course, a systematic theory which, however, still depended for its acceptance on the principle of mathematical simplicity. Galileo, sensing the importance of experimental verification, provided the last historic step by means of his telescope.

The Newtonian era probably represents one of the most significant and fruitful epochs in human thought. Relevant to our discussion here, the birth of scientific inquiry was accompanied by a formulation of concepts which have determined and dominated thinking up to the present day. Copernicus meditated "upon the mobility of the earth." Newton, age 23, "began to think of gravity extending to ye orb of the Moon." Kepler gave support to the Copernican system because "I have attested it as true in my deepest soul," and "I contemplate its beauty with incredible and ravishing delight." Harvey "began to think whether there might not be a motion [of the blood], as it were, in a circle." Huygens and others formulated the principle of the conservation of what later was termed "kinetic energy." The list is virtually endless. In every area of human thought startling and productive contributions were made. Since there is no reason to suppose that the seventeenth century was especially propitious for the birth of genius, one wonders if the productivity of this period may not be attributed to a fortunate blending of unfettered speculation coupled with a new awareness of the need for empirical verification at every step. Remove the speculation and only barren measurement remains.

OPERATIONISM. In the past quarter century the basic tenets of operationism have so interested all science and have become so ingrained in the thinking of most scientific investigators that no discussion of the role of experimentation in scientific inquiry can be complete without a consideration of the place of operationism, which is, historically, a "recent formulation of some of the essential features of the experimental method and of empiricism generally" (19, p. 250).

The impetus for operationism came from Bridgman in physics with the recognition that concepts such as distance have different meanings when used in different contexts. The concept is, therefore, a construct of the observer and not "a thing in itself." It follows that, if the variables with which an experimenter deals are products of the experimenter's ingenuity and cannot be specified by pointing to them, then they must be specified by pointing to the procedures employed by the experimenter in creating his constructs. It is only by pointing out the procedures employed in experimentation that the investigator can convey to others the constructs he is dealing with.

Unfortunately, however, the generality of Bridgman's approach has sometimes been lost sight of. There is nothing in the general statement of operationism which delimits, or in any way prescribes, the defining operation to be used. Bridgman himself has asserted that "any method of describing the conditions is permissible which leads to a characterization precise enough for the purpose in hand, making possible the recovery of the conditions to the necessary degree of approximation" (2, p. 246). Those writers who assert that defining operations must necessarily be "physicalistic" are gratuitously adding a restriction not inherent in the operational approach. This insistence probably traces back to the feeling that physicalistic constructs are somehow more "real" than others and has led to a fundamental misconception and perversion of the operational approach as originally stated.

The inhibiting effect of this artifical restriction has probably not been severe in those sciences that are more closely concerned with the physicalistic. In psychology, however, this has tended to exclude the use of psychological constructs and, as Pratt has stated, "to place a stamp of approval on certain limited fields of research in which hypotheses can

be neatly formulated in the language of the older sciences" (28, p. 268).
We have indicated that a study of relationships alone does not constitute
scientific research. Real research must always involve constantly higher-
order abstractions. In the field of psychology many of these abstractions
cannot possibly be "pointed to" in any narrow operational sense, and
many of them are not easy to manipulate experimentally. While a scientific investigator must rely upon operational concepts, he must remember
at the same time, as Feigl has said, that "operationism is not a system
of philosophy. It is not a technique for the formation of concepts or
theories. It will not by itself produce scientific results. These are brought
about by the labor and ingenuity of the researchers" (19, p. 258).

SELECTIONS OF STANDARDS. A major problem confronting any investigator is the selection or discovery of the standards to use in his investigation. The dictionary defines a standard as "that which is set up and
established by authority as a rule for the measures of quantity, weight,
extent, value, or quality."

The problem of selecting standards is much more complicated than
is often realized, for the reason that the conditional relationships we
abstract out of a total situation and except for which the situation would
not exist do not themselves exist in their own right, nor is there any
adequate intellectual explanation of their existence. These conditional
relationships or aspects of a total phenomenon that the scientist calls
"variables" are not God-given and are not limited. Einstein and Infeld
point out that "physical concepts are free creations of the human mind,
and are not, however it may seem, uniquely determined by the external
world" (17, p. 33). Any adjective or any adverb can serve as a potential
basis for a variable. Variables that provide the bases for standards are
purely the creations of man, enabling him to formulate an abstract,
common, determined, phenomenal world. The variables employed in
any scientific research are based on intuitive judgments and in any
concrete investigation depend upon the way in which the investigator
has formulated his problem. Since problems are formulated differently
in different fields of inquiry, the aspect of a phenomenon that we choose
in one field to serve as the basis for a standard in that field will not
necessarily be applicable in another field of inquiry. Furthermore, the
aspects of a phenomenon that may serve as a basis for standards within
any one field will vary according to the nature of the hitch in a concrete
situation.

Here words play their familiar tricks even with the thinking of the
scientist, who may tend to forget that in his necessary use of word symbols for his thinking and communication (space, time, IQ, attitude, etc.)
he is employing abstractions which he cannot, as a scientist, implicitly

or unconsciously assume as real in investigation. It is only to the extent that the investigator is aware of his own transformation of adjectival or adverbial relationships into noun qualities that he maintains the possibility of discovering new conditional relationships except for which a phenomenon would not exist. If abstracted characteristics of the situation are unconsciously reified, complacency or a defensive attitude results.

When we decide on a standard we take some aspect of a phenomenon, some variable, as a basis for measurement. Since the phenomena with which science deals are so enormously varied, the quantitative units employed in any investigation will depend on the nature of the problem at hand—e.g., distance will be measured in angstrom units or in light years. Also, obviously, we cannot necessarily quantify one standard in the same way that we do other standards. While precise units of measurement may be applicable in the physical sciences, in psychology, if we are using some aspect of experience as the basis for a standard, we may have to be satisfied with crude introspective measures such as "more than" or "less than." Whitehead has pointed out that "we must entirely separate psychological time, space, external perception, and bodily feeling from the scientific world of molecular interaction. This strange world of science dwells apart like the gods of Epicurus, except that it has the peculiar property of inducing our minds to play upon us the familiar antics of the senses" (32, p. 62).

Since every standard is based on a man-made assumption, and since it is possible for man to use an infinite number of abstracted subphenomena as bases for standards, the criterion for the selection of what shall be used as the basis for a standard is essentially its usefulness in determining whether or not the abstracted subphenomenon with which we are dealing is constant, verifiable, and potentially helpful in solving our original problem. Also, of course, the basis to be used for our standards must be subject to voluntary recall and to intellectual manipulation.

How do we proceed to select the standards we will use in actual empirical investigation? Since we must start with the nature of the particular hitch we have experienced, abstract generalizations or rules cannot be given. The best that can be done is to describe the apparent functional process that goes on.

It seems to be something like this: In the course of following an acquired interest in understanding why certain phenomena occur (in physics, biology, psychology, and other sciences), we encounter a difficulty which no previous investigator has resolved to our intellectual satisfaction or perhaps has faced as we face it now. The assumptive world we have built up from experience (which includes the abstracted scientific concepts that have a bearing on the problem) proves inadequate as we try to intellectualize the hitch we have run into. There is no empirical evidence we can find that describes all the conditions except for which the phenomenon that puzzles us would not exist.

In trying to intellectualize the inadequary of our assumptive world, we discover that a certain condition or set of conditions has not been taken into account. We abstract out of the hitch situation those aspects we believe are probably necessary to our understanding of the original hitch. We use these aspects of a phenomenon as the bases for our standards, and we vary their "amount." We may have an understanding of why such conditions are important at the time we think of them or we may only have a vague hunch that they are important and may intellectualize them much later. If we have an immediate understanding, we can design our investigation rather precisely. If we have only a hunch, a certain amount of trial and error in experimentation is necessary. But this trial and error takes place within boundaries we set and is not to be mistaken for a shotgun approach. In either case, we design the empirical test of our new basis for a standard with reference to other phenomena that have already been established as bases for standards. We do this in an attempt to determine whether or not the variation in the new basis we have selected for a standard affects old standards and is affected by them according to our formulation.

Our formulation may be validated in some circumstances if the new aspect of the phenomenon we have introduced is affected by other functional aspects. Or, under other circumstances, our formulation may be confirmed if the new aspect we have introduced is not affected by other standards. If our empirical test confirms our formulation and we find that we have abstracted out an aspect of the phenomenon that is the necessary condition for the existence of the total phenomenon, then we can say that we have the basis for a new standard and can proceed to think of it quantitatively.

Once an investigator has discovered new aspects of a phenomenon that can serve as the bases for standards, it is only too easy for him to slip into the misconception that the particular operation on which he has settled as suitable to the problem at hand exhausts the subject and says all there is to be said about it. This leads to reification of the very construct which operationism, for example, was devised to avoid. Any science becomes stagnant if it does not regard the discovery of new variables as its primary concern.

We cannot agree with those investigators who believe that the basic variables of all sciences are the same if we can only find them. As we have already pointed out, in psychology this leads to an artificial restriction of the problems dealt with, sometimes to the extent of eliminating from consideration the most pertinent variables. For example, in the attempt to study certain perceptual phenomena, emphasis has been placed on such easily defined variables as "farther than" and "bigger than," where the more psychologically meaningful variable in many cases is probably the subjective feeling of "surer than." If our awareness of a change in an external event is to be considered at all functional in nature, then the subjective sense of surety accompanying the perception must be of primary psychological significance. In the case of those perceptions that we label attitudes, investigation of the surety with which attitudes are held under different conditions has lagged far behind our interest in measuring the "direction" of the attitude or opinion.

A NOTE ON ANALYSIS. The use of the term "analysis" is a poor and misleading way by which to describe the processes involved in determining the variables we will use in our scientific thinking. For analysis assumes the existence of entities existing in their own right, which together make up a total phenomenon, and suggests that all we have to do is somehow isolate them, by analysis, for manipulation. Analysis becomes synonymous with the classification of variables in terms of abstracted, fixed, and reified standards.

As we have already indicated, there is an infinity of variables that provides the bases for an infinity of standards. We have said that all adjectives and adverbs furnish a potential basis for standards. From a study of the history of our language we know that emerging situations bring their own new bases for standards—e.g., the "snafu" of the GI. When we analyze by using existing standards we make nouns out of adjectival or adverbial relationships often without knowing. For analysis is possible only by using existing standards. Analysis, thus, does not add anything to our understanding of the functional activities involved in transactional relationships. Hence, analysis is not at all similar to what must be regarded as the scientist's constant obligation to discover those aspects of a phenomenon except for which it would not exist. Likewise synthesis—the putting together of that which we have taken apart—is a process by means of which we cannot get any more into the synthesis than is included in the standards made use of in analysis.

The functional activities we pick out for attempted intellectual understanding are those related to the immediate hitch we face. This means, then, that although an infinite number of conditional relationships exist, in any concrete scientific pursuit the range of conditional relationships an investigator might pick out as important will be limited and will be bounded by the nature of the hitch he has encountered. Scientific progress results from the ability to pick out the most relevant conditional relationships for empirical investigation, not by further analysis of established variables alone.

III. THE TRANSACTIONAL VIEW
IN PSYCHOLOGICAL RESEARCH

WHEN PSYCHOLOGY emancipates itself from dependence on interactionism alone by taking a transactional view of the phenomena which come within its province, we should expect that the division of psychologists into schools would rapidly disappear. Schools (Gestalt, behaviorism, psychoanalysis, etc.) would disappear not because they are "wrong" or "have been overthrown" but because the formulations of each school that meet empirical tests would be encompassed within wider formulations of problems. What are some ways to speed this development?

First of all, the psychologist not only must realize intellectually but must make a part of his functional assumptive world the idea that man's thought and behavior can be understood only as processes of a "full situation of organism-environment." The point has been made by H. A. Murray and collaborators in their contention that "the main body of psychology started its career by putting the wrong foot forward, and it has been out of step with the march of science much of the time. Instead of beginning with studies of the whole person adjusting to a natural environment, it began with studies of a segment of a person responding to a physical stimulus in an unnatural laboratory environment" (25, p. 466). Brunswik, in his "ecological analysis," has pointed out the need to understand the complete "representativeness of circumstances" operative in any situation under observation (3). But while an increasing number of psychologists are calling for a revision in traditional psychological procedure, their voices are still those of men crying in the wilderness of the universe which constitutes so much of psychological inquiry today. The psychological investigator, of all people, cannot separate the observer from what is being observed, the process of knowing from what is known, what is "out there" from whatever goes on in the experiencing organism. Psychology must disavow completely any "field theory" which implies that an environmental field acts *on* a person rather than *through* a person.

Because man inevitably builds up for himself an assumptive world in carrying out his purposive activities, the world he is related to, the world he sees, the world he is operating on, and the world that is operating on him is the result of a transactional process in which man himself plays an active role. Man carries out his activities in the midst of concrete events which themselves delimit the significances he must deal with.

In the process man is himself changed in greater or lesser degree by having his own assumptive world changed through confirmation or denial as a result of action. In his immediate activity man abstracts from the immediate situation certain determined aspects according to his assumptive world. This, as we indicated, includes far more than the immediate occasion; it is a continuum which includes the past and the future, a storehouse of both past experience and ideals. As Bentley has pointed out, "Behaviors are present events converging pasts into futures. They cannot be reduced to successions of instants nor to successions of locations. They themselves span extension and duration. The pasts and the futures are rather phases of behavior than its control" (1, p. 485). Psychologists must be constantly aware of the effects man's own actions have both on his assumptive world—confirming or denying certain aspects of it—and concurrently on the "environment out there" as it is perceived and experienced.

Another implication of the transactional mode of observation is that the psychologist, like any other scientific investigator, must be sensitive to the pitfalls involved in reifying anything as an entity that has been given a proper name—a pitfall that philosophers since Plato have inveighed against. Psychologists, like other scientists, must become increasingly self-conscious of the dangers to their scientific progress inherent in catchwords, whose use, as Dewey and Bentley point out, "shatters the subject matter into fragments in advance of inquiry and thus destroys instead of furthering comprehensive observation for it" (13, p. 243). Any uncritical use of traditional abstractions makes it difficult or impossible to see together what has already been taken apart.

While academic psychologists have long since given up the entity of the *soul,* and while most of them, at least in their professional writing, refuse to talk of the *mind,*[8] many other entities have slipped into the professional jargon of psychology to make transactional observation difficult. We have, for example, *need, IQ, schizophrenic, trait, attitude, Oedipus complex,* and *mesomorph.* The uncritical use of such words as specifications can easily lead to redundancy and double talk.

Psychology runs the risk of retarding its discovery of new bases for psychological standards through the use of bases for standards employed successfully in the past by the physical sciences. For example, psychologists refer to "the size of the retinal image," "visual angles," "intensity of

---

[8] A good example of a scientist who used the transactional method of observation was G. E. Coghill, who taught himself to see every organism in terms of a manifold of three inseparable constituents—structure, function, and mentation. The word "mentation" Coghill used as a substitute for "mind" to connote the constant organism-environment transaction (7, p. 198).

opinion," "field forces," "gradients," "positive or negative valences," "vectors," "depth psychology," and some even search for the physical dimensions of consciousness, limiting physical dimensions to a handful of constructs. Psychology has by no means emancipated itself from the standards of the physical sciences and is not rapidly enough discovering standards appropriate for the phenomena with which it deals.[9] By refusing to place firm reliance on standards whose bases are necessarily subjective, psychology sometimes complacently throws out some of the most important problems with which it should be concerned. Nouns such as *surety, anxiety, ego-involvement, expectancy, happiness* imply adjectival or adverbial relationships that are purely subjective. There are plenty of bases available for standards if the psychologist dares use them as he becomes sensitive to the importance of the problem of selecting bases for standards appropriate for the inquiry at hand.

It has become increasingly clear in recent years in the fields of chemistry and biology, for example, that standards appropriate to the subject matter of investigation must be sought and that reliance on the standards of classical or modern physics alone will hamper investigation. For example, J. G. Hoffman, a professor of biophysics, has recently noted that "the word biophysics . . . is a ridiculous combination of incongruous extremes. Disciplined scientific thought has never taken more diverse forms than it has in the fundamental modes of thinking in biology and in physics" (22, p. 7). In pointing out the limitations of a physical mode of observation for the study of living systems, Hoffman quotes Delbrück's statement that "instead of aiming at the whole of the phenomena exhibited by the living cell, we now expect to find natural limits, and, thereby, implicitly, new virgin territories, on which laws may hold which are independent of those of physics, by virtue of the fact that they relate to phenomena whose appearance is conditioned on *not* making observations of the type needed for applying atomic physics" (22, p. 14).

There is also a tendency in psychology to use catchwords in labeling the fields of social, clinical, educational, or industrial as "applied" fields of psychology, and to separate them from the more traditional "experimental" psychology. Any such division is absurd unless the person who uses it consciously reserves it for rough descriptive purposes. Investigators in these fields must, of course, also rely on experiments. But,

[9] It is significant that psychological terms describing capacities of human beings are occasionally used by natural scientists as rough specifications of certain phenomena they encounter. For example, mathematical physicists, in describing the behavior of some of their electronic computing machines when they become overloaded, call them "neurotic"; while biologists occasionally speak of the phenomenal "memory" which the cells of the body exhibit for certain stimuli.

beyond that, any such distinction acts as a deterrent in the search for more adequate formulations which will better account for human behavior, whether in the laboratory, the clinic, the factory, or in everyday social life. It is especially in fields such as these that one encounters hitches in interpretation because of the huge number of variables involved in the concrete situations that constitute each of the areas of inquiry. When such hitches are encountered, the investigator does not merely "apply" to their resolution some theory he has read in a book or learned from laboratory experiments. To be sure, he brings such knowledge and experience into the process of hypothesis formation. But the chances are very high indeed that any theory which is not itself based in large part upon the understanding of similar full-bodied concrete situations will turn out to be extremely inadequate.

We can illustrate the way in which psychological inquiry has been restricted by the use of terms with reference to the field of perception, which has so often been a weather vane in psychology. In working on perception, psychologists early found that certain variations in objective or physiological factors produced marked subjective variations. This naturally led to the idea of correspondence between subjective factors, on the one hand, and objective and physiological factors, on the other hand. Since an alteration of objective and physiological factors could so easily be shown to cause subjective effects, and since the converse could not so easily be demonstrated, the assumption was built up that the subjective aspects of perception had their origin largely in the corresponding objective factors and the accompanying physiological disturbances they caused. Studies of perception have thus concentrated largely on the analysis of objective and physiological factors. Since these objective or physiological factors could be varied quantitatively, scientific methodology in psychology tended to become identified with measurement alone.

This led to a long neglect of those factors not amenable to precise measurement: These neglected factors were, of course, subjective factors described by such symbols as past experience, loyalties, expectancy, and purpose, whether these were operating consciously or unconsciously. This methodological dam has recently been cracked, largely through research in social and clinical psychology, where the effects of subjective factors on perception are especially obvious. More recently, in an attempt to liberate investigators somewhat from correspondence between subjective and objective or physiological factors, demonstrations of perceptual phenomena have been designed which deliberately make use of illusions. By using illusions the investigator gains more freedom to understand the nature of the functional activities involved in the scientific inquiry of perception and thereby gets a better toe hold on the function of perception in man's purposive behavior. For example, it can be demonstrated that the perception of *where* a thing is depends upon the perception of *what* a thing is and on *when* it is perceived. Carr has pointed out that "illusions contrasted with correct perceptions are the experimental variants that reveal the common principle involved in both" (5, p. 326).

On the basis of an interactional view alone, an investigator could study the interdependence of various aspects of a perception forever and never get at the reason for such relationships until he asked himself what function such an interrelationship of phenomena served in the transaction of living. When he asks himself this question it appears that variables such as size and distance are experientially related because it is only through their relationship in past experiences that high prognostic reliability is built up. Prognostic reliability becomes itself, then, a new dimension of experience, a new basis for a standard the psychologist can use for experimentation. If the investigator continues, as he must, to ask the next question concerning the function of prognostic reliability in a life transaction, the apparent answer is that prognostic reliability of a perception increases effective action. So the effectiveness of action becomes another variable that can be used as a basis for a standard in experimentation. There must follow, of course, the question: Effective action for what? We then see that we cannot understand even the simplest perception without bringing in the variable of purpose.

The transactional mode of observation seems, then, to be peculiarly appropriate for psychologists if they are going to seek what Collingwood has called more abstract, more universal "logical grounds" for the understanding of subordinate abstractions or phenomena (6). Obviously, if we do not understand the logical ground that causes relevant variables to be relevant, then our scientific methods will be sterile indeed. Hence, progress in psychology is to be measured largely in terms of the discovery of logical grounds which increase our understanding because of their intrinsic reasonableness and the possibility they hold out of verification by experimental methods. Many of the abstractions Freud created are a case in point.

The transactional view has a third implication for psychology which concerns the method of experimentation that must be involved in real research. Different subjects for scientific inquiry pose different kinds of problems that can only be solved by adapting or creating methods appropriate to them. In saying that any one scientific discipline has special circumstances of its own which determine the techniques to be used, we are not in any way denying the indispensability of the universal characteristic of scientific method: the controlled experiment. All we are saying is that we must increase our self-consciousness and our ingenuity concerning the use and meaning of *controlled,* and not claim that we are undertaking controlled scientific investigation when our assumptive world artificially limits the number of potential controls of which we are aware.

One difficulty in the use of experimental techniques in psychology and the social sciences is that of approximating in a controlled experiment any concrete situation in which thought and behavior normally occur. Although this has been pointed out many times, and although the difficulty is easily recognizable, psychologists must be particularly on their guard to see that, in the experimental situations they devise, they have not left out so many of the subjective variables involved in normal experience that their experimental results will have little subsumptive power.

A second and much less frequently realized difficulty is that in dealing with the human organism we are dealing with a particular variety of "world stuff" which perceives complicated significances. Unless we make a special effort to understand the particular significance a particular organism at a particular time and place attaches to all the stimuli involved in our investigations, we shall again have abstracted out of the situation perhaps the most important variables for study. In psychology it is imperative that the investigator be as aware as possible of the unconscious assumptions brought by his subject to any experimental situation. Otherwise he will not have the slightest idea of what aspects of the phenomenon under investigation are most important. This awareness of assumptions is as important for the psychologist to have in mind in understanding the perception of a chair as it is in understanding social perceptions.

Still another difficulty facing the psychologist is the comparative lack of any agreed-upon bases for standards by means of which experimental situations can be described and repeated and results can be interpreted. The search for appropriate bases for standards is obviously one which requires great caution and wisdom in an area such as psychology because of the number of unknown variables likely to be involved in any standards set. Much careful research is still needed to discover what variables should be used as the bases for standards to provide the most useful analysis of man's experience.

Value Judgments and "Objectivity"

A great deal of discussion has taken place in recent years concerning the possibility or the desirability of complete "objectivity" in science.

The publication of Karl Pearson's *Grammar of Science* in 1892 (27), with its contention that an understanding of scientific method can train "the mind to an exact and impartial analysis of facts" and can free the individual from bias in the formation of judgments, gave a great boost to the myth that real scientific inquiry somehow goes on in a world devoid of personal judgments. The contrasting point of view has been expressed by Whitehead (31, pp. 228 f.):

> Judgments of worth are no part of the texture of physical science, but they are a part of the motive of its production. Mankind has raised the edifice of science, because they have judged it worth while. In other words, the motives involve innumerable judgments of value. Again, there has been conscious selection of the parts of the scientific fields to be cultivated, and this conscious selection involves judgments of value. These values may be aesthetic or moral or utilitarian; namely, judgments as to the beauty of the structure or as to the duty of exploring the truth or as to utility in the satisfaction of physical wants. But whatever the motive, without judgments of value there would have been no science.

It is becoming increasingly clear that the process of mentation involved in scientific inquiry is not a simple one of bringing "impartial analysis" to bear on a set of conditions. The scientist's own value judgments are involved in (1) sensing the inadequacy of his conceptual structure—posing a problem for himself; (2) sensing the functional activities or subphenomena which may be involved in the phenomenon that has caused the original hitch; (3) deciding on which aspects of a phenomenon (variables) can fruitfully be used as bases for standards in experimentation; and (4) designing an experimental procedure to test the validity of these bases for standards. Scientific research thus involves an elaborate process of weighing and integrating which may take place largely on an unconscious level.

In this process, all the unconscious assumptions, all the awarenesses, and all the conceptual abstractions of the individual investigator's assumptive world are operative. Whether any scientist likes to admit it or not, any interpretation he makes must be regarded as a value judgment. To be sure, rational thought and the conscious intellectual manipulation of abstracted variables can, often do, and obviously should play a most important role in the process of scientific inquiry. But to assume that rational thought and conscious manipulation alone are the determinants of the judgments involved in scientific research is to go against the overwhelming evidence already obtained from scientific research itself. The dictionary definition of the word "objective," in the sense that it is used in discussions concerning the objectivity of science, is: "Emphasizing or expressing the nature of reality as it is apart from self-consciousness; treating events or phenomena as external rather than as affected by one's reflections or feelings." For example, our knowledge of perception, showing that "the nature of reality" as we experience it would not exist *except* for the assumptive world we bring to a concrete situation, flatly contradicts the contention that the scientist can be objective in any such sense.

The objectivity of science can therefore only refer to the use of accepted rules of empirical research *after* the problem, the variables, and the experimental design have been decided upon. Here the scientific investigator takes every precaution he can to see that he does not misinterpret what he observes by allowing any subjective bias to enter into the actual conduct of the experiment itself.

Not only is objectivity illusory in the sense of eliminating personal bias, it is also undesirable. We cannot improve on the conclusion reached by Herrick (21, pp. 180 f.) after a lifetime of productive research in neurology:

> The bias which arises from unrecognized personal attitudes, interests, and pre-conceptions is the most treacherous of all the subversive enemies of sound, scientific progress; yet these attitudes and interests are the key factors in all really original scientific investigation. This issue must be faced frankly and courageously. The easy way out is to ignore the troublesome personal ingredients of the problem and say that science has no concern with them. This is now generally regarded as the standard, or normal, scientific method. But actually this cannot be done, and we cannot afford to try to do it; for the interests and the attitudes of the inquirer shape the whole course of the investigation, without which it is meaningless and fruitless. To neglect these components of scientific work and the satisfactions of a successful outcome is to sterilize not only the process but also the results of the inquiry. The vital germ of untrammeled imaginative thinking is thrown into the discard, and too often we seem quite content with the dead husk which is so easily weighed, measured, classified, and then stowed away in the warehouse.

In the social sciences, Robert Lynd has made the same point in his plea for "outrageous hypotheses" (23).

The myth that "science is objective" may tend to be fostered in most cultures today in an attempt to preserve whatever status quo exists by giving it scientific blessing. But any scientist will resent boundaries placed on his thinking by social, economic, political, religious, or any other ideological barriers and taboos. This danger is especially prevalent in the field of inquiry labeled "social psychology" and in the social sciences, where the data gathered have been largely determined and preconditioned by the purposes and conditions within which the investigator has worked.

Psychologists and social scientists who honestly try to bring their most mature value judgments to bear on concrete social problems are all too frequently labeled as biased, crackpot reformers if they even implicitly criticize existing social relationships. Yet it is because scientific inquiry is shot through with value judgments that no scientist can avoid some responsibility for the judgments he makes. Because value judgments play so important a role in scientific thinking, ways and means must be discovered of making value judgments themselves the subject matter for scientific inquiry (4). Value judgments concern the significance of the constant emergents which are not subject to explanation in determined and verifiable terms. Here the scientist has a freedom of choice; here conscience, the "sense of oughtness," must be recognized as the highest standard for effective action. When the subject matter with which the scientist deals consists of human beings trying to act effectively to carry out their purposes, then the social responsibility of anyone who pretends to be an expert obviously becomes very great indeed.

Our recurring theme has been that any truly scientific investigation involves much more than the use of an accepted methodology of experimentation. We have tried to show why the progress men hope for in their understanding of themselves can come about only to the extent that those who are professionally concerned with such an understanding become increasingly sensitive to the problem of problemization.

But the readers already sympathetic with our emphasis may be reminded of the drama critic who, after pointing out the second-rate quality of then current productions, ended his comments with the statement that what we need are better plays. Are there any concrete suggestions which might speed up the search for more and more adequate formulations that psychologists would seek to verify experimentally? A few have occurred to us and they are the subject matter of the chapters that follow.

REFERENCES—CHAPTER 1

1. Bentley, A. F. *J. Phil.*, 1941, *38*, 477.
2. Bridgman, P. W. *Psychol. Rev.*, 1945, *52*, 246.
3. Brunswik, E. *Proc. Berkeley Symp. Math. Statistics and Probability.* Berkeley, Calif.: Univ. Calif. Press, 1949. Pp. 143–202.

4. Cantril, H. *J. Psychol.*, 1949, *27*, 363.

5. Carr, H. A. *An Introduction to Space Perception.* New York: Longmans, Green, 1935.

6. Collingwood, R. G. *An Essay on Metaphysics.* Oxford: Clarendon, 1940.

7. Conant, J. B. *On Understanding Science.* New Haven: Yale Univ. Press, 1947.

8. Dampier-Whetham, W. C. D. *A History of Science.* New York: Macmillan, 1929.

9. Dampier-Whetham, W. C. D. *Shorter History of Science.* Cambridge, Mass.: Cambridge Univ. Press, 1944.

10. Darwin, F. (Ed.) *Life and Letters of Charles Darwin.* New York: Appleton, 1888.

11. Dewey, J. *Problems of Men.* New York: Philosophical Library, 1946.

12. Dewey, J. *J. Phil.*, 1948, *45*, 197.

13. Dewey, J., and Bentley, A. F. *J. Phil.*, 1945, *42*, 225.

14. Dewey, J., and Bentley, A. F. *J. Phil.*, 1946, *43*, 645.

15. Dewey, J., and Bentley, A. F. *J. Phil.*, 1946, *43*, 505.

16. Dewey, J., and Bentley, A. F. *J. Phil.*, 1946, *43*, 535.

17. Einstein, A., and Infeld, L. *The Evolution of Physics.* New York: Simon and Schuster, 1942.

18. Eysenck, H. J. *Dimensions of Personality.* London: Routledge, 1947.

19. Feigl, H. *Psychol. Rev.*, 1945, *52*, 250.

20. Fries, H. H. *The Cultural Function of Art Relative to the Conceptualization of Novel Problems.* University of Wisconsin. (Unpublished manuscript.)

21. Herrick, C. J. *George Ellett Coghill.* Chicago: Univ. Chicago Press, 1949.

22. Hoffman, J. G. *Physics Today*, 1949, *2*, No. 7, 6.

23. Lynd, R. *Knowledge for What?* Princeton, N. J.: Princeton Univ. Press, 1939.

24. Mead, G. H. *Mind, Self, and Society.* Chicago: Univ. Chicago Press, 1939.

25. Murray, H. A., *et al. Assessment of Men.* New York: Rinehart, 1948.

26. Oppenheimer, J. R. *Physics in the Contemporary World.* Little Memorial Lecture at Massachusetts Institute of Technology, Cambridge, Mass., 1947.

27. Pearson, K. *Grammar of Science.* London: Black, 1911 (3rd ed.).

28. Pratt, C. C. *Psychol. Rev.*, 1945, *52*, 262.

29. Randall, J. H., Jr. *Making of the Modern Mind.* Boston: Houghton Mifflin, 1926.

30. Whitehead, A. N. *Adventures of Ideas.* New York: Macmillan, 1933.

31. Whitehead, A. N. *The Aims of Education.* New York: Macmillan, 1929.

32. Whitehead, A. N. *The Principle of Relativity.* Cambridge, Mass.: Cambridge Univ. Press, 1922.

The Nature of Perception: Some Visual Demonstrations

F. P. Kilpatrick

THE PROBLEM OF PERCEPTION

LET US BEGIN with what would seem to be a simple case of visual perception. Look at any chair. If you give your attention to what you see, you can analyze your "total" impression into a great number of characteristics and qualities. For example, you see a chair, it is a specific distance from you, it is of a certain size, it is upright so you can sit on it, it is three-dimensional, the legs are parallel and at right angles to the seat, the various parts are of certain colors and textures, etc., etc. Where do all these characteristics and qualities come from? A naïve guess would be that they are properties of the thing you are looking at and come from it to you, and what you see, therefore, constitutes "reality." That the answer is not so simple, however, has been known for a long time. Its inadequacy may easily be demonstrated.

The apparatus shown in Figure 1 is provided with three peepholes,

[*36*]

FIG. 1. *Exterior view of chair demonstration. A, B, and C are peepholes through which the contents of each compartment can be viewed. D, E, and F are tubes, each containing a lens and an artificial ground-glass retina. By moving a tube into position over a peephole, the observer may see on the ground glass a rough likeness of the image which was on his retina when his eye was at that peephole.*

A, B, and C, through which you may look with one eye at objects on the other side of the screen. If you look first through A, then through B, and then through C, you see in each case what appears to be the same thing; that is, a chair (Figure 2, A, B, and C). It is true that it appears smaller and lacks the details of an ordinary chair looked at through a similar peephole, but that is simply because the demonstrational setup would be inconveniently large and complex if it were made to give the impression of a full-sized chair. But this smaller and simpler version has most of the essential features: it appears to be at a specific distance, of a specific size, upright, three-dimensional, with legs parallel and at right angles to the seat, etc.

Now, if you walk around behind the screen or look over the top of it, you will find that the three "things" you were looking at are entirely

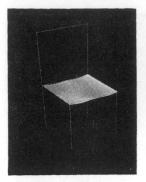 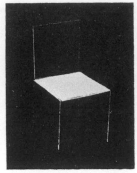 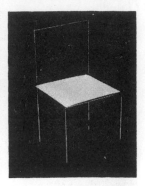

FIG. 2. *Views through peepholes A, B, and C of the chair demonstration (Figure 1).*

different. The "chair" behind peephole A is a set of strings and a piece of cardboard arranged much as the parts of a chair (Figure 3 A). The one behind B also is simply a set of strings, and a white diamond painted on the back wall. The strings are all of different lengths and at different angles (Figure 3 B) so that when seen from this new point of view they present no aspect of "chairness," and appear to be nothing but a bit of jumbled three-dimensional nonsense. Behind C, too, there is only a set of strings and a piece of cardboard (Figure 3 C), in this case arranged in a plane so as to constitute a perspective projection of a chair-shaped object.

The fact that in each of the three cases you saw approximately the same "thing" through the peepholes but were actually looking at three entirely different "things" cannot be reconciled with any notion that what you see is in objects themselves. It is apparent that you would not have visual perceptions except for the fact that something is out there

  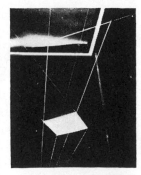

FIG. 3. *Contents of each of the three compartments of the chair demonstration, photos taken from above the front panel. A, B, and C in this figure correspond to A, B, and C in Figure 2.*

and except for the reflected light rays which impinge upon your eye; but of themselves, these factors do not constitute an explanation of perception.

A current, and more sophisticated, answer to the problem is to grant that visual perceptions are not determined by objects, but instead are determined by—can be derived from—the physiological stimulus patterns that result from the impingement of light rays on the organism. Unfortunately, however, that does not seem to be true either. Let us return to the chair demonstration.

Three tubes (D, E, and F in Figure 1), each containing a lens and a

FIG. 4. *An artificial "eye" in position over a peephole, showing the pattern cast on the ground-glass "retina."*

piece of ground glass, are provided. When these tubes are slid into position over the peepholes, the images cast on the ground glasses have essentially the same characteristic as the images formed on your retina when you look through the holes in the three screens (one of them is shown in Figure 4). An examination of these images reveals first of all that they are all alike. This means that the *same* physiological stimulus pattern is being produced by three entirely *different* sets of configurations in space. A bit of reflection on this fact leads to the formulation of an equally obvious, but more generalized, statement: *a given physiological stimulus pattern may be related to (produced by) an infinity of different external conditions.* Consequently, the particular external configuration perceived cannot be derived from the stimulus pattern alone; only a class of external configurations may thus be derived.

We may note further that the characteristics of the images on the ground glasses do not correspond to what you saw when you looked through the holes. If you consider just the characteristics of the images themselves, and not how you might interpret them, it is apparent that:

(1) In themselves they are not a chair.
(2) In themselves they have no indication of the specific distance of the chair you saw when you looked through the holes.
(3) Their actual dimensional size is much smaller than what you perceived when you looked through the holes. If you look at a chair about six feet away, the image on your retina is only about 1/100 the size of the chair.
(4) They are only two-dimensional.
(5) The lines corresponding to the legs are not at right angles to the seat.
(6) They are upside down.

Many other differences between percept and retinal image might be pointed out, but with just these few it becomes clear that, if the only data you had at your disposal were the stimulus patterns themselves, you could no more derive your perceptions from them than you could derive from Egyptian hieroglyphics the meanings that the Egyptians used to relate to them if all you ever had were the hieroglyphics.

We have not solved any problems with this demonstration, but we have succeeded in setting a direction for further inquiry. Some light may be thrown on the issue by a negative approach. Since what is perceived cannot be derived from either the *immediate* outside world or the *immediate* physiological stimulus pattern, it would seem reasonable to suppose that the explanation might profitably be sought in the realm of past events.

A convenient starting point is to consider the question of why we see any "thing" apart from any other "thing." It is apparent that in absolute darkness we could have no visual perception of a particular objective "thing," nor could we under any other conditions where our total field of view was undifferentiated; for instance, if it were all exactly the same color and brightness. That is, we can only have a sense of objective "thatness" when the impingements on our organism give rise to differentiated stimulus patterns to which differentiated significances can be related. This means that the very basis of perception is the capacity of the organism to be sensitive to differential stimulation, coupled with the capacity to relate differential significances to them.

The necessity for differentiating the part from the whole before the perception of a "thing" can occur is commonly experienced. Animals have protective coloration which serves the function of preventing other animals and man from having a perception of their "thingness" as differentiated from the background behind them. Only when we become aware of the "togetherness" of the animal apart from the "togetherness" of the background do we see the animal. "Togetherness" and "apartness" are therefore aspects of the same phenomenon.

As human beings we can only sense those "togethernesses" that have significance to us as human beings. There are infinities of other "to-gethernesses" that we can know nothing about. It will be generally agreed that it is impossible for us to experience all possible elements in any situation, let alone all the possible interrelationships of all the elements. This must be, if for no other reason than because our relationship to our environment through our senses is so limited. For example, of all the forces that are impinging on our physiology, we can record and take account of only an infinitesimal part. Because of our inherent nature as human beings we can take account of only very limited partial wholes out of the total whole. It is only in so far as we can do this that we can establish any relationships which give us directives for acting.

Brightness differences, color differences, differences in relative motion, differences between stimulus patterns on the two retinas, etc. are necessary for seeing one "thing," but in themselves they do not constitute what we see. When we perceive one object as different and apart from another object, two important aspects are involved. One is localization in space (they cannot be in the same place) and the other is the assignment of the characteristics which for us constitute the object.

In conducting our inquiry into these aspects, use will be made of visual illusions because they are excellent tools for determining the variables involved in the perception of "where" and "what" an object is. For example, if I set a water glass before you and you see it in its "true" shape and location, very little will have been revealed concerning the nature of your seeing; however, if one factor is varied and you now see the glass in other than its "true" shape or position, it may reasonably be inferred that the altered factor plays a definite, and perhaps determinable, role in your perception. Through a study of such factors we should gain some insight concerning the nature and function of the perceptual process, and thus make additional progress in the direction of a unifying theory which will make sense out of the enormously diverse and often apparently conflicting phenomena which are ordinarily included under the heading of perception.

LOCALIZATION IN SPACE

IT HAS LONG been known that there are many types of indications that play a role in determining the distance at which we see things. Color, softness of edge, size, perspective, shadows, parallax, brightness, and binocular disparity are a few examples. It is helpful to know that such indications are utilized in the perception of depth or distance, but it is far more important to understand the how and why of the process involved in, for example, the immediately given interpretation of some differences in size as differences in relative distance, while other equally great differences in size are not so interpreted. We shall begin our inquiry with some simple visual demonstrations.

One simple demonstration consists of two star points of light in an otherwise dark room. The light points are at equal distances from the observer, but of different intensities. When viewed with one eye with head stationary, however, they are not ordinarily perceived as being at equal distances; but rather, the point of greater intensity is perceived as nearer. Generally, but not always, it is also seen as being somewhat brighter. Apparently, the difference in intensity may be perceived as difference in brightness (which is what one would expect in purely physical terms), difference in distance, or an unlimited number of combinations of the two. Now, if we add a third star point which is midway between the two with respect to both position and intensity, the most intense point will appear to have moved much nearer than its former position, and the least intense point much farther away. Apparently the addition (in a line) of light points of graded intensity reinforces the perception of differences in intensity as differences in distance.

The explanation of such an apparently simple perceptual problem is not at all simple, and is further complicated by the fact that the perceived relative distance of such light points is not solely a function of intensity but is also related to direction from the observer. If two points of light of equal intensity, one about a foot above the other, are situated near the floor and observed with one eye (Figure 5 B), the upper one will generally be perceived as farther away than the lower one. However, if

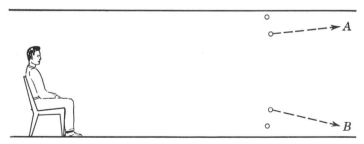

FIG. 5. *The circles represent points of light equidistant from the eye of the observer. Observed monocularly in an otherwise dark room, they are not ordinarily seen as equidistant. In pair A the* lower *one is seen as farther away. In pair B the* upper *one is seen as farther away.*

the same two lights are situated near the ceiling (Figure 5 A), the lower one will generally be perceived as farther away than the upper one.

Similar monocular distance perception phenomena may be obtained by varying the number, relative lengths, or spatial arrangements of small lines of light of equal intensity. Perfectly satisfactory apparatus for this demonstration might be constructed in a number of ways. A very convenient one is shown in Figure 6. It consists of a black-painted light box.

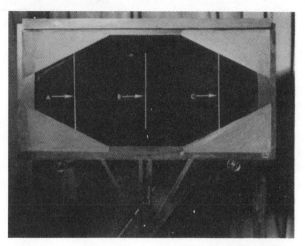

FIG. 6. *Apparatus for showing the depth-perception effects of altering the number, relative lengths, or relative brightnesses of lines of light. The front frame can be moved from left to right and vice versa, thus altering the amount seen of lines A and C, by means of a lever at the back of the box. Another lever operates a pair of rheostats connected to the lights behind A and C. Movement of the lever in one direction causes A to brighten and C to dim; opposite movement causes the reverse to happen. An independent switch and rheostat are provided for the light behind B. Although only static phenomena are described in the text, a considerable variety of continuous changes in perceived depth may be obtained by continuous movement of the levers in various ways.*

with three narrow strips (A, B, and C in Figure 6) cut in the front so that the interior light shines through. Frosted glass between the light source and the front of the box ensures equal diffusion all along the apertures. Movable opaque shields, also painted black, permit one to vary the lengths of the light lines within wide limits.

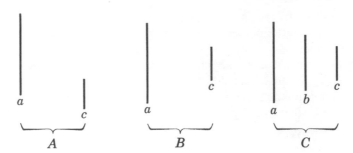

FIG. 7. *Lines of light in the three different arrangements discussed in the text.*

If only two lines of unequal lengths are used and arranged so the midpoint of the shorter line is considerably below the midpoint of the other, as in Figure 7 A, most observers, looking at them with one eye in an otherwise dark room, report that the lines appear to be at the same distance but of unequal lengths. However, if the shield over line (c) is now adjusted so that the midpoint of the shorter line is at the same elevation as that of (a) (Figure 7 B), the most common report is that the lines appear to be of about equal length, but at different distances, (c) being farther away. Simply murmuring "telephone poles" to the observer strongly reinforces this effect. It may be reinforced also by introducing line (b), length midway between those of (a) and (c) and midpoint at the same elevation (Figure 7 C). Ordinarily, this results in line (a) appearing much nearer and line (c) much farther away than when (a) and (c) alone are exposed. The effect may now be heightened even more by diminishing the height ratio of (c) to (a) either by lengthening (a), shortening (c), or both.

A somewhat more complex demonstration permits the analysis of the perceptual correlates of such cues in a nonstatic situation. The apparatus (Figure 8) consists of two partially inflated balloons (A and B) illuminated from a concealed source. The balloons are in fixed positions about one foot apart. A lever control (C) is connected to a bellows (E); movement of the lever in one direction causes one balloon to increase in size and the other to decrease in size; moving the lever in the opposite direction causes the reverse to happen. A second lever (D) controls the illumination of the balloons, permitting their relative intensities of reflected light to be varied in the same way. The two levers may be moved together, in opposition, or separately.

When the size and illumination of one balloon are about the same as the size and illumination of the other, an observer, looking at them monocularly, head stationary, from ten feet or more, sees them as two glowing spheres at equal distances from him. If illuminations are left

FIG. 8. *The balloon demonstration. Lettered items are identified and their uses explained in the text.*

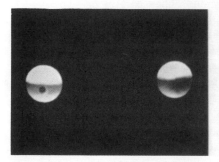

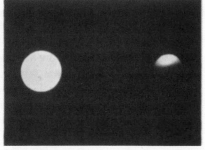

FIG. 9. *The balloons appear about equidistant when they are about the same size and brightness.* (Scientific American; *photo by David E. Scherman.)*

FIG. 10. *The left balloon appears closer when it is larger and brighter.* (Scientific American; *photo by David E. Scherman.)*

equal and the sizes fixed at their maximum possible difference, the large balloon appears to nearly all observers to be somewhat nearer and the smaller one somewhat farther away. Now, if the size lever is moved to cause continuous variation in the relative size of the balloons, they appear to move dramatically back and forth through space, the larger one coming much farther forward and the smaller one going much farther away than was the case when the size was fixed, and this is true even when both eyes are used. Results which are similar but lesser in degree may be obtained by keeping the sizes equal and making comparable alterations in relative illumination.

Clearly, then, size alone and intensity of reflected light alone are important in the perception of distance. But with this same apparatus the two may be combined in ways which are either supplementary or conflicting and the resulting alterations in perception noted. When both size and illumination are continuously varied so as to supplement one another, the variation in apparent distance is much greater than when either size alone or illumination alone is continuously varied. When conflict is introduced by varying size and illumination in opposition to one another, apparent change in relative distance is considerably less than when they are in harmony. However, in this conflict situation the apparent change in distance is, for most people, in the direction related to size change and opposite to that related to illumination change. These facts indicate that, although we do give some weight to relative intensity of reflected light as an indicator of relative distance, in this situation, at least, we assign less weight to it than we do to relative size.

Singly, or as a group, these phenomena present a major explanatory problem. They cannot be explained by referring to "reality," because "reality" and percept do not correspond. They cannot be explained by referral to the retinal pattern, because, for any given retinal pattern, there are an infinite number of light intensity-size-distance combinations to which the pattern might be related. Failing, thus, to find any sufficient explanation in the *immediate* occasion, we will follow our earlier suggestion and attempt an answer which involves the relation of processes in time. There is a reasonable explanation which would appear to cover all the facts. Apparently the organism, always forced to "choose" among the unlimited number of possibilities which can be related to a given retinal pattern, calls upon its previous experiences and "assumes" that what has been most probable in the past is most probable in the immediate occasion.

Thus, when presented with two star points of different intensities, the observer operates on the basis of an unconscious assumption that the two points, being similar, are probably identical (i.e., of equal intensity) and to a considerable extent uses the difference in intensity as an indication of their relative positions in space. The introduction of a third star point midway between the two in both position and intensity strongly reinforces the assumption of identity. We might occasionally have experienced two lights of differing intensities at the same distance, but seldom three of graded intensities. Much more common would be the experience of identical or nearly identical lights at different distances, as with street lamps, a line of oncoming automobiles, etc.

FIG. 11. *The left card appears closer than those at the center, and right in each of the three rows, especially if the lower half of the picture is covered. The true order from near to far is as follows: Left row—A, B, C; center row —C, B, A; right row—king, plain card, jack. The lower-left corners of B and C, center row, and of the king and plain card, right row, are cut out, giving false overlay indications. (Sci-*entific American; *photo by David E. Scherman.*)

Similarly, in the case of two star points placed one above the other, a reasonable explanation of the observed phenomena is that, when we look down we assume, on the basis of past experience, that objects in the lower part of the visual field are nearer than objects in the upper part; when we look up, we assume the opposite to be true. An analogous explanation can be made of the role of relative size as an indication of relative distance.

Why, in the case of the balloon demonstration, do the differences in distance appear so much greater when the relative size of the two objects is varied continuously than when the size difference is fixed? This phenomenon, too, apparently is based on experience. It is fairly common experience, though not usual, to find that two similar objects of different sizes are actually the same distance away from us. But it is rare indeed

FIG. 12. *The overlay apparatus. The photograph for Figure 11 was taken from a point slightly to the right of the small shield hanging down from the upper part of the headrest.* (Scientific American; photo by David E. Scherman.)

to experience two stationary objects at the same distance, one growing larger and the other smaller; almost always in everyday life when we see two identical or nearly identical objects change relative size they are in motion in relation to one another. Hence, under the experimental conditions we are much more likely to assume distance differences in the objects of changing size than in the case of fixed size. Again, when size and intensity of illumination conflict, the most reasonable explanation of its result in perception would seem to be in terms of some sort of averaging of our past experience. In general, when objects approach us they reflect more light energy on the retina, and vice versa, but this relationship is highly variable due to shadow, multiple sources of illumination, etc. The size-distance relationship, on the other hand, although probably not absolute, is much more invariant. Since in the past the prognostic reliability of size has been much greater than that of intensity of illumination, indications of size are given greater weight than are illumination indications in the extremely rapid, complex, evolving, and unconscious integration which is the perceptual process.

Overlay, or the obscuring of part of one object by another, is also a well-known cue to relative distance, but, as another of the demonstrations clearly shows (see Figures 11 and 12), the indications one gets from it are likewise probabilities and depend upon assumptions. Undoubtedly one necessary assumption is that of "wholeness"; that is, if any part of an object whose shape is known (through experience, certainly) is cut off by another object, it is probably behind the other object.

In other words, what we see is apparently a function of some sort of weighted average of our past experiences. It seems that we relate to a stimulus pattern a complex, probability-like integration of our past experience with such patterns. Were it not for such integrations, which have been labeled assumptions, the particular perceptual phenomenon would not occur. It follows from this that the resulting perceptions are not absolute revelations of "what is out there" but are in the nature of probabilities or predictions based on past experience. These predictions are not always reliable, as the demonstrations make clear. In the above instances, actions based on perception would be very unsuccessful.

THE ASSIGNMENT OF OBJECT CHARACTERISTICS

VISUAL PERCEPTION involves an impression not only of *where* an object is but of *what* it is. From the demonstrations already described we may guess that there is a strong relationship between localization in space ("thereness") and the assignment of objective properties ("thatness"). In the case of the lines of light of different length, the degree to which they are perceived as being at different distances is a function of their perceived "thatness"; that is, the extent to which they are seen as being lines of the same length. The importance of "thatness" in the demonstration is further emphasized by the effect of the suggestion "telephone poles." No lengthy discussion is needed to point out that the same principle applies to all the phenomena, both static and dynamic, observed in the balloon demonstration. As a means of exploring some of the important aspects involved in the "thereness"-"thatness" relationship, a specialized demonstrational apparatus [1] has been designed. Quite appropriately, Ames has named it the "thereness-thatness" demonstration (earlier it was somewhat vaguely called the "oak leaf table").

The apparatus (see Figure 13) provides two fields of view placed side by side. In the field of view on the observer's left there are numerous objects which give rise to a sufficient number of indications to provide a definite sense of the distance from the observation point of a series of objects. This is accomplished not only by permitting the observer to see that field with both eyes but by providing a multiplicity of monoc-

[1] Two quite different pieces of equipment have been designed for this purpose. They demonstrate the same phenomena, but vary in their usefulness for specific experiments. The one discussed here is shown in Figure 13. A description of the other is given in Chapter 4.

FIG. 13. *The thereness-thatness table. When the observer places his forehead against the headrest (A), the shield (B) cuts off the view through the aperture (C) from the left eye. Thus, the left alley with its numbered posts is seen binocularly while the right alley is seen monocularly. On the movable screen (D) in the monocular alley, pictures may be projected from the enclosed Clason projector (E). Movement of the lever (F) varies the size of the projected image. If desired, the screen may be removed, permitting the use of actual objects instead of projected images in the monocular field. The apparatus is used in a room which is dark except for the lights on the equipment. When in use, the entire top of the binocular alley is covered in the same manner as the rear portion (G).*

ularly useful indications, such as brightness, size, overlay, shadows, etc. The field of view which is on the right, and adjacent to the other, is concealed from the left eye by a properly arranged shield. There is nothing visible in this right-eye field except the test object or "thing" whose distance it is the observer's task to judge.

For convenience, we shall call the first field the binocular field and the second one the monocular field. In the binocular field there is a series of five evenly spaced posts on which there are large numbers running from 1 through 5 in order from near to far, so that post number 1 is about two feet away from the observer's eye, number 3 about six feet away, and number 5 about ten feet away. These provide a convenient way for the observer to compare and to designate various functionally sensed distances in the adjacent monocular field. Both fields are artificially illuminated, and there are convenient switches by which the lights illuminating either field can be turned off. When both lights are turned off, the entire field of view is completely black.

The method of conducting the initial demonstration with this apparatus follows: With the binocular field light off, an object is put up in the monocular field, for instance, at the same distance as post 3 in the binocular field. Since only the object itself is illuminated, the observer sees only the object against a completely black background. After he has looked at the object a short time, the binocular field is illuminated, and the specific distance at which the observer has perceived the monocularly seen object is disclosed by where it appears in the binocularly seen field of view. A number of objects of various types are put up one at a time in the monocular field of view, *all at the same actual distance as post 3* in the binocular field, judgments of distance being obtained for each in the manner just described.

A single star point of light is perceived as being farther away than its true position, generally at 5 or beyond 5. Four star points also are seen as farther away than 3, but nearer than in the case of the single star point—perhaps between 4 and 5. The position of an illuminated blur can also be "fixed" by the observer, generally somewhere beyond 3; the same holds true of a vertical line. An oak leaf is seen by some observers as nearer than 3; others see it as farther away. However, an ordinary playing card, as well as a cigarette package, are perceived by virtually all observers as being very close to number 3, the true position.

It seems that no matter what is put up in the monocular field, no matter how unstructured it may be, it is perceived as being at a specific distance. Further, it appears that the distance at which an object is seen depends on what the object "is"—"thereness" and "thatness" are inseparable in experience.

How does it happen that the playing card and the cigarette package are so accurately and consistently localized, while the localization of the oak leaf, an equally well-structured object, is so inaccurate and variable? For an answer to this question, we must inquire into the origin and nature of "thatness."

Where does one's sense of "thatness" of star points, blurs, lines, oak leaves, playing cards, and cigarette packages come from? Light can be thrown on this problem by altering the so-called "objective characteristics" of the various objects and observing the effect of such alterations on the distance from the observer at which they are perceived. In order to simplify our inquiry we will consider here only the characteristic of size, even though other of the demonstrations provides means of studying the effects of altering such factors as brightness, shape, etc.

It is technically difficult to alter in any easy, continuous, and rapid way the sizes of a variety of actual objects. However, the same effects (i.e., the impingements on a single retina of the observer) as would be produced by altering actual objects may be produced by altering projected pictures of the objects, provided such factors as brightness, sharpness of focus, etc. are adequately controlled. This may be accomplished by adding three items of equipment to the monocular side of the "thereness-thatness" table. The first of these is a projection screen which can be placed at any desired distance from the observer. The second is a Clason projector, enclosed on all sides to prevent light leakage from other than the projection opening, and placed in such a fashion that it will project on the screen but not impede the observer's view of the screen. With a Clason projector it is possible to change the size of a projected picture while keeping it in sharp focus. The third addition is a rheostat which provides a means of controlling the brightness of the projected image.

With the projection screen placed in the middle distance opposite post 3, a picture of a playing card is projected on the screen, and by means of the rheostat, its brightness is equated for the observer to that of the objects in the binocular field. The size-control lever of the projector is now moved back and forth, causing the image of the card to change continuously from large to small and vice versa. Under these circumstances, the observer sees the card change distance relative to the objects in the binocular field. As it is made larger, it appears to come closer; as it is made smaller, it appears to move away. When projected images of four star points, a blur, a vertical line, an oak leaf, and a cigarette package are thus altered in size, similar changes in apparent distance are experienced by the observer.

These facts suggest that no matter what we see we attribute to it a characteristic "thatness" in respect to size. Variations from this standard, in the absence of stronger conflicting indications, are perceived as variations in distance.

Let us continue with the demonstration. With the screen at 3, the observer is asked to move the control until the playing card appears opposite post number 3. For nearly all observers, the size at which the image is set corresponds almost exactly with the actual size of an ordinary playing card. This also holds true when the screen is placed at 2 and a 2 distance setting asked for, or when the screen is placed at 4 and a 4 distance setting asked for. When the picture is changed to that of an oak leaf, however, there is very little agreement between the settings of various observers, even though a single observer tends to be consistent in successive settings. In general, it has been found from the experiences of a large number of observers who have gone through these demonstrations that, although they agree very well as to their standard sizes of playing cards and cigarette packages, they vary greatly in their standard sizes of grouped star points, blurs, lines, and oak leaves. It is of interest to note that individuals who have had experience in the woods tend to have a larger standard for oak leaves than do those who have not.

It would appear, then, that the questions "How big is a blur?" and "How long is a line?" are not as silly as they sound. They make as much sense functionally for the individual as the question "How big is a playing card?"

What is the nature of these standards? Certainly they do not exist in "reality." There is no such thing as a standard length of line or a standard-size blur in any "objective" sense. The explanation would seem to be that the standard "sizes" which the observer brings to the situation are averages of some sort of his past experiences with objects of the various types. These averages can be roughly differentiated on the basis of the nature of the historical data from which they are derived. With playing cards and cigarette packages there would be very little variation in the history of experienced sizes for the same individual, or between individuals. With oak leaves there would be more variation in both cases, and with blurs and lines, still more. The standards brought to the occasion by the individual may conveniently be thought of in the form of probability curves. For example, probability curves for playing cards would be relatively high and narrow because the playing cards which we experience do not vary much in size. On the other hand, probability curves for leaves would be low and broad, simply because our experiences with the sizes of leaves have been so variable. For such objects as lines and blurs, the diversity in experience is even greater.

To continue the analogy, the standard "chosen" may be thought of as a point or area along such a probability curve. The particular point or area employed in a given situation is a function not only of the past experience of the individual but of all the various aspects of the immediate occasion, many of which are not customarily thought of as entering into the visual perception of size and distance. Examples of the latter are the observer's notions, generally unconscious, concerning the size of the room, the dimensions of the whole experimental apparatus, suggestions from any source concerning the nature of the object, etc. Obviously, such factors are of more importance in altering perception of the "where" and "what" of blurs or lines than they are in the case of a playing card.

It should not be supposed that these standards or assumed sizes are necessarily either conscious or expressible in linear dimensions such as inches or feet. Rather, they are generally unconscious and independent of any particular point of view in space or time, and are functional in the sense that you would have to open your fingers a certain amount to grasp a cigarette package, irrespective of its distance. The results of these unconscious processes are brought into operation in relation to the immediate impingements from sensory receptors. For purposes of thinking and communicating, we speak of object characteristics as though they existed independently of the perceiving organism. Actually, however, perceived object characteristics are assigned on the basis of past experience as it is related to the immediate occasion, which necessarily involves the particular point of view of the perceiving organism.

This thesis may be illustrated further by a demonstration which shows the effect of perceived distance on the assignment of characteristics to a three-dimensional object—in this case, a cube. Two solid white cubes are suspended on wires that are painted black so as to be invisible against a black background. One cube is about three feet from the observer and the other about twelve feet. The observer's head is in a headrest, so positioned that the cubes are almost in line with each other, but he can see both, the nearer cube being slightly to the right. A tiny metal shield is then placed a few inches in front of the left eye. It is just big enough to cut off the view of the far cube from the left eye. The result is that the near cube is seen with both eyes and the far cube with just the right eye. Under these conditions, the observer can fix the position of the near cube very well, because he has available all the cues that come from the use of the two eyes. But in the case of the far cube, seen with only one eye, localization is much more difficult and uncertain.

Now, since the two cubes are almost in line visually, a slight movement of the head to the right will cause the inside vertical edges of the cubes to coincide. Such coincidence of edge is strongly related to an assumption of "togetherness." Hence, when the observer moves his head in this way, the uncertainly located distant cube appears to have moved forward to a position even with the nearer cube. Under these conditions, not only does the mislocated cube appear smaller, but it is perceived as different in shape; that is, no longer cubical, even though the pattern cast by the cube on the retina of the eye has not changed at all.

In the demonstrations discussed so far, the only aspect of "thereness" treated in its relation to the assignment of object characteristics has been that of distance from the observer. "Thereness," however, involves

FIG. 14. *The movable projection screen in three different positions. By means of a mirror arrangement, the slide projector (to the right of the observer's head) focuses an image on the screen from a point a fraction of an inch to the right of the peephole through which the observer is looking with his right eye.*

not only distance but direction as well, and this latter factor cannot be excluded in the determination of the "what" of what we see. For verification of this fact we must turn to another demonstration.

The apparatus for this demonstration consists of a small slide projector mounted on a frame which can be rotated 45° above or below level about a horizontal axis, and a screen mounted about three feet from the projector on the same frame so that it rotates with it about the same axis (see Figure 14). The observer looks with one eye through a small hole equivalent to the nodal point of the projector. Thus, with suitable adjustment of the frame, he can look at a projected picture downward 45°, straight ahead, or upward 45°.

The two pictures observed in these three different directions are of a tower or steeple taken with the camera pointing upward 45°, and of a stairway photographed with the camera pointing downward 45°. When the viewing apparatus is set at 45° downward, an observer looking through the viewing hole sees the steeple in very distorted perspective; it appears to slant markedly back and away from him. If he looks at the same picture straight ahead, the perspective is still distorted, but not so badly. If he looks at it upward 45°, the perspective is perfectly normal and the steeple does not appear to lean at all. However, with the stairway picture taken with the camera pointing down 45° all the above phenomena are reversed. When the observer looks up at the picture, the effect is quite confusing and disagreeable, the perspective is bad, and he has trouble interpreting what he sees. Looking straight ahead improves the situation somewhat, and a shift to 45° downward results in a perception which appears perfectly natural in that perspective is good and there is a marked tri-dimensional effect.

It is apparent that, whether the observer using this apparatus is looking downward, straight ahead, or upward, the stimulus configuration on his retina remains absolutely the same. The only factor that is varying is the direction in which he is looking. In each case, though, what the observer sees—the characteristics he assigns to the object—is somehow a function of his past experience of directionality in dealing with such retinal patterns.

In order to round out the thinking behind the idea that what we see are constructs built up through experience, it should be pointed out that directionality itself probably is not the "objectively" determined phenomenon we commonly suppose it to be. Ordinarily, we think of visual direction as being determined entirely by the direction of impinging light rays, but this common assumption is denied by a variety of experiments, especially those dealing with the effects of acceleration or alteration of the "G" factor. For example, if an observer is strapped

in an upright position on a chair on a centrifuge and forward acceleration is produced by rotating the centrifuge, he will see a light which is
actually on a level with his eyes as being in an upward direction. How
high above eye level it appears to be depends on the speed with which
the centrifuge is rotated. He sees the light in a different direction from
where it actually is, and in a different direction than that from which
the light rays are coming to his eyes. This and numerous other oculo-
gravic and oculogyral illusions show the effects of radial and angular
acceleration on the perception of the direction of an object (1, 2, 3).
Thus the sense of direction cannot be accounted for here by so-called
objective factors; there must also be included the subjective factor of
the observer's sense of orientation to gravity. It seems likely that only
through experience in looking, reaching, walking, balancing, etc. do we
build up functional assumptions concerning direction as it is related to
our sense of egocentric localization.

With the aid of a number of demonstrations we have examined
certain aspects of the process of perceiving. These demonstrations
strongly suggest that distance, direction, and object characteristics do
not exist independently in their own right; that our perception of them
cannot be explained either by "what is there" or by any unique correspondence between physiological stimulus patterns and what is perceived.
A more satisfactory explanation began to emerge when we introduced
consideration of the time dimension and experience (assumptions) and
treated "thereness" and "thatness" not as objectively determined "things"
but as abstracted aspects of a total process which necessarily includes
past as well as present, organism as well as environment. It can be truth-
fully said, however, that the demonstrations presented in this chapter
are somewhat limited in that they are, for the most part, concerned
with quite simple, static, monocular situations. They are indeed a far
cry from the complex dynamic perceptions involved in our daily living.
One might fairly ask, then, "Do the principles derived from these simple
cases apply as well to more complex examples involving more factors,
motion, and the use of both eyes?"

REFERENCES—CHAPTER 2

1. Clark, Brant, and Graybiel, Ashton. "Apparent rotation of a fixed
target associated with linear acceleration in flight." *Amer. J. Ophthal,*
1949, *32,* 549–57.

2. Clark, B.; Graybiel, A.; and MacCorquodale, K. "The illusory

perception of movement caused by angular acceleration and centrifugal force during flight: II. Visually perceived motion of a fixed target during turns." *J. Exper. Psychol.,* 1948, *38,* 298–309.

3. Graybiel, A.; Hupp, D. I.; and Patterson, J. L., Jr." The law of the otolith organ." *Fed. Proc. Amer. Soc. Exper. Biol.,* 1946, *35,* 35.

C H A P T E R

3

The Perception of Movement[1]

F. P. Kilpatrick & William H. Ittelson

INTRODUCTION

I T SEEMS USEFUL at the outset to distinguish between two different principal directions of perceived movement. One, directly toward or away from the point of observation, can be labeled *radial movement*, while the other, at a constant radial distance, can be termed *tangential movement*. These principal directions of motion are clearly analogous to the familiar static *depth* and *direction*, and, just as in the static case, one would expect different types of cues to be utilized by the organism in the two different cases.

[1] Originally printed under the title "Three Demonstrations Involving the Visual Perception of Movement," *J. Exper. Psychol.*, 1951, *42*, 394–402. Printed here in slightly abridged form by permission of the authors and the publisher, The American Psychological Association.

DEMONSTRATION I: RADIAL MOTION

THIS DEMONSTRATION is concerned with the role of continuous change of size as an indication of continuous movement in a radial direction. That such an effect does take place was apparently first appreciated by Wheatstone (10), and has since been studied in a variety of contexts (1, 3, 4, 5, 7). The apparatus discussed below contains within it means for demonstrating virtually all that is known regarding this particular phenomenon.

A light box (A in Figure 1), on the front of which is a square dia-

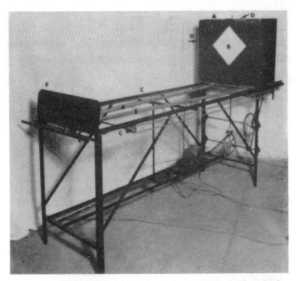

FIG. 1. *The radial motion apparatus. The light box A is driven back and forth on the tracks C and C. As it moves, the size of the diaphragm openings B changes in a manner determined by the setting of the tracks E and E.*

phragm opening (B), is driven back and forth on a track (C and C) through a distance of six feet by an electric motor. The opening is observed, in an otherwise dark room, from a distance of six feet from the shield (F) at the near end of the track. The square diaphragm opening is formed by two metal plates (D and D) moving in slots on the front of the light box. Each of these metal plates engages one of a second pair of tracks (E and E) whose inclination and separation can be varied. As the box moves back and forth, variations in the size of the diaphragm opening are controlled by the inclination of this second pair of tracks. If they are set parallel, the size of the opening remains constant. If the tracks are set so that they converge toward the observer, as in the figure, the size of the diaphragm decreases as it moves toward the observer; if they are set so that they diverge, the size of the diaphragm increases as it approaches the observer.

When an observer views this apparatus under various conditions of monocular and binocular observation and with various separations and inclinations of the tracks, certain consistent and predictable perceptions are experienced.

Situation 1: when the tracks are set parallel, an observer looking with both eyes sees a square of constant size moving back and forth at a constant speed, approaching to a distance from him of approximately six feet and receding to a distance of approximately twelve feet (condition I, Figure 2). His perception in this case corresponds to the actual objective situation.

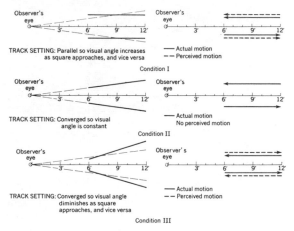

FIG. 2. *Perceived motion of the lighted diaphragm (B in Figure 1) under three conditions of observation. The actual motion is the same under all three conditions, but the perceived motion varies with the track setting.*

Situation 2: if the observer looks with one eye, he sees substantially the same thing (condition I, Figure 2).

Situation 3: if, under these conditions, the tracks are then converged so that the opening subtends a constant visual angle as it moves back and forth, the observer sees the square standing motionless at the apparent distance at which it was localized at the moment that the tracks were converged (condition II, Figure 2).

Situation 4: if the tracks are converged still more to just the right amount, the observer will again see a square of constant size moving back and forth at a constant speed through a distance from him of six to twelve feet, but the apparent direction of movement will now be opposite to that of the actual movement (condition III, Figure 2).

Situation 5: if both eyes are used under the conditions described in situation 4 above, the effect continues to be experienced by most observers to a greater or less extent, persisting even when stationary objects are placed in the field of view to provide more adequate binocular localization. Great individual variations are encountered here.

A further most interesting phenomenon can be illustrated with this apparatus. The tracks are first set parallel with a medium separation. Situations 1, 2, 3, and 4 above are then successively presented to the observer who, under situations 1, 2, and 4, sees a square of medium size moving at a constant speed from a point six feet away to a point twelve feet away and back again. It should be noted that the apparatus is so designed that the sequence 2–3–4 can be carried out smoothly, without any sudden jumps in the size of the moving diaphragm. The tracks are then set parallel but with a greater separation than under the original situation 1. Under these conditions, using both eyes, the observer's perception of the distance, direction, and speed of movement remains unchanged; he simply sees a larger square. After the observer has looked for a few moments, one of his eyes is blocked off, but, as before, he experiences no significant change in his perceptions. Without giving the observer any indication of exactly what is being done, the tracks are then shifted back to the original situation 4, the apparatus being so designed that this can be accomplished smoothly without introducing any sudden jumps in the size of the stimulus. This situation provides exactly the same external situation and retinal stimulus pattern which had previously been perceived as a square of fixed size moving at a constant speed from six to twelve feet. But now the observer perceives it as a *larger* square, moving through a *greater* distance, *farther* away from him, and at an *increased* and *variable* rate of speed. This effect continues even when the original situation 2 is presented again, which may be accomplished by presenting situations 4–3–2 in that order.

Many variations of this basic effect are possible, involving, for example, a shift toward rather than away from the observer. All these variations, however, seem to involve the same process. When the observer first looked at the smaller square he perceived a square of constant size moving back and forth at constant speed from six to twelve feet, which in fact corresponded to the actual external situation. In terms of retinal stimulation, this means that a square retinal pattern (disregarding distortion) continuously changing in size was related to the perception of a square of constant size continuously moving in space. When the shift was made to the larger square, the same effect was obtained, reinforced initially by the use of binocular indications. The interesting point, of course, occurs when, in monocular observation, the actual size of the square is reduced to the original, smaller size. It should be noted that the procedure is such that the observer is unaware of this change and assumes that he is still looking at the larger square. As a result of this assumption, the identical pattern of retinal stimulation, which just previously had been related to the perception of a small square moving at constant speed through a certain distance, is now related to the perception of a larger square, farther off, moving through a greater distance, and at a variable speed. To state this more generally, there are an unlimited number of objective, external events which will produce the same sequence of retinal patterns. Which one of these external events will in fact be perceived depends on the particular assumptions (in this case, primarily that of size) which the individual brings to the occasion.

DEMONSTRATION II: CIRCULAR MOTION

THE SECOND APPARATUS to be described involves the perception of circular motion. It is photographed in Figure 3 and schematically represented in Figure 4. As shown in the diagram (Figure 4), this ap-

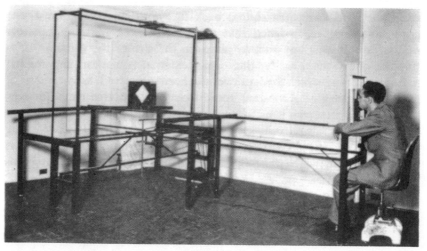

FIG. 3. *Circular motion apparatus showing the light box with variable size square diaphragm opening in place on the oscillating mount.*

paratus contains a mount (A), which is electrically driven so that it oscillates through an arc (BCD) of about 40° at a distance of 8′ 9″ from the observer's eye (E). The rate of angular movement about this point (E) is mechanically controlled to be the same as that which would result from an object describing a hypothetical circle (BFDG) with a three-foot radius at a constant angular velocity about a center (C) 8′ 9″ from E. This means that the angular velocity about the obser-

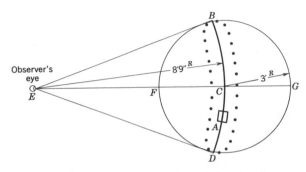

FIG. 4. *Schematic representation of the circular motion apparatus.*

vation point (E) is variable, being zero at the two end points (B and D) and reaching a maximum halfway between them. This maximum, furthermore, is greater for movement in one direction (in our case, left to right or BCD) than in the other direction (right to left or DCB).

When a small star point of light is placed on the oscillating mount (A), an observer using one eye in an otherwise dark room sees it moving in a shallow ovate arc approximately as indicated by the dotted lines in Figure 4. Its apparent speed of movement is variable, being considerably greater in one direction (left to right) than in the other direction. We stress here that the star point does not appear to swing from side to side at a constant distance from the observer as it is actually doing, but rather, it is seen appreciably nearer the observer during the period of higher angular velocity and appreciably farther away during the period of low angular velocity, resulting in a roughly elliptical path of perceived movement.[2]

We now replace the star point with a light box having a variable

[2] It is worth noting also that a star point which remains at the same height as the observer's eye and is actually moving in the circle BFDG at a constant speed is perceived in exactly the same way; that is, as moving in the roughly elliptical path indicated by the dotted lines in Figure 4.

size square diaphragm opening similar to that used in the radial motion demonstration described above. If the size of this opening is kept constant as the square swings from side to side, an observer using one eye sees a constant size square swinging from side to side at variable speeds at a constant distance from him; i.e., true tangential movement at variable speed, which in this case corresponds to the actual movement. It is possible, however, by means of a mechanical linkage, to vary the size of the diaphragm opening in such a way that the angle it subtends to the observer's eye exactly corresponds at all times to the angle that would be subtended by a square surface normal to the observer's line of sight moving in a counterclockwise direction about the hypothetical circle pictured in Figure 4. When the observer now looks at this square diaphragm, which is changing its size at a variable rate and swinging in a shallow arc at variable speed, he sees a square of constant size moving in a circle at a constant rate of speed.

It is evident from the above-described effects that objective tangential movement can be related to a number of perceived movements, depending on the other indications available. In the case of the star point, relative angular velocities at different times served as an indication of relative apparent distances at these times. This effect is clearly related to the familiar depth cue of parallax, with the important modification that the relative angular velocities occur at different times rather than simultaneously. It would seem evident that a perceptual integration along a temporal dimension is involved here. However, if angular velocity serves as an indication of distance, even more striking is the effect of apparent distance in determining apparent velocity. Apparent circular movement at constant speed resulted from the addition of appropriate indications of relative distance. Or, to state this more precisely, circular movement at constant speed was the correlate in experience of appropriate indications of tangential movement at variable speed plus radial movement at variable speed.

TANGENTIAL MOTION: A CASE OF CONFLICT

A GIVEN MOVEMENT across the retina—for example, movement in a constant direction at a constant speed—can be produced by an infinity of external, objective movements; and of course, this relationship becomes even more complicated when eye and head movements and bodily orientation are taken into account. The related perception, however, can obviously be of only one of this infinity of objective conditions. Ordinarily other aspects are available, such as size, brightness, etc., to determine the particular perception, but these other indications are themselves not unequivocal and may even be in conflict. The demonstration described below shows how real, objective tangential movement [3] may be perceived as a variety of apparent movements when some of the other indications are systematically altered.

A thin metal trapezoidal shape with openings corresponding to window panes (inset, Figure 5) is placed, related to the observer's eye, in the position of A'B' (Figure 5). When viewed monocularly under these conditions, the physically near edge (A') becomes the apparently far edge (A), and the physically far edge (B') becomes the apparently near one (B). The resulting perception is of an approximately rectangular "window" in the position AB. The photographs in Figure 6 will give an idea of the way in which the trapezoid is perceived.

A small electric motor drives a fine thread in such a way that light objects suspended from it—e.g., a small card cut out of paper—can be driven across the field of view at a constant speed along the straight path CD (Figure 5), passing through one of the near openings of the trapezoid, which to the observer is one of the apparently far openings.

However, it is not perceived as moving in such a straight path; it is seen as following the approximately S-shaped course indicated by the dotted line EF (Figure 5). The nature of this illusory movement is dependent on the fact that the observer sees the trapezoid as a rectangular shape in a position different from its true position. As the card moves across the field of view, it is initially to the right of the "window" and appears against a homogeneous background (I in Figures 5 and 6). Under these conditions it is seen as constant in size moving from right to left at a constant speed in a direction parallel to the observer's frontal plane. When it moves to a position such that part of it is behind the near edge of the trapezoid, it appears to be passing behind the far edge of the apparent rectangle (II in the figures). As the card moves completely through the near opening of the trapezoid, it comes between the observer and successively farther parts of the trapezoid. To the observer, however, it appears to be passing in front of successively nearer parts of the apparent rectangle (III and IV in Figures 5 and 6). The card, therefore, appears to be moving toward the observer parallel to the apparent plane of the rectangle and at the same time decreasing in apparent size. It finally appears to pass completely in front of the rectangle and continue to travel in a straight line at a constant speed

[3] The movement employed in the demonstrations is not, strictly speaking, tangential. It is straight-line movement at right angles to a fixed line of sight, with consequent variation in radial distance. However, since the variation in radial distance is very small in the demonstration, it seems fair to speak of the motion as tangential.

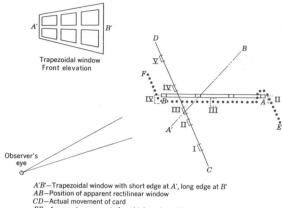

FIG. 5. *Diagram showing the real and apparent positions of the trapezoid and the real and apparent paths of the moving card in the tangential motion demonstration. Direction of movement is from the positions I to V along the line CD.*

FIG. 6. *Photographs showing eight successive positions (A through H) of the card in the tangential motion demonstrations. The frame appears to be tipped back with the right side farthest from the camera; actually, the reverse is true. The Roman numerals indicate the five positions corresponding to those shown in Figure 5.*

and size (V in the figures). The distance from the observer at which the card is moving before and after it passes the trapezoid cannot be judged accurately.

In summary of this particular effect, movement of a constant-size object traveling at a constant speed in a constant direction at a virtually constant distance from the observer is perceived as an object of varying size traveling in varying directions and at varying speeds and distances. This perceived movement through an approximately S-shaped path is, as indicated earlier, only one of an infinite set of movements which might be perceptually related to the given objective movement. Broadly speaking, this particular effect is achieved by placing the constant size, speed, and direction of the moving object in conflict with the overlay indications from the falsely localized trapezoid. Overlay proves more effective for all observers, and the above-described movement is perceived.

Not all observers, it should be added, see the apparent size change. Many continue to see the moving card as constant in size even when specifically questioned, and in spite of the fact that they perceive the movement in depth quite dramatically. This is merely evidence that, in any perceptual situation involving conflicts, differential individual behavior is to be expected, with greater differences occurring the more nearly the two, or more, possible ways of perceiving are equated in terms of probability of occurrence. This can be most startlingly illustrated with the apparatus described here by placing not only the object but also the trapezoid in motion (2, 6). The resulting effects are described in Chapters 12, 13 and 14.

[Because of the importance of apparent movement in the recent history of psychology, note should be made of the role played by past experience in the perception of apparent movement. This was studied experimentally and analyzed by Toch (8) and by Toch and Ittelson (9). They demonstrated that the direction in which a "stimulus" object appeared to move depended on what an observer assumed the object was. For example, when a photograph of a vertical row of three bombs was flashed on a screen, six out of the eight observers saw movement in a downward direction, the other two observers not recognizing the objects as "bombs." Similarly, a slide picturing airplanes arranged vertically with their noses pointed upward produced an upward apparent movement on the part of the observers who recognized the objects as airplanes.

[In Chapter 4 experimental investigations of some of the points made in Chapter 2 concerning size and distance perception, and in this chapter on radial motion, are reported.

[In Chapter 5, the underlying variables (assumptions) are studied in relation to visual accommodation and convergence.—Ed.]

REFERENCES—CHAPTER 3

1. Ames, Adelbert Jr. *Some Demonstrations Concerned with the Origin and Nature of Our Sensations (what we experience). A laboratory manual.* (Preliminary draft.) Hanover, N. H.: Hanover Institute, 1946. (Mimeographed.)

2. Ames, Adelbert Jr. "Visual perception and the rotating trapezoidal window." *Psychol. Monogr.,* 1951, Vol. 65, No. 7 (whole No. 324).

3. Calavrezo, C. "Uber den Einfluss von Grossenänderungen auf die scheinbare Tiefe." *Psychol. Forsch.,* 1934, *19,* 311–65.

4. Hillebrand, F. "Das Verhältnis von Accommodation und Convergenz zur Tiefenlokalisation." *Z. Psychol.,* 1894, *7,* 97–151.

5. Ittelson, W. H. "Size as a cue to distance." *Amer. J. Psychol.,* 1951.

6. Kilpatrick, F. P. *Some Aspects of the Role of Assumptions in Perception.* Unpublished Ph.D. thesis, Princeton Univ., 1950.

7. Metzger, W. "Tiefenerscheinungen in optischen Bewegungsfeldern." *Psychol. Forsch.,* 1934, *20,* 195–260.

8. Toch, Hans H. "The perceptual elaboration of stroboscopic presentations." *Amer. J. Psychol.* 1956, *69,* No. 3, 345–58.

9. Toch, Hans H., and Ittelson, W. H. "The role of past experience in apparent movement: A revaluation." *Brit. J. Psychol.,* 1956, *47,* Part 3, 195–207.

10. Wheatstone, C. "Contributions to the physiology of vision. Part the second." *Philos. Mag.,* 1852, Ser. 4, *3,* 504–23.

CHAPTER

4

Size as a Cue to Distance[1]

William H. Ittelson

STATIC LOCALIZATION

Introduction

THERE IS LITTLE experimental evidence to which one can turn when investigating many of the monocular cues to depth perception. Very few studies have been devoted, for example, to such cues as overlay, or light and shadow, to mention but two from a long list. The question of the relation between size and distance, however, is an instructive exception. The general outlines of this subject will be familiar to most readers and need not be repeated here. The literature is large and informative, but on close inspection is seen to deal almost exclusively with the special question of size constancy. While this aspect presents an interesting and fruitful field for investigation, it has often been quite removed from the question of size as a cue to distance. Most investigators in the field assert that for size constancy to function other indications of distance must be present, thereby implicitly denying what might

[1] Originally printed in the *Amer. J. Psychol.,* 1951, *64,* 54–67, 188–202. It is printed here, slightly modified with the kind permission of the author and of the publisher, the *American Journal of Psychology.*

well be the core of the problem, that size itself is a recognized cue to distance. Distance as determined from size is a problem quite distinct from, although obviously related to, that of size as determined by distance.

That size does serve as a cue to the localization of objects in visual space is recognized by virtually all writers on the subject. A survey of a large, though perhaps not representative, sample of texts ranging from the most elementary "introductory psychologies" to the most advanced treatises on visual space perception reveals only rare omissions and no denials of this generally accepted fact. Why, then, undertake to belabor the obvious?

The answer to this question calls for a statement of the aims of the first half of this paper. First we should provide a statement of, and evidence for, the conditions under which size serves as a cue to distance. Three cases may profitably be distinguished: (1) relative size as a cue to relative distance; (2) absolute size as a cue to absolute distance; and (3) change of size as a cue to change in distance. Of course, these three cases are not independent, and it seems reasonable to assume that similar processes are involved in all three. Nowhere, however, can these three cases be found described in detail with conditions for them analyzed and subjected to experimental investigation. The chief aim of this first half is to start in the direction of such a detailed analysis.

While almost all writers recognize size as a cue to distance, most restrict themselves to the first case alone, that of relative size as a cue to relative distance. The reason for this is not hard to find, for this case is undoubtedly the most easily conceptualized and does the least violence to traditional ways of thinking. Another aim is, therefore, to specify a mechanism adequate to account for all three observed cases.

In this section certain aspects of size as a cue to static localization are experimentally studied while the next section will be devoted to the question of size change as an indication of radial movement.

Method

The basic problem in the experimental study of distance cues is to find a means of measuring the apparent localization of a perceived object and to study changes in this localization as a function of the variable or variables under consideration. The accepted experimental procedure has generally been some variation of the classical psychophysical techniques in which the variable has been systematically altered and compared at each point with a "standard" consisting of the same variable held constant. This type of study has proved invaluable in yielding information concerning a wide variety of perceptual phenomena; but in the case of distance cues the results have by no means been entirely satisfactory. Such an approach does not readily lend itself to the study of the apparent absolute distance from the observer as the dependent variable under investigation. Yet this is exactly the variable which must be studied if one is seeking information about the distance cues.

This problem has been recognized by many investigators who have attempted to introduce absolute apparent distance explicitly as a variable to be studied. Bourdon, for example, used distance as judged in meters as a measure of apparent distance (4, pp. 279–90). He also had his observer approach the object to be localized until O believed himself to be near enough to touch it with his outstretched arm. Carr introduced in some of his experiments a more satisfactory objective measure of apparent distance, but the revolutionary nature of this contribution has not been grasped by later investigators (8, p. 250). His technique, used in connection with his mirror stereoscope, consisted of having O use his hand, which he did not see, to indicate the apparent distance of the object presented. This method yielded quite satisfactory results within the near distances to which it is necessarily limited. Attempts to extend the range of such measurements have involved the substitution of visual indications for the placement of O's hand. Fischer and Lowenbach, for example, used the setting of a vertical rod, which was visible to O, as an indication of apparent distance (12). Grant (14) has reported a technique in which apparent distance is measured by the placement of a monocularly viewed coin.

All such attempts to measure apparent distance, however, remain inconclusive until an adequate and generally accepted definition of apparent distance can be reached, a problem that has not received the attention devoted to other aspects, due probably to at least three contributing factors: the general neglect of the experimental study of distance cues, the all-too-frequent implicit assumption that physical and apparent distance are generally equal, and an unstated belief that an intuitive grasp of the meaning of distance is adequate to the problem. We shall attempt a somewhat more rigorous definition of two aspects of distance as they enter into our experimental studies:

Physical or objective distance: measured distance, in the external physical world, from a reference point on O to the physical object in question, expressible relative to such a standard as feet and inches.

Apparent or functional distance: the physical distance at which the object is functionally located for O, as determined by some specified operation.

The operation so specified can, in general, be any type of behavior in a "well-structured" field, a situation when, in popular terminology, the perception "resembles as nearly as possible the permanent object which is being perceived." What is meant by such loose terminology is simply that purposive behavior is normally successful.

What is proposed, then, is essentially an operational definition of apparent distance. It is not suggested that such a definition exhausts or adequately describes all aspects possible to O of perceived distance. We can only agree with James that "subjectively considered, distance is an altogether peculiar content of consciousness" (21, p. 40). It is maintained, however, that an operational definition is essential for experimental study. In the research reported here the apparent distance of an object will be measured in terms of some operation which O performs relative to that object. In this sense, the perception of apparent distance can be defined as an implicit awareness of what action or actions would be needed in order to carry out some purpose involving that distance.[2] It would be desirable to have workers in the field agree upon some standard measuring operation.

This measuring operation must meet at least two requirements: it must measure what we want to measure and it must not itself influence the results obtained. Our operational definition of apparent distance enables us to meet the first of these requirements. If the awareness of distance is an awareness of a functional relationship between O and the various objects in the field, then this distance can be measured in terms of some operation performed by O with respect to the particular object under consideration. For example, if O reaches out his hand to grasp the object, as in Carr's technique, the place to which he reaches may be taken as a measure of where he sees the object. Similarly, for greater distances, the placement of a pointer at the same distance as the perceived objects may be taken as a measure of the apparent distance, provided all normal indications of the position of the pointer are present and the distance is within the limit of the normal effective functioning of such indications.

If these requirements are met, the position of the pointer, expressed in terms of some physical co-ordinate system—say, in feet and inches from midway between O's eyes—represents the best obtainable measure of the apparent localization of the object.

The second requirement of the measuring operation, that it should not influence the results obtained, can only be checked experimentally. If the operation can be varied systematically without affecting the results, it may safely be said to meet this requirement. Failing this, the extent of interaction can be determined and a decision made as to its

2 For a more general application of such a definition to problems of perception, see Cantril (6, p. 19).

significance relative to the particular problem at hand. Such a check was conducted on the apparatus used in this study.

In addition to providing a means of measuring apparent distance, the apparatus must also allow control of the visual cues which are the independent variables under consideration. It is evident that the two requirements of control and measurement dictate entirely different properties which can only be met in different visual fields. Yet O must be able closely to compare these two fields. The apparatus, therefore, must have two visual fields which can be viewed in close juxtaposition in both space and time. One field, called hereafter the experimental field, can be used to present the carefully controlled stimulus situation which is being investigated. The other field, the comparison field, is designed to provide a measure of the effect of the conditions set up in the experimental field. Measurements in the comparison field must be accurate and reliable, and there must be no interaction between the two fields.

APPARATUS. The two fields [3] are provided by the two sections of an L-shaped room. O sits at their junction and looks directly into one field, the comparison field, while the experimental field extends to his right, at right angles to his line of view. Now O views the comparison field through an arrangement of half-silvered mirrors the effect of which is to superimpose the experimental field, which is actually to his right, on the comparison field directly ahead. Thus, by manipulating the lighting of the two fields, E can present—apparently directly in front of O—either the experimental field or the comparison field, or both together. Since, in general, the cues under investigation will be monocular, the half-silvered mirror arrangement is such that the comparison field is viewed binocularly while the experimental field is seen with one eye (although by a simple adjustment it too can be viewed binocularly). Binocular observation of the comparison field is used in order to provide reliable distance indications so that the earlier stated requirement of a "well-structured" field may be met.

It should be stressed that there is nothing in principle to prevent the use of this apparatus for the inverse situation; i.e., a well-structured monocular field used to measure the effect of an unstructured or anomalous binocular configuration.

The room which houses the apparatus forms an L roughly 50 feet by 25 feet. These dimensions are not regarded as ideal, being merely dictated by the space available. A satisfactory apparatus could be con-

[3] The present apparatus is a further development by Ames of his original thereness-thatness table (see Chapter 2, this volume). The two alleys have been completely separated physically, for simpler and more complete control of each, while they have been placed phenomenally closer together to increase the validity and accuracy of the results.

structed in considerably less space, and all dimensions can presumably be scaled up or down within limits, depending on the distances under study.

In the comparison field directly before O is a table 20 feet long on which is a small cart which moves on tracks the length of the table. A comparison object can be placed on this cart and illuminated in such a way that it is the only object in the comparison field visible to O. By manipulating a knob, O can move this comparison object the length of the track (*ca.* 2–19 feet). The setting of this comparison object, as measured on a scale fastened to the table, is used as an indication of the apparent distance of the object presented in the experimental field. In addition to the movable comparison object, any desired comparison situation may be set up. For example, the comparison field may consist of a series of rods relative to which the apparent distance of the experimental object can be judged.

The experimental field is completely empty and may have any desired stimulus configuration placed in it by E. A headrest is provided, together with shields containing apertures which allow O to see only that part of each field actually required by the experiment. Careful control of the illumination prevents O from being aware of these apertures. The details of the illumination used will vary with each individual experiment, but a master switchboard is available which provides for six separately controlled light sources. Black draperies, which prevent light from leaking from one field to the other, complete the setup.

This apparatus was subjected to exhaustive tests in the control of the experimental field and interaction between the experimental and comparison fields.

CONTROL OF THE EXPERIMENTAL FIELD. The effects of general illumination, perspective, and parallax can be adequately controlled with proper care. The chief remaining cues which might affect the experimental field are brightness, accommodation, and convergence. No simple means of controlling one or more of these can be used without interfering with accurate localization in the comparison field. The most effective means of control, therefore, is either to keep all constant or systematically to balance them out in any specific experiment.

INTERACTION BETWEEN THE EXPERIMENTAL AND COMPARISON FIELDS. The effects of perspective, movement parallax, and general lighting conditions can be adequately controlled. Binocular convergence, which is determined by the objects in the comparison field, was studied by means of converging and diverging prisms and was not found to be a major determinant of the apparent distance of objects in the experimental field.

A comparison of settings made while both fields were viewed simultaneously with others made while the fields were viewed alternately indicated the desirability of using "alternate presentation" with first one field and then the other viewed by O for approximately 1 second with a 1-second dark interval between, this sequence continuing until O was satisfied with his setting.

The effect of the size of the object placed in the comparison field, the setting of which is used as a measure of apparent distance of objects in the experimental field, was studied by using two different sizes of each of a variety of comparison objects. In order to minimize size-interaction effect, it was found desirable to use a well-defined, specific comparison object; i.e., not merely a meaningless or ambiguous geometrical figure, and one which will be readily identifiable within the distance range employed. Two such objects which gave satisfactory results were an ordinary pack of cigarettes and a checkerboard pattern of black and white squares. Each of these comparison objects was used in part of the experiments described below.

Size and Static Spatial Localization

HISTORY. That the relative sizes of objects of visual space serve as a cue to their relative positions is generally accepted. It is to be found listed among the depth criteria in virtually all texts, although actually little relevant experimental work has been conducted.

Some positive evidence is to be found in the studies of the role of accommodation; e.g., Bourdon (4), Peter (25), and Bappert.[4] Studies more specifically concerned with the size cue have been reported by Pouillard (27), Petermann (26), and Carr (8); while Vernon (30) and Hirsch (19) have studied the role of relative size in relation to binocular disparity. Chapter 2 of this volume describes demonstrations of the effect of relative size on relative distance for one-, two-, and three-dimensional objects, using pairs of lines, squares, and balloons. The findings are all in substantial agreement. Relative size is, in fact, utilized as an indication of relative distance; of two similar objects, the one subtending the larger visual angle will, in the absence of other indications, be seen as closer.

That the absolute size of an object provides a cue to its absolute localization in space is by no means as well established or as generally accepted. Virtually all discussion pro and con has been on a theoretical, rather than an experimental level. Many authoritative writers have

[4] For a summary of this and other studies, see Woodworth (32, pp. 665–80).

argued affirmatively and present a picture of general agreement as to the broad outlines of the process involved.[5] O must *know* the size of the object of regard. This enables him to *infer* its distance.

While some of Bourdon's work on the localization of a single disk of light is relevant (4), the first specific experimental test of this generally held hypothesis was provided by Ames when he showed that a single monocularly viewed object can be definitely localized with respect to a binocular comparison field (1). Ames refers to this as the "thereness of the thatness demonstration," thereby laying stress on the fact that the apparent distance of the perceived object (its "thereness") is determined by the perceived nature of the object (its "thatness"). The basic apparatus used by Ames has been described earlier in this book, and modifications may be found described in more detail by Lawrence (23) as well as by Hastorf (15), who provides the first relevant quantitative evidence.

Hastorf presented his Os with identical stimulus configurations on two successive sessions differing only in the meaning of the stimulus E suggested to O. For example, a white rectangle was on one occasion a calling card and on another an envelope. Os performed significantly differently under these two conditions in a setting dependent on apparent distance. Hastorf concluded that "the size of a stimulus can be used as a distance cue. Moreover . . . the distance of this stimulus depended on the assumed size attributed to it." The efficacy of this "assumed size" cue was shown by Ittelson and Ames (20) in their study of the role of apparent distance in determining the accommodation and convergence of the eyes (see chapter 5).

The experimental evidence, therefore, while scanty, is consistent in showing that the absolute size of an object can be utilized as an indication of absolute distance.

DEFINITIONS. It seems imperative, before proceeding, to clarify terms. The ways in which distance will be used in this paper have already been defined. Size poses still further problems. Some of the many uses of this term in the study of visual perception will be briefly reviewed:

Physical or objective size: measured size in the external physical world, expressible in relation to such a standard as feet and inches.

Visual angle: the angle, expressible in degrees, which a physical object subtends at the nodal point of the eye.

Retinal or physiological stimulus size: the physical size of the stimulus pattern on the retina. In general, this must be estimated from other data.

Visual angle and retinal size are often treated as synonymous. This

[5] Representative statements may be found, for example, in Donders (10, p. 154); Helmholtz (16, p. 282); Hering (17, p. 203); Carr (8, p. 278); and Duke-Elder (11, p. 1061).

useful practice has potential disadvantages. It is most important, for example, in any theoretical interpretation, to recognize the fact that, since there are no physiological processes relating the nodal point to the retinal elements, the organism has no basis for determining visual angle, which is merely a convenient abstraction created by the conductor of the experiment.

These three definitions represent the physical and physiological aspects of size; its experiential aspects must now be defined. This question dates at least to Berkeley, who identified two types of size, "visible" and "tangible," and asserted that "the judgments we make of the magnitude of objects by sight are altogether in reference to their tangible extension. Whenever we say an object is great or small, of this or that determinate measure, I say, it must be meant of the tangible and not the visible extension" (3, sect. 61). We can see in this statement an early progenitor of the current emphasis on the "distal" as opposed to the "proximal" stimulus.

Both aspects do, to be sure, intrude themselves into experience. Joynson sums up contemporary views of this problem by describing two types of perceptual attitudes, the phenomenological and the analytic, and showing how two meanings for apparent size derive from these two modes of observation, thus requiring two definitions.

> Apparent absolute size: the impression of "real" size which we obtain when we look at an object in normal, practical perception. (Phenomenological attitude: attention directed to "bodily size," as Brunswik terms it.)

> Apparent angular size: the proportion of the visual field an object appears to fill. (Analytic attitude: attention directed to "projective size," as Brunswik terms it (22).

These two definitions are admirable in that they fix once and for all the fact that there are two equally valid meanings for apparent size related to two equally valid modes of observation. To state this in other words, visual space perception represents a transformation from polar to Cartesian co-ordinates. Attention can be directed toward either.

The concept of apparent absolute size, nevertheless, remains somewhat amorphous, as defined above, since it relies on an essentially intuitive grasp of what is meant by the undefined term "real." It may be suggested, without elaboration, that the way out of this difficulty lies in terms of "functional size" along the lines already indicated in defining apparent distance. It should be noted, however, that any attempt to achieve such a behavioral definition must recognize that an object (a far-off man, for example) may look small and yet be judged big. Hering, who first explicitly stated this problem (17, p. 171), therefore introduced the concept of estimated size, which is a deliberate, conscious, intellectual judgment of the physical size of an object.

Assumed size is another useful concept which was suggested by Ames (1) and elaborated by Hastorf (15), who defines it as "the entirely subjective sense of size which the observer might relate to a specifically characterized physiological stimulus-pattern. Most people, for example, have some concept of the size of a playing card or of an oak leaf. It is to these concepts of the sizes of familiar objects which the term assumed size refers. Assumed size can, naturally, only relate to objects with which we have had concrete experience." The size used in this definition is presumably our physical size.

Occasionally, in this paper, it will be found convenient to generalize this concept of assumed size into assumed objective referent, which can be defined as the sum total of objective properties, the specific "thingness," that an observer attributes to a particular characterized stimulus pattern.

A final use of size should be recorded to round out this account. The term "real size," introduced by Thouless (28) and developed by Vernon (30), "relates to an abstract idea of the size of an object based upon deductions from the apparent size of the object when it is quite close to the observer, in comparison with the apparent sizes of other near objects." As thus defined, "real size" would seem to lie somewhere between Hering's estimated size and Hastorf's assumed size. As actually used, the term seems to drift somewhat uncertainly between these two with occasional sorties in the direction of physical size.

It will sometimes be convenient to use here the simple, unmodified term "size" to refer most generally to all aspects and processes involved in the study of size as a cue to distance. The word will be appropriately modified to conform to one of the above definitions whenever specific reference to a specific aspect is intended.

The Experiments

The experiments here reported were designed to study the general question of the absolute localization in space of a single monocularly viewed object. Two series of data were taken under essentially identical procedures. Several objects were presented to O, one at a time, at a constant physical distance, in the experimental field of the apparatus. The apparent distance of each object was determined in the manner already indicated.[6]

[6] The author is indebted to A. H. Hastorf for assistance in the design and conduct of this part of the experiment.

Series I examines the general relationships existing between retinal size and apparent distance by measuring the apparent distance of each of two physical sizes of three different objects presented one at a time at the same physical distance and viewed monocularly. Series II more directly studies the role of assumed size by controlling the assumed objective referent. Assumed size is changed while both physical size and distance remain constant, and both assumed size and physical size are changed with physical distance constant.

STIMULUS CONFIGURATIONS. The test objects used in Series I are given in Table I. The diamonds and inkblot figures were cut out of white cardboard, while the playing cards were obtained by photographing a card and printing it in reverse to appear normal when reflected by the mirroring arrangement. The objects were presented one at a time at the fixed distance of 9 feet. The comparison object was a cigarette package of standard size.

The test objects in Series II (Table II) were presented one at a time at the fixed distance of 7½ feet. It will be noted that all five test objects are rectangles with the same width-to-height ratio. The only distinction between the large card and the letter, or between the small card and the matchbox is the pattern or design, which suggests to O a specific objective referent.

TABLE I

EFFECT OF SIZE ON APPARENT DISTANCE
Physical distance 9 ft.; monocular observation
(N = 24)

TEST OBJECT	SIZE (in inches)	MEAN APPARENT DISTANCE (in feet)	SD	DISTANCE RATIO	SD
Small playing card	1¹¹⁄₁₆ x 2⅝	11.88	1.77	1.92	0.21
Large playing card	3⅜ x 5¼	6.19	0.81		
Small inkblot	*	10.72	2.27	1.84	0.24
Large inkblot	*	5.83	1.17		
Small diamond	3½ x 3½ †	7.93	2.38	1.73	0.33
Large diamond	7 x 7†	4.59	1.67		

* These were irregular cutout figures. Maximal vertical dimension of the large inkblot was 7 inches, maximal horizontal dimension 5¼ inches. The dimensions for the small inkblot are 3½ inches and 2⅝ inches.

† These squares were presented with diagonals vertical and horizontal: thus they appeared as diamonds. The dimensions given are for the sides of the squares.

The comparison object used was a checkerboard pattern viewed binocularly.

PROCEDURE. In Series I, O was led to the apparatus in complete dark-ness, his head placed in the headrest, and then given instructions as to the nature of his task, which was to set the comparison object at the same distance as the test object. At the end of the trial, O was questioned upon the difficulty of the task, his estimated accuracy, and the apparent sizes of the test objects. The experimental design provided for control of the effect of order of presentation of the test objects, order of presenta-tion of size, level of brightness, order of presentation of brightness, and initial position of the comparison object. In analyzing the effect of any one of these, the effects of all others can be canceled out.

The Os were twenty-four college students who were completely un-aware of the nature of the experiment or of the apparatus and had never previously served as a psychological O.

The procedure in Series II differed from Series I only in that a simplified experimental design was used, the test objects being presented in the same order for all five Os, who varied from thoroughly experienced to completely naïve in this field.

RESULTS. In response to the questions asked at the end of Series I, only one O indicated any real difficulty with the task. Most believed that they had made their settings easily and within an accuracy of 4–8 inches. None was aware that two different sizes of each object had been used, although objectively the sizes, and hence the visual angles, varied in a ratio of two to one. Four reported that, in some cases, possibly differ-ently sized figures had been used.

The mean setting of apparent distance of each of the six test objects used in Series I is given in Table I. It will be noted that a ¾-size playing card at 9 feet was, when viewed monocularly, seen at approximately 12 feet, while a 1½-size card, also at 9 feet, was seen at approximately 6 feet. Each card was therefore seen at that distance at which a normal-size playing card would have to be placed in order to provide a retinal image of the given size. In this case the assumed objective referent is known. Presumably, the other figures also were seen at distances appropriate to their objective referents, which varied more widely from individual to individual, as is indicated by the greater coefficients of variation of the settings. Just what the objective referents of these figures were for the various Os is an open question, although all instantly and unequivocally localized them in space.

A further point of interest in Table I is given by the distance ratios, which refer to the far apparent distance divided by the near apparent distance. This provides a measure of the extent of the change in distance independent of the actual magnitudes of the distances involved. It will be noted that the two-to-one ratio of objective size was seen as a 1.92 distance ratio for the playing cards, 1.84 for the inkblots, and 1.73 for the diamonds. This suggests the possibility that the consistency with which a specific assumed objective referent was maintained in each of the three cases decreased in that order.

Of the experimental controls, only the effects of the level of brightness, the order of presentation of size, and the initial position of the comparison object were significant.

The mean settings of apparent distance for each of the five test objects used in Series II are given in Table II. The significance of the differences of the various means was checked by means of a t-test with indicated results. It will be noted that the apparent distances of the normal playing card, the letter, and the matchbox are not significantly different. These three objects, of very different physical size and presenting differently sized retinal images, were perceived at the same apparent distance.[7] A comparison between the apparent distances of the double-size playing

TABLE II

APPARENT DISTANCES OF OBJECTS DIFFERING
IN SIZE AND OBJECTIVE REFERENT
Physical distance 7.5 ft.; monocular observation
(N = 5)

TEST OBJECT	SIZE *(in inches)*	MEAN APPARENT DISTANCE *(in feet)*	SD
Normal playing card	3½ x 2¼	7.46	0.51
Double playing card	7 x 4½	4.61	0.49
Half playing card	1¾ x 1⅛	14.99	2.51
Typewritten business letter	7 x 4½	8.58	1.01
Matchbox	1¾ x 1⅛	8.96	1.73

Tests of the significance of difference between above means

MEANS COMPARED	t*	SIGNIFICANCE	INTERPRETATION
Normal card and letter	2.19	No	Three different size objects seen at the same apparent distance.
Normal card and matchbox	1.41	No	
Letter and matchbox	0.39	No	
Double card and letter	6.14	Yes	Same size objects seen at different apparent distances.
Half card and matchbox	8.63	Yes	

* t = 4.60 for significance at 1% level.

[7] Actually, the letter and the matchbox were seen slightly, though not significantly, farther away than the normal card. Both of these test objects, in order to equal the size of respectively the double-size card and the half-size card, had to be made somewhat smaller than "normal." Their somewhat greater apparent distances, therefore, are entirely consistent with the other results.

card and the letter or between the half-size playing card and the match-box reveals just the opposite effect. In these cases two objects of identical physical size and presenting retinal images of the same size were, never-theless, seen at greatly different apparent distances. These results become completely consistent when interpreted in the light of the known assumed objective referent in each case.

Summary and Conclusions

The apparent distance of each of a variety of test objects was meas-ured for several observers in an apparatus designed for this purpose. The test objects consisted of playing cards of various sizes, matchbox, typewritten business letter, and cutout geometrical shapes. They were viewed monocularly at a fixed distance. An analysis of the results leads to the following conclusions:

(1) A single object viewed monocularly is perceived at a definite radial distance.

(2) This apparent distance is primarily determined by the size cue.

(3) Size operates as a cue to distance in the following manner: A perceptual integration is reached between the physiological stimulus size and the assumed size related to that particularly characterized stimulus pattern. The object is localized by O at the point at which an object of physical size equal to the assumed size would have to be placed in order to produce the given retinal size.

(4) This dependence is not absolute but varies from individual to individual.

(5) When the assumed size related to a specifically characterized stimulus configuration tends to be the same for a group of Os, they will tend to see the object related to that configuration at the same dis-tance. When the assumed size varies from individual to individual, the apparent distance also will vary. The assumed size may also presumably vary for a single individual from time to time.

(6) Discrete changes in the size of the physiological stimulus related to a physical object will be perceived as discrete changes in the apparent distance of that object, provided the assumed size remains constant.

(7) These discrete changes in the size of the physiological stimulus related to a physical object can be compensated for or completely over-ridden by changes in assumed size.

(8) Discrete changes in the characteristics of the physiological stim-ulus pattern resulting in changes in assumed size will be perceived as discrete changes in apparent distance even though retinal size remains constant.

RADIAL MOTION

Introduction

The visual perception of motion has long been a subject of theoretical interest in experimental psychology. The question of the existence of a "sensation of motion" may be almost as old as the concept of sensation itself. While the emphasis on specific theoretical considerations has shifted throughout the years with the gradual development of psychological concepts, the general area remains today, as almost a century ago, a fertile ground for speculative debate. Further incentives for the study of the perception of motion have arisen more recently in the widespread use of fast-moving vehicles, with their operation dependent in the last analysis on some individual's perception of moving relationships. These highly practical considerations, underlined by the experiences of World War II and the continuing emphasis on military applications, have resulted in an intensification of the effort to gain an understanding of the basic phenomena involved in the visual perception of movement.

A great volume of experimental work has been conducted upon many aspects of the problem. There are classical studies in the literature covering such aspects as the phi-phenomenon, perceived speed of motion, thresholds of movement, aftereffect of seen movement, autokinetic movement, and numerous illustrations of movement, to mention only a few of the areas that have been investigated. The history of this experimentation is too long and complex to be covered here, and a complete integration which should provide a working theory of all the perceptive facts of motion is still lacking.

This section is devoted to an experimental investigation of a phase of perceived movement which has not received the attention given to some of the above-mentioned aspects; namely, movement directly toward or away from the observer (hereafter to be called radial motion). The specific experimental problem is that of size change as a cue to radial motion. In view of its central importance for any complete understanding in this field, it is perhaps astonishing to note that there is only scattered evidence bearing on the problem.

That continuous change of retinal size is perceived as continuous movement in space was early noted by Wheatstone (31), but it remained for Hillebrand (18) to report a simple, practical laboratory demonstration. He found that, if the size of an illuminated diaphragm, viewed monocularly in an otherwise dark room, was continuously increased or decreased while its actual distance from O remained constant, a distinct impression of approach or recession was aroused. Further, if the diaphragm actually approached while at the same time its aperture was rapidly decreased, O reported an impression of movement away from him, or in a direction opposite to that of the actual movement.

Although these facts are referred to in many reference works on visual perception, the theoretical significance of Hillebrand's observations does not seem to have been generally recognized. Knowledge of the phenomenon remains today essentially as Hillebrand stated it. Its existence is nowhere denied, nor has it received any further systematic experimental or theoretical treatment.

Recently, however, Ames has extensively investigated this phenomenon, which we can subsume under the general heading of apparent radial movement. He has demonstrated its existence for one-, two-, and three-dimensional objects and has combined these effects with others to produce a wide variety of apparent movements which cannot be directly distinguished from real movement. Most important for our purpose, he has shown qualitatively that the region in space through which the aperture apparently moves and the apparent distance of its movement depend on the assumed size which O attributes to it.

In addition to this evidence, analogous observations have been reported in investigations of other problems. Gamma movement, for example, refers to the apparent swelling in size of a suddenly illuminated object. Under favorable conditions, this increase in apparent size is accompanied by an apparent movement toward O (2).

Phi movement directly toward O has been demonstrated by Calavrezo by stroboscopically presenting forms of similar shape but different sizes (5). Under optimal conditions, his Os experienced apparent movement in depth, seeing a single object continuously moving toward them.

Metzger has reported an arrangement by which moving shadows are cast upon a screen (24). As the size of the shadows changes continuously, there is a strong tendency to interpret this fact as movement-in-depth of objects of constant size and shape.

Hastorf, whose Os themselves varied the size of a stimulus, found "that almost all the subjects reported that they had a very real feeling of movement as the stimulus was increased or decreased in size . . . . an alteration in the objective size of the stimulus was perceived as a change in apparent distance of the stimulus" (15).

In addition to the above published reports, the author would like to include some personal observations made when he was privileged to witness a private demonstration of a new art form which is being developed by James Davis of Princeton. In part, this consists of casting on a screen multicolored reflections which continuously move and change shape and size. The experience is aesthetically and emotionally quite impressive. In the immediate context, however, it is of interest to report the dramatic depth effects which are achieved. Objects appear to recede into the far distance or to rush spectacularly into the foreground. It is impossible to see the entire movement as taking place on a two-dimensional surface. The changes in shape and position, as well as overlay indications, are all contributing factors, but the effect seems to be largely dependent upon the size changes. The factor of continuous change is crucial. If the movement is stopped, the apparent depth shrinks or disappears completely.

From the above evidence it may be concluded that the phenomenon of apparent radial movement resulting from continuous size change is quite well established. At least four important questions can never the less be posed for which there is little evidence and with which the experiments reported in this section are concerned. What are the conditions which favor and which inhibit this phenomenon? What is the relation of apparent to real radial motion? What are the conditions which determine the apparent distance of such movement? And finally, what mechanism can be proposed which will be adequate to account for all the observed cases of size as a cue to distance—static localization as well as radial movement?

Terms must be first clarified. "Size" and "distance" as used in this paper have previously been defined. The consideration of radial motion, however, necessarily introduces some new terminology.

POLAR REFERENCE SYSTEM. Space, depth, tri-dimensionality, the third dimension, are all descriptive terms commonly used to convey the idea that "we see a three-dimensional world through a two-dimensional retina." As such they are admirable, but as well-defined scientific concepts they would seem to be useless. For the purpose of experimentation we shall express spatial localization in terms of a polar co-ordinate system; i.e., radial distance and angular direction from O. The origin of this co-ordinate system will be, for monocular observation, the nodal point of the viewing eye and, for binocular observation, a point midway between the two eyes. "Radial distance" refers to distance along a straight line passing through this origin point, and "radial motion" refers to movement along this line.

This polar reference system is useful primarily because its "radial" aspect, although analogous to the classical "depth," enables us more definitely to study experimentally the effect of distance from O. Helpful though it is for this purpose, the polar system is not adequate to describe phenomenological space perception. We may view the world about us from the center of a polar system, but we interpret it in terms of a behavioral reference system which is essentially Cartesian. Any space perception, and especially the perception of motion, can be shown to be a complex integration of the polar and the rectilinear. Indeed, the very term "depth" carries implicitly this dual reference. The polar reference system, therefore, is an experimental tool and is not intended to be descriptive of phenomenal space perception.

PHENOMENAL ASPECTS OF MOTION. The perception of motion is a complex phenomenon which can be analyzed in many different ways. For the purpose of this analysis it seems useful to distinguish the following four aspects:

(a) Awareness of movement. The awareness of continuous displacement in space of a definite object. This is not intended to imply that such a definition exhausts all possible meanings of the awareness of movement —it clearly does not—but merely that this is the use to which the term will be put in this discussion.

(b) Apparent distance of travel. The apparent distance through which the moving object appears to move. If the movement is in the radial direction the apparent distance of travel may be determined by subtracting the apparent distance of the farthest point of movement from the apparent distance of the nearest point, provided movement is continuous in one direction.

(c) Apparent direction of movement. No general definition of this term will be given here. In the experiments to be reported, movement resulting from a change in size without change in angular direction is studied. Hence, this movement is in the radial direction; i.e., directly to or from the viewing eye.

(d) Apparent velocity of movement. This aspect is mentioned only for the sake of completeness. It will not be defined here since it is not explicitly included in this study.

Experiments

Two experiments were performed dealing with various aspects of radial motion. Experiment I is concerned with the factors that influence the awareness of radial movement resulting from a continuous change of retinal size and seeks to determine whether continuous size change actually is seen as continuous radial movement, whether such movement can be distinguished from objective radial movement, and what the effect is of placing continuous size change in conflict with other indications. To answer these questions, various measures of the apparent motion of a stationary diaphragm which continuously changes in size are compared with the same measures for a similar diaphragm which remains of constant physical size but is in actual movement.

Experiment II deals with the factors that influence the apparent distance of travel of movement resulting from continuous size change. A comparison is made between various measures of apparent movement taken for a variety of objects all having the same actual motion.

APPARATUS. Both experiments utilize the basic apparatus previously described—a two-alley setup, one alley containing the experimental field in which the stimulus situation being studied can be placed, and the other alley containing the comparison field relative to which apparent distance can be measured. A system of mirrors enables O to see both alleys simultaneously and apparently directly in front of him.

The comparison field, as used here, contained a checkerboard comparison object on a movable cart. In addition, parallel to the path of the comparison object and just to the left of it was a row of vertical posts placed at distances of 5, 10, 15, 20, and 25 feet from O. These posts were ½-inch wood dowels 4 feet in length, each of which was provided with a small spotlight which directly illuminated about a foot in the middle of the post. The illumination gradually decreased beyond this point until the ends of the posts were not visible.

STIMULUS CONFIGURATIONS. The stimulus situation used in Experiment I consisted of two parts. The first was a cart bearing a light box with a square aperture 3¼ inches by 3¼ inches illuminated from behind, Target A. This cart was motor driven on tracks in such a way that the target moved back and forth, between two points 6 and 12 feet in a radial direction from O, at a constant speed of 36 feet per minute, requiring 10 seconds to cover the 6 feet of travel.

The second part consisted of a light box at a fixed distance of 9 feet from O, containing a similar illuminated aperture of variable size, Target B. The size of this target was controlled by the motion of the cart carrying Target A, so that the size change of B was always synchronized with the motion of A. Target B varied from a 2½-inch to a 4¾-inch square, subtending the same range of visual angles as Target A.

Both targets were placed with their diagonals vertical and horizontal, appearing to O as illuminated diamonds against a black background.

For Experiment II both targets were removed, and the test objects indicated in Table IV were placed one at a time on the reciprocating carriage which had previously carried Target A. The physical movement of these objects was therefore the same as that described for Target A. It will be noted that these test objects are the same as those for which data on apparent static localization have already been given.

PROCEDURE. Experiment I was divided into several parts which will be described separately.

(1) The comparison field was viewed binocularly and was continu-

ously illuminated while O was making a setting. The experimental field was viewed monocularly. The half-silvered mirror arrangement was so adjusted that whichever target was in view appeared directly before O, the path of its perceived movement being parallel to the row of posts and to their right. Each O was first shown Target A and asked to set the comparison object at the nearest point of movement, and then at the farthest point. These settings were repeated. O was asked to attend the moving object, but not to fixate it while making settings. No time limit was made for a setting, the target moving back and forth continuously until O was satisfied with each setting. O was then shown Target B and the procedure repeated.

(2) The procedure was the same as in Part 1, and the same data were taken. In this case, however, the stimulus targets were viewed binocularly and the comparison field monocularly. In order to improve accuracy of localization in this monocular comparison field, playing cards were suspended from each post and a playing card was used as a comparison object. (It should be noted that this comparison field does not completely meet the requirements stated previously for such a field and therefore does not give an entirely accurate measure of the apparent distance. It does, however, provide an objective means of comparing reactions to the two conditions.)

(3) Conditions were the same as in Part 2, except that both experimental and comparison fields were viewed binocularly. O was asked for verbal reports.

(4) The comparison field was not used. Both targets were illuminated at the same time and viewed binocularly. The half-silvered mirror was so adjusted that the apparent paths of the perceived movement of each target made equal angles with the median plane of O, who was asked to estimate the distance of travel of either target relative to the other, under three conditions: viz., (a) Target B going through the same range of visual angle as A, angle increasing as A approached; i.e., apparent motion of both targets in the same direction; (b) same as (a), but the visual angle of B decreased as A approached; i.e., apparent motion in opposite directions; (c) size of B constant.

The procedure in Experiment II was identical to Part 1 of Experiment I. (Data have previously been reported for the same Os using the same test objects.)

RESULTS: EXPERIMENT I. The results of Experiment I will be reported separately for each part.

(1) O viewed monocularly first an actually moving target and then a similar target which was fixed in space but varied in size. Verbal reports under the two conditions were identical. The target in each

case was perceived as moving back and forth in space. No apparent size change was reported.

The mean settings of the apparent nearest and farthest point of travel of each target are given in Table III. Those of the near and far points of Targets A and B are not significantly different. O not only perceived both targets as moving in space but also failed to distinguish between them in terms of the apparent position of the end points of this movement. It should be noted, however, that the standard deviations for Target B are almost twice those of Target A. Performance relative to the two targets was not identical, even though it was not significantly different in this study.

TABLE III
APPARENT DISTANCE OF NEAREST AND
FARTHEST POINT OF MOVEMENT (MONOCULAR)
(N = 5)

Target A actually moving from 6 to 12 feet. Target B fixed at 9 feet but changing in size through same range of visual angle as A

POSITION	TARGET	MEAN APPARENT DISTANCE (in feet) *	SD	t	SIGNIFICANCE
Near point	A	6.41	1.26	1.91	No
	B	7.26	2.03		
Far point	A	13.96	2.88	0.08	No
	B	14.05	4.12		

* The distance ratio, obtained by dividing the apparent far point of movement by the apparent near point, is, for Target A, 2.18; for Target B, 1.93.

(2) O viewed the same two targets binocularly and made settings in a fairly well-structured monocular comparison field. Verbal reports from all Os indicated that Target B appeared to move back and forth in space. Table IV gives the mean settings made. It will be noted that the means for the far positions are significantly different, although those for the near positions are not. In other words, while O perceived a binocularly viewed stationary object, which changed in size, as moving in space, he nevertheless distinguished in terms of the given task between this object and an actually moving binocularly viewed object.

(3) O binocularly viewed Target B, changing in size, in a well-defined binocular field. Reports indicated a very equivocal situation. Size change

TABLE IV

APPARENT DISTANCE OF NEAREST AND
FARTHEST POINT OF MOVEMENT (BINOCULAR)
(N = 5)

Target A actually moving from 6 to 12 feet. Target B fixed at 9 feet but changing in size through same range of visual angle as A. Both targets viewed binocularly, apparent distances measured in monocular comparison field

POSITION	TARGET	MEAN APPARENT DISTANCE *(in feet)* *	SD	t	SIGNIFICANCE
Near point	A	5.61	0.22		
	B	6.16	0.54	1.46	No
Far point	A	11.21	1.56		
	B	10.29	1.71	4.12	.01

* The distance ratio, obtained by dividing the apparent far point of movement by the apparent near point, is, for Target A, 2.00; for Target B, 1.67.

was reported in all cases but was always accompanied by statements regarding the appearance of movement. ("It seems to be moving without getting anywhere." "It looks as if it's moving, but it isn't. Yes, it is. No, it isn't.") In general, fixating the target resulted in a conviction of a slight amount of radial movement, while fixating some other part of the field resulted in "movement without getting anywhere." In all cases, a lack of surety was experienced and the situation was described as anomalous.

(4) The two targets, viewed binocularly, were compared under three conditions: (a) Target B changing with A; (b) Target B changing opposite A; and (c) Target B constant. Reports for five Os are given in Table V.

When the two targets appeared to be moving in the same direction, four of the Os gave almost identical reports. Target A came farther forward than Target B and went farther back, but B moved back and forth within roughly the middle third of the travel of A.

When movement was in opposed directions, the reported apparent movement of B approached much more closely than of A. This judgment, however, is much more difficult to make, and no controls were used in terms of two actually moving objects. It may well be, therefore, that there is no real difference between these two cases.

The third condition was introduced to determine how much, if any, of the movement seen in the other two cases might have been due to induced movement.[8] The results show at best a very slight induced-movement effect.

TABLE V

APPARENT MOVEMENT OF TARGET A RELATION TO THAT
OF TARGET B (BINOCULAR)

*Target A actually moving from 6 to 12 feet. Target B fixed at 9 feet, but
changing in size through same range of visual angle as A.
Targets viewed simultaneously*

Condition of observation: Direction of movement

O	(a) opposed	(b) together	(c) B not changing
WI	B moves ¾ of distance of A	B moves ⅓ of distance of A	No movement of B
BM	B moves same distance as A	B moves ⅓ of A	Slight movement of B in random direction
HC	B moves ¾ of A	B moves ½ of A	Zero to very slight movement of B
AW	B moves a little farther than A	B moves ⅓ to ½ of A	No movement of B
DR	B same as A	B same as A *	No movement of B

* In view of this performance, this O was subsequently given a standard clinical stereoptical test. She attained 100% on the Keystone DB6 card.

TABLE VI

THREE MEASURES OF THE PERCEIVED MOVEMENT OF OBJECTS
DIFFERING IN SIZE AND OBJECTIVE REFERENT

Physical movement 6–12 ft.; monocular observation
(N = 5)

TEST-OBJECT	SIZE (in inches)	MEAN APPARENT DISTANCE OF MOVEMENT (in feet)	MEAN APPARENT DISTANCE OF MIDPOINT OF MOVEMENT	MEAN DISTANCE RATIO*
Normal playing card	3½ x 2¼	9.16	10.77	2.55
Double playing card	7 x 4½	6.06	6.95	2.58
Half playing card	1¾ x 1⅛	15.01	17.39	2.52
Typewritten business letter	7 x 4½	7.01	9.36	2.23
Matchbox	1¾ x 1⅛	9.17	11.31	2.34

* Distance ratio here (as elsewhere in this paper) refers to the apparent far point of movement divided by the apparent near point.

[8] The term "induced movement" has been used to refer to a phenomenon which can be observed when a moving and a stationary object are viewed simultaneously. Under some conditions the movement may be entirely attributed to the actually stationary object which then appears to move relative to the actually moving object which appears stationary. This effect has been reported only for movement in a plane perpendicular to the line of sight. Induced movement in the radial direction has not been studied.

EXPERIMENT II. Table VI gives the means for three measures of performance in Experiment II. The first is the apparent distance of travel, obtained by subtracting the apparent near point of travel from the apparent far point. The second is the apparent distance of the midpoint of this travel, taken as a measure of the specific radial localization of the object. The third is the perceived movement expressed in terms of ratios of apparent distances from O. It should be noted that both the objective movement and, hence, the visual angle varied in the ratio of two to one.

This table shows extremely wide and significant variations in distances and midpoints of travel for the five test objects but a great consistency in the ratios of movement.[9] None of the mean ratios was found to be significantly different from any of the others, although there was evidence of individual differences.

Correlation between the apparent distance of travel and the apparent localization in space, as measured by the midpoint of travel, was very high, 0.98. The ratio of the movement, however, was unrelated to either of these measures, the correlation with the midpoint being −0.30, and with the distance of travel −0.18.

SUMMARY OF EXPERIMENTS (1) The awareness of radial movement is the result of a continuous change in one or more indications of radial distance. Apparent radial motion resulting from a continuous change of retinal size is indistinguishable from objective radial movement in monocular vision and tends to dominate even well-structured binocular effects.

(2) The apparent distance of travel of radial movement resulting from continuous size change depends on the specific apparent radial localization of the perceived object, which has previously been shown to depend on the assumed objective referent.

(3) The ratio of the apparent near point of travel to the apparent far point of travel depends on the ratio of the visual angles. It is not completely determined by this ratio, since individual differences exist in tendency to inhibit or encourage movement.

(4) There is evidence for the hypothesis that dynamic cues will, in general, override static cues, if these stand in conflict.

GENERAL DISCUSSION

A GLANCE AT the history of speculation and experimentation regarding size as a cue to distance shows that the conclusions reached both in this section and in the previous one in no way contradict any of the existing evidence. In the case of radial movement, our findings extend and verify

---

[9] As may be expected, the great differences in apparent distance of travel were accompanied by differences in apparent velocity which O spontaneously reported.

earlier data. The general experimental and theoretical agreement that relative size serves as an indication of relative distance has already been noted. With regard to absolute size as a cue to absolute localization, discussion has been largely speculative, with virtually no experimental evidence up to the present time. There is no need for a detailed comparison of the conclusions reached here with those of each of the many writers who have dealt with these topics. These experiments have attempted to fill in some of the experimental gaps with pertinent quantitative data, and to show that these three effects, often considered as isolated and mutually independent, are in fact different aspects of the same phenomenon and depend on the same perceptive mechanism.

It has been traditionally argued that the so-called monocular cues to depth perception require explanation in terms of some "higher" perceptual process, that they cannot be understood as simple physiological responses to a stimulus. It is not sufficient, however, simply to classify them as "psychological cues" which depend on an undefined past experience. A more detailed theory is certainly needed. The mechanism which is here proposed as being adequate to account for the evidence reported in this paper and elsewhere is to be found, as already intimated, in the assumptions which an observer makes as to the nature of the world about him. Retinal size, for example, can become an indicator of distance only if coupled with some information as to the physical size of the external object. This information is provided in the form of an assumption of that physical size. Assumed size, coupled with retinal size, provides sufficient information to determine distance. Similarly, the relative retinal sizes of two simultaneously viewed objects can become meaningful in terms of relative distance only if some assumption is made as to the relative physical sizes of objects. This process is adequate to account for all the reported evidence. There is no contradictory evidence.

The notion that some assumption must be made as to the nature of the external configuration before size can function as a cue is not new. It is implied by all the writers earlier cited with regard to the problem of absolute localization. It has, furthermore, been more or less explicitly stated in one form or another by several writers. Hering, for example, was clearly expressing a similar view when he said that "the apparent alterations in form and place, of objects, which result from the manner of their projection upon the retinal surface, are well known after much experience. Hence, it becomes possible that very diversified forms of retinal images of a single object bring to reproduction the image of its real form which our memory retains more or less clearly" (17, p. 200). Here the "image of its real form" is obviously a forerunner of our "assumed-objective referent." Similarly, Helmholtz referred to the dependence of monocular depth perception on "some previous acquaintance with the special nature of the perceived object" (16, p. 282). The treatment by Thouless of the role of "real" size is also a case in point (28), while Vernon has explicitly referred to the assumptions which the observer must make in order to account for the effects of size on the apparent distance of an object. "Conclusions as to its distance must in general be based," she writes, "on some knowledge of or assumption as to its 'real' size, or, in cases of relative localization, of the relative 'real' sizes of the two objects" (29).

In discussing the operation of relative size as a depth cue, Ames has also specified what he feels are the assumptions which one must necessarily make in order to account for the observed effect (1). As he expressed it, "you presume identity of size (length in this case) from similarity, and use the appearance of difference in apparent length as an indication of distance." Or, as more generally stated by Ames, the basic assumption involved is that "similar things are identical."

The relevance of Hastorf's work in this context is obvious (15). He has specifically defined "assumed size" and made it the independent variable in his experiment.

The need to postulate some such mechanism of assumption to account for the functioning of size as a cue to distance is inescapable. Efforts to formulate theories without doing so have been unsuccessful. No attempt will be made at this point to discuss in detail all such theories. A recent systematic presentation by Gibson may, however, serve as a case in point. Gibson sets forth a stimulus-response theory of depth perception in which the "stimulus correlates of continuous physical distance" are various retinal gradients. This leads him to speak of "the retinal gradient of size-of-similar-objects."

Commonly there are classes or types of similar objects scattered about or lined up in the environment. Houses, fence posts, telegraph poles, fields, and even hills tend to be of similar physical size and shape, as do chairs, tables, and people. If there are more than a few of these similar objects in the visual field, there can exist a gradient of decreasing retinal size (13).

Gibson then goes on to insist that such gradients "are to be distinguished from the traditional 'cue' for distance perception of the apparent size of familiar objects; i.e., of objects whose real size is remembered from past experience . . . The explanation proposed here does not assume the perceiving of absolute sizes as such, but only the ability to react to a continuous gradient of retinal sizes." But it does assume the subjective identification of "classes or types of similar objects." This "subjective factor," having thus quietly sneaked in by the back door, quickly finds its way to the front parlor. For "gradients of size and gradients of texture are obviously analogous and the one merges into the other." Even the basic "gradient of texture" is therefore clearly seen to depend on the identification of its elements as belonging to the same class of objects. Or, in Ames's terminology, on the assumption that "similar things are identical."

The impossibility of formulating a theory of size as a cue to distance without building on some such foundation of subjective factors has led some writers tacitly to deny the existence of such a cue. One means of denying it has been to ignore it. Many reference works, for example, give but scant and passing mention to the role of size in distance perception, limiting themselves to some simple statement that "relative size may be a criterion of distance."

Another more effective, and more pervasive, way of accomplishing the same object lies in asserting the primacy of distance. Apparent distance is, for these writers, determined by other cues; then apparent size emerges as the result of a combination of this apparent distance with the retinal size. This approach has developed as a natural outgrowth of the size-constancy studies. That it is often true cannot be denied. To claim that it is always true is to fall into error. Our results, as well as the evidence from other sources, show that such an interpretation is simply not in keeping with the facts. As one author has written, "It is usually stated that in such cases the idea of distance is the primary one, but it is questionable if this can be dogmatically affirmed; the relation is probably reciprocal, for when size is definitely known the illusion affects the perception of distance" (11). The fact that size serves as a cue to distance cannot be effectively refuted.

The foregoing discussion, however, is primarily relevant to static localization and still leaves unanswered the question of the applicability of the assumptive mechanism to the problem of size change as an indication of continuous radial motion. Certainly movement perception is not a completely unique case, and it is clear that everything that has been said about assumptions in the static cases holds in this instance. The apparent radial localization of the moving object at any given moment is just as clearly dependent on the assumed size which the observer attributes to it as is the localization of a stationary object. An assumption of size is therefore necessary; but it is not sufficient to explain the fact of apparent movement, since the changing retinal size might conceivably result in a changing assumed size with apparent distance remaining constant. In the experiments reported this did not happen. It therefore becomes necessary to postulate an additional assumption of constancy of objective properties to account for the observed results.

The assumption of "thing" constancy is essential for the perception of radial motion.

This assumption of the constancy of physical properties need not necessarily be made by every observer in every situation. It will, however, in general be made whenever the observer subjectively places the perceived external configuration in the general class of inorganic, physical objects. From the perceptual point of view, the chief characteristic of this class of objects is the constancy of the properties of its members. As Dewey and Bentley have expressed it in another context, "object is chosen as the clearly indicated name for stabilized, enduring situations, for occurrences that need so long a span of time, or perhaps so minute a space change, that the space and time changes are not themselves within the scope of ordinary, everyday perceptual attention" (9). In ordinary, everyday perception, objects are assumed to have constant properties.[10]

This attribution of specific objective properties to a particularly characterized stimulus configuration, however, is at best never an absolute certainty. It is always subject to empirical modification. It is for this reason that the term "assumption" has been chosen, and because such processes as are involved in perception operate "below the level of awareness," these assumptions have been specified as "unconscious." Whether or not there is any relationship between these unconscious assumptions and the conscious intellectual assumptions of reasoning need not concern us here.

We can, however, define an assumption, as used here, as an unconscious attribution of specific objective properties to an external configuration. One's assumptive world (see 7) then becomes that galaxy of assumptions which an individual makes as to the nature and significances of the objective world about him. "Properties," "nature," and "significance" as used here are definable only in terms of some behavioral reference. "Assumption" does not, therefore, refer to a conscious, intellectual, mentalistic concept, but rather to a specific mode of behavior

---

[10] It may, of course, be argued that the experiments on which these conclusions are based are laboratory experiments which severely limit the data available to the observer and therefore are not representative of ordinary, everyday perception. This objection can only be answered experimentally, but the available evidence clearly indicates that, under "normal" conditions, with all the usual cues present, size serves as a cue to distance in precisely the manner demonstrated in the laboratory, that the assumptive mechanism functions just as completely, and just as necessarily, under normal as under laboratory conditions. This does not imply that the apparent distance of an object in normal observation will often be entirely, or even largely, determined by its assumed size, as was the case in the laboratory. Under such condition assumed size probably accounts for only a small part of the variance in apparent distance.

in a specific situation which has been learned and which has become characteristic of the behavior of the particular individual in that situation.

REFERENCES—CHAPTER 4

1. Ames, A. Jr. *Some Demonstrations Concerned with the Origin and Nature of Our Sensations (what we experience). A laboratory manual.* (Preliminary draft). Hanover, N. H.: Hanover Institute, 1946. (Mimeographed.)

2. Bartley, S. H. *Vision.* New York: Van Nostrand, 1941.

3. Berkeley, G. *An Essay Towards a New Theory of Vision* (1709). (In *Berkeley: Essay, Principles, Dialogues.* New York: Scribner's, 1929.)

4. Bourdon, B. *La Perception visuelle de l'espace.* Paris: Schleicher frères, 1902.

5. Calavrezo, C. "Über den Einfluss von Grössenänderungen auf die scheinbare Tiefe." *Psychol. Forsch.,* 1934, *19,* 311–65.

6. Cantril, H. *Understanding Man's Social Behavior* (preliminary notes). Princeton: Office of Public Opinion Research, 1947.

7. Cantril, H.; Ames, A., Jr.; Hastorf, A. H.; and Ittelson, W. H. "Psychology and scientific research." *Science,* 1949, *110,* 461–64, 491–97, 517–22.

8. Carr, H. A. *An Introduction to Space Perception.* New York: Longmans, 1935.

9. Dewey, J., and Bentley, A. F. *Knowing and the Known.* Boston: Beacon, 1949.

10. Donders, F. C. *Accommodation and Refraction of the Eye.* (Trans. from the author's manuscript by W. D. Moore.) London: New Sydenham Society, 1864.

11. Duke-Elder, W. S. *Textbook of Ophthalmology.* St. Louis: Mosby, 1936, Vol. 1.

12. Fischer, M. H., and Löwenbach, H. "Messende Untersuchungen über Sehferne und Sehtiefe." *Arch. f.d. ges. Physiol.,* 1935, 235, 609–37.

13. Gibson, J. J. (Ed.) *Motion Picture Testing and Research.* (Army Air Forces Aviation Psychol. Program Report No. 7.) Washington: Government Printing Office, 1947.

14. Grant, V. W. "Accommodation and convergence in visual space perception." *J. Exper. Psychol.,* 1942, *31,* 89–104.

15. Hastorf, A. H. "The influence of suggestion on the relationship between stimulus size and perceived distance." *J. Psychol.,* 1950, *29,* 195–217.

16. Helmholtz, H. *Psychological Optics* (1866, trans. by J. P. C. Southall). Optical Society of America, 1925, Vol. III.

17. Hering, E. *Spatial Sense and Movements of the Eye* (trans. by C. A. Radde). Baltimore: American Academy of Optometry, 1942.

18. Hillebrand, F. "Das Verhältnis von Accommodation und Konvergenz zur Tiefenlokalisation." *Z. Psychol.*, 1894, *7*, 97–151.

19. Hirsch, M. J.; Horowitz, M. W.; and Weymouth, F. W. "Distance discrimination. III. Effect of rod width on threshold." *Arch. Ophthal.*, 1948, *39*, 325–32.

20. Ittelson, W. H., and Ames, A., Jr. "Accommodation, convergence, and their relation to apparent distance." *J. Psychol.*, 1950, *30*, 43–67.

21. James, William. *Psychology, Briefer Course.* New York: Holt, 1892.

22. Joynson, R. B. "The problem of size and distance." *Quart. J. Exper. Psychol.*, 1949, *1*, 119–36.

23. Lawrence, M. *Studies in Human Behavior.* Princeton: Princeton Univ. Press, 1949.

24. Metzger, W. "Tiefenerscheinunger in optischen Bewegungsfeldern." *Psychol. Forsch.*, 1934, *20*, 195–260.

25. Peter, R. "Untersuchungen über die Beziehungen zwischen primären und sekunären Faktoren der Tiefenwahrnehmung." *Arch. ges. Psychol.*, 1915, *34*, 515–64.

26. Petermann, B. "Über die Bedeutung der Auffassungsbedingungen für die Tiefen- und Raumwahrnehmung. *Arch. ges. Psychol.*, 1924, *46*, 351–416.

27. Pouillard, G. "Contribution à l'étude expérimentale de la notion spatiale de la profondeur." *J. Psychol. Norm. & Path.*, 1933, *30*, 887–929.

28. Thouless, R. S. "Phenomenal regression to the real object." *Brit. J. Psychol.*, 1931, *21*, 339–59; *22*, 1–30.

29. Vernon, M. D. "The perception of distance." *Brit. J. Psychol.*, 1937, *28*, 1–11, 115–49.

30. Vernon, M. D. *Visual Perception.* Cambridge, England: Cambridge Univ. Press, 1937.

31. Wheatstone, C. "Contributions to the physiology of vision. Part II." *Philos. Mag.*, 1852, *3*, 504–23.

32. Woodworth, R. S. *Experimental Psychology.* New York: Holt, 1938.

5

Accommodation, Convergence,

& Apparent Distance [1]

William H. Ittelson & Adelbert Ames, Jr.

A. INTRODUCTION

A COMMON EXPERIENCE of any keen observer is that objects can be, and often are, seen at distances quite different from their actual distances. While such instances are often limited to far objects, laboratory workers have shown that careful control can produce similar results at any distance, however near. One of the first demonstrated, and still the most striking, of these effects results from the rapid decrease in size of an illuminated diaphragm which, while actually approaching, is seen to recede into the distance (10). While the effect of size change remains the most easily demonstrated, similar situations have been constructed utilizing many other cues to distance. The pronounced depth seen in stereoscopic pictures as well as the distances experienced in flat paintings, and more dramatically in motion pictures, are familiar cases in point.

[1] Reprinted from *J. Psychol.*, 1950, *30*, 43–62, by permission of the authors and the publisher. (Copyright, 1950, by the Journal Press.)

The fact of experienced discrepancies between the apparent and the measured distance of visually perceived objects is amply documented and needs no further elaboration here. Obviously, the implications of even so simple a fact as this reach to the very soul of any theory of space perception.

In this paper we are concerned only with the special problems arising from an attempt to determine the relationship of the mechanisms of accommodation and convergence (hereafter referred to as the image-producing mechanisms) to apparent distance and to actual distance when these two distances differ. Three pertinent questions can be asked: (a) What is the effect of change of the image-producing mechanisms on apparent distance, i.e., do accommodation and convergence act as cues to distance; (b) what is the effect of change of actual distance on the image-producing mechanisms, i.e., to what extent do the eyes accommodate and converge for the actual distance of the object of regard; and (c) what is the effect of change of apparent distance on the image-producing mechanisms, i.e., do apparent "nearness" and apparent "farness" influence accommodation and convergence? These questions are obviously not mutually exclusive; no one can be experimentally answered without knowing or controlling the effects related to the other two. Although only the third question is specifically studied in this research, it is nevertheless necessary to consider the evidence relevant to all three questions in order to determine what experimental and conceptual information they may yield which will aid us in understanding our selected problem.

[1] Image-producing Mechanisms as Cues to Distance

The history of accommodation and convergence as cues to distance starts with Descartes's analogy of the blind man feeling out space with two staves and continues to the present day. This early history can be found in Boring (3), and the more recent experiments have been adequately reviewed by Woodworth (18) and Grant (8). While these experiments need not be described in detail here, it may be worth while briefly to indicate their general nature.

The first experiment on accommodation as a cue to distance was performed by Wundt, who had his observer view a vertical thread under such conditions that accommodation was presumably the only cue to its distance. He then moved the thread either toward or away from the observer, who reported any change in apparent distance. Correct reports were presumed to be evidence of utilization of accommodation as a distance cue. This early experiment is representative of the general procedure followed in all later work, the chief addition being the use of binocular observation in which convergence is controlled by forcing fusion of the images for some distance other than the actual distance. The mirror stereoscope of Carr (5) and as modified by Grant may be taken as examples.

Most recent work has further attempted to study accommodation and convergence as cues to absolute distance from the observer, as well as to changes in this distance. In general, the effort is made, as in all previous work, first, to eliminate by a priori considerations all cues to distance other than accommodation and convergence and, second, to find if distance can be judged under these conditions.

Out of the welter of conflicting results from these experiments there seems to emerge general agreement that (a) the image-producing mechanisms can function as cues to apparent distance and (b) their effectiveness in this role varies from primary through minor to virtually nonexistent. A statement of what may be regarded as a typical position on this question holds that "accurate vision involves constant motor adjustment of the eyes to the distances of the stimulating objects. . . . This adjustment requires a pattern of muscular contractions and tensions characteristic of every distance. It is generally believed that these contractions and tensions give rise to proprioceptive clues to the distance of the fixated object" (6).

While we do not propose at this point to take exception to this conclusion, we do feel it imperative to question much of the experimentation on which it is based, and this because all reported work has explicitly or implicitly assumed a priori answers to the other two pertinent problems; answers which are either unproven or invalid. Specifically, it is assumed that apparent distance has no effect on the image-producing mechanisms and that these mechanisms are in fact always adjusted for the actual distance of the object of regard. Grant (8, p. 89), for example, states that "for objects 'within infinity,' which by optical convention means within six meters, accommodation and convergence vary in amount with the distance of the object." Let us consider evidence of the validity of this assumption.

[2] Actual Distance as a Determinant of Accommodation and Convergence

It is generally agreed that the function of the image-producing mechanisms is to produce a sharp image on the foveal region of each retina. This requires accommodating and converging for the actual distance of the stimulus object. There is an extensive literature, chiefly reported in ophthalmological and optometrical journals, in which the distance of accommodation and convergence has been most carefully measured and correlated with the actual distance of the stimulus. The findings indicate that in binocular vision fusion generally forces convergence to the actual distance of the viewed object within the limits of fixation disparity. This term has been used to refer to the fact that under certain conditions a single, fused image will be experienced, although "the retinal images of the point of fixation may be actually disparate" (16, p. 1070). However, both binocular and monocular accommodations as well as convergence in monocular observation can, and frequently do, differ quite widely from that required for the actual distance. Indeed, much of the work in clinical refraction has always been devoted to attempts to correct anomalies occurring when these mechanisms for one reason or another do not perform their functions properly. Extreme examples of such anomalies are squint, in which one eye is radically diverged from the point of view of the other eye, and cases in which accommodation is for distances other than the actual distance, which can reach the point of causing severe pathology. A lack of correspondence between distance of accommodation and actual distance even for normal observers was pointed out by Ames and Gliddon (1), who concluded that in most cases actual distance and accommodation distance coincide at only one point.

These and other anomalies, together with the findings for normal eyes, force us to conclude that it is unwise to assume that the condition of the image-producing mechanisms can be determined solely from a knowledge of the distance of the stimulus and that any experimental findings based on such an assumption must be open to doubt. However, we hasten to add that much of the work on which this conclusion is based itself neglects the possible role of apparent distance as a determinant of accommodation and convergence.

[3] Apparent Distance as a Determinant of Accommodation and Convergence

This problem, which is the particular one of interest to us in this analysis, has received but little mention and virtually no systematic study. Most writers leave the question open by implying but never explicitly discussing it. A typical statement says that "it appears that the three innervations (for accommodation, convergence, and pupillary contraction) . . . are released by the impulse for clear vision of near objects." Here "clearness" and "nearness" are both mentioned, and, since no distinction is made between actual and apparent nearness, the statement would seem to reflect general uncertainty as to the role of apparent distance in controlling the action of the image-producing mechanisms.

There is, nevertheless, some evidence on this question. Luckiesh and Moss (14, p. 495) claim that "the proximity of the hand to the eyes when operating the sensitometer may tend to stimulate accommodation reflexly due to the impression of 'nearness' arising from propriocepter phenomena." Elsewhere, under the heading "A paradox of accommodation," these same authors assert that "when an observer looks at a two-dimensional picture of a three-dimensional scene, such as a landscape, changes in accommodation not infrequently take place as different parts of the picture are viewed, notwithstanding the fact that all parts of the picture would be in focus for the same accommodation" (14, p. 108). Unfortunately, Luckiesh and Moss do not cite any reference or data for this interesting observation, and most other recent writers would seem to disagree with them. Walls (17), for example, holds that "the stimulus to converge seems to be the psychic impression of nearness" but makes no such claim about accommodation, which seems to him to be controlled by the need for sharp focus.

The most extensive recent experimental study of this question is that of Hofstetter (11), to which the reader is referred for a detailed discussion and history. Hofstetter presented similar targets monocularly at two distances, 5 meters and 0.345 meters, and varied the demands on accommodation by means of lenses. Apparent distance was not measured but was considered determined by the relation of the targets to other visible parts of the room. Haploscopic measures of accommodation and convergence were taken. Hofstetter concludes that "awareness of nearness of the point of fixation is effective in bringing about changes in convergence," but "the data provides no evidence for proximal accommodation" (11, p. 76). This is modified, however, by the statement that "the failure to obtain evidence of proximal accommodation can probably be attributed to the fact that the subjects were experienced in the use of optical instruments and had previously performed a number of experiments that dealt with the problems of accommodation" (11, p. 75).

Similar conclusions were reached by Morgan (15) on the basis of a very similar approach. He states that "the psychic influence of the subject's awareness of the nearness of objects has little influence upon accommodation, but it does influence convergence" (15, p. 194).

While these references are certainly suggestive of the fact that apparent distance plays a role in determining the functioning of the image-producing mechanisms, they would not appear to be an adequate foundation on which to base any comprehensive formulation. It seems desirable, therefore, prior to any experimental investigation, to subject the question to a more detailed theoretical analysis.

[4] Analysis of the General Problem

As pointed out earlier, a complete consideration of all the questions that should be asked when an observer visually locates an object at other than its actual distance would be far beyond the scope of this discussion. However, it is possible to abstract out of this complex situation those aspects which seem to be significant to the particular problem under consideration. That is, to decide on those aspects except for which the phenomena would not exist.

It is necessary at the outset to distinguish between two groups or classes of these aspects, which we can for convenience label primary and secondary. By primary we mean those aspects with which the observing organism has direct contact; those which can be considered, for purposes of the particular question under discussion, data of direct experience of the organism. In this sense they may be thought of as "subjective." By secondary we refer to those aspects which, for the particular problem at hand, may not be considered part of the direct experience of the observer. In this sense they are "objective," although this is not meant to imply that for another problem these same aspects may not be considered primary. Thus the primary aspects represent the data available to the organism. They must be studied and understood before a satisfactory solution to the particular problem can be reached. The secondary aspects represent the remaining conditions which are necessary for the specific situation to exist and be studied.

We may now briefly list what seem to us to be the important primary and secondary aspects of the situation, following which an experimental approach will be indicated.

I. PRIMARY ASPECTS

a. Apparent distance: enters into awareness.

b. Condition and characteristics of the retinal images: are they blurred or sharp, fused or not fused, one or two? Partial awareness.

c. State of the image-producing mechanisms: accommodation and convergence, binocular and monocular. Generally no awareness. No useful purpose would be served at this point by an elaboration of the great differences in both this and the preceding aspect in binocular as opposed to monocular observation. However, it must be borne in mind that the apparent great strength of the impulse to fusion and the close link between accommodation and convergence make these two cases quite dissimilar and, therefore, different experimental designs and analyses are called for.

II. SECONDARY ASPECTS

a.   Indications of apparent distance: size, overlay, parallax, etc.—static or moving.

b. Measurement of apparent distance: in general, apparent distance is a subjective datum which cannot be observed or measured by the experimenter. However, we can achieve a satisfactory approximation of it by measuring an "equivalent apparent distance." By this is meant the actual measured distance of an object whose apparent distance is reported to be the same as the unknown apparent distance. This can be taken as an adequate measure provided sufficient normal, supplementing indications are available on which the judgment of the equivalent apparent distance is based. Under these conditions, it is assumed that the measured and apparent distances are in some sense equal.

c.   Actual distance for which the eyes are accommodated and converged: this can be measured by deliberately bringing into awareness certain aspects of the condition of the retinal images. By this is simply meant that the various instruments which have been devised for measuring accommodation and convergence require some subjective awareness on the part of the observer of conditions directly related to the characteristics of his retinal images, such as lining up two points of light, or setting a single point of light to appear sharpest.

d. Actual distance of the stimulus object: measured from some reference point on the observer. For purposes of comparison this should be the same as that used in measuring the equivalent apparent distance. The actual distance of the stimulus object really enters into the problem in two quite distinct ways. First, it determines the optical properties of the light traveling from the object to the eye, which, together with the state of the image-producing mechanisms, determines the characteristics of the retinal images. Secondly, the actual distance of the stimulus object may be related to its apparent distance. However, this relationship is often quite tenuous, and any work which uncritically asumes actual and apparent distance to be equal is open to doubt. Actual distance may, of course, be related to one or more indications of apparent distance, such as the size of the retinal image. In addition to this direct influence, the actual distance is related to apparent distance only indirectly; for example, by the observer being aware of the details of the experimental setup. In our experiment, those observers who were aware of the experimental details did not perform consistently differently from those who were not. This is, of course, not always the case. It should be added that, in a situation requiring some action on the part of the observer with respect to the stimulus object, actual distance enters into the problem in another most important way.

[5] Experimental Approach

The specific problem to be experimentally investigated in this paper asks: will a change in apparent distance induce a change in the state of the image-producing mechanisms, while the actual distance of the observed object is held constant? It remains, therefore, to indicate whether and to what extent we can experimentally measure and control these aspects and by what means this may be most effectively accomplished.

a. THE APPARENT DISTANCE can be inferred from a measurement of an "equivalent apparent distance" in the manner already outlined. In our experimental setup the observer placed a post, binocularly viewed under normal conditions, to appear at the same distance as the apparent distance of the stimulus object. Apparent distance can be varied by altering one or any combination of well-known distance indicators. In the experiments reported here we have made use of the fact that, in the absence of other indications, a familiar object is seen at a distance appropriate to its familiar or assumed size, independent of its actual size or distance (9, 12, 13). We have, therefore, used only a single distance indication. Hindsight enables us to question the wisdom of this. It seems probable that, if more supplementing indications were used, the greater would be the subjective sense of surety associated with the particular perception and, hence, the greater the effect. In addition, the specific indication chosen may not have represented the wisest choice, being demonstrably less effective than, for example, overlay. Only the great ease with which it can be experimentally manipulated argues in favor of our decision.

b. THE CHARACTERISTICS OF THE RETINAL IMAGES, depending as they do on the functioning of the image-producing mechanisms, are not easily controlled, and in this experiment no attempt was made at direct control. While these characteristics of the retinal images can, under certain conditions, be directly observed, we have rather inferred them from a comparison of the measured distance for which the eyes are accommodated and converged and the actual distance of the stimulus.

c. THE STATE OF THE IMAGE-PRODUCING MECHANISMS cannot be directly observed, but may be inferred from the actual distances for which the eyes are accommodated and converged.

As indicated earlier, quite different considerations enter into the study of binocular rather than monocular functioning. We shall report quantitative data only for the monocular case, followed by a qualitative experiment using binocular vision.

B. EXPERIMENTAL

[1] General Experimental Method

THE EXPERIMENTS reported in this paper consist essentially of presenting the observer with a size cue of a distance which is different from the actual distance, and then measuring the apparent distance, and the accommodation and convergence. Various conditions of monocular and binocular observation will be studied, using both stationary and apparently moving stimuli. In all cases, the experiment requires two essential pieces of apparatus: first, the apparatus for measuring accommodation and convergence and, second, that for providing the various stimulus configurations.

a. APPARATUS. Haploscopic measurements were made of accommodation and convergence. A detailed account and description of an instrument similar to the one used can be found in Ames and Gliddon (1). A photograph of the specific instrument used in this experiment, together with further information concerning it, appears in Ames, Gliddon, and Ogle (2). In view of these detailed references, only a brief description of this apparatus is considered necessary at this point.

The stimulus object is viewed through two half-silvered mirrors, one placed before each eye. Each mirror is connected to its own arrangement of a lens and star point so that the image of the star point is reflected to the corresponding eye of the observer. Therefore, the observer sees two star points superimposed on the stimulus object in front of him. The mirror, lens, and star point on each side are rigidly connected to an arm which rotates about the center of turning of each eye. Two scales are provided. One scale reads the optical distance of the star point from the eye along the line of regard through the lens, the mirror, to the object. This scale, the accommodation scale, is calibrated directly in diopters. Another scale, the convergence scale, is calibrated in prism diopters, and reads the deviation from dead ahead at which each star point may be set. A small shield, inserted beyond the left mirror, prevents the left eye from viewing the stimulus object during monocular tests.

b. MEASUREMENT OF ACCOMMODATION. This procedure can be more easily understood initially if we do not consider the function of the lenses in the instrument. If a star point were viewed without any intervening optical mechanism by an eye accommodated for some fixed distance, it would appear sharpest when it was at the distance of accommodation of the eye. Within or beyond this distance, the point would appear blurred. This is equivalent to what is done in this instrument, except that a lens is introduced in order to reduce the distance through which the star point must be moved; a star point at the focal length of the lens being equivalent to a star point at infinity. Thus the actual accommodation of the eye while looking at the stimulus object can be measured by moving the star point back and forth until it appears sharpest, and then read directly from the scale. At each session, under each experimental condition, ten settings of accommodation were made, five with the star point initially at its farthest position and five with it initially at its nearest position.

c. MEASUREMENT OF CONVERGENCE. The convergence of the eyes is primarily effected by so-called fusional innervations which cause the eyes to converge or diverge to bring similar images on corresponding retinal areas of the two eyes. In monocular vision this factor is not operative, and in general the two eyes will not be converged on the object of regard, as is shown by the horizontal phoria tests. Such tests disclose the relative direction that the two eyes take when "dissociated." The procedure is to have an observer fixate an object, situated in his median plane at a particular distance, with one eye, make the image to his other eye so dissimilar that he has no impulse for fusion, and then determine the converging or diverging position which the other eye takes. This measures the esophoria or exophoria, which usually varies somewhat with the distance of the fixated object and varies greatly with different individuals.

In this experiment very similar measurements are taken. However, in this case we are concerned with the actual direction in which the nonfixating eye is pointed, rather than with the deviation of this direction from that required for the fixated object. Inasmuch as the stimulus object is placed directly ahead of the right or fixating eye, we shall refer to the direction in which the left or nonfixating eye is pointed, as measured in terms of deviation from its dead ahead position, as simply the convergence of the eyes.

The procedure is as follows: The small shield is placed in position so that the left eye does not see the stimulus object. The star point seen by the right eye is directly centered on the stimulus object. The arm carrying the star point seen by the left eye is rotated so that the star point appears far to the left or the right of the stimulus object. The arm is then rotated until the two star points appear, one somewhat above the other, in the same vertical line. The convergence of the left eye can then be read directly from the appropriate scale.

d. STIMULUS CONFIGURATIONS. Two different types of stimulus configuration were used in this experiment. These are described below:

(1) Static size change. The stimulus objects used in this part were three playing cards of different sizes: a normal-sized playing card, a double-sized playing card, and a half-sized playing card. (In this paper, a normal-sized playing card is taken to be 3½ inches by 2⅝ inches, so that a double-sized playing card is 7 inches by 5¼ inches, while a half-sized playing card is 1¾ inches by 1⁵⁄₁₆ inches.) These cards were presented to the observer in that order, one at a time, at a constant distance of 32 inches. They were viewed monocularly in an otherwise completely dark room and were illuminated to 0.5-foot candles, as measured by a Macbeth illuminometer. Black draperies were used to conceal the small spotlight used for illumination and to trap all stray light.

(2) Continuous size change. The stimulus used in this experiment consisted of the image of a playing card projected on a screen 16 inches from the observer's eye. The image was reflected onto this screen by means of a mirror and was projected from a Clason projector. The size of the image could be changed continuously from that of a normal-size playing card to that of a one-third-size playing card. The observer viewed the screen continuously and watched the playing card as it changed size. Both binocular and monocular observations were used with this stimulus condition.

e. GENERAL PROCEDURE. Although the specific details of procedure varied in the different parts of the experiment, the general procedure was as follows: First, in an otherwise completely dark room, the observer viewed the stimulus object at a fixed distance. The accommodation of his eyes was measured as well as the convergence. The stimulus object was then changed in size, while the distance remained constant, and the measurements of accommodation and convergence were repeated. Finally, measurements of the apparent distance of the stimulus object were taken.

f. OBSERVERS. Five of the six observers used were chosen simply because they were available. Three, ML, HC, and WI, were experienced observers, while the others had never served as subjects before. Two, MI and RB, had never worn corrective lenses; the remaining four wore their habitual glasses throughout the experiment. At 15 years of age, RB was the youngest observer, with the others ranging from two to three times his age. He was specially selected in order to include representation of a younger age group.

[2] Experimental Results

a. STATIC SIZE CHANGE—MONOCULAR. The observers were instructed to fixate the stimulus object and try to see it as clearly as possible. Ten measurements of accommodation and ten of convergence were made for each stimulus object at each session for each observer. Four observers made two such settings on two different days, while the remaining observer, RB, came for only one session. In addition to accommodation and convergence measurements, the apparent distance of each card was determined in the following manner: The observer was asked to view the card and obtain as good an idea as possible of the distance of the card from him. He then removed his head from the instrument, looked to his right, and, in full general illumination, told the experimenter where to set a post in order that it appear at the same distance from him as the card he had viewed. As many references back to the stimulus were allowed as the observer desired. All observers made this determination without any difficulty and reported a high degree of surety in making the setting and satisfaction with it after it was made.

Table I presents the results obtained in this experiment. This table shows: (a) apparent distance in all cases was in the direction of that determined by assumed size, and, for all observers except one, this relationship is almost perfect, i.e., the assumed size cue was completely effective in determining the apparent distance at the viewing distance of 32 inches; (b) in all cases except one, accommodation shifted in the direction of the apparent distance; (c) convergence, in all cases except one, shifted in the direction of the apparent distance.

It may also be noted that the absolute values of convergence vary widely for the various observers. This is indicative of the varying amounts of phoria present in each observer. It further provides evidence of the unreliability of convergence innervations as a cue to distance.

TABLE I

EFFECT OF STATIC SIZE CHANGE

(Actual distance: 32 inches; apparent distance on basis of size: 16, 32, 64 inches, or 2.50, 1.25, and .625 diopters.)

OBSERVER	ACCOMMODATION (Diopters)			CONVERGENCE (Prism diopters)			APPARENT DISTANCE (Inches)		
	Large	Normal	Small	Large	Normal	Small	Large	Normal	Small
ML	.91	.83	.59	6.4	5.8	4.7	18	28	69
HC	.75	.52	.59	10.6	9.9	8.7	16	34	66
NP	.92	.82	.69	8.2	7.7	6.9	14	22	55
WI	.91	.82	.72	12.1	9.1	7.8	17	30	65
RB	.91	.95	.99	13.7	13.4	13.4	22	30	50

The one observer who did not show a shift in accommodation and convergence is an interesting exception. It will be noted that he alone showed a distinctly restricted range of apparent distance for the different sizes of the stimulus object. He was the youngest observer, with the best visual acuity and the widest range of accommodation, and was specially selected after the original four observers had been run, in order to determine how such an observer would behave in this situation.

b. CONTINUOUS SIZE CHANGE—MONOCULAR. In this case, one measurement of accommodation was made with the card at one extreme size. The observer then viewed it as it continuously changed its size to the other extreme. Another measure of accommodation was made, and so forth. Then the same procedure was repeated for convergence settings.

The apparent distance was not measured, but the observers were asked to give introspective reports as to the change or lack of change in apparent distance. All observers volunteered the information that the card appeared to be a constant-sized playing card that was moving back and forth in space. This information, together with that obtained for apparent distance (Table I), justifies the conclusion that the apparent distance of the playing card varied with its objective size in such a way that it at all times appeared at approximately the distance a normal playing card would have to be in order to subtend the same angle. That is, the assumed size cue continued to be effective even at a viewing distance of 16 inches.

Table II presents the measured accommodation and convergence for each observer at the large and small position. It will be noted from Table II that all observers again showed a shift of accommodation in the direction of the apparent movement. Furthermore, the change in accommodation was, in three of the cases, sufficient to cause blurring of the image; these observers reporting that, as the card apparently receded into the distance, it became blurred. One observer even accused the experimenter of having his projector out of focus.

TABLE II

EFFECT OF CONTINUOUS SIZE CHANGE
(*Actual distance: 16 inches; apparent distance range on basis of size:
16–48 inches, or 2.50–.833 diopters.*)

	ACCOMMODATION (Diopters)		CONVERGENCE (Prism diopters)		BLURRING	
OBSERVER	Large	Small	Large	Small	Large	Small
ML	1.26	.89	7.5	5.6	No	Yes
HC	2.15	1.59	15.1	12.7	No	No
WI	.99	.62	14.0	10.4	No	Yes
MI	1.12	.59	7.1	4.7	No	Yes

It was felt that this blurring phenomenon deserved further consideration. Therefore, several visitors to the laboratory, in addition to the four subjects for whom data are presented, were asked to view this stimulus configuration. No measurements were taken for these observers, but they were asked to report on apparent movement and on blurring. With occasional exceptions, these observers reported blurring of the image as the playing card apparently receded into the distance. If it was stopped at its small size, or apparent far position, the image for most of these observers then slowly, and completely beyond their control, cleared up. For all, repeating the apparent movement resulted in a repetition of the blurring experience.

c. CONTINUOUS SIZE CHANGE—BINOCULAR. The stimulus configuration used in this experiment was the same as that reported above. Three observers viewed this configuration binocularly while the size was rapidly and continuously being changed, with the following results:

1. Distinct impressions of distance change were reported. As the card was made smaller, it definitely appeared to move away and to get smaller at the same time.

2. Convergence remained constant within the limits of measurement throughout this apparent movement, as measured by the constant relative positions of the two star points, as well as by the fact that no double images were reported.

3. All three observers reported a feeling of strain about the eyes to the extent of becoming quite uncomfortable after a few moments, and lasting for approximately one hour after the end of the experiment.

4. Accommodation varied as the object appeared to move back and forth. This change in accommodation was reported by setting one accommodative star point so that it appeared sharp and distinct when the stimulus card was normal size. Then, as the stimulus was rapidly changed in size and appeared to move away from the observer, the appearance of this star was noted by the observer.

An interesting effect was reported with regard to the accommodation change. All observers noted that the initial change in size of the stimulus did not result in a very pronounced change in apparent distance. Nor did it affect the appearance of the accommodative star point. However, as the change in size continued regularly for a few moments, the effect of apparent movement became fairly strong, and with this effect the appearance of the accommodative star point began to change. Under these conditions, all observers reported that, as the stimulus appeared to move away, that is, actually was made smaller, the star point appeared to blur, and as the stimulus appeared to approach, the star point became sharp again, thus indicating that accommodation was changing in this situation. Attempts to measure the extent of this accommodatory change were not successful, however, due to the fact that no provision was made on the instrument for dynamically changing the appearance or the position of the accommodatory star point, so that the setting had to be made while the card was stationary. However, the effect noted depended upon the continuous apparent movement of the stimulus object. Measures of the accommodatory change, therefore, must await a more refined apparatus. However, additional evidence of the fact of a change in accommodation is provided by the report of all observers that, as the card appeared to recede, it also appeared to blur, and as it appeared to approach, the image cleared again. This blurring, reported by all three observers, was particularly pronounced for one. There would seem to be ample evidence, therefore, suggesting that change in accommodation took place for all observers in the direction of the apparent movement.

[3] Summary of Experimental Results

a. STATIC SIZE CHANGE—MONOCULAR. Different sizes of a familiar object (playing card) were presented one at a time at a distance of 32 inches. Measures of apparent distance, accommodation, and convergence were taken. For four out of five observers, apparent distance of the double-size card was an average of one-fourth that of the half-size card, accommodation when viewing the double-size card was an average of .25 diopters nearer than when viewing the half-size card, and convergence followed the same pattern.

b. CONTINUOUS SIZE CHANGE—MONOCULAR. The projected image of a playing card which continuously changed size from normal to one-third size was viewed from a distance of 16 inches. Introspective reports of four observers indicated that apparent distance changed continuously with the size of the image, the card appearing to move back and forth as it grew smaller and larger. Measures of accommodation showed an average of .46 diopters nearer for the large size than for the small size. Convergence measurements indicated similar results.

c. CONTINUOUS SIZE CHANGE—BINOCULAR. The same stimulus configuration was used as above. Introspective reports indicated a distinct impression of movement. Some blurring of the images suggests a shift in accommodation. Severe feelings of muscular strain about the eyes were reported after a few minutes.

C. DISCUSSION

THE SPECIFIC EXPERIMENTAL problem posed in this study was that of determining whether a change in apparent distance alone will induce a change in accommodation and convergence. The results of the experiments reported above suggest an affirmative answer to this question.

The two cases involving monocular vision gave clear-cut evidence of changes in both accommodation and convergence, and the binocular results certainly tend to supplement these findings. We cannot emphasize too strongly, therefore, that for our observers *the muscular efforts of accommodation and convergence were related to a subjective change of apparent distance with all other things remaining constant.*[2]

However, it is important to add that this statement is based on the results of an exploratory study. Our findings need to be duplicated under carefully controlled conditions involving several different distance indications, both singly and in combinations. And more especially, they need to be generalized to a larger population and norms established for that population. These most important questions are not touched in the experiments reported here; indeed, they require much more extensive facilities than we find available. It is hoped that workers who have such facilities will verify and expand along these lines the findings reported in this study. Nevertheless, our findings, while frankly exploratory in nature, are sufficiently clear-cut to force a consideration of their implications in various contexts as well as an attempt to understand them conceptually.

Most immediately relevant is, of course, the general question of the conditions which are necessary to bring about a change in accommodation and convergence. That there is a definite and consistent pattern of muscular reactions involved in shifting from far to near vision is not subject to controversy. The fact that this pattern, involving changes in accommodation, convergence, and pupillary contraction described by Duke-Elder as the "near reflex" (7), is elicited in every such shift is accepted by all writers, although there remains debate on the extent to which the three functions are mutually independent. However, as has been pointed out earlier, there is considerable question concerning the nature of the stimulus which brings about this "near reflex." Two possible answers have been suggested: one, characterized by "clearness," emphasizes the characteristics of the retinal patterns related to near and far objects, while the other, characterized by "nearness," stresses the role of apparent distance. Our findings would seem to indicate that these two factors are complexly interrelated. The fact that in normal vision we

[2] Strictly speaking, of course, all other things were not constant. The indications of apparent distance, in this case the size of the retinal images, changed as did the total radiant energy falling on the retinas. However, there is no evidence to indicate that these two factors, in and of themselves without reference to their possible effect on apparent distance and within the ranges used, are capable of producing the observed effects on accommodation and convergence. We therefore feel justified in stating that all other relevant factors remained constant. In further work more careful control of these factors should settle this point experimentally.

seem automatically to converge and accommodate upon the object of regard has led many writers to state that these functions are reflexly controlled. However, if apparent distance is a factor in determining ocular adjustment, as we have shown it to be, then the reflex concept must be greatly modified. A more truly correct statement of the general process would seem to call for (a) some aspect of the perceptual situation which will initiate a change in the image-producing mechanisms and (b) an effort of these mechanisms until an adequate image is obtained.[3] In normal everyday vision, the aspect of the perceptual situation which initiates ocular adjustment appears to be the subjective sense of the apparent distance of the object of regard.

This conclusion, which would seem to follow directly from our experimental findings, has important implications for the clinical treatment of ocular problems. The fact that little is known as to the factors which control accommodation and convergence has generally been overlooked in determining the procedures applied by ophthalmologists and optometrists in diagnosing and correcting visual anomalies or the character of research in the applied fields in general. As far as is known, no account is taken of the relative roles played by subjective criteria of apparent distance in investigating the etiology of visual disorders such as refractive or motor anomalies. But this very factor, as we have shown, can be responsible for activating anomalous ocular adjustment. Therefore, it would seem to be of primary importance to determine whether and to what extent visual and ocular anomalies are related to anomalous apparent localization. In this connection, one is further led to ask whether incorrect apparent localization can be caused by the alteration of the size of the retinal images by corrective lenses, and if so, whether this may not itself induce further anomalies. Or, even in the absence of corrective lenses, is it possible that there may be a conflict between binocular and monocular apparent localization with resulting malfunctioning of the ocular mechanisms? Indeed, the demonstration that

[3] This view adequately accounts for our obtained results. An "adequate image" must be defined in terms of the experience of the individual. The young person, equipped with unimpaired ocular apparatus, will be more likely to exert the extra effort required to produce the type of sharp image to which he is accustomed than will the older person for whom an adequate image is often quite blurred indeed. In terms of our experimental results, it will be noted that Observer RB did not achieve a maximum accommodation any greater than that of the older observers. However, they were quite willing to settle upon a far less sharp image as adequate. Indeed, they might well have been surprised had they produced a sharp image of the faraway object. In this connection it would be interesting to determine experimentally whether greater shifts in accommodation and convergence would result from a combination of many supplementing distance indications. As an extreme case, our results strongly suggest that fusion might even be broken by sufficiently compelling indications of an incorrect distance.

changes in apparent distance can by themselves effect the innervations to the accommodative and extrinsic eye muscles opens up a virtually endless list of problems of primary importance in the applied fields.[4]

However, although these practical questions undoubtedly are both interesting and important, the chief challenge of this fact lies in the need to incorporate it into a systematic psychological interpretation. It is evident that the reported results cannot be incorporated within the classical view of accommodation and convergence. We are forced to conclude that it is not possible to explain them in terms of such a simple spatial and temporal ordering of events, starting with the actual object, then to the optical properties of the light rays reaching the eyes, followed by automatic responses of the eyes appropriate to these optical properties, and eventually ending up with an apparent distance. The evidence is overwhelming that all these factors, and many others, are at once affecting and being affected by each other in a continuing process to which neither spatial nor temporal limits can be set. We can in no way consider accommodation and convergence as automatic responses of the organism to the enviroment, but rather as one of the results of a complex integrative process in which presumably each factor influences the ultimate outcome to the extent of the weight given it in terms of its past reliability as well as its present relationship to the inherited structure of the organism.

If this is true of the "physiological cues" of accommodation and convergence, what must it imply for the other so-called cues of space perception? Does it not become impossible to speak of the visual cues as given offered up by the environment to the waiting organism? Rather, must they not be treated as abstractions created by the organism as it carries out its purposeful activity in an ever-changing relationship with its environment? A visual cue, then, would be a particular aspect of the total situation of organism-environment, which has proved useful in determining response in that situation and which is utilized by the organism for that purpose.

This conclusion is in agreement with the more general conclusion (see 4) reached by the authors from other evidence, that a visual perception, no matter how well structured, is not a disclosure of the external situation but is rather a prediction made by the organism of what it is probably looking at; i.e., a perception is a prognostic directive for purposeful action. The reliability of this prognosis will be related to the

----

[4] One wonders, for example, whether this fact cannot be made use of in orthoptic treatment.

It may be appropriate at this point to inquire whether the effects observed in our experiments, especially those for binocular observation, may not be sufficient to account for some of the eyestrain and general ocular fatigue reportedly attendant upon the prolonged close viewing of a television screen.

reliability and number of the indications or abstracted aspects whose integration constitutes the perception. Presumably, the relative reliability of these indications is learned from experience while carrying out purposeful activity.

The findings reported in this study have an important application to this general theoretical picture. Great emphasis has often been placed on the movements of the eye muscles as an explanatory principle underlying much, if not all, of the development of visual space perception. Explanations making use of this principle have, in general, not been successful simply because the actions that take place when the image-producing mechanisms are functioning are quite different from the actions involved in carrying out a purpose involving movement in space. The function of the activity of the image-producing mechanisms is solely to provide differentially characterized stimulus patterns. These patterns are translated into perceptions that predict the probable significance of the environment and are used as directives for action. Thus, it seems evident that while one could learn the significance of space cues from action whose purpose involved behavior in a spatial environment, it would be much more difficult, if not impossible, to learn this from the action of the image-producing mechanisms. For apparently these mechanisms have served their purpose as long as they produce stimulus patterns that are sufficiently differentiated to provide the related perceptual indications.

In the broadest sense, these findings show that even the organism's physiological response in a given situation depends not on that situation as it might be conceived to exist, independent of the organism, but rather on the total organism-environment complex *as perceived by the participating organism*. Human behavior and experience can be understood, not as simple interplay of isolated and independent entities but only by recognizing that the environment in which man carries out his purposes, "the world he is related to, the world he sees, the world he is operating on, and the world that is operating on him is the result of a transactional process in which man himself plays an active role" (4, p. 517; also Chapter 1 of this volume).

REFERENCES—CHAPTER 5

1. Ames, A. Jr., and Gliddon, G. "Ocular measurements." *Trans. Sec. Ophthal. Amer. Med. Assn.,* 1928 (June 15), 1–68.

2. Ames, A. Jr.; Gliddon, G.; and Ogle, K. N. "Size and shape of ocular images." *Arch. Ophthal.,* 1932, *7,* 576–97.

3. Boring, E. G. *Sensation and Perception in the History of Experi-*

mental Psychology. New York: Appleton-Century, 1942, pp. 271–82.

4. Cantril, H.; Ames, A. Jr.; Hastorf, A. H.; and Ittelson, W. H. "Psychology and scientific research." *Science,* 1949, *110,* 461–64, 491–97, 517–22.

5. Carr, H. *An Introduction to Space Perception.* New York: Longmans, 1935, p. 248.

6. Dimmick, F. L. In Boring, Langfeld, and Weld, *Foundations of Psychology.* New York: Wiley, 1948, p. 300.

7. Duke-Elder, W. S. *Textbook of Ophthalmology.* St. Louis: Mosby, 1933, Vol. I, pp. 553 f.

8. Grant, V. W. "Accommodation and convergence in visual space perception." *J. Exper. Psychol.,* 1942, *31,* 89–104.

9. Hastorf, A. H. "The influence of suggestion on the relationship between stimulus size and perceived distance." *J. Psychol.,* 1950, *29,* 195–217.

10. Hillebrand, F. "Das Verhaltnis von Accommodation und Konvergenz zur Tiefenlokalisation." *Z. Psychol.,* 1894, *7,* 97–151.

11. Hofstetter, H. W. "The proximal factor in accommodation and convergence." *Amer. J. Optom.,* 1942, *19,* 67–76.

12. Ittelson, W. H. "Size as a cue to distance." *Amer. J. Psychol.,* 1951, *64,* 54–67, 188–202.

13. Lawrence, M. *Studies in Human Behavior.* Princeton: Princeton Univ. Press, 1949, pp. 81–89.

14. Luckiesh, M., and Moss, F. *The Science of Seeing.* New York: Van Nostrand, 1937.

15. Morgan, M. W. "The clinical aspects of accommodation and convergence." *Amer. J. Optom.,* 1944, *21,* 185–95, 301–13.

16. Ogle, K. N.; Mussey, F.; and Prangen, A. de H. "Fixation disparity and the fusional processes in binocular single vision." *Amer. J. Ophthal.,* 1949, *32,* 1069–87.

17. Walls, G. L. *The Vertebrate Eye.* Bloomfield Hills, Mich.: Cranbrook Inst. of Science, 1942, p. 315.

18. Woodworth, R. S. *Experimental Psychology.* New York: Holt, 1938, pp. 665–80.

CHAPTER

6

Aniseikonic Glasses [1]

Adelbert Ames, Jr.

[This report by Ames is the basic descriptive and analytic document concerning the phenomenological results of wearing aniseikonic lenses. Besides their usefulness in correcting defective vision (aniseikonia), these lenses have proved extremely useful as devices for perceptual experimentation. Illustrations of some of their many experimental uses are given in Chapter 7 and in Chapter 11.—Ed.]

I T HAS LONG BEEN known that binocular spatial localization becomes abnormal if the normal [2] relation of the dioptric images on the respective retinas is altered by refractive lenses or by prisms (17, 18, 24, 25, 37). The earlier investigators in this field were handicapped by the fact that the lenses they used for distorting the images were refracting lenses which, besides altering the shape of the images, also put them out of focus, so that the images from given object points stimulated extended areas of the receptor mosaic and were blurred. Such blurred

[1] Published originally as "Binocular Vision as Affected by Relations Between Uniocular Stimulus-Patterns in Commonplace Environments," *Amer. J. Psychol.,* 1946, *59,* 333–57. Reprinted in slightly abridged form by permission of the author and the publisher, The American Journal of Psychology.
[2] The image conditions for normal spatial localization may be said to occur when the difference between the respective uniocular images is due solely to interocular separation (interpupillary distance).

images not only tend to prevent stereoscopic interpretation (except when weak lenses are used) but, even where stereoscopic interpretation does exist, the blurring makes it impossible to establish definite relations between a particular stereoscopic interpretation and the stimulation of particularly circumscribed areas of the receptor mosaic.

The development of aniseikonic or size lenses provided (4, 27), for the first time, means by which sharply defined dioptric image patterns of various types could be precisely altered in size and shape by known amounts, thus permitting a more thorough investigation than had heretofore been possible of the relation between the dimensions of the uniocular stimulus patterns and binocular spatial appearances. The results of the studies employing this new tool appear significant.

These lenses were first used in exploring their effect on the binocular spatial localization in connection with the so-called frontal plane horopter apparatus. Determinations were made of the actual positions in which the horopter elements had to be placed in order that they would appear in a frontal plane, with the various size lenses before the eyes.

The relation of the appearances to the particular alteration of the stimulus patterns of the respective eyes was then evaluated on the basis of the classical "corresponding point" theory, following in the main geometrical analytical reasoning (6, 26, 28).

Later, instruments called Ophthalmo-Eikonometers (2, 5) were built, which measured with considerable exactitude the linear differences in the size and shape of the uniocular stimulus patterns. By means of these instruments, inherent ocular defects similar to abnormal stimulus relations artificially introduced with size lenses could be determined, and it was possible by the correction of same to give relief to many patients.[3]

The definite relations between the anomalous appearances of horopter test targets and the specific incongruities produced in the retinal images by size lenses suggested an explanation of the positive clinical results obtained from "correcting" anomalous differences in size and shape of ocular images with the above-mentioned instruments. The explanation is that the symptoms in aniseikonic subjects which are relieved by corrections which bring about correspondence are due to ineffectual functioning resulting from discrepancies between visual appearances and the actual position of objects.

The inevitable question arose, however, as to how natural everyday environments would appear to a person having abnormal incongruities, whether inherently or artificially imposed. Theoretically, it might be presumed possible to analyze such environments at least into their principal components and thus to determine their typically abnormal

[3] The following are some of the more important published papers on the clinical aspects of aniseikonia: 7, 8, 9, 10, 11, 12, 13, 14, 15, 16, 20, 21, 22, 23, 24.

appearance on the basis of the classical "corresponding point" theory, following geometrical reasoning. This possibility could, of course, be put to a practical test by wearing size glasses of different types in natural environments and by comparing the actual appearances as experienced with the theoretically expected results. Such comparison forced upon the investigator the conclusion that, while the binocular appearances experienced in some environments followed theoretical expectations fairly well, others certainly did not.

It appeared possible that investigations with especially controlled environmental conditions would disclose a hypothesis that would account for these appearances that could not be explained on the basis of the accepted theories of vision. Accordingly, controlled objective test fields embodying specific characteristics of commonplace environments yet permitting an analytical approach were developed. First, the so-called "Tipping Field" (1, 19, 29) was developed, and later the "Leaf Room" (34). Finally, the "Space Eikonometer" (3, 35, 36) was developed for determining the presence and characteristics of anomalous uniocular stimulus patterns on the basis of spatial localization instead of subjectively judged lateral distances, the methodology used in the Ophthalmo-Eikonometer. The results of these investigations have, it is believed, disclosed a satisfactory explanation of some of the apparently unexplainable phenomena.

The purpose of the present discussion is to acquaint the reader with the general characteristics of these visual phenomena that are experienced in commonplace environments, especially their salience and infinite variation.

BINOCULAR VISION IN COMMONPLACE ENVIRONMENTS AS AFFECTED BY ANOMALOUS RELATIONS BETWEEN THE DIOPTRIC IMAGES ON THE TWO RETINAS

THERE IS, APPARENTLY, an infinity of anomalous appearances that can be experienced when the relationship between the stimulus patterns received by the two eyes is altered in different ways by all the various different types of size lenses.

In the following pages an attempt will be made to describe only those visual experiences which result from three types of alteration of the relation between the stimulus patterns produced by three types of size lenses.

The first type of alteration of the stimulus patterns is an outward or inward declination of the vertical meridians of the two ocular images, as diagrammatically shown in the drawings on the right of Figure 1, A

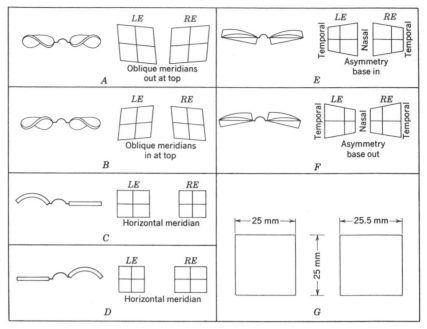

FIG. 1. *Types of differences between the dioptric images produced by various types of size lenses.*

In order to make the difference in the size and shape between the dioptric images of each eye apparent in drawings, they have had to be greatly exaggerated. The reason for this is that the differences in the size of the dioptric images produced by the size lenses, with which marked anomalous localization is related, are too little to produce any apparent change in the form of the object as seen by the two eyes, or to be shown in a drawing. For instance, consider the difference in the dioptric images in the horizontal meridian (see row D). The size lenses increase the horizontal dimension of the dioptric image of the right eye by 2 per cent. If the dioptric image of the left eye is represented by a square 25 mm. on the side, the rectangle that represents the increased size of the dioptric image in the right eye would be only 0.5 mm. larger in the horizontal, which could not be noticed (see G).

The approximate relation between mean variation of settings and least perceptible differences of binocular disparity differences and sense of form briefly stated are as follows:

Mean variation of binocular disparity settings		0.06%
Least perceptible disparity differences		0.12%
Mean variation of settings of form	around	1.25%
Least perceptible form differences		two or three times these figures

and B. This type of alteration results from looking through meridional size lenses positioned before the eyes as shown on the left of A and B in Figure 1, the axes of these lenses being positioned obliquely 45° for the right eye and 135° for the left eye, or 135° for the right eye and 45° for the left eye.

The second type of alteration of the stimulus patterns is a magnification of one of the ocular images in the horizontal meridian, as diagrammatically shown on the right of C and D, Figure 1. This type of alteration results from looking through a single meridional size lens as shown on the left of C and D, Figure 1, the axes of the meridional size lens being positioned vertically (i.e., axis 90°).

The third type of alteration of the stimulus patterns is an increase of the nasal parts of both images relative to the temporal parts or vice versa (4). This type of alteration results from looking through so-called "asymmetric distortion lenses" positioned before the eyes as shown on the left of E and F, Figure 1.[4]

The characteristic influence on the visual field seen binocularly of each of these types of image-relation change will now be described. It must be emphasized here that the nature of the phenomena to be described, i.e., the way things look, can be thoroughly appreciated only if the individual actually experiences them. As the next best means, drawings have been resorted to, since it is impossible to reproduce the experiential effects even with stereoscopic photographs.

Fortunately, it was possible to interest Mr. Walter Humphrey, a well-known artist, who happened to be in Hanover in 1938 painting the murals in Thayer Hall, to make the drawings herein reproduced. The advantage in having these done by a trained artist is that the appearances, to be fairly convincing, can only be rendered by a skilled draftsman; for example, the effects observed in many cases have to be shown by including the observer in the picture, and, in some cases, by introducing perspective features and shading which are not actually seen.

There follows a set of seven drawings by Mr. Humphrey, showing the characteristic appearances of a number of environments selected advantageously to illustrate the most important variations of the phenomena.

The legends of these figures describe the lens or lenses used and the abnormal differences which they cause between the uniocular stimuli.

---

[4] Anomalous appearances also result from looking through "aniseikonic" lenses that increase the image in one eye in the vertical dimension. Anomalous appearances of this type are in general similar to those that are experienced when the image of the other eye is increased in the horizontal meridian. For this reason, and also because they are less marked, their description is not included in this paper. Readers who are interested in this phenomenon are referred to the following publications: 29, 30, 31, 32, 33.

They also quote Mr. Humphrey's descriptions of the effects as they appeared to him, which are included to give the reader an idea of the dramatic nature of the appearances.

The following general remarks by Mr. Humphrey may well serve as a foreword to his drawings and his more specific explanations of each drawing.

> These various effects which I have picturized are truly startling to one who has always seen square things square and flat things flat. Though it is an acknowledged fact that in modern art some perspective distortion is deliberately done for effect, nevertheless, the experiencing through the aid of special glasses of these visual abnormalities leads to the conjecture that some of the present-day tortured representations might have a physical, rather than a psychological origin. Certainly it would be interesting to test the vision of some of our modern painters for incongruities between the ocular images.

FIG. 2. *Variations in the appearance of a level grass lawn when observed through different types of aniseikonic lenses.*

(A) With 2.00 per cent meridional aniseikonic lenses, axis 135°-right eye, and axis 45°-left eye. The optical effect of these lenses is a rotation of the vertical meridians of the dioptric images formed on each retina outwardly 1.14° at the top.

"The ground appears to rise up in front at a severe angle of 45° or more, and one has the feeling of being about nine feet tall. Looking directly downward, one sees the toes pointing upward with the sloping ground. All details on the ground appear increased in size."

(B) The same lenses as in A with axis 45°-right eye, and axis 135°-left eye, causing opposite rotation of the meridians of the dioptric images formed on each retina.

"The ground slants in the opposite direction but with a less severe slope, about 30°. One feels dwarf-like in stature, three or three and a half feet in height, and the toes are noticed pointed downward with the ground. All details in the ground appear reduced in size."

(C) With 4.00 per cent meridional aniseikonic lens axis 90° before the left eye. The optical effect of this lens is to increase the size of the dioptric image formed in that eye 4.00 per cent in the horizontal meridian.

"The ground appears to curve over and downward with extreme steepness on the left and slant upward with slightly less steepness on the right. The left leg seems to be longer and the right leg seems to be shorter."

(D) The same lens as in (C) before the right eye.

"The appearance is the same as in (C) but in the opposite direction."

(E) Before each eye a 5-prism diopter lens ground on a 6-diopter base curve, convex side toward the eye, apex in; the prismatic effect of these lenses being compensated by similar prisms, convex side out, and with apices out. The optical effect of these combinations is an asymmetrical distortion of the dioptric images formed on the retinas, with the temporal parts of the images spread out relative to the nasal parts.

"The ground appears concave, as if one were looking into a hollow. The curvature, though definite, is not as marked as the tipping described above."

(F) Similar lenses to those described in (E) with apices in the opposite direction, producing the opposite asymmetrical effect.

"The ground appears convex in all directions, as if looking at a mound, the amount of curvature being the same as in (E)."

FIG. 3. *Variations in the appearance of a vertical leaf-covered wall.*

(A) Lenses that cause the vertical meridians of the dioptric images to be rotated outward at the top. (See Figure 2, A, for lens data.)

"The wall appears to slant forward at the top at a sharp angle."

(B) Lenses that cause the vertical meridians of the dioptric images to be rotated inward at the top. (See Figure 2, B.)

"The wall appears to slant backward at the top at a sharp angle."

(C) Lenses that increase the size of the dioptric image formed in the left eye in the horizontal meridian. (See Figure 2, D.)

"The wall appears to slant at a sharp angle near on the right and far on the left."

(D) Lenses that increase the size of the dioptric image formed in the right eye in the horizontal meridian. (See Figure 2, C.)

"The wall appears to slant at a sharp angle far at the right and near at the left."

(E) Lenses that cause an asymmetric distortion of the dioptric images, the temporal parts being spread out relative to the nasal parts. (See Figure 2, E.)

"The wall appears concave; that is, farther away at the center where one looks."

(F) Lenses that cause an asymmetric distortion of the dioptric images, the nasal parts being spread out relative to the temporal parts. (See Figure 2, F.)

"The wall appears convex; that is, near at the center where one looks."

FIG. 4. *Variations in the appearance of a leaf-covered ceiling.*

(A) Lenses that cause the vertical meridian of the dioptric images to be rotated outward at the top. (See Figure 2, A.)

"The ceiling appears to be sloping at an angle of 20° to 30°, the near end downward."

(B) Lenses that cause the vertical meridians of the dioptric images to be rotated inward at the top. (See Figure 2, B.)

"The ceiling appears to be sloping at an angle of 20° to 30°, the near end upward."

(C) Lenses that increase the size of the dioptric image formed in the left eye in the horizontal meridian. (See Figure 2, D.)

"The ceiling appears to be tipping down on the right side and up on the left side."

(D) Lenses that increase the size of the dioptric image formed in the right eye in the horizontal meridian. (See Figure 2, C.)

"The ceiling appears to be tipping down on the left side and up on the right side."

(E) Lenses that cause an asymmetric distortion of the dioptric images, the temporal parts being spread out relative to the nasal parts. (See Figure 2, E.)

"The ceiling appears concave."

(F) Lenses that cause an asymmetric distortion of the dioptric images, the nasal parts being spread out relative to the temporal parts. (See Figure 2, F.)

"The ceiling appears convex."

FIG. 5. *Variations in the appearance of a head.*

(A) Lenses that cause the vertical meridians of the dioptric images to be rotated outward at the top. (See Figure 2, A.)

"Compared with the normal, the features appear to be pulled together, the brow is enlarged, sloping strongly back in the upper part and jutting forward below—with a jaw to invite a heavy-weight's right."

(B) Lenses that cause the vertical meridians of the dioptric images to be rotated inward at the top. (See Figure 2, B.)

"With these glasses, a very different effect is produced. The brow appears shortened and more vertical, the features spreading down and back in a general fade-away effect, the receding chin and out-thrusting turtle-like neck."

(C) Lenses that increase the size of the dioptric image formed in the right eye in the horizontal meridian. (See Figure 2, C.)

"Compared with the normal head, which was fairly symmetrical, the face appeared to be cramped together on one side and stretched out on the other. The symmetrical arrangements of the planes of the head also come out of line, the small side of the head advancing and the large side sloping away. The ear on the large side appears much larger and farther back, and the ear on the small side appears much smaller and nearer."

FIGURE 6

FIG. 6. *Variations in the appearance of the human figure.*

(A) Observer standing at X, wearing lenses that cause the vertical meridians of the dioptric images formed on each retina to be rotated inward at the top. (See Figure 2, B.)

"The figure appears to be long-waisted; i.e., stretched out from the hips up with short legs, and to be leaning backward as shown in (A). The head and features are distorted as described in Figure 5, B."

(B) Observer standing at X, wearing lenses that cause the vertical meridian of the dioptric images formed on each retina to be rotated outward at the top. (See Figure 2, A.)

"The figure appears to be short-waisted; i.e., short from the hips up, with long legs, and to be leaning forward as shown in (B). The head and features are distorted as described in Figure 5, A. If the subject raises his right arm above his head and lowers his left arm to his side, as shown in one aspect of Figure E, the upper arm will appear short with a small hand, and the lower arm will appear long with a large hand. If he now swings his two arms together so that his right hand is a few inches above his left, it will appear much nearer to the observer than the left, as shown."

(C) and (D) Appearance of the extended arms of a subject to the observer wearing lenses that increase the size of the dioptric image in the left eye in the horizontal meridian. (See Figure 2, D.)

"Drawing C shows the appearance with the arms stretched sideways. The right arm appears longer with a large hand, slanting slightly backward; the left arm appears shorter with a very small hand slanting slightly forward. The entire figure partakes of the same asymmetric distortion, the face appearing as described in Figure 5, C."

"When the arms are stretched forward as shown in (D), the right arm appears shorter and the left arm appears longer, the left hand appearing to be much nearer the observer."

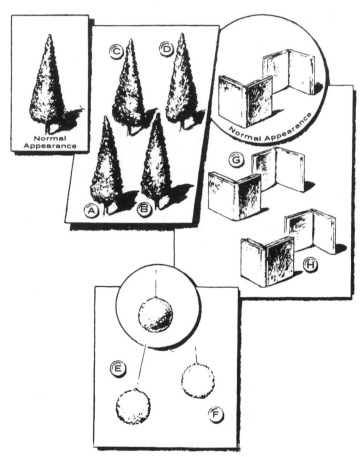

FIG. 7. *Variations in the appearance of a tree, a sphere, and a book.*

(A) and (B) A vertical cone-shaped tree as appearing to observer wearing lenses that cause the vertical meridians of the dioptric images to be rotated outward or inward at the top. (See Figure 2, A and B.)

"With lenses that rotate the vertical axes of the images, a vertical tree will appear tipped forward or backward, as shown. These are the same phenomena as described in Figure 3, A and B."

(C) and (D) Lenses that increase the size of the dioptric images in the right and left eye in the horizontal meridian.

"When round objects, like the tree, that have roughened surfaces are looked at through such lenses, they appear flattened and slanted, as shown in drawings C and D. If the strength of the lenses is increased, they appear almost perfectly flat like paper cutouts."

(E) and (F) A sphere as appearing to observer wearing lenses that cause the vertical meridians of the dioptric images to be rotated outward or inward at the top. (See Figure 2, A and B.)

"With lenses that tip the vertical meridians outward at the top, the sphere appears like a canteen or lozenge tipped forward at the top, as shown. With lenses that rotate the vertical meridians inward at the top, the ball appears similarly flattened but tipped back at the top."

"Actually, the shading on the disks appears the same as that on the sphere, and the strings appear vertical. The shading has been falsified as shown, and the strings put on a slant, as this was the only way to show that one disk appeared to be tipped forward at the top and the other tipped forward at the bottom."

(G) and (H) A book as appearing to observer wearing lenses that increase the size of the dioptric images in the right or the left eye in the horizontal meridian.

"When wearing lenses which increase the image in the left eye in the horizontal meridian, the right half of the book appears larger than the left half when the book is opened toward the observer. The right half of the book appears smaller than the left half when the book is spread away from the observer. This difference cannot be corrected by changing the angle of either or both halves. When the image in the right eye is increased, the opposite effect results."

FIG. 8. *Variations in the appearance of a rectilinear room and a brook.*

(A) With a lens that increases the size of the dioptric image formed on the left eye in the horizontal meridian. (See Figure 2, D.)

"A perfectly rectangular room, all surfaces of which are covered with leaves or some textured material, will appear with these glasses to come out of a square in all rectilinear lines; the flat back wall angled, the right part farther away, and the left nearer. What is most extraordinary is that the perspective is reversed, the length of the side which retreats being long, and that of the side which advances being shorter. The floor slants down on the left, and the ceiling slopes up on the left. Though one is standing with the side walls equidistant, the left one slopes away from the observer and increases in size; moreover, all the units of its textured surface are enlarged and outstanding. On the other hand, the right wall slopes in close to the observer and decreases in size, and the units of its textured surface are reduced in size and flattened."

"In general, the projected planes and perspective lines of the floor, back wall, and ceiling appear to form an apex 15 or 20 feet outside the right wall; while those of the two side walls interact in the middle distance slightly to the right of the plane of the right wall. The top and bottom lines of the side walls do not co-ordinate perspectively in converging on a common vanishing point. Those of the right wall seem to have a slight convergence; those on the left a violent convergence."

"The observer while standing halfway between the left and right walls, seems to be much nearer the right wall."

The change in appearance of this room to an observer wearing lenses that rotate the vertical meridians outward or inward at the top is also very marked. See Figure 2, A and B.)

"If outward, the room remains symmetrical right and left. The floor tips down at the near end, up at the far end; the back wall tips forward at the top, and the ceiling tips—the near part downward. The side wall slants in at the top. The detail on the floor appears large, that on the ceiling small."

"If the vertical meridians are rotated inward, these effects are just the opposite."

(B) Appearance of a brook to an observer wearing a lens that increases the size of the dioptric image formed in the right eye in the horizontal meridian. (See Figure 2, C.)

"The effect of many of these visual experiences with the different glasses are difficult to render pictorially. In the case of a rapidly flowing brook, it is possible (with glasses described in Figure 2, B) to look directly upstream and see the water as flowing violently *up* toward the observer, or with other glasses (described in Figure 2, A) to look downstream and see the water running *up* as it flows away. With the glasses described above, the unnatural slope of the water is as startling as I have tried to make it appear in the drawing."

It is hard to imagine what one's situation would be, had one always suffered from one or another of these defects; but I cannot imagine how one could produce representations which look true to the normal eye, nor could I imagine a person with such a defect once corrected by glasses ever trusting himself again to work without their aid.

The pictures and the accompanying text will have acquainted the reader with the general nature of the appearance that will be experienced under the particular commonplace environments described above, while wearing the particular types of aniseikonic lenses described.

The infinite number of possible appearances that might be experienced in different natural environments while wearing the various size lenses prevents their description. It is believed worth while, however, to attempt to describe briefly some of the appearances that result in six typical everyday situations; viz.:

(1) observing comparatively small moving objects,

(2) observing manipulated objects at near viewing distances,

(3) observing natural scenes at greater viewing distances,

(4) phenomena in the woods,

(5) phenomena on the water, and

(6) phenomena while driving an automobile.

(1) OBSERVING SMALL MOVING OBJECTS. A convenient setup for this purpose is the following: A light stick, about six feet long, is pivoted near one end on a universal bearing. On the other end of this stick, and at right angles to it, a card about six inches square is fastened. By placing the bearing close to a point between the eyes of the observer, the distance of the card, as it is moved through an arc, can be kept constant; its speed can also be kept relatively constant.

If the observer wears glasses that increase the image of one eye in the horizontal meridian (Figure 2, C and D), and the card is swung in a horizontal plane, typical misinterpretations of size, distance, and speed become apparent. For instance, with the image of the left eye increased, if the card is swung with approximately constant speed from a position at the left to the right, the card appears to decrease in size, to come nearer, and to move with constantly decreasing rate of speed. As it appears to come nearer, the length of the stick also appears to decrease, and the path of its movement, instead of following the arc of a circle as it should, is ovate in form. With glasses causing the image in the right eye to be relatively increased, the appearances are just the opposite.

With vertical movement of the card, similar effects become apparent if glasses rotating the vertical meridians of the dioptric images (Figures 2, A and B) are worn. These glasses, however, do not effect appearances of horizontal movement. When glasses are worn that rotate the vertical meridians outward at the top (Figure 2, A) and the card is swung up from below, it appears to become smaller, to come nearer, and to move slower. With glasses that rotate the vertical meridians inward at the top (Figure 2, B), the effects are just the opposite.

If the center of rotation is placed four to six feet in front of the observer, slightly below the level of the eyes and to one side of the median plane, these phenomena become, for many observers, even more pronounced.

In carrying out this experiment, it is convenient to put cards on both sides of a stick pivoted in the middle and heavy enough to keep rotating at fairly constant speed. When the stick is spun, the cards appear to move through an ovate course, with a marked change in their apparent rate of motion. As the length of the stick on one side appears to shorten, the card on that end appears to move more slowly, while, at the same time, the card on the other end of the other half of the stick, which appears to lengthen out, speeds up. The phenomena are substantially the same, with the proper glasses, with both horizontal and vertical movement.

(2) OBJECTS MANIPULATED AT NEAR DISTANCES. Phenomena such as described with reference to Figure 6, D and E, and Figure 7, G and H, are in general more marked for near than for distant vision.

To test what bearing these misinterpretations of spatial localization might have on our functional performances in near work, blocks and cards were manipulated on a table in ways that involved judgment of alignment, and evaluation of distance and size. Marked misjudgments were experienced concerning all three factors, their magnitude and exact nature depending upon the glasses worn.

(3) NATURAL SCENES OBSERVED AT GREATER VIEWING DISTANCES. For the purposes of empirically testing appearances of objects seen from greater distances, the glasses were worn while looking down from a bridge crossing a chasm about two hundred and fifty feet wide at the top and two hundred feet deep, with sides at inclinations of 60° to 70°, and at the bottom of which flows a stream.

To most persons, the effects of the glasses are immediately apparent, to others they come more slowly, and some observers with poor binocular vision do not experience them at all.

Looking down from a point in the middle of the bridge through glasses of the type described with reference to Figure 2, A, B, C, and D, the wall on one side or the other would appear almost horizontal, while the opposite wall would appear nearly vertical, the top but a few feet away. There are marked macropsia-micropsia effects associated with these apparent displacements. For example, pine trees on that wall of the chasm which tips up appear as diminutive shrubs.

Depending upon the glasses worn, the flowing stream appears slanting almost directly up or falling away very steeply; depending upon whether one is looking up or downstream, the water may appear either as a steep waterfall or as flowing uphill.

Glasses of the asymmetry type change the apparent depth of the chasm.

If the observer wearing any of these glasses and observing the corresponding abnormal appearances raises his head and looks out at the distant landscape, it appears perfectly normal. This is an example of the effect of the particular nature of environmental conditions upon subjective sensation.

(4) PHENOMENA IN THE WOODS. In general, the effects of these glasses when worn in the woods are most marked.

The ground tips very markedly in the direction called for, according to the horopter theory, by the particular glasses worn. By quickly turning or by parallax movements of the head, this tipping can be greatly reduced. However, while one is standing or walking along as one ordinarily does, the tipping is always present to a greater or lesser degree. This is especially so in thick, bushy undergrowth.

With glasses that cause the ground to tip away to one side or the other (analogous to Figure 2, C and D), one misjudges the distance of the trees on the right and left. With the glasses that tip the ground down on the right, the trees on the right side of the median plane appear farther away than they actually are and those on the other side appear nearer. In reaching out to take hold of a tree trunk or to push a branch aside as one does when walking through thick young growth, one will reach too far on one side and not far enough on the other.

It might be expected that this misjudgment of apparent distances to the right and left of the median plane might prevent one from walking in a straight line. In open woods, where one can look a long distance ahead, the glasses have no such effect, but in thick, bushy undergrowth, there is a tendency to deviate one way or the other, depending upon which glasses are worn.

In general, wearing these glasses in the woods is quite distressing and disagreeable, markedly so in thick underbrush. A sense of relief is experienced when they are taken off.

(5) PHENOMENA ON THE WATER. Preliminary observations were made concerning the effect of wearing these glasses while on small sailing boats.

If glasses are worn which on land cause the ground to appear tipped up (Figure 2, A), the surface of the sea appears much farther away and the apparent size of the waves and all floating objects is very much increased. At the same time there is a marked apparent increase in the speed of moving objects. One feels way up from the water as one would in a boat with very high sides. With the glasses that tip the ground away (Figure 2, B), the waves appear to be flattened out, there is an apparent decrease in the rate of motion, and one feels very close to the water as one would in a boat with very low sides. With the glasses that cause the ground to appear tipped sideways, the waves appear high on one side and low on the other.

It was thought that the glasses which make the waves appear higher than they actually are might cause nausea. Contrary to expectation, they tend to have the opposite effect. It is the glasses that make the waves appear flattened out that cause marked symptoms of nausea which quickly disappear when the glasses are taken off. A possible explanation may be that, when the waves appear flatter than they actually are, no visual signals are received as to the extent of the motion of boat and body which takes place when the waves rock the boat. One is battered around, so to speak, without forewarning or apparent cause. In the other case, when the waves appear steeper, more than ample notice is received of what is going to happen.

In this connection, the following observation is quite interesting. If, while wearing size lenses that produce an outward rotation of the dioptric images at the top, one stands on a level grass lawn close to a large body of water with a disturbed or roughened surface so that the bottom cannot be seen, and looks at the grass, the lawn will appear approximately at the same distance but tipped up; however, the water surface will appear level and farther away. An explanation of this phenomenon must be based on the fact that the observer knows from past experience that grass surfaces can be inclined, but that the surfaces of bodies of water are always horizontal.

(6) PHENOMENA WHILE DRIVING AN AUTOMOBILE. In driving an automobile, a most pronounced effect results from wearing the glasses described with reference to Figure 2, A and B. There is only the very slightest or no apparent tipping of the road. However, with the glasses that cause the lawn to appear tipped up (Figure 2, A), one feels elevated, almost as if sailing along ten or fifteen feet above the road. The glasses that cause the lawn to appear tipped away (Figure 2, B) have the opposite effect, as if one were driving in a child's cart with his feet almost dragging on the road.

Contrary to what might be expected, movement of the car enhances these effects. Preliminary tests have disclosed that under particular environmental conditions similar anomalous localization is experienced in airplanes.

With the glasses that cause an apparent tipping sideways of the lawn (Figure 2, C and D), no apparent tipping is noticed on an ordinary dirt or paved road. However, on a rough, grass- or snow-covered road, there is a marked apparent tipping. With these glasses a much more significant misinterpretation takes place. One is unable correctly to judge one's lateral position in the road. It is the same phenomenon that is described with reference to Figure 8; namely, misjudgment of the distances from the two side walls of a room.

Some preliminary observations were made as to the quantitative amount of this lateral misjudgment caused by lenses that increase the relative size of the image of one eye about 4 per cent in the horizontal meridian. When one is driving down what appears to be the middle of the road, one will, in fact, be off to one side or the other from around a foot to a foot and a half, depending upon which eye the lens is worn over.

If one tries to drive on one's own side of the road, in one case one will drive too near the ditch and in the other one will "hog" the center.

The effect of these lenses when one drives into a garage is most marked. A driver wearing an axis 90° size lens stronger than 4 per cent will probably hit the jamb of a standard garage opening. However, it will appear to the driver wearing these lenses that he is exactly in the middle of the opening.

With all types of lenses, a noticeable misinterpretation of the planes of the instrument board is apparent.

In general, there is a marked sense of uncertainty associated with driving an automobile while wearing these glasses and a sense of relief when they are removed.

OBSERVATIONS ON THE GENERAL NATURE OF THE PHENOMENA

THE ABOVE PHENOMENA have been experienced by many observers, both trained and untrained. Apparently, all persons with normal binocular vision have similar visual experiences when wearing the same size lenses in the same environmental conditions, the magnitude of the effects being directly related to the magnitude of the distortion produced by the size lenses.

There were a few observers who failed to get any effect at all, but there was evidence that they did not have normal binocular vision. There was also a small group of observers who got effects from observing near environments but did not get them from observing distant environments.

The rapidity with which the abnormal appearances develop varies with different observers. Some experience the effects immediately, others with more or less delay. There is also a greatly varying personal factor in the correcting effect of movement of the head upon the anomalous appearances. For instance, the phenomenon of short grass appearing tipped to the observer wearing axis 90° lenses tends to disappear with some persons upon even a slight movement of the head, while with others it will remain even if they walk or run. In the case of long grass or low brush, motion has no corrective effect even for the first-mentioned class of observers.

An appreciable anomaly of appearance results from a lens that produces a difference in the size and shape of the images received in the two eyes which is of the order of magnitude of the retinal resolving power. It is of special interest, however, that no anomaly of appearance is experienced if the magnitude of the distortion produced is greater than a certain amount which varies with the particular environmental conditions being observed. Furthermore, roving binocular fixation has no appreciable effect on the anomalous appearances, nor do certain head positions.

In view of the unequivocal and most marked, one might say, dramatic nature of these anomalous appearances, it might be expected that looking through the above-described glasses should produce similar anomalous appearances under all conditions. Actually, however, this is not the case. The nature and degree of the anomalous appearances that are experienced depend not only upon the particular environmental conditions but also upon the observer. At present there is not enough known of the relationships between environmental conditions and visual appearances to permit more than the mentioning of a few more important factors that play a role.

Of first importance is the presence in the field of view of those factors that give rise to uniocular stimulus patterns with which visual significances are related. If such factors are sufficiently predominant, no anomalous appearances will be experienced. For instance, if any of the above-mentioned size lenses are worn in an ordinary room, everything appears substantially normal to most observers, due to the presence of what, for the sake of brevity, may be called uniocular "clues." To what extent uniocular "clues" will be taken account of and binocular "clues" neglected apparently depends not only on their relative dominance but also on the "sensitivity" of the particular observer to the two types of "clues."

The observer has the capacity for taking account of or neglecting binocular clues in different parts of the field of view at the same time. An illustration of the capacity is furnished by the following experiment:

If the observer wears say a 4 per cent axis 90° cylindrical magnification lens before the right eye, in an ordinary room in which there are perspective features such as a fireplace and mantel, everything will appear practically normal to most observers, in spite of the abnormal binocular stimulus pattern relation produced by the size lens. If, now, another person stands in front of the fireplace with arms extended toward the observer, one arm will appear longer than the other (Figure 6, D). Why a human figure with the form of which we are so conversant should appear distorted whereas the room remains normal is not too clear. The only apparent explanation is that rectilinear geometrical patterns give rise to more definite spatial clues than irregular forms.

A second factor in the environmental conditions that plays a role in anomalous appearances is the distance of the objects in the field of view. This is due to the fact that spatial significances related to a given binocular stimulus pattern vary with the distance at which they are localized. For example, the apparent tipping of surfaces related to a given size difference in the horizontal meridians of the uniocular stimulus patterns increases with the distance at which the surface is seen. These relationships are shown in Figure 9. It will be noted that the amount of apparent tipping increases very rapidly with distance.

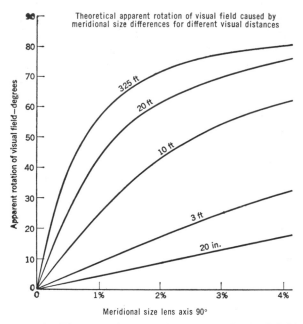

FIG. 9. *Theoretical apparent rotation of visual field caused by meridional size differences for different visual distances.*

A third factor in the environmental conditions that plays a role in determining spatial localization is knowledge of the spatial significance of the objects in the field of view. An example of the effect of such knowledge is the different appearance of grass and water viewed through the same size lenses as described.

Another important question for consideration is whether or not the above-described anomalous localization continues to be experienced if the glasses are worn for protracted periods. This matter was investigated and reported by Burian (12). Briefly stated, the findings showed that, in environmental conditions giving rise to uniocular clues which have sufficient spatial significance, the anomalous localizations due to the anomalous binocular relation of the stimulus patterns ceased to be experienced with protracted wearing of the glasses. However, in environments where there was a minimum of uniocular stimuli of this type, the anomalous localization became apparent, although in some instances there was evidence of a fractional reduction thereof.

These findings indicate that persons with an anomalous binocular stimulus-pattern relation can, through experience or practice, develop normal vision. They also indicate that this is not due to an alteration of the anomalous binocular stimulus-pattern relation, but is due to neglect of its visual significance and reliance on the significances related to the uniocular stimulus patterns. This, in turn, means loss of the advantage of the added accuracy of spatial localization derived from binocular vision.

That alteration of anomalous binocular stimulus patterns cannot be brought about by experience and practice is evidenced by the fact that there are many persons with inherently anomalous stimulus incongruities who experience anomalous spatial localization of a nature that would be expected from the character of their aniseikonia; i.e., anomalous binocular stimulus pattern.

REFERENCES—CHAPTER 6

1. Ames, A. Jr. "Aniseikonia—a factor in the functioning of vision." *Amer. J. Ophthal.,* 1935, *18,* 1014–20.

2. Ames, A. Jr. "Aniseikonia," in *The Eye and Its Diseases,* edited by Conrad Berens, 1936, pp, 258–59, 284–86.

3. Ames, A. Jr. "The space eikonometer test for aniseikonia." *Amer. J. Ophthal.,* 1945, *28,* 248–62.

4. Ames, A. Jr.; Gliddon, G. H.; and Ogle, K. N. "Lenses for changing size and shape of the dioptric images." *Annals Distinguished Service Foundation of Optometry,* 1932, *1,* 61–70.

5. Ames, A. Jr.; Gliddon, G. H.; and Ogle, K. N. "Size and shape of ocular images. I. Methods of determination and physiologic significance." *Arch. Ophthal.,* 1932, *7,* 576–97.

6. Ames, A. Jr.; Ogle, K. N.; and Gliddon, G. H. "Corresponding retinal points, the horopter and size and shape of ocular images." *J. Opt. Soc. Amer.,* 1932, *22,* 538–632.

7. Bannon, R. E. "Practical aspects of aniseikonia." *Amer. J. Optom. & Arch. Amer. Acad. Optom.,* 1942, *19,* 239–60.

8. Berens, C., and Loutfallah, M. "Aniseikonia. A study of 836 patients examined with the Ophthalmo-Eikonometer." *Amer. J. Ophthal.,* 1939, *22,* 652–41.

9. Bielschowsky, A. "The etiology of squint." Amer. J. Ophthal., 1937, *20,* 478–89.

10. Bielschowsky, A. "Die Störungen im Bereich der Vertikalmotoren der Augen." *Acta Ophthal.,* 1938, *16,* 235–70.

11. Burian, H. M. "Clinical significance of aniseikonia." *Arch. Ophthal.,* 1943, *29,* 116–33.

12. Burian, H. M. "Influence of prolonged wearing of meridional size lenses on spatial localization." *Arch. Ophthal.,* 1943, *30,* 645–66.

13. Burian, H. M., and Ogle, K. N. "A study of the aniseikonia in a case of increasing unilateral index myopia." *Amer. J. Ophthal.,* 1943, *26,* 480–90.

14. Carlton, E. H., and Madigan, L. F. "Size and shape of ocular images: II. Clinical significance." *Arch. Ophthal.,* 1932, *7,* 720–38.

15. Doane, H. C. "Analysis of clinical data on aniseikonia with case reports. *Amer. J. Optom. & Arch. Amer. Acad. Optom.,* 1941, *18,* 404–17.

16. Fisher, H. M. "Aniseikonia." *Amer. J. Optom. & Arch. Amer. Acad. Optom.,* 1941, *18,* 362–69.

17. Friedenwald, H. "Über die durch corrigierende Gläser hervorgerufene binokulare Metamorphopsie." *Arch. f. Augenheilk.,* 1893, *26,* 362–70.

18. Green, J. "On certain stereoscopic illusions evoked by prismatic and cylindrical spectacle glasses." *Trans. Amer. Ophthal. Soc.,* 1888–1890, *2,* 449–56.

19. Herzau, W. "Demonstration des Ameschen Kippfeldes." *Zentralbl. f.o. O.,* 1938, *41,* 396.

20. Hughes, W. L. "Report of a series of cases examined on the Ophthalmo-Eikonometer." *Arch. Ophthal.,* 1935, *14,* 146–59.

21. Lancaster, W. B. "Aniseikonia." *Arch. Ophthal.,* 1938, *20,* 907–12.

22. Lancaster, W. B. "Nature, scope and significance of aniseikonia." *Arch. Ophthal.,* 1942, *28,* 767–79.

23. Lancaster, W. B. "A reply to criticisms of aniseikonia." *Trans. Amer. Ophthal. Soc.,* 1942.

24. Lippincott, J. A. "Über die durch corrigierende Gläser hervorgerufene binokulare Metamorphopsie." *Arch. f. Augenheilk.,* 1891, *23,* 96–108.

25. Lippincott, J. A. "On the binocular metamorphopsia produced by optical means." *Arch. Ophthal.,* 1917, *46,* 397–426.

26. Ogle, K. N. "An analytical treatment of the longitudinal horopter; its measurement and application to related phenomena, especially to the relative size of the ocular images." *J. Opt. Soc. Amer.,* 1932, *22,* 665–728.

27. Ogle, K. N. "Correction of aniseikonia with ophthalmic lenses." *J. Opt. Soc. Amer.,* 1926, *26,* 323–37.

28. Ogle, K. N. "Die mathematische Analyse des Längshoropters." *Arch. f. d. ges. Physiol.,* 1938, *239,* 748–66.

29. Ogle, K. N. "Induced size effect: I. A new phenomenon in binocular space perception associated with the related size of the images of the two eyes." *Arch. Ophthal.,* 1938, *20,* 604–23.

30. Ogle, K. N. "Induced size effect: II. An experimental study of the phenomenon with restricted fusion stimuli." *Arch. Ophthal.,* 1939, *21,* 604–25.

31. Ogle, K. N. "Induced size effect: III. A study of the phenomenon as induced by horizontal disparity of the fusion centers." *Arch. Ophthal.,* 1939, *22,* 613–35.

32. Ogle, K. N. "Induced size effect with eyes in asymmetric convergence." *Arch. Ophthal.,* 1940, *23,* 1023–38.

33. Ogle, K. N. "The induced size effect." *J. Opt. Soc. America,* 1940, *30,* 145–61.

34. Ogle, K. N. "Association between aniseikonia and anomalous binocular space perception." *Arch. Ophthal.,* 1943, *30,* 54–64.

35. Ogle, K. N. "Theory of the space-eikonometer." *J. Opt. Soc. Amer.,* 1946, *36,* 20–32.

36. Ogle, K. N., and Ellerbrock, V. J. "Stereoscopic sensitivity in the space-eikonometer." *Arch. Ophthal.,* 1945, *34,* 303–10.

37. Wadsworth, O. F. "The effect of a cylindrical lens, with the vertical axis placed before one eye." *Trans. Amer. Ophthal. Soc.,* 1873–1879, *2,* 342.

C H A P T E R

7

The Temporal Course of

Perception

William H. Ittelson

[This paper, not previously published,* was presented by Ittelson a number of years ago to a meeting of psychologists at Princeton University. It is printed here because the thoughts it presents aid in understanding some of the temporal processes introduced for discussion in Chapters 8 and 9. In addition, it serves as excellent introduction to Chapters 10 and 11, because the experiments described in those chapters deal systematically with some aspects of temporal delay in perceptual change and show the influence of Ittelson's thinking in both design and analysis.—Ed.]

I T IS PROBABLY A truism that behavior somehow reflects or is related to a temporally extended process in which both the real and the experienced "now" elude definition. It is nevertheless possible to analyze behavior into various stages, necessarily arbitrary, which succeed each other in

---

* Since this note was written, Professor Ittelson has informed me that he has used this article as a base for an expanded chapter including references and experiment material in his book *Visual Space Perception*, New York: Springer Publishing Company (in press).

definite temporal order and to determine characteristic time durations for these various stages. Having done this, we can ask ourselves questions about the temporal order of events within any single stage. In this paper we shall be concerned with such a question related to that stage in the process which can for the moment loosely be termed "perceptual."

Every one of us has repeated countless times a primitive experiment which consists of first closing our eyes and then opening them. Two observations are consistently made. First, as soon as one opens one's eyes, one sees something. Second, what this something is depends upon what one happens to be looking at. These are facts of observation. They are related to two principles which have historically played an important role in psychological thought—one, the immediacy of perception, and two, the stimulus determination of perception. Immediacy as used here typically carries a double meaning of "without intermediary stages" and "instantaneous in time." The common-sense conclusion drawn from the experiment I have just described is that a perception is uniquely determined by the stimulus, that this perception is experienced exactly simultaneously with the stimulation, and that the perception necessarily emerges in one fell swoop, without passing through any successive stages.

Now this view is manifestly naïve in the extreme and is supported as thus and baldly stated by very few theorists today. The argument of immediacy has tended to degenerate into an argument of spontaneity, while that of stimulus determination has similarly degenerated into an argument of intransigence.

That is, perceptions seem to arise spontaneously, and to resist change vigorously. These arguments of spontaneity and intransigence sum up the thinking of many contemporary perception theorists. They lead to what seems on the surface to be a more sophisticated statement, linearly descended from the earlier, which might read something like this:

"Perception is a process, extended in time, which is initiated by a stimulus, and each step of which is uniquely determined by a combination of the initiating stimulus and the inherent properties of the organism."

This is a statement which I believe would be subscribed to by many perceptual theorists today. It has only one serious drawback. It is incorrect at several important points.

The error, I think, stems primarily from the mistaken belief that something which occurs extremely quickly therefore occurs inevitably. One way of putting this assumption to experimental test is to study in detail the time interval between a change in stimulation and the appearance of a changed stable perception. In order to define this time interval a little more specifically, it may be worth while to discuss the various stages into which the process can be analyzed, as mentioned earlier.

Let us consider a hypothetical experiment. A light is turned on. Our subject is given a key which he presses and which turns off the light. Starting arbitrarily with time equals zero when the light is turned on we can roughly enumerate the sequence of events. The first stage is that of transit of the energy from the light source to the receptor, in this case the retina. There follows excitation of the peripheral receptor, then nerve transmission to various central areas. The next stage can, for the moment, be called central elaboration which is followed by the appearance of an impulse along the efferent nerve which initiates motor activity which then alters the condition of the external light source. Characteristically, the time consumed in each one of these stages is quite short. The total process may take as little as the order of a quarter of a second and the great bulk of this time is undoubtedly consumed in the motor phase. The remaining stages probably occupy durations in the order of milliseconds or less. One fact to be noted, however, is that, while these times are characteristically short, they are not necessarily so. If the stimulus is auditory and the source is far distant, the transit time may be appreciable. The state of sensory adaptation may lengthen the excitation time considerably. If we tell our subject to press the key when he feels like it, the period of central elaboration may extend to many seconds, minutes, or longer.

Nevertheless, it remains true that the time elapsed in the perceptual part of the sequence, defined here as the time between a change of excitation and the appearance of a changed stable perception, is characteristically extremely short. It is to this time interval that we shall devote our attention from here on. It might be parenthetically pointed out that by extremely short we mean extremely short relative to normal human functioning. And it is perhaps no more than a tautology to say that a part of a process takes place in a time which is short relative to the total process. The time duration is very large indeed relative to high-speed computing devices, for example. However, for experimental purposes this time may be considered short. It is of the order of ten milliseconds. It has usually been assumed that this time cannot be greatly extended, and the chief tool for studying this part of the process has been the tachistoscope, in which exposure times of durations comparable to that occupied by the process itself are used. While much useful work has been done by this technique, it still remains desirable to approach the problem from the other direction, that is, artificially to extend the duration of the process into a length of time amenable to examination and study. It is desirable to do this both for experimental reasons and because as long as one is forced to rely on tachistoscopic experiments one is implicitly supporting the arguments of spontaneity and intransigence, the very arguments which much tachistoscopic work attempts to refute. If we cannot, in the laboratory, extend the duration of the perceptual process beyond the few milliseconds commonly occupied, we can scarcely expect much credence to be given to our protestation that, nevertheless, in normal functioning outside of the laboratory this process is frequently temporally quite extended.

Fortunately, we now have at our disposal several experimental techniques which do just this. The same general sequence of events can be observed in all the techniques.

First, the stimulation on the retina is altered suddenly. Then at some appreciable time later a changed stable perception is reported. The fact that this time interval is appreciable, sometimes being in the order of minutes, is in itself significant, as well as offering us an opportunity for observing in detail the changes in perception over this period which normally take place in a small fraction of a second.

I will now describe one such experiment in some detail. An 8-foot cube, open on one side, and with the interior walls lined with leaves, which for obvious reasons we call the "leaf room," can be viewed through the open side by an observer who for this experiment is provided with a pair of aniseikonic glasses. These glasses produce a change in the binocular disparity pattern from that provided normally by the cubical room to the disparities which would be provided by some distorted, that is, noncubical, room. At eye level along the back wall of the leaf room is placed a rod whose tilt can be controlled by the observer and automatically recorded as a function of time. The observer is seated looking into the room. He is wearing either no glasses or his normal corrective lenses. He is told to set the rod so that it appears parallel, for example, to the ceiling of the room and to maintain the rod apparently parallel to the ceiling at all times. He is then given some practice adjusting the rod from various pre-set tilts. As soon as he is familiar with the apparatus, he again sets the rod apparently parallel to the ceiling and the aniseikonic glasses are suddenly placed over his eyes. The apparent distortion of the room as a function of time can then be read directly from the recording of the position of the rod as a function of time.

Certain results are uniformly obtained with all observers. *First,* the room does not appear altered immediately after putting on the glasses. *Second,* some finite time later an alteration of the shape of the room is perceived. *Third,* this new apparent shape is not stable but continues gradually to change. *Fourth,* finally the room is perceived in a stable, altered shape. What are the time durations related to these various stages? The period of no apparent change at all varies from a minimum of one or two seconds up to as high as thirty seconds or even more. The duration between the first appearance of change in the shape of the room and the attainment of a final, stable apparent shape again varies widely from a minimum of two or three seconds up to commonly as long as two minutes or more.

These results are easily and universally obtained by the technique I have just described, as well as by other techniques. From these results we may draw some fairly definite conclusions. It is quite clear, first, that a finite time intervenes between a change of the stimulus and the appearance of a changed stable perception. Secondly, this time interval which is commonly quite short can experimentally be greatly extended for study. And third, the transition from one stable perception to another involves not only a finite time but also successive intermediary stages. In sum, we can conclude that it is possible for extensive and protracted changes of perception to take place over a period of time during which all sensory stimulation remains constant and unchanging and we have an effective experimental technique for studying such changes.

While such a conclusion has manifestly far-reaching implications, it is nevertheless just a start. Many questions remain to be answered. I will attempt to offer a few hypotheses about this process based on as yet insufficient evidence. These hypotheses are not to be taken too seriously but are the best guesses we can make at the moment. The first question is undoubtedly, "What are the conditions under which this great extension of the temporal duration of the perceptual process can be observed?" I am not sure that I can specify sufficient conditions but a necessary condition quite clearly seems to be the sudden introduction of a perceptual conflict. By this I mean that perceptual indications are provided which are capable, figuratively, of diverse interpretations which are mutually incompatible; that is, they cannot successfully be maintained simultaneously. While this is the general condition for this effect, many other factors are involved. There are wide individual differences in the duration of the various stages. These may be partly related to such factors as stereoscopic acuity, eye dominance, etc., although it is not clear whether these enter inherently or experientially. Perhaps of more interest to many people is the evidence, fairly conclusive, that there is a relationship between this time interval and personality factors. We have, for example, considerable evidence that stress increases the time to attain a new stable perception. Not only the time but also the magnitude is definitely influenced by affective relationships between the observer and what he is looking at. It is conceivable that this technique may eventually lead to a new diagnostic test. More certainly, and more importantly, it will throw light on questions of personality theory.

Investigation of these and other areas remains for the future. It is perfectly clear, however, that the temporal course of perception can be characterized as a continuous succession of changes, all of which occur a finite time after stimulation has changed, each step in the process being affected by diverse factors, including, among others, at least such things as the personality structure of the individual and, further, that the time duration of this process can be quite long.

8

The Monocular and Binocular

Distorted Rooms

William H. Ittelson & F. P. Kilpatrick

[Of all the demonstrations, the distorted rooms have received the most publicity, but tend to be regarded as "interesting," with little appreciation of their significance for perceptual theory and experimentation. This chapter makes clear that they were constructed as critical expreiments testing specific aspects of perceptual theory and Chapters 9 and 10 offer examples of their value as experimental devices for studying numerous other aspects of the perceptual process.—Ed.]

INTRODUCTION

TWO CONFIGURATIONS in the physical world can be defined as visually equivalent if they provide an observer with exactly the same visual cues.[1] Conversely, a given visual cue can be said to define two or more

[1] Visual cue, as used here, refers most broadly to any characteristic of the impinging light rays to which the organism is sensitive, or with respect to which it can make a discrimination. In this chapter we will be concerned specifically with distance cues, i.e., those characteristics of the impinging light rays which provide the organism with spatial information.

equivalent configurations if it can be shown that there exist two or more physical configurations which produce exactly the same cue. The proof of the existence of equivalent configurations is primarily a problem in geometry. It is asserted and will be demonstrated in this chapter that each of the already identified visual cues to depth defines an infinite family of equivalent configurations.

This assertion means that identical incoming "messages" can come from quite different external spatial arrangements. It is clearly essential that the organism which receives these identical messages be able to distinguish between them. Presumably, this can only be done on the basis of additional information from some other source.

After proving geometrically the existence of equivalent configurations, we shall describe the *monocular distorted rooms* as evidence that two or more monocularly equivalent configurations, in the absence of any additional information, are in fact perceived as being identical in monocular vision. Following that, the *binocular distorted rooms* will be described as a means of presenting the same sort of evidence for binocular vision.

EQUIVALENT CONFIGURATIONS

The proof of the existence of a family of equivalent configurations involves two steps:

1. The identification of a visual cue. This involves the specification of a particular characteristic of the impinging light rays which the organism utilizes in making distance discriminations.

2. The determination, usually by means of geometry, of the physical configurations which are adequate to account for any unique instance of the cue identified above. If these configurations are found to constitute an identifiable family, then it can be stated that the particular visual cue defines a family of equivalent configurations.

Equivalent Configurations Defined by Certain Cues: I. Size

The particular characteristics of the impinging light rays with which we are here concerned are those which determine the size—and shape—of the retinal area stimulated. If, for the sake of simplicity, we consider only a single plane passing through the nodal point of the eye, this characteristic can most conveniently be expressed in terms of the visual angle, α. It is immediately clear from Figure 1 (p. 158) that the statement $\alpha = $ constant defines a family of surfaces. Some of these are indicated in the figure. If we limit our consideration for the moment to plane surfaces, the equation

$$\tan \alpha = \frac{S \cos \delta}{D - S \sin \delta}$$

where α = visual angle
D = Distance along line of sight
S = Size
δ = inclination to the vertical

[1]

specifies the entire family, using the vertical to the line of sight as reference. It is possible, but not particularly useful for the present discussion, to generalize this equation for a fixed reference system independent of the observer and for curved as well as plane surfaces.

Any surface which satisfies Equation [1] provides exactly the same size cue, specified by α, as does any other surface which satisfies this equation. Similarly, if the value of α is changed by changing one or more of the characteristics of the surface, e.g., its distance, slant, or size, then a wholly new family of surfaces is defined, the characteristics of which can be determined again from Equation [1].

II. Illumination

If the illumination of an object, viewed monocularly in a dark room, is increased, the object appears to approach the observer. The particular characteristics related to illumination which are critical for this discrimination are not well established. Two characteristics, intensity per unit area and total intensity, will be discussed here. As will be seen, both define families of equivalent configurations.

Let us consider a surface of area A, normal to the line of sight, at a distance D, sufficiently great so that the solid angle β subtended by A at the point of observation O is given approximately by A/D^2. The surface A is reflecting (or emitting) light uniformly in all directions. Let i be the brightness, or intensity of reflected light per unit area, and $I = iA$ be the total intensity of light reflected by A, in the direction of the observer.

The intensity of light reaching the observer per unit area of the source decreases as the square of the distance of the source from the observer. The total intensity of light at the point of observation, I_o, is given by multiplying the received intensity per unit area of the source by the area of the source. Hence,

$$I_o = C \frac{iA}{D^2} = C \frac{I}{D^2}.$$

[2]

If i_o is the intensity per unit angle at the point of observation, then

$$I_o = \beta i_o.$$

Substituting

$$\beta = \frac{A}{D^2}$$

$$I_o = \frac{i_o A}{D^2}.$$

Therefore, substituting in Equation [2]

$$I_o = \frac{i_o A}{D^2} = C \frac{iA}{D^2}$$

or

$$i_o = Ci. \qquad\qquad [3]$$

Equation [3] states that the brightness, or intensity of light per unit angle, at the point of observation is dependent only on the brightness of the observed object. This means that the family of equivalent configurations defined by a given impinging brightness, expressed by $i_o =$ constant, consists of any and all surfaces of a given brightness i. Conversely, the impinging brightness of an object is independent of the distance of that object from the observer.

Equation [2] provides a more serious limitation. For a given total intensity of illumination impinging on the point of observation, the expression

$$\frac{iA}{D^2} = \text{constant}$$

defines the family of equivalent configurations. For a constant brightness, i, the surface must decrease in size as the distance decreases in such a way as to maintain a constant visual angle. Or, considering a constant-size object, its brightness must vary with the square of the distance.

III. Movement Parallax

An observer moving with respect to objects which are themselves also moving with respect to each other represents the most general, and most common, condition of observation. The very fact of relative movement itself provides an important distance cue—movement parallax. Graham (2) has suggested that the characteristic of impinging light rays which represents the cue can be expressed in terms of a relative angular velocity. He has derived expressions for this relative angular velocity for two cases: (a) moving objects and a stationary observer and (b) stationary objects and a moving observer. This restriction is not necessary, however, and the following derivation, following Graham closely, provides an expression for the general case in which both observer and objects are moving.

Referring to Figure 2, and assuming D to be very much greater than all other dimensions, the angular velocity of point M, relative to O, is given approximately by

$$^{\omega}M = \frac{^{v}M - {}^{v}O}{D}.$$

Similarly,

$$^{\omega}N = \frac{^{v}N - {}^{v}O}{D + \delta}.$$

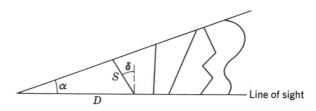

FIG. 1.

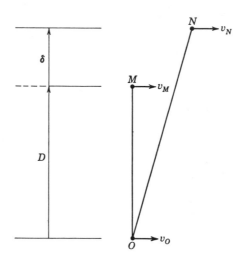

FIG. 2.

The differential angular velocity, which provides the parallax cue is,

$$\omega = {}^{\omega}M - {}^{\omega}N = \frac{^{v}M - {}^{v}O}{D} - \frac{^{v}N - {}^{v}O}{D + \delta}.$$

Simplifying, and noting that $\delta << D$,

$$\omega = \frac{\delta}{D^2} ({}^{v}M - {}^{v}O) + \frac{1}{D} ({}^{v}M - {}^{v}N). \qquad [4]$$

It is immediately clear from Equation [4] that any specific case of movement parallax, i.e., $\omega = $ constant, defines a family of equivalent configurations.[2]

Let us consider, for example, the case of stationary objects and a moving observer. Equation [4] reduces to

$$\omega = \frac{\delta\ ^{v}o}{D^2} \ .$$

If the velocity of the observer is constant, the criterion that ω be constant is met by a family of objects whose spacing increases with the square of their distance from the observer.

Another case of interest is that in which both objects are moving at the same speed. Equation [4] reduces to

$$\omega = \frac{\delta}{D^2} \ (^{v}M - {}^{v}o) \ .$$

The same parallax cue, i.e., $\omega = $ constant, is provided by a family of objects whose spacing varies inversely with the difference between their speed and that of the observer.

IV. Binocular Disparity

"Stereoscopic perception of the difference in depth between the point of fixation and any other point in space depends on the disparity between the two retinal images of those points" (4, p. 18). Although the determination of physiological or of functional disparity is a complex and controversial topic, thoroughly covered in the authoritative discussion by Ogle (4), specification of geometric disparity is a relatively straightforward problem on which general agreement has been attained. Referring to Figure 3,

$$\eta = \text{Disparity} = \alpha_2 - \alpha_1, = \theta_1 - \theta_2.$$

It is generally agreed that binocular disparity provides a cue to the distances of objects relative to each other and not of their absolute distances, i.e., relative to the observer.[3] This fact immediately suggests the

[2] Since the "configurations" referred to in the case of movement parallax include such aspects as the movement of the observer, equivalent "conditions" might be a better expression. For the sake of simplicity the earlier term will be continued in this section.

[3] For example, Fry (1, pp. 11–12) has written that, "Although stereopsis aids one in judging the relative distances of two or more objects, it does not give any information about the absolute distance of the objects." Similarly, Ogle (4, p. 159) states: "The angles α_1 and α_2 themselves (corresponding to retinal dimensions) do not provide sufficient means for the judgment of the *absolute* distance of either F or P from the eyes, but their difference does provide the stimulus for the *relative* localization (depth) of the two points."

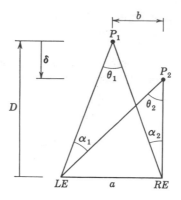

FIG. 3.

possibility of stereoptically equivalent configurations, which can easily be verified. Referring again to Figure 3, and assuming

$$\delta, a, \text{ and } b \text{ are all } < < D,$$

$$\theta_1 = \frac{a}{D}$$

$$\theta_2 = \frac{a}{D - \delta}$$

$$\eta = \theta_1 - \theta_2 = \frac{a}{D} - \frac{a}{D - \delta} = \frac{a\,\delta}{D(D - \delta)}$$

$$\eta \cong \frac{a\,\delta}{D^2}.$$

It follows directly from this equation that a given binocular disparity, $\eta = $ constant, defines a family of pairs of points whose spacing relative to each other is very nearly proportional to the square of their distance from the observer.

It is possible, however, to establish a more general, and more rigorous, statement of binocularly equivalent configurations. The following presentation is condensed and modified from Luneberg (3).

In the co-ordinate system indicated in Figure 4, let us consider an observer with his eyes located at the points $y = \pm 1$. In Cartesian co-ordinates, a point P can be characterized by (x, y, z). We now introduce a bipolar co-ordinate system in which θ is the angle of elevation of the plane through the y axis and the point P, and α and β are the angles between the Y axis and lines drawn to P from the right and left eye, respectively. The positive directions of α and β are as indicated in the figure.

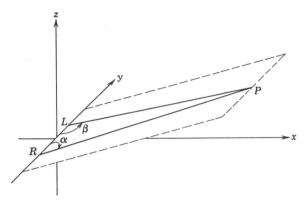

FIG. 4. *Diagram from R. K. Luneburg,* Mathematical Analysis of Binocular Vision. *(Princeton, N.J.: Princeton Univ. Press, 1947. By permission of the publisher.)*

The relation between the x, y, z co-ordinates and the α, β, θ coordinates is given by

$$x = \frac{2 \cos \theta}{\cot \alpha + \cot \beta}, \quad \cot \alpha = \frac{y + 1}{\sqrt{x^2 + z^2}}$$

$$y = \frac{\cot \alpha - \cot \beta}{\cot \alpha + \cot \beta}, \quad \cot \beta = \frac{1 - y}{\sqrt{x^2 + z^2}}$$

$$z = \frac{2 \sin \theta}{\cot \alpha + \cot \beta}, \quad \cot \theta = \frac{x}{z}.$$

We now consider a line element (dx, dy, dz) attached to point P. It will be projected on the right retina as a line element $(d\alpha, d\theta)$ and on the left retina as $(- d\beta, d\theta)$. The physiological significance of this is clear: $d\alpha + d\beta$ represents the horizontal disparity of the line element (dx, dy, dz).

It follows that two line elements in space (dx_1, dy_1, dz_1) and (dx_2, dy_2, dz_2) will present identical binocular indications if

$$d\,\alpha_1 = d\,\alpha_2$$
$$d\,\beta_1 = d\,\beta_2$$
$$d\,\theta_1 = d\,\theta_2$$

Such line elements are *binocularly equivalent*. Furthermore, since most external objects can be considered as configurations of line elements, this is readily generalized to curves and surfaces. It is evident that the transformation

$$\alpha' = \alpha + \delta$$
$$\beta' = \beta + \epsilon$$
$$\theta' = \theta + \lambda$$

satisfies the conditions for binocular equivalence. Hence, any two surfaces in space such that one can be transformed into the other by a transformation of this type are *binocularly equivalent surfaces*.

In general, this simple transformation in the α, β, θ co-ordinate system leads to a complex transformation in the x, y, z co-ordinates. We shall illustrate this with one simple, but by no means trivial, example. Let the problem be to determine the curves which are equivalent to the straight line $x = x_o$ lying in the xy plane.

We first introduce the new co-ordinates

$$\gamma = \pi - \alpha - \beta$$
$$\phi = \tfrac{1}{2} (\beta - \alpha)$$
$$\theta = \theta$$

which retain the physiological significance of the α, β, θ co-ordinates, $- d\gamma = d\alpha + d\beta$ being the binocular disparity.

The transformation

$$\gamma = \gamma + \tau$$
$$\phi' = \phi + \sigma \qquad\qquad [5]$$
$$\theta' = \theta + \lambda$$

satisfies the conditions for binocular equivalence or, in other words, binocular disparity is invariant with respect to this transformation.

It is easily shown that, in the xy plane, the relation between the x, y co-ordinates and γ, ϕ co-ordinates is given approximately (i.e., for distances large compared to the interpupillary distance) by

$$\gamma = \frac{2_x}{x^2 + y^2}$$

$$\tan \phi = \frac{y}{x} .$$

Applying the transformation

$$\gamma' = \gamma + \tau$$
$$\phi' = \phi$$

we obtain

$$\frac{x'}{x'^2 + y'^2} = \frac{x}{x^2 + y^2} + \frac{\tau}{2}$$

$$\frac{y'}{x'} = \frac{y}{x}$$

Substituting $y' = \frac{y}{x}x'$ in the first equation leads directly to

$$x = x'\left(1 + \frac{\tau}{2}\ \frac{x^2 + y^2}{x}\right).$$

The inversion of this formula is obtained simply by replacing τ by $-\tau$.

$$x' = x\left(1 - \frac{\tau}{2}\ \frac{x'^2 + y'^2}{x}\right).$$

Since we are concerned with the transformation of the line $x = x_{o'}$ we can write directly (substituting x, y for x', y')

$$x = x_o\left(1 - \frac{\tau}{2}\ \frac{x^2 + y^2}{x}\right).$$

Hence the straight line $x = x_o$ transforms into a family of binocularly equivalent conic sections, hyperbolae if $\tau < o$ and ellipses if $\tau > o$.

Generalized Statement of Equivalent Configurations

The foregoing proof of the existence of equivalent configurations for four isolated distance indications does not constitute a generalized statement. In order to achieve generalization two additional steps are needed.

1. Proof of the existence of equivalent configurations for every distance indication in isolation. As yet it is difficult to specify mathematically the exact characteristics of the impinging light energy which describe many of the cues. However, it seems reasonable to assume that once this is done, equivalent configurations can be derived, as was done for the four cases treated in detail above, for all cues with the possible exception of those which may be provided by accommodation and convergence innervations.[4]

2. Following the proof of the existence of equivalent configurations for each isolated cue, the next step in generalization would consist of showing that various combinations of these cues do not result in a restriction of the freedom allowed by each cue individually. It can easily be shown, for example, that the combination of size and illumination results in no restriction, and a family of equivalent configurations can still be derived. Similar proofs for all possible combinations of cues could undoubtedly be worked out eventually. Such a procedure would

---

[4] These cues would seem to be unique to the stimulating situation. However, there remains considerable doubt as to whether such cues actually are utilized in distance perception. Even if they are, their contribution is undoubtedly small. The role of accommodation and convergence in depth perception has been discussed elsewhere in this volume.

be needlessly time consuming and a completely general proof seems to be needed.

Such a proof might be developed along the following lines: First, a proof that every cue or combination of cues can be expressed mathematically in terms of no more than two independent co-ordinates. Second, a proof that any statement in two independent co-ordinates must necessarily be ambiguous with respect to a third independent co-ordinate. While this general proof must await more accurate specification of all the cues, it seems reasonable to believe that it can eventually be provided. Until this can be done, we shall simply assert, on the basis of the preceding discussion, that visual distance indications are *always* ambiguous. This statement has been formally proven for the cases of size, illumination, movement parallax, and binocular disparity.

THE MONOCULAR DISTORTED ROOMS

THE MONOCULAR DISTORTED rooms provide an empirical test of the equivalence in monocular vision of three-dimensional configurations derived from equations of which Equation [1] is a special two-dimensional case. Even though the actual construction of such rooms takes considerable skill, the principle dictating their construction is quite simple. Each part of a distorted room must subtend the same visual angle at the nodal point of an eye placed at the chosen observation point [5] as would the corresponding part of an undistorted room observed from the same point. If this prescription is followed, the stimulus patterns on the retina will be the same for the distorted and undistorted rooms. In this fashion, a whole "family" of distorted rooms of vastly different shapes could be built, yet all of them, if our reasoning is correct, should be seen as "normal" instead of some other way because our past experience has made it a "better bet" to perceive level floors, upright walls, rectangular windows, etc.

Figures 5 and 6 show distorted versions of the same 4-foot by 4-foot rectangular reference rooms. As of this writing, several hundred observers have been led blindfolded to these rooms, placed in the proper position for viewing, and have reported their monocular observations. Without a single exception, the observers, under these conditions, have described the rooms as being "normal" or very nearly "normal" in shape; that is, with level floors and ceilings, upright walls, windows the same size and shape, etc. An example of how such a room is perceived is shown in

[5] This condition is only approximated in actual viewing, as one can ensure only that the observer's eye is *near* the reference point arbitrarily chosen for the room's construction.

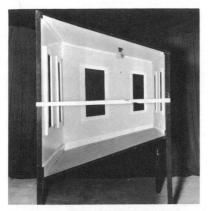

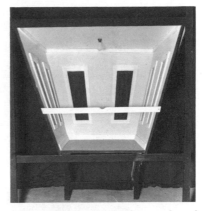

FIG. 5. *A monocular distorted room based on a 4-foot by 4-foot reference room. When viewed with one eye with the chin in the hollow place on the horizontal crossbar, the room is perceived as shown in Figure 7.*

FIG. 6. *Another distorted room based on the same 4-foot by 4-foot reference room.*

Figure 7, which is a photograph of a room of the same design as that shown in Figure 5, but taken with the camera lens at the observation point.

When people or objects are observed in such a distorted room, the assumptions the observer has built up concerning their shapes and sizes come into direct conflict with his assumptions as to the "normal" shape of the room. Ordinarily this conflict is resolved by perceptual distortion of the object or person in the room (as shown in Figures 7 and 8), but the kind and degree of exceptions to this generalization appear to be very revealing of the ways in which social and other factors enter into the process of perceiving. A pilot study of some of these relationships is reported in Chapter 10.

Also worth noting are certain aspects of the relationship of action to the perception of the distorted room. A naïve observer with his eye at the observation point can look at the room for an unlimited amount of time and never suspect that it is at all unusual in shape—if he does nothing but look. However, if he attempts to touch certain parts of the room with a stick, he quickly becomes aware of the lack of correspondence between his perception and the consequences of his action. As he continues to explore with the stick, he becomes more and more successful in his actions. More importantly, there is a growing body of evidence which indicates that, as he continues to act and experience the

FIG. 7. *A distorted room the same size and shape as the one shown in Figure 5, but taken with the camera lens at the prescribed viewing point. (From M. Lawrence,* Studies in Human Behavior [*Princeton, N.J.: Princeton Univ. Press, 1949.*] *By permission of the author and the publisher.)*

FIG. 8. *The large monocular distorted room shown in these photos is the one referred to in Chapter 10.*

consequences of his action, he sees the room more and more in its true shape even though the stimulus pattern on his retina has remained unchanged.

An analysis of this modification of visual perception through action with retinal stimulus pattern constant is extremely important in view of our hypothesis stated earlier (Chapter 2), that actions and their consequences are instrumental in the "construction" of what we see. Present evidence suggests that this modification occurs in two phases, probably overlapping, but distinguishable nevertheless.

The first phase consists of a modification of the assumptive *complex* alone, in the sense that already established assumptions are weighted more heavily or less heavily in their relationships to the visual cues available. The result is that "give-away" cues which square better with the consequences of action receive an emphasis in perception which they did not have at first and would not have yet if no "testing" of the perception had taken place. The "give-away" cues referred to are those which are present because of imperfections in construction, failure to place the observer's eye exactly at the reference point, etc.

The second phase of modification of perception is far more crucial than the first in terms of perceptual theory. It consists of an actual alteration in the weighted averages of experience (the assumptions) related to the pattern reflected to the eye by the class of external configurations of which the reference room and the distorted room are examples, with a consequent alteration in perception even though the retinal pattern does not change. This sort of perceptual alteration does not depend on the presence of "give-away" cues.

A further point worthy of mention is that an observer who knows in advance and even has seen the true shape of a distorted room will, when placed at the observation point, still see the room as "normal," or almost "normal." In most cases advance knowledge results in a small amount of phase one change; that is, the informed observer takes account of "give-away" cues, but only to a limited extent. Also, given a stick and asked to touch various parts of the room, he will be little if any more successful than a completely naïve observer. Apparently, intellectual knowledge and unconscious assumptions built up through experience must be distinguished. Apparently, too, we tend to act in terms of the world as we perceive it, even when our perceptions do not square with our "knowledge."

THE BINOCULAR DISTORTED ROOMS

IN THIS PART we shall be concerned with the binocular distorted rooms as examples of equivalent configurations in which all the cues normally available to a stationary observer are utilized. It will be shown that two such equivalent configurations, which are grossly different in their physical properties, are nevertheless indistinguishable to an observer who has no additional information concerning them.

The principles for designing binocular distorted rooms have already been indicated in the discussion of binocularly equivalent configurations. In principle, the same procedure can be followed for the three-dimensional case in which the transformation is applied to the vertical and horizontal planes comprising the walls, floor, and ceiling of some arbitrary reference room. The actual computation is long and laborious. The rooms described here were computed by Dr. Anna Stein as transformations of a reference room 8 feet by 6 feet by 6 feet. Two binocular distorted rooms were computed and constructed, one an "interior" room, i.e., dimensions smaller than those of the reference room, and one an "exterior" room, i.e., dimensions larger than the reference room. Mathematically, these two rooms are represented by positive and negative values of τ in the transformation Equation [5].[6]

Horizontal cross sections of the rooms are shown in Figure 9. As can

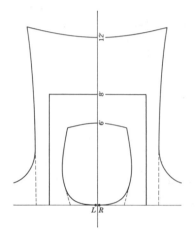

FIG. 9. *Nonexact diagram showing a horizontal cross-sectional view of the large and small binocular distorted rooms in relation to the 8-foot rectangular reference room. Dashed lines indicate the departures in actual construction from theoretical form. L and R indicate the viewing positions for the left and right eyes. The solid vertical line in the center is merely a reference line and not part of the construction.*

be seen, the surfaces from which these rooms are formed are complex, three-dimensional curves. The task of constructing such surfaces proved to be quite difficult and was finally solved by enlisting the aid of a shipbuilding concern. The rooms are, literally, built like a ship, with the curves cut in vertical and horizontal members and plywood bent and molded to these members. A third, rectangular room of the dimensions of the reference room was also constructed.

It was predicted, as already stated, that these three rooms would appear identical. This prediction in practice reduces to the prediction that the two distorted rooms will look like the same rectangular room.

[6] The computation of these rooms was actually not based on the transformations derived in the first part of this paper, but rather on the somewhat more complex procedures stemming from Luneberg's hyperbolic metric (3). However, as Luneberg pointed out, these two procedures yield substantially the same results at fairly great viewing distances, and rooms derived under the two procedures do not differ greatly. The derivation of binocular equivalence presented earlier, resting as it does only on the generally accepted definition of binocular disparity, seems preferable at this point to the hyperbolic metric, which depends on several less well-accepted assumptions.

When the rooms were initially assembled they were painted a uniform, neutral color. Under these conditions they were viewed by the authors and others, all of whom had been actively working with the rooms. Both rooms appeared to be rectangular, but they appeared to be of quite different sizes, which closely approximated their actual sizes. It was concluded that this partial failure of the prediction might be due to the fact that such factors as the grain of the wood, nail heads, dirt marks, etc. did not conform to the criteria for equivalence. This difficulty could not be overcome by providing the surfaces with a perfectly uniform, flawless covering, since this would at the same time remove all stereoscopic stimuli, except from the intersections of the surfaces.

It was, therefore, decided to paint identical patterns on both rooms; and simulated floor boards, sills, windows, window frames, etc. were provided. Whether this rather laborious step was essential remains doubtful. When the same observers now viewed the rooms from the proper position, the same results were obtained. Both rooms appeared rectangular, but of approximately their true sizes.

The rooms were then shown to five observers who had no knowledge of the nature or aims of the experiment. Each observer was blindfolded and led to the "interior" room. A headrest was provided which prevented him from seeing anything other than the room itself. When the observer's head was in the rest, the blindfold was removed and he was asked to describe what he saw. No further questions were asked except, "Anything else?" When the subject exhausted his description, he was again blindfolded, led to the "exterior" room, and the procedure was repeated. He was then blindfolded while he was being led away from the rooms, after which he was interviewed searchingly with respect to the apparent sizes and shapes of the rooms. The above viewing procedure was then repeated, with the exception that the observer was now questioned about the size and shape of each room while he was viewing it, using such comments as "Are you sure?" and "Make absolutely certain." The results for the five observers are summarized in Table I.

An examination of this table shows that on the first viewing there were no important differences in the appearance of the two rooms. No difference in shape was reported by any observer, either in the first viewing or during the interview. One observer reported no size difference, one observer reported a slight size difference which he later repudiated, and one observer reported a size difference in a direction opposite to that of the actual difference. The remaining two observers reported minor size differences in the direction of the actual difference. The reported magnitudes of these differences, one foot and two feet, are considerably smaller than the actual difference, which is of the order of six feet.

TABLE I

SUMMARY OF NAÏVE OBSERVERS' COMMENTS ON BINOCULAR ROOMS

OB-SERVER	FIRST VIEWING (Spontaneous Comments) Interior room	Exterior room	INTERVIEW	SECOND VIEWING (Critical Comments) Interior room	Exterior room
I	Six windows, no locks, wide panel floor, home paint job. Square, vacant room	Not identical, but similar; little longer, not much different	Hard to compare the two; they are identical	Same as first viewing	Ditto
II	Six windows, black lines, three walls	Six windows, same kind of floor, etc. Doesn't seem to be any different than other	Exterior room seemed two feet larger than interior, otherwise the same. Walls flat, square, at right angles to floor. Both rooms same proportion	Windows seem larger; floor quite a bit larger	Looks identical but larger than interior room
III	A square room, six feet long. Colors, etc., described	Exactly the same but painting and lighting different	Both rooms same size. Walls and floor flat, floor horizontal. Both rooms almost square but longer than wide	Much smaller, otherwise the same. Seven by eight feet	Much bigger, ten by eleven or twelve feet, otherwise the same. Floor looks tipped down toward left corner
IV	Six windows, black lines on floor, etc. Floor wider in front than in back	Same room but deeper and bigger. Floor boards wider, colors, etc., same	Both rooms seemed the same and square but exterior about one foot larger. Both rooms normal, no bumps or strange angles	Looks lot tinier, four by five feet, Well proportioned	Much bigger, deeper, wider. About seven by eight feet. Floor slants toward back
V	Six windows, three walls, etc. Perfectly flat and square	Same type room, windows look larger but room seems smaller all around	Both square, walls parallel and flat, at right angles to floor. Exterior room looked smaller, five or six feet square; other, seven feet square	Square but smaller than said before; five and a half to six feet	Looks larger than other; six and a half to seven feet. Walls flat and at right angles

FIG. 10. *Stereo photos of the small, or interior (upper), and the large, or exterior (lower), binocular distorted rooms. Each stereo pair may be cut out and mounted as a unit on cardboard for viewing with a stereoscope.*

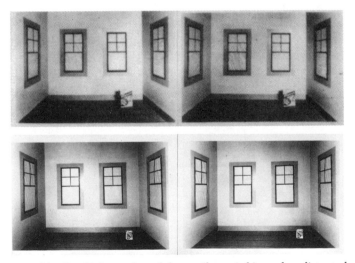

FIG. 11. *Small (upper) and large (lower) binocular distorted rooms, with the same Bisquick box appearing in both stereo pairs. The box, by its apparent alteration in size and shape, reveals to some extent how different the two rooms are in size and shape. These photos may be cut out and mounted for stereoscopic viewing.*

The reports on the second viewing show slight shape distortions of the "exterior" room apparent to two observers. In addition, two observers reported small size differences and two reported major size differences, all in the direction of the actual difference. Only one observer did not change his report on the second viewing.

The results following the second viewing have not been replicated, and it cannot be stated whether they are due to a "critical" viewing attitude or to an experimental artifact. The findings on the initial viewing have, however, been repeated and appear to be reliable. It is possible to summarize what seem to be the well-established reactions of observers to the binocular distorted rooms as follows:

1. Subjects who are led to the rooms blindfolded, with precautions taken to avoid any sensory indications of the sizes of the rooms, report that the two rooms appear substantially identical, i.e., rectangular rooms of the same size. (This has been true even for observers who knew that the rooms were of different sizes. Dr. Stein, herself, who computed the rooms but did not see them during construction, reported no apparent difference between them on initially viewing them under these conditions.)

2. Subjects who catch even a glimpse of the exterior dimensions of the rooms report them to be rectangular but of different sizes which closely approximate their true sizes.

3. Even complete familiarity with the rooms, such as that of the author and others who worked intimately with them, results in only occasional and minor deviations from apparent rectangularity.

REFERENCES—CHAPTER 8

1. Fry, Glenn A. "Visual perception of space." *Amer. J. Opt. & Arch. Amer. Acad. Opt.,* November, 1950, Monogr. No. 110.

2. Graham, C. H. "Visual perception." Chapter in Stevens, S.S. (Ed.), *Handbook of Experimental Psychology,* New York: Wiley, 1951.

3. Luneburg, R. K. *Mathematical Analysis of Binocular Vision.* Princeton, N. J.: Princeton Univ. Press, 1947.

4. Ogle, K. N. *Binocular Vision.* Philadelphia: Saunders, 1950.

9

Two Processes in Perceptual

Learning [1]

F. P. Kilpatrick

STATEMENT OF THE PROBLEM

IT WAS BRIEFLY suggested in Chapter 8 that the perceptual modification that occurs in the monocular distorted rooms involves at least
two learning processes, overlapping and affecting one another but logically and perhaps experimentally distinguishable nevertheless.

REORGANIZATIONAL LEARNING. The first process is one in which an
unconscious reweighting of visual cues occurs. Unavoidably present in
every such room are cues that we are able to perceive in ways not in
harmony with the dominant percept; thus they have the potential of functioning as "give-away" cues. These cues, which "give away" to some
degree the distortions present in the room but are not at first utilized,
are given greater and greater weight as the incompatibilities between
the original percept and the consequences of the practice continue to

[1] Reprinted from *Journal of Experimental Psychology,* Vol. 47, No. 5, May,
1954, by permission of the publisher, The American Psychological Association.

be registered, with the result that changes in the apparent shape of the room occur. The cues referred to are those which are present because of minor, and almost impossible to correct, defects in construction, lighting, placement of O's eye, etc.; also, of course, they may be deliberately introduced. Probably "reorganizational learning" is not the ideal name for this process, but it does suggest that what is learned is a new way of organizing into a whole the complex of previously established cue-percept relationships. It is the usual explanation offered for perceptual modification such as that in the distorted room, and probably few people would argue that such a process does not occur.

FORMATIVE LEARNING. The second process, which we shall call "formative learning," is, however, far more crucial than the first in terms of perceptual theory. It is believed to consist of an actual learned alteration in the way in which a given stimulus pattern is perceived, a new perception which is not dependent on the utilization of give-away cues. It is a learning process in which the perception of the basic configuration related to that particular distorted room, the reference room, or equivalent distorted rooms of any shape is modified. Reorganizational learning shakes up and rearranges the marbles in the bag; formative learning puts new marbles into the bag, and, if we are correct in our view, explains how most, if not all, of the marbles got in the bag in the first place.

From this two-process theory certain deductions concerning perceptual learning in distorted rooms may be made and tested as a means of checking the adequacy of the theory. If one had two or more equivalent rooms of different shapes and O were given sufficient training at one of them (Room 1) to perceive to some degree its true shape, and were then transferred to an equivalent room of an entirely different shape (Room 2), one would expect the following:

(a) If the only learning that took place was reorganizational, that is, dependent on give-away cues, there would be no transfer of the newly learned percept from Room 1 to Room 2, because no give-away cues to the Room 1 shape could be available in Room 2. Thus, Room 2 would be seen as normal after the Room 1 learning.

(b) If, on the other hand, as the theory states, formative learning is also involved, there should be some transfer of the newly learned percept. That is, one would expect Room 2 to be seen as "normal" no longer, but to be seen at least to some degree as being shaped like Room 1.

The major purpose of this experiment was to show, if possible, that formative learning does occur in visual space perception.

A second problem in theory was included in the experiment since a rough check on its adequacy could be included without much trouble. This second problem is concerned with the role of action. The author

(6, 7) and others (1, 3, 4) with a similar point of view have stated that actions and their consequences are instrumental in the "construction" of what we see. What exactly is meant by action has not been well specified, but the implication has always been, probably intentionally, that it means gross, overt bodily activity, the doing of something. This implies that one's perception of a distorted room would remain unmodified, or very nearly so, if one merely observed the room's interior while someone else carried out the prescribed action, such as feeling around the interior of the room with a wand. Of course, O would not be completely inactive under these conditions. There would be eye movement and minor bodily adjustments, but generally speaking his activity would be minimized to an extent that, on the basis of theory as stated, the author would be forced to predict that little or no perceptual learning would occur under such circumstances.

METHOD

APPARATUS

THE BASIC APPARATUS consisted of three rooms designed to be monocularly equivalent, two of them distorted and one a 4-foot by 4-foot cubical room (the "normal" or N room). One of the distorted rooms is larger on O's left than on his right (the L room), and the other is larger at the

FIG. 1. *The cubical "normal," or N, room; caster-mounted chair with face piece in place against the front panel.*

FIG. 2. *The left-distorted, or L, room, with the spotlight in place.*

FIG. 3. *The top-distorted, or T, room, with the front panel removed.*

top than at the bottom (the T room).[2] In constructing the three rooms used in this experiment great care was taken to eliminate nonequivalent visual cues such as grain in the wood, nail or screw heads, shiny reflecting surfaces, etc. The interiors were painted a flat gray with the exception of the window panels, which were painted a flat black. Plywood panels

[2] Construction drawings are contained in (5).

were placed over the fronts of the rooms. The rooms were arranged in a blacked-out experimental room so that their fronts formed a U, the distorted rooms facing one another, and the front of the N room forming the bottom of the U.

Lighting for each room was from a number of 7-watt bulbs placed inside the room along the top of the front panel, above O's head and out of his visual field. Extreme care was taken to equate the brightnesses of all parts of each room, and to equate the rooms with each other.

An armless, straight-back swivel chair on casters, on which O sat straddling the seat and facing the back of the chair, was provided. A face piece at the top of the chair back provided a means of guiding O's face to the observation position and of preventing undue head movement. In the front panel of each room an oval opening was cut that was just large enough to admit O's nose and allow him to observe the interior of the room with the right eye when his nose was as far down and to the left as it would go. This use of a nose rest permitted more accurate placement of the eye than would a chin rest. Since these observation holes were at the same height in each of the rooms, a single adjustment of the face piece sufficed for all. Thus O could be moved from room to room while seated on the chair, and in each case simply putting his face back in the face piece ensured the proper observational position.

The L room, which was to be the practice room, was provided with some additional equipment. A number of sponge rubber balls, covered with scotch tape so as not to mark the interior of the room when thrown against the walls, were provided. A small spotlight on a swivel was pointed into the room through a hole slightly to the left and above the observation hole. It was placed as near to the observation point as possible so that the alteration in the visual angle subtended by the spot as it was aimed at various parts of the room would be very little from O's point of view. This spot of light, about 3 inches in diameter when the spotlight was aimed at a point directly opposite the hole into which it was inserted, served as a target at which to throw the balls. A light bamboo wand 4 feet long and covered with several thicknesses of flannel at one end was also provided. In addition, most of the bottom third of the front panel was cut out to permit both Observer and Experimenter to have free access to the interior of the room with their hands.

A tape recorder was also used.

OBSERVERS

The Os were 12 young adults, 10 males and 2 females, all with normal vision without glasses.

EQUIVALENCE TESTING. In order to be sure that any distortions in appearance of the rooms following the learning sessions could be attributed to learning, it was necessary first to establish for each O that the L, N, and T rooms were, in fact, equivalent and all seen as "normal" under the prescribed conditions. This was done through equivalence testing conducted immediately prior to the learning sessions for each O.

The O first was shown line drawings of the L, T, and N rooms, and their shapes were fully described. He was told that he would be seated in a chair and moved from room to room, that he would be given two looks at each of them, and that his task in each case was simply to identify the room as L, N, or T. Then a mask was placed over his left eye, he was led with his eyes closed into the blacked-out experimental room, seated in the chair, and given two 10-second looks at each of the three rooms, the order of these six looks being randomly determined. Following the viewing and attempted identification, he was asked to describe how the rooms looked and, if he had felt he could tell them apart, the ways in which they looked different.

The results show that the rooms are seen as normal and are monocularly equivalent under the prescribed viewing conditions;[3] thus, any different results following a learning session may be treated as change in perception, provided one trusts O's reports in both instances. Of the 72 room identifications, 51 were incorrect and 21 were correct. This is just slightly worse than chance. Of the 21 correct identifications, 15 were of the N room; this is not surprising in view of the fact that all 12 of the Os stated after viewing that the rooms all looked alike, that is, quite normal. In fact, almost half of the Os either "gave up" or else disbelieved E, three responded "normal" all six times and two others did so five times in spite of having been told in advance that they would view each of the three rooms twice. The L room was correctly identified four times, twice by the same O. He stated, however, that he was just guessing and that it looked normal. The T room was correctly identified only twice, and then by different Os.

THE LEARNING SESSIONS. All learning sessions were conducted at the L room and consisted of a number of throws of the ball at the spot of light at various locations on the back wall, and of tracing the outline of the back wall four times with the wand. Half of the Os, the action group (Group A), tossed the ball and manipulated the wand themselves.

[3] As far as the author knows, this is the first time that the equivalence of monocular distorted rooms has been demonstrated in a controlled experiment. The equivalence of binocular distorted rooms was experimentally verified and is reported in Chapter 8.

The other half, the no-action group (Group NA), merely observed the interior of the L room while E or his assistant threw the ball or handled the stick. The O was asked to call out "hit" when he saw the ball hit the spot. This was not done for data purposes, but simply as a device to maintain O's interest and motivation.

There were four learning sessions separated by rest periods of about two minutes. Immediately after each learning session, O was asked to observe and describe the interior of one of the three rooms: the L room after Session 1, the L room again after Session 2, the N room or the T room after Session 3, and the remaining room after Session 4. Half of the Os saw the T room after the third session and the N room after the fourth; for the other half the order was the reverse. All assignments to groups and orders were random.

Room descriptions were elicited in a standard way with the request, "Please describe the shape of the room as you see it, that is, not as you might guess or know it to be, but as you actually see it." It was desired that every O describe at least the back wall, the windows in the back wall, the floor, and the ceiling, so omissions were filled in with questions in the form, "How does (the back wall) look to you?" All instructions, questions, and answers were tape-recorded and transcribed verbatim for analysis.

When the Os were moved from the L room to one of the others, they knew they were being shifted to either the N or the T room but not which one.

The four learning sessions differed only in the ball throwing; in Session 1 there were five throws at each of five positions of the spot, in Session 2 there were five throws at nine positions, in Session 3 there were three throws at nine positions, and Session 4 was the same as Session 3.

POSTEXPERIMENTAL INTERVIEW. Following the final observation, O was asked to discuss the nature of his experiences, particularly any alterations in what he saw and any discrepancies that he felt existed between what he saw and what he otherwise judged to be so. This material also was tape-recorded and transcribed.

RESULTS

THE MAIN RESULTS of the experiment are summarized in Table I. Of the six Os in Group A, five reported modification in the appearance of the L room after the first learning session. All six reported such modification for the L room after the second session. There were marked individual differences in both amount and type of change reported, but in all cases the change was in the direction of the true shape of the room. All six reported seeing to a marked degree the slope of the floor, and five of the six reported additional changes, such as the slope of the ceiling, the shape and slant of the back wall, the difference in size and shape of the two windows in the back wall, etc.

These alterations in appearance carried over to both the N and the T room,[4] according to Os' reports, for five of the six Os in the case of the N room, and for all six in the case of the T room. Both the N and the T room were seen, at least to some degree, as having the shape of the L room, with only a single exception. In 9 of the 11 instances in which there was such carry-over, the Os said that they saw slightly less of the L-room appearance at the N or T room than they had at the L room, but that it was clear and unequivocal nevertheless. In the other two instances no reduction in perceived L-room shape was reported. In Os' reports the N and T rooms were described as looking as though the

TABLE I

REPORTED CHANGES IN APPEARANCE OF THE THREE ROOMS AFTER
LEARNING SESSIONS FOR THE ACTION GROUP (N = 6)
AND THE NO-ACTION GROUP (N = 6)

CONDITION OF OBSERVATION	REPORTED ROOM APPEARANCE			
	A GROUP		NA GROUP	
	No Change	Changed in One or More Aspects	No Change	Changed in One or More Aspects
L ROOM				
After 1st learning session	1	5	2	4
After 2nd learning session		6		6
TRANSFER				
At the N room	1	5	2	4
At the T room		6	1	5

floor sloped down to the left, and in most cases one or more other L-room appearances such as ceiling sloping up to the left, back wall receding to the left, etc. were described.

A few illustrative excerpts from the protocols follow:

1. Observer C.S. viewing N room after Learning Session 3:
     E. How does the floor look?

---

[4] Perhaps it should be pointed out that this phenomenon is not at all analogous to classical figural aftereffect. The "transferred" configuration is not different, "compensatory," or "opposite," but is, to the degree that transfer occurs, like the learned configuration. In addition, visual fixation is not involved. Satiation or statistical theories of figural aftereffect should not be invoked as explanations for this phenomenon, as they clearly do not apply.

O. It looks as if it slants down to the left.

E. How does the ceiling look?

O. It slants up to the left some.

E. How about the windows?

O. The left window of the center panel looks larger and like it is slanting down to the left on the bottom.

E. Anything else you can tell me about the appearance of the room?

O. Well, I think it does give the appearance of being like the room that slants to the left, quite a lot.

2. G.S. viewing the T room after Learning Session 3:

E. How does the floor look?

O. The floor seems to tilt down toward the left.

E. How about the ceiling?

O. The ceiling tilts up and to the left.

E. How about the back wall?

O. It seems to slant quite a little bit. Back to the left.

3. P.B. viewing the N room after Learning Session 4:

O. Well, the floor slopes down toward—down toward the bottom left hand, you know, the far left-hand corner. Again the corner up at the right looks closer to me than the corner at the left and it looks shorter than the corner at the left. The ceiling looks like it's going up toward the left-hand side.

The results for Group NA were substantially the same as for Group A. Four of the six Os reported alterations in the appearance of the L room after Learning Session 1, and all six did so after Learning Session 2. Four of the six reported carry-over to the N room, and five of the six to the T room. However, these results plus a comparative examination of the protocols strongly suggest that the perceptual alteration was slightly less in speed and amount and that there was somewhat less carry-over to the N and T rooms than for Group A.

The replies to questions in the postexperimental interviews provide convincing evidence that Os experienced marked changes in visual space perception and reported what they saw. Here is an example that is perhaps more concise than most, but otherwise typical:

O. It progressively got more distorted as the experiment went on. I could tell some difference in the back wall and in the ceiling and floor. The ceiling seemed to be the slowest to come along, though. It seemed to be normal for quite a time there and then I began to see a difference—it began to slope, I think, upwards and to the left.

E. This is an actual change in how it looked?

O. That's right.

The evidence obtained in this experiment would seem to point to several rather clear-cut conclusions:

1. Marked alterations in visual space perception did occur as a consequence of the learning sessions. Every O did learn to see the L room in more nearly its true shape even though the stimulus configuration presented to his eye remained unchanged, thus confirming earlier findings.

2. This perceptual learning tends to increase with increasing amounts of practice in this situation.

3. The almost unanimous carry-over of the newly learned percept to both the N and the T room provides strong confirmation for the basic hypothesis that formative learning does occur. The Os did learn to see differently the basic visual configuration related to all three rooms, independently of give-away cues. We may infer that any properly constructed room based on the same reference room would have been seen the same way, regardless of its actual shape.

4. The evidence that the carry-over from the L room to the N and T rooms was not complete suggests that give-away cues functioning below the level of awareness also payed a role in the learning. It seems likely that reorganizational learning did occur in the L room, but the cues on which it depended were not available in the N and T rooms. Only give-away cues to the N or the T shape would be available in those rooms. Also, the protocols provide some evidence that the learning sessions resulted in a generalized increase in the saliency of give-away cues, not only for the L room but for the other rooms as well. These factors would work against the carry-over of the newly learned percept.

5. The notion that gross overt action is necessary for such perceptual modification to occur is clearly wrong. The amount of action indulged in by Group NA was at a minimum, yet there was very little less perceptual learning than in Group A. A more adequate formulation of the role of action in perceptual learning is called for.

DISCUSSION

IT WOULD BE easy to speculate at length concerning the signficance of these findings and conclusions for perceptual learning in general. However, it is felt that much more evidence is needed before any such ambitious project is undertaken. This discussion will be confined to a very few notions concerning reorganizational and formative learning, and the use of the distorted rooms in the controlled study of factors involved in learning in visual space perception.

It appears probable that both the reorganizational and formative processes are at work in almost any instance of perceptual learning; however, the formative process may be thought of as more fundamental in the sense that it is the one on which the expansion and development of our perception of our world depends. If we consider perceiving as acting, as responding, then we might say that reorganizational learning is simply the reshuffling of old previously learned responses; formative learning is the acquiring of new ones. Of course, the matter is not this simple, as there is no doubt an intimate and complex relationship between the two processes so that they affect one another differently under different circumstances. Perhaps if give-away cues are sufficiently available to permit an adequate and stable perceptual reorganization to be arrived at easily and quickly, formative learning related to the basic configuration may not occur because it becomes unnecessary. On the other hand, when the reorganizational process occurs to some degree but not enough to provide such adequate reorganization, it probably facilitates formative learning through helping to stabilize the learned modification as it occurs.

Implicit in the above is the suggestion that formative perceptual learning is gradual and not subject to sudden shifts; for it, continuity is the rule. Reorganizational learning, on the other hand, probably proceeds in sudden shifts. A hitherto unutilized cue becomes effective, with a consequent sudden alteration in perception. Reorganizational learning *need not* give the impression of discontinuity since the shifts may be so small as to conceal their nature; but it *may* do so, as in the case of hidden pictures, the rotating trapezoid (see Chapters 12, 13, and 14), etc.

Let us turn now to the problem of the role of action in perceptual learning. A more adequate formulation might be that some degree of perceptual modification occurs whenever certain aspects of the total process of perceiving are out of harmony with others in terms of carrying out some purpose, and this means both across modalities and within a single modality. Action merely serves the function of bringing the organism into contact with the cues that give rise to the disharmony; if the cues are made available in other ways, e.g., through the actions of others, the conditions necessary for perceptual learning will have been fulfilled. One might also add that probably the modification generally tends toward an organization which has more functional value in the sense of providing a better bet based on experience about "what happens next."

It should be pointed out that this reformulation does not appreciably diminish the importance of the role of action in perceptual learning.

Apparently, perceptual learning requires that a relevant set of sequential events be set in motion in such a way that successive impingements on the learning organism will be attended to and related over time to one another, to expectations, and to purposes. Only in rare circumstances, such as in an experiment, will these conditions even be approximated unless the learner is the operator. An operator other than the learner can provide the necessary sequence of conditions if he knows enough about what the learner perceives, what he expects, what he is attending to and will attend to, etc., but these factors will be known imperfectly in the first place and are continually changing in a unique way for the learner as the sequence of events proceeds. Thus, only when the learner is the operator can the conditions for perceptual alteration be maximized.

Discussion of the use of the distorted rooms as a means of investigating learning in visual space perception necessitates some preliminary remarks about previous work. Research involving postoperative cataract cases, the use of prism, aniseikonic, and inversion lenses, and the employment of unstructured or ambiguous pictures or objects would seem to have contributed most heavily to our knowledge in this area. However, certain limitations in these investigations must be noted. The cataract and lens researches are, in general, characterized by lack of experimental control of the factors involved in the perceptual learning; the other experiments have generally involved rather sudden shifts from one fairly stable perceptual organization to another and made analysis of the processes involved in the change rather difficult. Perhaps a valuable supplement to these would be the use of the distorted rooms. They provide a clear-cut instance of learning in visual space perception gradual enough to be described or measured at intervals as it proceeds, and one in which such factors as amount of practice, kind of practice, motivation, advance knowledge, number and kind of conflicting visual cues available, etc. might be varied systematically and checked for effects. Also, they permit reorganizational and formative perceptual learning to be separated for experimental treatment.

[Using the same distorted room equipment, two further sets of experiments were conducted, one by Bagby (2) and the other by Perrine (9). Both verified the findings reported above and offered some additional findings.

[Among other things, Bagby's experiments showed that advance intellectual knowledge concerning the "true" shape of a distorted room has no helpful effect on perceptual learning; in fact, it has an initial inhibiting effect on perceptual reorganization. Apparently the clues being generated through action are initially checked against a set of abstract concepts if they are available and only later does the observer actually

get down to the business of attempting to correlate them with concreteness, i.e., the perceived ("seen") shape of the room.

[Perrine has summarized his research as follows (8):

The general purpose of the present study was to investigate the
hypothesis that perceptual learning can occur without gross overt
physical action on the part of an individual if he shares the assumptions and purposes of another individual who is in turn acting. Sharing
was defined in terms of participating with others at some level. If
sharing is to occur, something must be observed and participated in,
which implies gross overt physical action. It was hypothesized that
some such action is a necessary condition for perceptual modification
and learning.

The apparatus consisted of three model rooms, one cubical and two
distorted. It was experimentally demonstrated that all three rooms
were monocularly equivalent and appeared cubical or "normal" initially. It was found that after the learning sessions, the Os identified
the rooms significantly more accurately than they had initially.

The experiment consisted of two general parts. In the first, seven Os
in the No Sharing Group were instructed to watch clinically the psychological reactions of their partner as he performed a ball-throwing
task in one of the distorted rooms. These seven Os were subsequently
asked to describe the appearance of the cubical room. None reported
any alteration in its appearance. The 14 Os in the Sharing Group
were also paired for the same ball-throwing task, but in this case co-
operation and team spirit orientation were openly encouraged. Only
two of these Os reported no alteration in the subsequent appearance
of the cubical room. These results were interpreted as supporting the
hypothesis that the sharing of the assumptions and purposes of another who is acting is a necessary condition for perceptual learning
without self-action.

In the second part, the 14 Os in each of the four groups were run
individually on the same general ball-throwing task. Half of these Os
threw the ball themselves, the other half watched while E threw the
ball. Two learning sessions, one at each of the two distorted rooms,
were given to all Os. After the first learning session, 24 of the 28 Os in
self-action groups reported alterations in the subsequent appearance of
the cubical room, but only four of the 28 Os in no-action groups reported alterations. These results were interpreted as supporting the
hypothesis that in the absence of "sharing" gross overt physical action
is a necessary condition for perceptual learning.

The increased post-learning accuracy of the room identifications
was discussed as being evidence for the occurrence of reorganizational

learning, one of the two hypothesized processes in perceptual learning. On the basis of data showing that self-action does not facilitate the post-learning accuracy of room identifications, it was suggested that this lack of the necessity of action may be the basis of the functional difference between reorganizational and formative learning. Evidence for formative learning, the other hypothesized process, was found in the fact that most of the self-action Os reported alterations in the appearance of the cubical room. Evidence was also discussed for the notion that sharing is a necessary condition if formative learning is to occur in an individual who just observes and does not himself act. It was mentioned that these findings have implications for education, interpersonal relations, and mass communications.

—Ed.]

REFERENCES—CHAPTER 9

1. Ames, A. Jr. "Visual perception and the rotating trapezoidal window." *Psychol. Monogr.*, 1951, *65,* No. 7 (whole No. 324).

2. Bagby, James. *The Relative Roles of Information and Action in the Genesis of a Perception.* Ph.D. Thesis, Columbia University, 1955.

3. Cantril, H. *The "Why" of Man's Experience.* New York: Macmillan, 1950.

4. Ittelson, W. H. "The constancies in perceptual theory." *Psychol. Rev.,* 1951, *58,* 285–94.

5. Ittelson, W. H. *The Ames Demonstrations in Perception.* Princeton, N. J.: Princeton Univ. Press, 1952.

6. Kilpatrick, F. P. "Assumptions and perception: three experiments." In F. P. Kilpatrick (Ed.), *Human Behavior from the Transactional Point of View.* Hanover, N. H.: Institute for Associated Research, 1952, pp. 153–73.

7. Kilpatrick, F. P. "Statement of theory." In F. P. Kilpatrick (Ed.), *Human Behavior from the Transactional Point of View.* Hanover, N. H.: Institute for Associated Research, 1952, pp. 1–15.

8. Perrine, M. W. Personal communication to the Editor, 1959.

9. Perrine, M. W. *Sharing, Action and Perceptual Learning.* Unpublished manuscript, 1959.

C H A P T E R

10

The Honi Phenomenon: A Case of Selective Perceptual Distortion [1]

Warren J. Wittreich

S TABILITY AND CONTINUITY are the rule rather than the exception in ordinary perception. In spite of constantly shifting impingements upon its sense organs, the human organism does perceive the world in an orderly and sensible manner. However, the facts of everyday perception are not explanations, and it is often only by deliberately distorting or changing the commonplace that we can shed any light on the processes which allow anything to become "commonplace" in the first instance. Perceptual distortions have therefore come to play an important role in the understanding of basic perceptual processes. Recently a number of devices have been developed which deliberately place cues in conflict

[1] Published originally under the same title in *J. Abnorm. Soc. Psychol.*, 1952, *47*, 705–712. Printed here with the permission of the author and the publisher, The American Psychological Association.

to such an extent that strikingly dramatic perceptual distortions can be obtained.

A number of distorted rooms have been constructed in which the floor slopes up to the right of the observer, the rear wall recedes from right to left, and the windows are of different sizes and trapezoidal in shape. When an observer looks at any of these rooms from a certain point with one eye, the room appears normal or almost normal, as if the floor were level, the rear wall at right angles to the line of sight, and the windows rectangular and of the same size.

One of these rooms has been built large enough so that people can enter the room and walk about in it (see Figure 8, Chapter 8). What the observer typically sees when he watches someone moving about in this room is a striking alteration in the observed individual's size. When standing in the corner to the observer's left, the person appears abnormally small; in the other corner he appears abnormally large. When walking from one corner to the other he appears to grow or shrink in size, depending upon the direction in which he is traveling. A smaller model of this room permits hands or faces to appear through the rear windows. As with the larger room, the hands or faces appear abnormally large or abnormally small, depending upon whether they are in the window to the observer's right or left.

The study to be reported here received its impetus from an unusual instance in which this typical pattern of observation was not reported. In 1949, a woman observed the faces of her husband and another man through the rear windows of the smaller room. The face of the other man was described as distorted in the usual manner, but no size changes whatsoever were reported for the husband; his face was described as being perfectly normal no matter which window it appeared in. Similar results were obtained in the large room. Again the other man was described in the usual manner; he appeared to grow or shrink and looked large or small, depending upon the corner in which he was observed. But again no such size changes were reported for the husband. No matter which corner he stood in, he was reported as looking perfectly normal— his usual size. This unusual observation was named the "Honi phenomenon" following the family nickname for the woman who first experienced and reported it.

This instance of a deviation from the typical pattern of observation of people in the room raises at least two specific questions. Is this observation simply a unique and isolated case or is it reproducible with other individuals? What are the psychological conditions which account for such a performance?

This paper reports two experiments which answer the first question by producing the Honi phenomenon in unmistakable fashion with a number of other people. The obvious and outstanding relationship between the woman and her husband in the original situation was simply the fact that they were married. It should also be noted that both were over sixty years of age, and that he was a very distinguished man whom she greatly admired and to whom she was devoted. The assumption was made that, if the phenomenon has been observed in this couple, it might very well be observed in certain other couples. A group of couples, the majority of whom had been married for a relatively short time, were selected as subjects primarily because of their availability and willingness to participate in the experiment.

In the first experiment an attempt was made to reproduce conditions under which the phenomenon had originally been observed, with the addition of needed experimental controls. All that was required of the S was a description of people observed in the room. It was assumed that if a description of what appeared to be a case of selective perceptual distortion had been obtained in the original situation, it could be obtained again. The prediction was simply that an individual, when observing both a stranger and his or her marital partner in the room, would report less distortion in the description of the marital partner than in the description of the stranger. The second experiment was an attempt to confirm what was found in the first experiment, and to obtain a quantitative measure of the difference in the relative distortion of the marital partner as compared to the stranger.

EXPERIMENT I

TEN MARRIED COUPLES provided a sample of 20 Ss in this experiment. At the time of the experiment six of the couples had been married less than one year. The remaining four couples had been married two, three and a half, five, and ten years, respectively (see Table I).

Both the small and the large rooms were employed in this experiment. Both rooms were viewed with one eye only. With the small room, the S was asked to describe: (a) the room itself, (b) the hands of the experimenter placed through the rear windows, (c) a marble which ran across the room and gave the appearance of rolling uphill, (d) two situations with two people putting their heads through the rear windows: two strangers, and one stranger and the marital partner. (Each person was seen once in each window in each of the above situations.) Descriptions a, b, and c were requested primarily to see if the S was initially observing the room and objects in the room in the typical manner.

With the large room the S was asked to describe: (a) the room itself; (b) two situations with two people standing in the corners of the room: two strangers, and one stranger and the marital partner (each person was seen once in each corner in each of the above situations); and (c) two different people walking from the corner on the observer's left to the corner on his right and back again: a stranger and the marital partner. The entire experiment was recorded on a wire recorder and transcribed.

Results

An analysis was then made of each individual protocol to determine whether or not the S had spontaneously described a definite difference between the appearance of the marital partner and the appearances of both of the strangers, and whether this difference was in the predicted direction. Table I indicates that 6 out of the 20 Ss did report a difference in the expected direction in the small room and 7 out of 20 reported a similar difference in the large room. Not once did an S report a difference other than in the expected direction, i.e., not once was the marital partner described as being more distorted than either or both of the strangers. It is also of interest to note that, although the exact same people did not display the phenomenon in both rooms, there are a few striking cases of overlapping. Taking both situations together, it can be seen that at least one member of all the couples married under one year displayed the phenomenon to some degree in one of the two rooms, but, with a single exception, no member of the couples married over one year displayed the phenomenon. That single exception was a man married only two years.

Because of space limitations only selected portions of the individual protocols which contain material specifically relevant to the hypothesis will be presented. In reading these protocols it is worth noting a number of things. First of all, when an S reports a difference, he does so in a spontaneous manner, and he, himself, often appears to be struck by both the existence of this difference and the direction it takes. Second, it will be noted especially in protocols D and E in the large room that, while the marital partner is maintaining some degree of constancy, the room itself is undergoing a process of increasing distortion. It appears almost as though the S is faced with a choice of distorting either the marital partner or the room, and he chooses to distort the latter. In all of the following protocols the marital partner is capitalized.

SMALL DISTORTED ROOM

A. Male, married 3 months: HERS looks bigger, but it doesn't look as much bigger than Bruce's did to yours although the windows look the same. It still looks bigger, but it doesn't look a great deal bigger. I think her head is bigger than Bruce's anyway naturally.

B. Female, married 7 months: I can't get over it. BOB'S head appears to be far away and Bruce's head appears to be close, and BOB'S head appears normal—uh, fairly normal—it's small, but it's more in proportion than Bruce's. That's all.

TABLE I

MEMBERS OF MARRIED COUPLES REPORTING
DIFFERENCES BETWEEN MARITAL PARTNER AND
STRANGER WHEN OBSERVED IN THE DISTORTED ROOMS

| | | DIFFERENCE IN APPEARANCE OF MARITAL PARTNER AND STRANGER REPORTED BY HUSBAND OR WIFE * | | | |
| | | LARGE ROOM | | SMALL ROOM | |
COUPLE	LENGTH OF MARRIAGE	Husband	Wife	Husband	Wife
1	3 mo.	x		x	
2	4 mo.	x		x	
3	7 mo.		x		x
4	3 mo.	x			
5	11 mo.	x	x	x	x
6	11 mo.			x	
7	2 yr. and 3 mo.	x			
8	3 yr. and 6 mo.				
9	5 yr.				
10	10 yr.				

* All differences reported are in the predicted direction, i.e., marital partner distorting less than stranger.

C. Male, married 4 months. BUNNY'S head looks normal, but Bruce's head is much larger than you would expect. (Heads reversed) Now BUNNY'S head is larger too, because of the size of the window; but not so much as it was the other way around. Bruce's head looked much larger than BUNNY'S does.

D. Male, married 11 months: I guess your (NANCY) head has grown, but it hasn't grown much. You're (Bruce) like you were before, I guess. I guess NANCY'S is mostly bigger and Bruce looks smaller and NANCY'S head is closer to me. (Heads reversed) That's right. That's amazing. Bruce's head looks larger but NANCY'S looks—your (NANCY) head doesn't seem to have shrunk much. Bruce's head has grown.

E. Female, married 11 months: DAVID'S head looks very big now. And Bruce's head looks the way it did before—when I looked at it the first time. Your head looks, darling; darling, you can't even get your head through that thing. But uh, I guess that's all. They both look in proportion. (Heads reversed) Gee. Golly. Well, Bruce's head looks bigger now than it did the last time when he had his head on this side, and uh, and DAVID, I don't know about you. Your head looks big too, but you look normal in size—I think—whereas Bruce looks bigger than he is. I think that's all.

F. Male, married 11 months: Well, now it's reversed. As a matter of fact, Bruce looks larger in comparison to CHARLOTTE than CHAR-LOTTE did to Bruce in the previous situation. Other than size I can't see anything unusual. The faces appear normal, except Bruce seems closer and his face looks larger.

LARGE DISTORTED ROOM

A. Male, married 4 months: BUNNY'S head looks about the size or smaller than this light bulb in the room, and Bruce's looks twice as large. Bruce looks like he's about—yeah, yeah he looks twice as tall as BUNNY. Twice as large, not only in height, but in width and every-thing. And uh—the left window's grown larger than the right. Bruce looks much—of course, that is, in relation to the people—the left win-dow dwarfs BUNNY and the right window is dwarfed by Bruce. When I look at the feet, the slant isn't as pronounced as you might think it is. But it is a terrific slant. But it doesn't look too bad from here. (Change places) Oh geez. It's the same relationship, but BUNNY looks—Bruce looked much taller than he should have—and BUNNY looks about her size. I mean I could get in and stand beside BUNNY and look the same way she does—about the same size. Bruce looked much taller than BUNNY does, but Bruce at the same time looks as small as BUNNY did. The same holds with his head in relation to the light bulb and BUNNY'S too. But the fact is, I think more of it is tied up with the fact that you know one person so much more, you know. I mean I can put myself in BUNNY'S place and I know darn well that—uh—that's just about the size she would look. Doesn't make her look much larger, but Bruce it makes look smaller. Bruce looked like a giant standing in the corner and BUNNY looks normal, but at the same time I know darn well Bruce can't be that much smaller than BUNNY is. I mean on the street, for example. She doesn't look like a giant and Bruce did. Put it that way. And now BUNNY looked like a midget and so does Bruce. Geez when I think back—even smaller he looks. I have to look at BUNNY in that corner again to tell you if Bruce looks smaller.

(Walking from corner to corner—marital partner) Well, BUNNY went from—everybody looks the same in that other corner—but BUNNY went from half her size to her normal size. I mean she looks normal now; she doesn't look any larger than she usually does. She got larger, but she didn't reach proportions which were beyond her normal. Geez, that's amazing. She doesn't start to get very much smaller until about two steps away from that very far corner there. All of a sudden she gets real small. And she's much further away now, too. Everybody looks the same size in that corner. (Stranger) Bruce gets larger and he gets larger than I know his size is, whereas BUNNY didn't. When he stands over in that other corner he looks the same size; I mean they both look very small. Now he looks larger than he usually does—you know—I mean when we're standing outside here. I notice his feet look larger than they did in the other corner—about size twelves up here and size fours down there. I guess he looks closer, but I can't remember. Yeah, he does look closer than he did in the other corner. He got smaller again, but he didn't get smaller until he got practically two steps before the corner. Have him stand in the middle. Now he looks his normal size. Now he looks like BUNNY did when she was way up in that corner.

B. Female, married 11 months: DAVID? DAVID looks small too. He doesn't look—uh—really as small as Bruce did the last time, but he still looks considerably smaller than he is. And Bruce looks the way he did last time. Oh Bruce looks a lot bigger. DAVID'S farther away though. (Change places) Hah. Hah. Hah. DAVID, DAVID—uh—darling, you look pretty much normal except you aren't standing up in the corner as much there so you're closer to the middle of my eyes so you don't look tall. And Bruce looks very small. DAVID looks big.

(Walking from corner to corner—stranger) Bruce is walking uphill. And now he is very tall, and he was small when he started. Now he's walking down hill, and now he's small again the way he started. (Marital partner) Well, DAVID just walked uphill too, but he looks . . . I guess that's all. (He looks what?) Well, he looks more normal to me because I feel I am a lot closer and its more in proportion. Oh, my, this is horrid. Well, now he looks very far away. And he looks smaller, but he doesn't look awfully small. I mean he doesn't look awfully small. I mean he doesn't look—uh—sort of very little. He looks more average size only much farther away.

C. Female, married 4 months: Good night! Well, now the difference is tremendous because Bruce is so small. You see, I can't be objective about it. I know BOB is tall; therefore the difference between his and Bruce's height seems tremendous, more so than the other two. (Does BOB look taller than usual?) Yes, I think. Uh, that's hard to say; he doesn't look taller than usual. Not especially. It's just that Bruce looks so small. He's just minute. That's just about it.

D. Male, married 11 months: Bruce is large. NANCY is small. She is, how you say, Lilliputian. Well, as a matter of fact the floor has become, it seems even more slanted. Her feet seem at more of a slant than the floor would indicate. You're (NANCY) just about belt size. Just an armful. You're quite small. When I look at NANCY without looking at Bruce, she looks normal, but when I look at Bruce, NANCY becomes smaller. NANCY is farther away too, and downhill. (Change places) Well, I'll be jiggered. NANCY looks, uh, this way, just looking at NANCY she looks quite normal. Just, I'd say, normal. Bruce looks smaller to NANCY. I think maybe Bruce looks smaller now than he did to Warren, though NANCY is farther away from the ceiling than Warren. Bruce looks very small and downhill too. I guess not as much. The same thing with his feet. His feet seem to be at more of an angle than the floor would indicate. When I look at them both, NANCY looks quite large, though further—no. NANCY looks quite normal actually.

E. Male, married 2 years: SALLY appears about normal to me. Of course Bob looks smaller. But SALLY doesn't look any different. When Bob gets down there and SALLY gets up here it seems to change the appearance of the room slightly. The back wall there—it seems to make that window next to Bob seem a lot larger to me than the window on the right behind SALLY, a lot bigger than if I were just looking into the room without anyone in it.

F. Male, married 3 months: SHE looks about normal size. They look about equal in height. LOUISE is much—just bigger. HER face is larger, but in height SHE is about equal to Sally. Sally looks about ⅘ her normal size.

G. Male, married 3 months: SHE not only goes from left to right, SHE grows big and SHE also comes a little bit toward me. SHE grows small but it looks so funny to hang on to things. SHE seems to go away from me just a little. Now SHE seems to be down and away from me just a little. Bruce looks the same as last time. When I look between the windows he looks like a midget in a small room. When I look at him he seems like a guy standing in a far corner—not a normal far corner. Jan is very tall. SHE is right up to the ceiling. SHE seems to be more in proportion than Bruce.

EXPERIMENT II

As MENTIONED PREVIOUSLY, this experiment was designed both to confirm the results of the first experiment and to provide a quantitative measure of the phenomenon. A number of assumptions underlie the procedure employed in this experiment. A person walking from the left to the right corner in the large room appears to go from very small, through a point of actual size, to very large. The reverse happens if he goes from the right- to the left-hand corner. If an S is set the task of subjectively determining the point at which the observed individual looks his normal size when walking from either corner, we would expect, on the basis of what was found in the first experiment, that a stranger would have to walk a greater distance from either corner than the marital partner in order to appear normal size. Conversely, since in either corner the marital partner appears normal, or more normal than a stranger, the partner will not have to move as far from that corner as the stranger will in order to appear of normal size. Furthermore, the magnitude of the difference between the distances traversed by the stranger and by the partner can be used as a quantitative measure of the magnitude of the phenomenon. At one extreme would be the case in which both stranger and partner had to walk the same distance; we would assume here that the phenomenon did not occur. The other extreme would be when the partner looked perfectly normal in the corner and did not have to move at all.

Hence the major prediction made in this experiment was that when the S is set the above task in the large room the point at which the marital partner appears normal will be significantly closer to the starting corner than will the point at which a stranger appears normal. It was also decided to specify the sex of the stranger, i.e., provide a comparison of the partner with both a stranger of the same sex and a stranger of the opposite sex, in order to see if a sex difference might be observed. This specification as to the sex of the stranger had not been controlled in the first experiment; the strangers used were males.

In this experiment six married couples provided a total of twelve Ss. All couples but one had been married one year, and that couple had been married one year and three months.

Again, the S was first asked for a description of the empty room, observing the room from the specified point. Then an individual (either the partner or stranger) was introduced into the room and stood in one of the two corners. The S was asked what this person looked like. If the individual was described as being either too large or too small, S then received the following instructions: "When I tell (the individual in the room) to do so, he is going to walk slowly across the back wall. I want you to tell him to stop walking as soon as you feel that he looks his normal size, that is, the same size as if he were standing out here (outside the room)."

After E obtained assurance from S that he understood the instructions, S was asked to make two such judgments, once from the left corner and once from the right, for each of the following:

1. One person in the room only: (a) the marital partner, (b) stranger of same sex as the subject, and (c) stranger of opposite sex to that of S.

2. Two people in the room, each one standing in a corner, but only

one person moving across the wall at a time: (a) the marital partner and stranger of same sex as S, (b) the marital partner and stranger of opposite sex to that of S, and (c) stranger of same sex and stranger of opposite sex.

Each judgment was recorded as the reading of the observed individual's position on a measuring tape which had been placed on the rear wall of the room. The tape read from left to right, and the readings were obtained directly from the tape by noting the point reached by the toe of the advancing foot, regardless of whether the individual had come from the left or the right corner.

As soon as the S saw his or her marital partner in the room for the first time the experimenter asked for a further description of the room: "Before you go any further, I want you to describe the room to me again in as much detail as you possibly can." This was done to see if the introduction of the marital partner into the room would be accompanied by an increase in the distortion of the room itself as reported by S. Both descriptions of the room, before and after the introduction of the marital partner, were recorded on a seven-point distortion scale, which provided one point for each of the following which was described as being distorted in any way whatsoever: the floor, ceiling, walls, windows, doors, furniture, and miscellany (e.g., the lighting fixture).

The readings on the tape measure provided the raw data for the experimental results. The S made a total of 18 judgments: 6 each for the marital partner, the stranger of the same sex, and the stranger of the opposite sex. Also available were the before-after distortion scores.

Because of the slant of the back wall it was necessary to convert the measurements in inches on the tape measure into angular displacement. This was done through the following steps:

1. The hypothetical center point on the rear wall was obtained by determining the point on the tape measure which was intersected by the median plane of the observer.

2. All readings were then converted into angular displacement from this center point, all readings to the right of center receiving a plus designation.

3. Reference points of 15° to both the left of the center point and to the right of the center point were selected. All readings coming from the left had a constant of plus 15 added to them; all readings coming from the right were first multiplied by minus 1, and then had a constant of plus 15 added to them. Consequently all minus numbers were canceled out and comparable distance scores were obtained for all Ss coming from either corner. It should be pointed out here that, in terms of the original hypothesis, the actual distance traversed by each individual

was not of primary interest. It was the difference between the points reached by different individuals that was of interest, and this difference remains unchanged no matter where the reference point is selected. The reference point is used for computational convenience.

4. For each individual observed by an S a mean position score was obtained by averaging the judgments (transformed as described above).

Results

The results for the experiment are presented in Table II. An examination of this table indicates that the basic hypothesis is borne out: the marital partner was required to walk a shorter distance to be judged his or her normal size than either of the two strangers. The difference of 1.45° between the marital partner and the stranger of the opposite sex is significant at the .001 level of significance (t = 3.48). The difference of 1.17° between the marital partner and the stranger of the same sex is significant at the .10 level of significance (t = 1.95). The difference of .28° between the two groups of strangers is negligible (t = 0.83). The differences of 1.45° and 1.17° represent approximately

TABLE II

DIFFERENCES IN MEAN POSITION SCORES FOR GROUPS OBSERVED—
MARITAL PARTNERS, STRANGERS OF SEX OPPOSITE TO OBSERVER,
AND STRANGERS OF SAME SEX AS OBSERVER

GROUPS COMPARED	RESPECTIVE MEAN POSITION SCORES		DIFF	p
Stranger opposite sex-M.P.	17.09°	15.64°	1.45°	.001
Stranger same sex-M.P.	16.81°	15.64°	1.17°	.10
Stranger opposite sex-stranger same sex	17.09°	16.81°	.28°	.50

8 per cent and 7 per cent, respectively, of the observer's visual field within which the defferences were observed, and correspond roughly to a six-inch difference on the tape measure.

An examination of the before-and-after room distortion scores, obtained as previously described, indicates that the mean room distortion score for the sample of Ss increased from 2.5 to 4.0 after the introduction of the marital partner, and this increase is significant at the .001 level of significance. This must be interpreted with care, however, since the nature of the cues offered by the introduction of *anyone* into the room would tend to make the room more distorted, certainly not less distorted. Yet it is interesting to compare the before-after distortion scores for the four Ss whose "measured distance" results are most in accord with the basic hypothesis with the four Ss whose "measured distance" results are least in accord with the hypothesis. The former group has mean distortion scores of 2.25 and 4.25, a difference of 2.00 in the predicted direction. The latter group has mean scores of 1.75 and 2.50, a difference of only 0.75 in the predicted direction. Naturally such a small sample precludes drawing any definite conclusions from such a comparison, but it is suggestive of the possibility that the room distortion score does have meaning in so far as it aids in selecting those Ss whose reported perceptions are most in accord with the basic hypothesis.

DISCUSSION

THE PHENOMENON under study in this paper represents a particular instance of behavior in which an observer reports a lesser degree of distortion of his marital partner than of a stranger, when observed under conditions which normally produce visual distortion, e.g., in the large and the small distorted rooms. This has been termed the "Honi phenomenon." The results from both experiments point to the conclusion that the Honi phenomenon is a reproducible instance of behavior which can be described adequately in both a verbal report and a quantitative measure and which is capable of having the variables associated with it roughly specified. This reported difference in distortion is capable of being quantified to the extent that a measurable difference can be obtained from the points on the back wall at which the marital partner and the stranger are judged to be of normal size when moving from either corner. In addition to the mere occurrence of the phenomenon, it should be pointed out that within the groups of S used marked individual differences were found which apparently were not due to chance factors, but seemed instead to be due to certain variables, as yet unspecified, contained within the situation itself.

The confirmation of the phenomenon plus the likelihood that the observed individual differences are real raise a very fundamental question which this paper cannot and does not attempt to answer. What are the psychological variables which can adequately explain both the phenomenon and the individual variations within the range of behavior provided by the phenomenon? The variable employed in both of the experiments is marriage, or various lengths of marriage. It may be assumed or inferred that this variable implies certain interpersonal, emotional, and valueful relationships between those married which cannot be assumed or inferred from the relationships of those not married. But the variable is itself a psychologically meaningless one, and no amount of assumption or inference can adequately specify those variables which are psychologically meaningful and which can adequately explain the observed behavior. Such information is obviously not contained in the experiments reported here, and only further experimentation can provide such information.

However, the experiments reported here do provide some hints as to possible hypotheses which can provide a basis for further experimentation. In the first experiment all of the instances of the phenomenon but one were reported by Ss who had been married less than one year. The differences obtained in the second experiment were from a sample of twelve in which all but two had been married less than one year. This would seem to suggest that the meaningful variables might be found through an examination of the relationships which are typical of the very earliest stages of marital life, although it must be remembered that the phenomenon was first observed in a couple that had been married over twenty-five years. It would also indicate that any explanation of the results reported here simply in terms of frequency would have to be rejected, since the results indicate a negative correlation between length of marriage and size of the reported or measured difference. In other words, the fact that one person has looked at another person more often does not explain the difference, and the results appear to contradict such an explanation.

Furthermore, it should be pointed out that any explanation of the experimental results must take account of something other, or something more, than just the nature of the retinal pattern and/or the nature of the stimulus configuration. The observer in this situation is faced with a definite conflict; apparently he cannot make both the room and the people in it look normal at the same time. Presumably one of the two has to be seen as distorted. The typical instance is to see the room as normal, and the people as distorted. In the atypical instance, the Honi phenomenon, the reverse appears to hold true: the room is seen as distorted and the marital partner as normal. The fact that both instances can and do occur indicates that in no sense can either instance be considered as "stimulus bound"; the stimulus and its retinal impingement are not, in and of themselves, an adequate explanation of the observed behavior.

It can readily be seen that the work reported here is entirely compatible with a great deal of experimental work which has been done within the framework of the so-called "transactional" viewpoint. As such, this experiment provides another instance in which a truly adequate and satisfactory explanation of the results must come from a consideration of the total "transaction" in which the perceiving mechanism and the stimulus configuration are merely integrally related parts, and in which the assumptions, needs, values, and purposes of the perceiver are equally as important.

[At the time the above experiment was completed numerous hypotheses were advanced to explain the Honi phenomenon, but none rested on a solid base of evidence. Subsequent experimental work on "stress," "anxiety," and "insecurity" in visual perception led to an increased understanding and to an explanation which seems to fit all aspects of the results obtained.

[It should be pointed out that stress is a very general, and probably inaccurate, name for a general class of phenomena with which we have been dealing. It is merely a descriptive term employed in lieu of more accurate specifications of the physiological and psychological factors involved.

[The first experiment in this general line is one in which Hastings (1) used a paper-and-pencil personal-security inventory as a means of selecting contrasting groups of secure and insecure subjects, and obtained size-distance judgments from them on the "thereness-thatness" apparatus (see Chapters 2 and 4). The differences between the settings given by the two groups were marked and highly reliable. It appears that even in such simple aspects of perceiving as of size and distance some sort of tension or general stress level which might be presumed to be different for the two groups of subjects must be taken into account. Further work of a somewhat different kind by Smith (2) tends to confirm this conclusion.

[Perhaps even more confirmation is offered by the preliminary work of Slack and Calloway on the effects in perception of "stress" artifically induced by cold-pressor or amyl-nitrite. They found that size-distance judgments in the laboratory and outside, in a normal environment, were reliably affected by putting one's foot in a bucket of ice water or by inhaling amyl-nitrite. Slack also conducted preliminary studies using the technique of one-dimensional tracking as a means of continuously recording alterations in perceptual-motor behavior. In testing the effects of cold-pressor and amyl-nitrite, he found that both conditions result in a change in what is called the "range effect," a sort of regression toward the mean.

[Another bit of research in this line involved the use of aniseikonic glasses in the "leaf room." For almost every observer there is an appreciable time lag between putting on these distortion-producing glasses and the appearance of any distortion of the room, and even more time elapses while the apparent shape of the room gradually alters until it finally reaches a fairly stable maximum (see Chapters 6 and 8). A device for measuring the speed and amount of this perceptual alteration has been designed by Ittelson. One of the experiments in which it has been used also involves the use of cold-pressor and amyl-nitrite. Both of these seem to result in an appreciable reduction in both the speed and the amount of perceptual alteration.

[Comparable results emerged from the use of aniseikonic size lenses with children. These lenses, referred to previously, alter the relative sizes of the retinal images in the two eyes, usually resulting in marked distortion in the perception of whatever is being viewed. In one experiment with children such glasses were put on the child and he was asked to look at both his parents and to describe how they looked. In a number of instances one parent was reported as distorting markedly in appearance while the other remained either normal or almost normal. Similar results were obtained when the children observed their parents in the monocular distorted room.

[In looking over this group of experiments one is tempted to generalize. If one merely postulates that among newly married couples, and among elderly couples for whom loss of the loved one is an ever-present possibility, distortion in the appearance of the marital partner is somehow threatening and tension-arousing in many instances; that for children the same thing is often true with respect to one parent more than another, then it would appear that this variety of studies could be subsumed under a single generalization. The generalization would be that whenever tension or stress is aroused, the individual tends in his perceptual organization to resist the change called for by new impingements from the environment, and to hold on to a stable perceptual construct, or constancy. Probably this resistence occurs because the constancy, in spite of the fact that it may not be appropriate or reliable in this immediate situation, has proved reliable in the past.

[In the next chapter, three studies offering evidence for this hypothesis are reported in detail.—Ed.]

REFERENCES—CHAPTER 10

1. Hastings, P. K. "An investigation into the relationship between visual perception and level of personal security." In *Human Behavior from the Transactional Point of View*. F. P. Kilpatrick (Ed.). Hanover, N. H.: Institute for Associated Research, 1952.

2. Smith, G. H. "Size-distance judgments of human faces (projected images)." *In Human Behavior from the Transactional Point of View,* F. P. Kilpatrick (Ed.). Hanover, N. H.: Institute for Associated Research, 1952.

II

Three Experiments in Selective Perceptual Distortion

Warren J. Wittreich, Marea Grace,

& Keith B. Radcliffe, Jr.

EXPERIMENT I:
BODY IMAGE DEVELOPMENT [1, 2]

KILPATRICK HAS MADE the point that we cannot perceive an object as "out there" in space without some reference to the self, i.e., what we are potentially capable of doing with or to that object. "Object constancy" is therefore dependent upon "self-constancy," each constancy representing an abstraction from a total process or transaction involving perceiver and perceived. Furthermore, all behavior is based upon a prediction by the individual as to what the situation *will be* when

---

[1] By Warren J. Wittreich and Marea Grace.

[2] The authors wish to express their gratitude to the following members of the Princeton school system whose assistance and co-operation made this study possible: Mr. Chester Stroup, Mr. Howard Waxwood, and Mr. Frederick S. Coffman. Thanks are also due to those teachers who willingly contributed their time and effort, and special thinks are due to Mr. Stroup, whose assistance enabled the study to get under way.

the act takes place, not what the situation *is* when the act is initiated. Consequently, the individual is making two sets of predictions: (1) a prediction about the object, (2) a prediction about the self. [For a more complete discussion see Chapter 21.—Ed.]

In many situations the major component of the prediction about the self is what has commonly been termed the "body image" or "body scheme." We can therefore define the body image as "a set of probable behaviors or expectancies of an individual, specifically referred to his body, and inferred from his past and present behaviors." Hence, in every percept, or in every act, the individual is making some prediction as to what his body can or will do.

Recent studies by Wittreich (11, 12) have indicated that induced optical distortion of an individual's mirror image may provide a means of studying the body image concept. From a knowledge of just the optics of the distortion-producing situation, we would predict that certain characteristic changes or distortions in the perceived mirror image would be reported by the individual. This is not the case. There is a discrepancy between our prediction and what is actually reported, and this discrepancy varies among individuals. Hence it is not unreasonable to assume, and evidence indicates this to be the case, the expectancies held by the individual are of major importance in determining the manner in which he perceives his mirror image in such a situation.

It is generally agreed that the major changes in body image occur in either (1) clinical instances of bodily malfunction or (2) the growth process that occurs from birth into late adolescence. Cases of the former genre were not available to the investigators; hence the latter area was chosen for study. The purpose of the experiment to be reported here was essentially to answer the following questions:

1. Can a direct measure such as induced optical distortion of an individual's mirror image be used as a method of investigating body image?
2. How does this method compare with another major technique of investigating body image, the Draw-a-Person test?
3. What bearing does such a new definition and new method have upon the general body of evidence already collected in past studies of body image?

Experiment

SUBJECTS. One hundred forty school children served as subjects in this study. Ten children—five male and five female—were represented at each of the fourteen grade levels. The grade range was from prekindergarten to high school senior; the age range was from four to seventeen.

PROCEDURE. A large mirror, 5 feet by 4 feet, was placed approximately 4 feet from a double booth arrangement constructed entirely of black drapery material. A child could stand in one of these booths, a contemporary of the child in the other. By having the child or the contemporary stand in a designated position, it was possible for the child to view his own image alone, or the image of the contemporary alone.

The child was first given a pair of "control lenses," i.e., a pair of frames with no lenses in them. He was told that these were extremely delicate lenses and that he was not to touch them. He was to allow E to put them on and take them off. With them on, he viewed either himself followed by his contemporary or vice versa. (The order was balanced within each grade level.) While viewing each image, he was asked if any of the following parts of the body image appeared to be changed in any way whatsoever: feet, legs, hands, arms, shoulders, face, nose, and finally the over-all image itself.

Then a pair of 4 per cent ex-cyclo aniseikonic lenses (axes rotated 135°–45°) was put on the child. Again he viewed his own image and the image of the contemporary (in balanced order) and again he was asked the set of questions described above for each of the two images.

Subsequent to the above procedure, the DAP test was administered to each child in the manner prescribed by Machover. Each child drew two pictures: one of a person of the same sex and one of the opposite sex. The associational questionnaire used by Machover was not administered. The pictures alone served as data.

Machover's scoring and classification system for the DAP is not amenable to IBM coding or statistical checks on reliability. It was therefore necessary to devise a scoring system which was amenable to the requirements of this investigation.

Two scoring keys were worked out. One was entitled the "Body Maturity Rating" or BMR. This is basically a modification of scoring keys used by Goodenough (3) and Modell (7). The scale gives increasing credit to increasing recognizability and differentiability of important parts of the body as well as increasing correctness in the proportions of these parts.

Each picture initially drawn by the child was scored independently by the senior author and by a colleague.[3] The rank order correlation between the two scorers was .89, indicating a high reliability of the scoring key.

The second scoring key was entitled the "Sexual Differentiation Rating" or SDR. This was a modification of the scoring key used by

---

[3] The authors are indebted to Mr. Edward Engel for his assistance in this phase of the investigation.

Modell. This scale gives increasing credit to increasing indications in the two drawings of an awareness of those parts and aspects of the body which differentiate male from female. Again, all drawings were scored by the senior author and his colleague. The rank order correlation between raters in this case was .83, again indicating high reliability of the scoring key.

Finally, each child was rated on each of seven "personality" criteria assumed to be related to the child's body image concept. The rating was done by the child's teacher. In the lower grades, where each child spent the entire day with a single teacher, the child was rated by this teacher alone. In the upper grades, the child was rated by three teachers, and the three ratings on each criterion were pooled to give the child a single rating. (The mean coefficient of concordance, according to the method devised by Kendall [5], for the independent ratings was .54.)

The technique of rating utilized in this study is an adaptation of the Stapel scalometer technique (9). The Stapel scalometer is a small white card measuring 3 inches by 4 inches. Printed on the card are ten squares of identical size lying along a vertical continuum. The top five squares are white with black outline; the bottom five squares are solid black. A single horizontal line divides the two sets of squares. A black plus figure is placed at the top left-hand corner of the card and a black minus figure at the lower left-hand corner.

The teacher was simply asked to point to the appropriate one of the ten squares which best expressed her feelings about the child on any given criterion. Each child was rated on the following:

1. Abilty to verbalize spontaneously
2. Ability to verbalize when directed
3. Gracefulness and co-ordination in large movements such as walking and running
4. Gracefulness and co-ordination in small movements such as drawing and finger painting
5. Quality and wholeheartedness of participation
6. Level of maturity
7. Qualities of leadership.

RESULTS. The following five questions were asked concerning the data obtained in the aniseikonic lenses situation:

1. Is there a difference between the control and the aniseikonic condition?
2. Is there a difference in the degree to which different parts of the body will change under either of the two conditions?
3. If 2 is answered affirmatively, is this difference in the degree to which the different parts of the body change a function of age?

4. Do boys differ from girls?

5. If 4 is answered affirmatively, is this difference between the sexes a function of age?

These questions were answered as follows:

1. Test: The eight parts of the body were treated separately. The number of times that a specific part was reported as having changed for the aniseikonic condition was compared to the number of times for the control condition. This comparison was made for each of the 14 age levels. Ties were divided equally. These results are presented in Table I. It is apparent that more change is reported for each part under the aniseikonic condition.

TABLE I

COMPARISON BETWEEN THE CONTROL AND ANISEIKONIC CONDITIONS FOR EACH PART OF THE BODY FOR THE 14 AGE LEVELS.

PART	NO. AGE LEVELS REPORTING MORE CHANGES UNDER ANISEIKONIC CONDITION	NO. AGE LEVELS REPORTING MORE CHANGES UNDER CONTROL CONDITION	TOTAL NO. AGE LEVELS
Feet	11	3	14
Legs	14	0	14
Hands	11.5	2.5	14
Arms	13	1	14
Shoulders	12.5	1.5	14
Face	9	5	14
Nose	10.5	3.5	14
Over-all	13.5	.5	14

2. Test: An 8 x 14 table of rankings was set up. The eight parts of the body were ranked at each of the 14 age levels. The rankings at each age level were made in terms of the number of times that a particular part of the body was reported as having changed as compared to each of the other parts. The part which changed the least was ranked first; the part which changed the most was ranked eighth. Then, the coefficient of the concordance was calculated to see if there was any significant agreement on rankings for the 14 age levels.

Low but significant agreement was found for the aniseikonic condition for both self and contemporary;[4] no significant agreement was found for the control conditions. These results are presented in Table II.

Kendall states that if significant agreement is found among rankings, then the mean rankings can be treated as the best "estimates" in a least square sense. Consequently, the 8 mean rankings which were obtained

[4] It should be noted that self and contemporary aniseikonic conditions are not significantly different from one another.

TABLE II

W, AS CALCULATED FOR THE RANKINGS OF THE 8 PARTS OF
THE BODY AT THE 14 AGE LEVELS FOR THE 4 CONDITIONS

CONDITION	W	SIGNIF.
Self-aniseikonic	0.252	.01
Contemporary aniseikonic	0.379	.01
Self-control	0.130	n.s
Contemporary control	0.139	n.s

for the 14 age levels for the aniseikonic conditions were then converted into, or treated as, actual rankings from 1 to 8. These rankings are presented in Table III.

TABLE III

RANKINGS OF THE 8 PARTS OF THE BODY ACCORDING TO
THE DEGREE OF RESISTANCE TO CHANGE FOR THE 2 CONDITIONS

RANK	SELF-ANISEIKONIC	CONTEMPORARY ANISEIKONIC
1	Shoulder	Nose
2	Face	Shoulder
3	Nose	Hands
4	Hands	Face
5	Feet	Arms
6	Arms	Feet
7	Over-all	Over-all
8	Legs	Legs

3. Test: Ranks 1–4 were considered separately as one score; ranks 5–8 were considered separately as another score. Each subject thus received two scores, each score based on the sum of parts reported as having changed for that set of 4 parts of the body. Naturally, the sum of scores for the parts of the body ranked 5–8 will be higher than the sum of scores for the parts of the body ranked 1–4 and, in general, subtracting the score of the latter from the score of the former for any given S should produce a positive number.

The question then is asked: does the size of the difference between scores increase as age increases? This was answered by taking the mean difference between scores for each age level and ranking these differences from 1–14. Then a simple rank order correlation was calculated between age and score differences, giving a positive figure of .663 (significant beyond the .05 level). Hence we can conclude that the difference between scores is related to age.

4. Test: The boys and the girls were treated as independent groups. Their scores for ranks 1–4 were compared as were their scores for ranks

5–8. There is no significant difference between the scores for ranks 1–4. However, the mean score for the boys on ranks 5–8 is 2.58, and the mean score for the girls on these ranks is 1.54. This difference of 1.04 is significant beyond the .01 level ($t = 4.41$ at 138 d.f.). In other words, for the four parts of the body which distort most readily, the boys report distortion significantly more often than do the girls.

5. Test: The mean difference between the boys' scores and the girls' scores for the ranks 5–8 was calculated at each of the 14 age levels. These mean differences were then ranked from 1 to 14; the smallest difference being ranked as 1; the largest difference being ranked as 14. A simple rank order correlation was then calculated between score differences and age. This correlation is .001, and hence we must conclude that the difference in scores between boys and girls is not related to age.

The results obtained from the Draw-a-Person test are presented in Table IV. Examination of this table indicates that both BMR and SDR scores are positively related to age. As the child becomes older, the score becomes greater.

TABLE IV

RELATIONSHIP BETWEEN DRAW-A-PERSON SCORES AND AGE

DAP MEASURE X AGE	RHO	SIGNIF.
BMR x Age	.802	.01
SDR x Age	.853	.01

Graphic analysis reveals that the BMR shows a steady increase from ages 4 through 11 and after that a leveling-off process occurs. On the other hand, the SDR shows a steady gradual progression over the entire age range.

The relationship between the DAP scores and the aniseikonic scores previously discussed is presented in Table V. No significant differences were obtained between the DAP scores obtained by boys and girls.

TABLE V

RELATIONSHIP BETWEEN DRAW-A-PERSON
SCORES AND ANISEIKONIC SCORES

MEASURES	RHO	SIGNIF.
BMR x High-Low ranks	.723	.01
SDR x High-Low ranks	.598	.05

The personality ratings were not significantly related to any of the measures obtained in either the aniseikonic lens situation or on the

Draw-a-Person test. Hence these results are not presented. It should be noted in passing that a nonsignificant relationship between "ability to verbalize" and amount of change reported in the mirror-distortion situation would tend to rule out the former as an influence in the latter. The same is true of the nonsignificant relationship obtained between "gracefulness and co-ordination in small movements such as drawing and finger painting" and the DAP scores.

DISCUSSION. When a child views his mirror image while wearing aniseikonic lenses, he reports certain changes in the appearance of his body. These changes are not randomly related to the different parts of the body. Rather, certain parts seem to be more "susceptible" to changes than are others. The legs are most likely to be reported as having changed; they are followed by the over-all image itself, the arms, and the feet in the order indicated. Then come the hands, the shoulders, the nose, and finally the face which is least likely to be reported as having changed.

The very young child does not seem to show this pattern of change as markedly as the older child. As the child increases in age he shows a greater tendency to report more change in the first four parts listed above, and a concomitant tendency to see less change in the latter four parts. Furthermore, if the child is a boy, he will tend to see more change in those first four parts than a girl will at any age level.

How can we account for these results? To begin, previous analyses of the experimental situation generally have agreed that the degree to which change is reported for any one thing viewed under conditions of aniseikonic distortion is directly proportional to the degree of security or certainty one has in relation to predicted effective behavior with that particular thing. Experimental evidence has substantiated this analysis.

Anything with which we have had very little experience; which is in any way threatening or anxiety-provoking; in short, which makes us highly uncertain as to the reliability of our future action in relation to it, is likely to resist change under conditions of optical distortion. To accept the optical change would be to increase the lack of reliability of future action beyond the point of individual tolerance. Hence, the induced change is, so to speak, "rejected," and that thing—whatever it may be—is seen as unaltered or only slightly altered.

If, on the other hand, we have had a great deal of experience with something; if it does not threaten us or provoke fear and anxiety; if, in short, we feel quite certain as to the reliability of our future action in relation to that thing, then it is quite likely to be seen as altered under conditions of induced optical distortion. We still feel capable of effectively operating in relation to that thing in spite of its being seen as changed.

As the child grows older, the meaning or functional significance of various parts of the body undergoes certain alterations. In addition, the various parts differ not only in the meaning of the part for the child but in the degree to which this meaning may be tested out or continually experienced in terms of overt behavior.

For instance, as the child grows older, the meaning of his facial appearance is changed. "Looks" and "good looks" come to have an increasingly significant importance for the child in the successful carrying out of his everyday social behavior. However, overt testing out and active experiencing of this meaning is not possible. What testing out does occur is due largely to the building up of a set of attitudes based on the reflected appraisals of others.

On the other hand, the meaning of the child's limbs also undergoes certain changes. Take the legs as an example. For both boys and girls the legs must function basically as a means of effective locomotion. For this fundamental purpose a constant overt testing-out process occurs. As a result of this process, a very solid and secure set of expectancies is built up which has little or nothing to do with the reflected appraisals of others.

As the girl grows older, the factor of looks comes into play. A girl with nice shapely legs is more attractive than one with bony, muscular, or fat legs. However, for this particular meaning which the legs acquire, no overt testing out is possible. As with the face, the testing out is dependent to a very large degree upon the reflected appraisal of others.

For the boys at any age, the aesthetic appearance of the legs is of very little importance. We might sum up their particular problem as one of basically being able to travel rapidly and successfully from home to first base. Unlike the girls, the added meaning which the legs take on is not dependent upon the reflected appraisals of others. It can be, and is, constantly tested out and experienced in terms of overt behavior.

This overt testing-out process which occurs with certain parts of the body would tend to make our predicted behaviors with these parts highly reliable. The experiental background for these parts is such that their particular functional significance is more certain and secure than those parts where no overt testing out is possible. Consequently, we would predict that parts such as the legs or arms would tend to change more readily under conditions of induced optical change than parts such as the face or nose. These are exactly the results we obtain. The legs change most readily; the face changes least readily. This becomes increasingly so as the child grows older. And the boys consistently are more willing to see change in their limbs than are the girls.

What relationship do these findings have to the data we have obtained from the Draw-a-Person test? The positive relationship between the BMR and age indicates that as the child grows older he increases his ability to differentiate the parts of the body and to place each part in its proper proportionate relationship to every other part. But the DAP test does not tell us what the nature of this differentiation process is, i.e., it fails to indicate what are the different meanings these parts take on in relation to one another.

Similarly, the positive relationship between SDR and age indicates that as the child grows older he becomes increasingly aware of those observable physical characteristics which distinguish the male from the female. But again, the test fails to tell us what are the different meanings which various parts—in common to both sexes—take on as age increases.

There is some relationship between the measures taken from the two situations—as indicated in the results. This relationship between independent sets of data is not the truly important thing. What is of the utmost importance is that an objective experimental situation has provided us with reliable data from which we are able to draw inferences about the body image and its development. The data and the inferences go significantly beyond what we are able to conclude from a so-called projective technique. In short, the results of our study have demonstrated in a clear-cut manner both the feasibility and the advantages of testing out a clinical concept in the experimental laboratory.

EXPERIMENT II: THE INFLUENCE OF STIMULATED MUTILATION UPON THE PERCEPTION OF THE HUMAN FIGURE [5, 6]

Introduction

THE PERCEPTION OF a severely injured or mutilated individual provokes a profound emotional reaction in the perceiver. This is a phenomenon which seems to be universal. It is probably the basis for the social problem of the acceptance of the mutilated person by society.

A number of studies have been carried out on this problem (e.g., 1,

[5] By Warran J. Wittreich and Keith B. Radcliffe, Jr.
[6] First issued as Naval Medical Research Institute Research Report, Project NM004 008.04.02. Published originally under the above title in *J. Abnorm. Soc. Psychol.*, 1955, *51*, 493–95. Printed here by permission of the authors and the publisher, The American Psychological Association.

4, 6, 8, 10). The majority of the studies have been based upon an analysis of evidence obtained in the clinical situation. These studies have been fruitful in suggesting various hypotheses related to the phenomenon. However, there still is not enough clear-cut data available on the basis of which one may adequately specify the relevant variables which can account for any of the findings presented to date.

This study represents an attempt to observe one facet of this phenomenon in an experimental setting. It is based primarily upon preliminary findings reported by Gilder *et al.* (2). This work indicates that when an observer views both an amputee and a person with normal body configuration under conditions of induced optical distortion, the observer tends to report less distortion in the appearance of the amputee. Gilder also reports that a pretended amputee tends to produce the same response from the observer as does the amputee.

These studies were carried out using a single set of aniseikonic lenses (4.00 ex-cyclo) as the distorting instrument. The means of measuring the difference in the amount of distortion reported for the amputee and the normal by the observer was through an analysis of the descriptions provided by the latter.

These findings by Gilder are in line with earlier studies done by Wittreich. The latter has shown that under conditions of induced aniseikonic distortion a child will tend to report less distortion observed in the parent than in a stranger (11). He has also shown that when a person observes his own image and the image of a stranger in a mirror while wearing aniseikonic lenses he reports different amounts and types of distortion for his own image as compared with the stranger's image (11, 12). However, both the studies by Gilder and Wittreich have been restricted to qualitative observations and reports and therefore must be characterized as preliminary or exploratory. The establishment of these findings as reliable scientific data depends upon their being reproduced under rigidly controlled experimental conditions.

Wittreich has developed a method of scaling the "resistance to induced aniseikonic distortion" of various objects for a given subject (13). The method involves the use of 14 sets of aniseikonic lenses of increasing power. Objects are scaled in terms of the point on the optical scale at which they are reported as first appearing to distort by the subject. Hence, any object can be given a threshold for distortion and compared with other objects according to this threshold.

The purpose of the study to be reported here is to reproduce the differences observed by Gilder utilizing the scaling method developed by Wittreich.

Experiment

SUBJECTS. Twelve white male naval enlisted personnel randomly selected from the crew of the Naval Medical Research Institute.

APPARATUS AND PROCEDURE. The subject was seated in front of the open side of a five-sided room measuring 7 feet x 7 feet, all surfaces of which were covered with black drapery material. Illumination was provided by four 200-watt floodlights mounted at the four corners of the open side of the room.

The subject observed the same individual standing in front of the rear wall of the room under two different conditions: (1) Normal—the observed individual appeared under conditions of normal body configuration. He was wearing a white lab coat. (2) Simulated mutilation—the observed individual appeared with the right sleeve of the lab coat pinned to the shoulder. The right arm was tied behind the observed individual's back. He also wore a black eye patch over his left eye.

Under each of these conditions, the subject was presented with a series of 14 aniseikonic lenses ranging in power from 0.25 per cent to 4.50 per cent. A total of 12 series of lens presentations was given for each condition: six of the series were ascending; six were descending. The subject attended three experimental sessions over a three-day period. At each session the subject was presented with four series for each condition.

The observed individual was visible to the subject only during the actual presentation of each single lens power. After a lens had been inserted into the viewing apparatus, the subject pressed a button which illuminated the room. He then observed the individual in the room for a period of 25 seconds, at which time an electronic timer shut off the light. Following each lens presentation the subject reported the appearance of the individual in the room for that particular lens presentation.

The experimenter gave the following specific instructions concerning the reports of the appearance of the observed individual to the subject: "Each time the light goes on you are to observe the appearance of the individual in the room as closely as possible. After the light goes off, I want you to tell me what he looked like when the light was on. If he looked the same as usual, I want you to tell me that. If he appeared to be changed in any way whatsoever, I want you to tell me that. I also want you to tell me in what way he changed. Now, he may change in a number of ways. He may change in size; he may appear to tilt forward or backward; he may change in his distance from you; he may change in specific parts of his body. Any one or a combination of these changes may occur. It usually depends upon the observer as to which ones do occur. In any event, please tell me after each lens presentation what his appearance was while the light was on."

The experimenter recorded the point on the optical scale (lenses numbered 1 through 14) at which distortion of the observed individual was first reported when the series was ascending or the point at which distortion was no longer reported if the series was descending.

The starting point for any particular ascending or descending series was varied within conditions, but equated between conditions. Also, the order of presentation of the normal and mutilated conditions, as well as the order of presentation of the ascending and descending series, was balanced within the sample of 12 subjects so as to cancel out any possible effects due to order of presentation.

RESULTS. For each subject, the mean threshold for distortion for both the normal and the mutilated condition was calculated. These results are presented in Table VI.

It can be seen that for 11 of the 12 subjects the threshold for distortion for the mutilated condition is higher than for the normal condition. Of these 11 differences, t analysis shows 3 to be significant beyond the 0.05 level; one is significant beyond the 0.001 level. One subject showed a difference in the opposite direction; this difference is not significant.

For the sample as a whole, a difference of 0.76 exists between the two conditions. This difference is significant at the 0.01 level (t = 3.50, at 11 d.f.).

TABLE VI

DIFFERENCES IN THE THRESHOLDS FOR DISTORTION
FOR THE MUTILATED AND NORMAL CONDITIONS

SUBJECT NUMBER	MEAN THRESHOLD		DIFF.	SIGNIF.
	MUTILATED COND.	NORMAL COND.		
1	3.08	2.41	0.67	n.s.
2	3.92	2.66	1.25	0.05
3	3.67	2.50	1.17	0.05
4	4.67	4.83	−0.16	n.s.
5	4.08	3.16	0.92	n.s.
6	5.58	5.50	0.08	n.s.
7	4.25	1.66	2.58	0.001
8	1.58	1.41	0.17	n.s.
9	1.50	1.25	0.25	n.s.
10	2.00	1.58	0.42	n.s.
11	2.75	2.25	0.50	n.s.
12	8.91	7.50	1.41	0.05
Mean for total sample:	**3.83**	**3.06**	**0.77**	**0.01** (d.f. = 11)

DISCUSSION. The results of the experiment indicate that a greater amount of optical change is required to bring about a concomitant perceptual change in the appearance of an apparently mutilated figure as opposed to a figure with normal body configuration. This confirms the preliminary observations reported by Gilder.

It should be stressed that the subjects employed in this experiment were in daily contact with a hospital population which included a large number of injured, mutilated, disfigured, and amputated individuals. Furthermore, the nature of the experiment was such that the subject was aware at all times that the observed individual was not in fact amputated or disfigured in any way. One could reasonably assume that these two factors ought to decrease the size of the differences between the two conditions. Yet, significant differences were obtained and this indicates that larger differences might very well be obtained with either a different sampling of subjects or an experimental design where the subject had no knowledge that the observed individual was not actually mutilated.

It should also be noted that subject No. 7, who showed the largest and most significant difference between the two conditions, had a personal history which may provide some insight to his marked behavior. He had a male sibling younger by a year who, for approximately a three-year period, had worn an eye patch. Upon being questioned at the finish of the experiment as to his feelings associated with his brother's wearing of the eye patch, the subject replied, "I felt like slugging anyone who made any remark about his wearing the patch." This would seem to indicate that the wearing of the eye patch by the brother had powerful emotional implications for this subject. In turn, it may be generalized that an increase in the emotional cathexis associated with a mutilated figure results in an increase in the size of the differences between the mutilated and normal conditions.

Also suggestive is the fact that subject No. 4, who showed the only difference in the opposite direction, was the closest and most intimate friend of the observed individual. This is consistent with Gilder's statement that distortion will be seen when the relationship is a secure one between the viewer and the viewee.

The explanation as to why specifically a mutilated figure should distort less than a normal figure is obviously not contained in the data itself. In the distorting situation, the subject has a number of alternative cues available on the basis of which he can construct or create his percept. The binocular cues have been altered through the aniseikonic distortion; the uniocular cues have remained unaffected. When little or no distortion is perceived by the subject, he is utilizing the uniocular cues as the basis for his percept and in general is ignoring the binocular cues.

The crucial question is why the subject relies more heavily upon the uniocular cues when viewing the amputee than when viewing the normal figure.

Gilder, whose preliminary investigation provided the impetus for this study, leans toward an interpretation which accounts for this phenomenon in terms of the mechanism of identification. His reasoning is that the subject has a basic wish or desire for a normal integrated body image for the self. When the subject sees another body figure, he automatically identifies with it. If that body figure is changed, then this change is threatening to the subject's self-body image because of his identification. Hence, the amputee is held constant in order to preserve the integrity of the body image of the subject.

The authors' preference is for an explanation along more functional lines—one which does not rely upon the mechanism of identification as an explanatory concept. They would argue that the subject would basically tend to rely upon those perceptual cues which in the past have proven reliable and which therefore provide effective guides for future action. When the subject views an amputated or mutilated individual with no optically distorting factor introduced, he nevertheless becomes anxious and stressed because: (1) he has had little experience dealing directly with such body configurations in the past, and (2) he therefore has an unreliable set of assumptions from past experience on the basis of which he can predict future action. When optical distortion is introduced, the acceptance of the binocular cues would tend to increase the lack of reliability of future action, which is highly unreliable to begin with. This is primarily true when viewing the mutilated figure—certainly more important than when viewing the normal figure. Hence, when viewing the amputee, the subject relies more heavily upon those uniocular cues which have proved reliable in the past and which do provide some basis for effective action in the future.

In this experiment, it has been shown that the same amount of optical change does not produce the same amount of perceptual change in the mutilated as opposed to the normal figure. Consequently, the consideration only of the relationship between the stimulus configuration and the perceiving mechanism cannot possibly account for our findings. What has been demonstrated here in the more general perceptual sense is the interdependence of the processes of perceiving and of interpersonal relations. It would not be too unreasonable to assume that such evidence points in the direction of an eventual understanding of both the process of perceiving and the process of interpersonal relations, not as separately defined interacting factors, but rather as abstractions from a single process of "being" or "living" which is basic to both.

EXPERIMENT III: DIFFERENCES IN THE PERCEPTION OF AN AUTHORITY FIGURE AND A NONAUTHORITY FIGURE BY NAVY RECRUITS [7, 8]

THE NAVY RECRUIT is introduced into military discipline immediately upon his arrival in boot camp. He is taught that orders given are orders obeyed—the alternative being severe disciplinary action. He rapidly learns to recognize those individuals who represent authority, and he becomes aware of the implications these authority figures have for his own successful behavior.

In the early phases of training, when the recruit is still relatively unsure of himself, the appropriate visual configuration bearing stripes or bars is often sufficient to provoke fear and anxiety. As recruit training teaches him the appropriate forms of behavior in the appropriate situations, the element of fear is gradually diminished. Yet, seldom is that element completely eliminated. The comforting reliability of being in the presence of one's own peers is invariably preferred to the ever-present uncertainty involved in dealing with authority.

The question then arises: Does this element of fear involved in viewing and being with an authority figure actually influence the perception of that figure? Previous studies in this general area would indicate an affirmative answer. Gilder *et al.* (2) provide evidence which seems to indicate that a threatening figure changes less readily than a nonthreatening figure under conditions of induced optical change. In Experiment II, Wittreich and Radcliffe have shown that the human figure under the condition of simulated mutilation is less susceptible to induced optical change than the human figure under conditions of normal configuration.

Hence the hypothesis is advanced that under conditions of induced aniseikonic distortion a figure that represents authority is more resistant to perceptual change than a figure that does not represent authority. This hypothesis was tested in a study of navy recruits.

Method

Twenty-four white male navy recruits in their seventh week of training at the Naval Training Center at Bainbridge, Maryland, served as subjects. The subject was seated approximately 10 feet from a black back-

[7] By Warran J. Wittreich and Keith B. Radcliffe, Jr.

[8] Published originally under the above title in *J. Abnorm. Soc. Psychol.*, 1956, *53*, 383–84. Printed here by permission of the authors and the publisher, The American Psychological Association.

drop. During the experimental session the subject was able to view only a single figure standing before the backdrop. Illumination was provided by four 60-watt bulbs mounted in reflectors which were focused on the figure being observed.

Two figures were observed by each subject: (a) *Authority figure*. The observed individual was dressed in a white enlisted man's uniform. On his left sleeve was the rating badge of a 1st Class Boatswain's Mate and two hash marks. (It should be pointed out that the subjects used had 1st Class Petty Officers as their company commanders.) (b) *Nonauthority figure*. The observed individual was dressed in a white enlisted man's uniform with the identifying marks of a recruit: canvas leggings or "boots" and the stripes of a seaman apprentice. (At Bainbridge all seaman recruits wear the stripes of a seaman apprentice.)

Two different individuals played the roles of the authority and the nonauthority figure. Every effort was made to present these figures as genuine. Within each subsample of 12, one individual played the role of the authority figure 6 times and the nonauthority figure 6 times. The names assigned to the authority figure and the nonauthority figure remained constant. The two individuals employed were approximately the same size, weight, and body build.

Each figure was viewed by the subject through aniseikonic lenses in a series of 14 lenses ranging in power from 0.25 per cent to 4.50 per cent. Four series of lens presentations were given for each figure: 2 of the series were ascending, 2 were descending. The subject attended a single experimental session which lasted approximately 50 minutes. The observed individual was visible to the subject only during the actual presentation of each single lens power. After a lens had been inserted into the viewing apparatus, the subject pressed a button which illuminated the figure standing in front of the backdrop. He then observed that figure for a period of 25 seconds, at which time an electronic timer shut off the light. Following each lens presentation the subject reported the appearance of the observed individual for that particular lens presentation.

The experimenter gave the following instructions: "Each time the light goes on you are to observe the appearance of the individual in the room as closely as possible. After the light goes off, I want you to tell me what he looked like when the light was on. If he looked the same as usual, I want you to tell me that. If he appeared to be changed in any way whatsoever, I want you to tell me that. I also want you to tell me in what way he changed. Now, he may change in a number of ways. He may change in size; he may appear to tilt forward or backward; he may change in his distance from you; he may change in specific parts of his body. Any one or a combination of these changes may occur. In any event, please tell me after each lens presentation what his appearance was while the light was on."

The experimenter recorded the point on the optical scale (lenses numbered 1 through 14) at which distortion of the observed individual was first reported when the series was ascending, or the point at which distortion was no longer reported if the series was descending. The starting point for any particular ascending or descending series was varied within conditions. Also, the order of presentation of the authority and the nonauthority figure, as well as the order of presentation of the ascending and descending series, was balanced within each subsample of 12 subjects so as to cancel out any possible effects due to order of presentation.

RESULTS. For the total sample of 24 subjects, the mean threshold for distortion for the Boatswain's Mate was 3.28 (SD 2.29); for the Seaman Apprentice 2.16 (SD 1.32). For 22 of the 24 subjects, the threshold for distortion was higher for Boatswain's Mate than Seaman Apprentice. By sign test, this gives a two-tailed p value of less than .0001.

CONCLUSION. As predicted from previous work on fear-evoking objects and resistance to perceptual distortion, navy recruits viewing persons through aniseikonic lenses showed higher distortion thresholds when viewing an authority figure than when viewing a nonauthority figure.

REFERENCES—CHAPTER 11

1. Garrett, James F. (Ed.). *Psychological Aspects of Physical Disability*. Federal Security Agency, Office of Vocational Rehabilitation, Wash. 25, D. C., *Rehab. Serv. Series,* No. 210.

2. Gilder, R. Thompson, S. B.; Slack, C. W.; and Radcliffe, K. B. Jr. "Amputation, body image, and perceptual distortion." *U.S.N. Med. Res. Inst. Rep.,* 1955.

3. Goodenough, Florence. *Measurement of Intelligence by Drawings*. Chicago: World Book Co., 1926.

4. Grayson, Morris. "Concept of acceptance in physical rehabilitation." *J.A.M.A.,* 1951, *145,* 893–96.

5. Kendall, M. G. *Rank Correlation Methods*. London: C. Griffen, 1948.

6. Ladieu, G.; Adler, D. L.; and Dembo, T. "Studies in adjustment to visible injuries." *J. Soc. Issues,* 1948, Fall, 55–61.

7. Modell, Arnold. "The human figure drawing as a measure of integrative capacity." *Memorandum: Portsmouth Navy Hospital,* 1952.

8. MacGregor, F. C. "Some psychosocial problems associated with facial deformities." *Am. Soc. Rev.*, 1951, *16*, 629–38.

9. Stapel, Jan. *Scales Without Tears.* Amsterdam: Netherlands Institute of Public Opinion, 1951.

10. White, R. K.; Beatrice, A. W.; and Dembo, T. "Studies in the adjustment to visible injuries." *J. Abnorm. Soc. Psychol.*, 1948, *3*, 13–28.

11. Wittreich, W. J. "A preliminary investigation into certain aspects of perception, including the Honi phenomenon." In F. P. Kilpatrick (Ed.), *Human Behavior from the Transactional Point of View.* Hanover, N. H.: Institute for Associated Research, 1952.

12. Wittreich, W. J. "Aniseikonia and distortion of the self-image." *Amer. J. Psychol.*, 1953, *8*, 457–58.

13. Wittreich, W. J. *An Investigation into the Nature of Aniseikonic Distortion.* Unpublished Ph.D. Thesis, Princeton University, 1954.

CHAPTER

12

The Rotating Trapezoid:[1]

Description of Phenomena

Adelbert Ames, Jr.

INTRODUCTION

IT IS APPARENT from the earlier investigations that what we are aware of when we look at a rotating object is not a disclosure of what is "objectively" taking place, but is a prognosis whose nature is related to assumptions arrived at from prior experience. To increase our understanding of the origin and nature of our perception of motion, it seemed necessary to understand more about the nature of the assumptions which play a role in our perception of motion. A possible procedure to disclose more about the nature of our assumptions was to vary, under controlled conditions, certain "objective characteristics" of a rotating object (in this case a rectangular configuration, a window) and determine if and

[1] Published originally by *Psychol. Monogr.,* 1951, Vol. 65, No. 7 (whole No. 324), under the title, "Visual perception and the rotating trapezoidal window." Printed here in slightly altered form as Chapters 12 and 13 by permission of the author and the publisher, The American Psychological Association.

how such variation would alter our perception and thereby possibly disclose more about the nature of the related assumptions.

The problem then arose as to what "objective characteristics" to vary. There are, of course, innumerable "objective characteristics" of a rotating window that could be varied, such as its chemical-physical make-up, weight, hardness, motion, form, shape, color, etc. It is apparent that light could be thrown on the nature of our visual processes only by varying visual aspects. It had become apparent from our earlier investigation that significant disclosures might result from variation of particular aspects of the objective form. The form of a rectangular configuration can be varied in a number of different ways. It can be varied from a long rectangle to a square form or vice versa by varying its length or height, or it can be varied in its over-all size by changing its length or height, or it can be varied in thickness. But with this type of variation of form, there would only be the expected alteration in perception "corresponding" to the "objective" variation. With such corresponding alteration of perception, nothing is disclosed as to assumptions or the role they play in the situation.

A rectangular configuration can also be changed into a trapezoidal form. It had been found that with such type of variation there are related marked unexpected perceptual phenomena that might throw light on assumptions and the role they play. It was for this reason that it was decided to vary it into trapezoidal form.

This brings us to the explanation of why the form was varied in the particular way in which it was varied. There are innumerable trapezoidal projections of any given rectangle (see Figure 1, top). However, it seemed advisable to use a particular trapezoidal form which, at a particular angle of inclination to the observer's line of sight, produces light-ray impingements essentially the same as those produced by a rectangular configuration at some particular inclination to the observer's line of sight. There are innumerable trapezoidal forms that meet this specification (see Figure 1, bottom). A'B', representing a trapezoidal window, is a projection of AB, representing the rectangular configuration, and is an example of one of the innumerable possible forms. The particular form of A'B' depends upon the inclination of the rectangular configuration AB to the observer's line of sight OG and also upon the inclination of the plane CD.

In the earlier investigations it had been empirically found that, when certain trapezoidal figures were rotated, they appeared through half of their rotation to rotate in a direction opposite to their actual rotation. A further preliminary investigation was carried out to determine what degree of trapezoidal variation of what objective configurations would

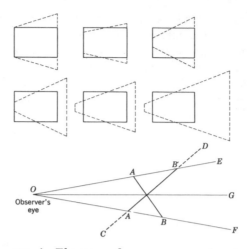

FIG. 1. *The upper figures are examples of the innumerable trapezoidal projections of a rectangular configuration. The lower figure shows that there are innumerable trapezoidal forms that will produce the same impingement patterns as a given rectangular form.*

be most effective in producing (so to speak) alterations in the observer's perception. The following different objective configurations were tested: white ⅛ inch thick aluminum plane surfaces with various trapezoidal variations (see Row a, Figure 2); white frame-shaped plane surfaces (see Row b, Figure 2); white mullioned plane surfaces (see Row c, Figure 2); white mullioned plane surfaces on which shadows were painted to represent a three-dimensional window frame (see Row d, Figure 2); white mullioned plane surfaces with shadows with a different number of mullions or panes (see Row e, Figure 2); and finally, white mullioned plane surfaces with shadows to represent a three-dimensional window frame with a different degree of trapezoidal variation (see Row f, Figure 2).

It was found that white plane surfaces (see Row a, Figure 2), although they "produced" alteration of the observer's perception, were least effective, irrespective of the degree of trapezoidal variation; that more effect was "produced" by the frame-shaped surfaces (see Row b, Figure 2); still more when mullions were added (see Row c, Figure 2); and still more when shadows were painted on the surface to represent a three-dimensional window frame (see Row d, Figure 2); and still more when there were more mullions or panes (see Row e, Figure 2). It was

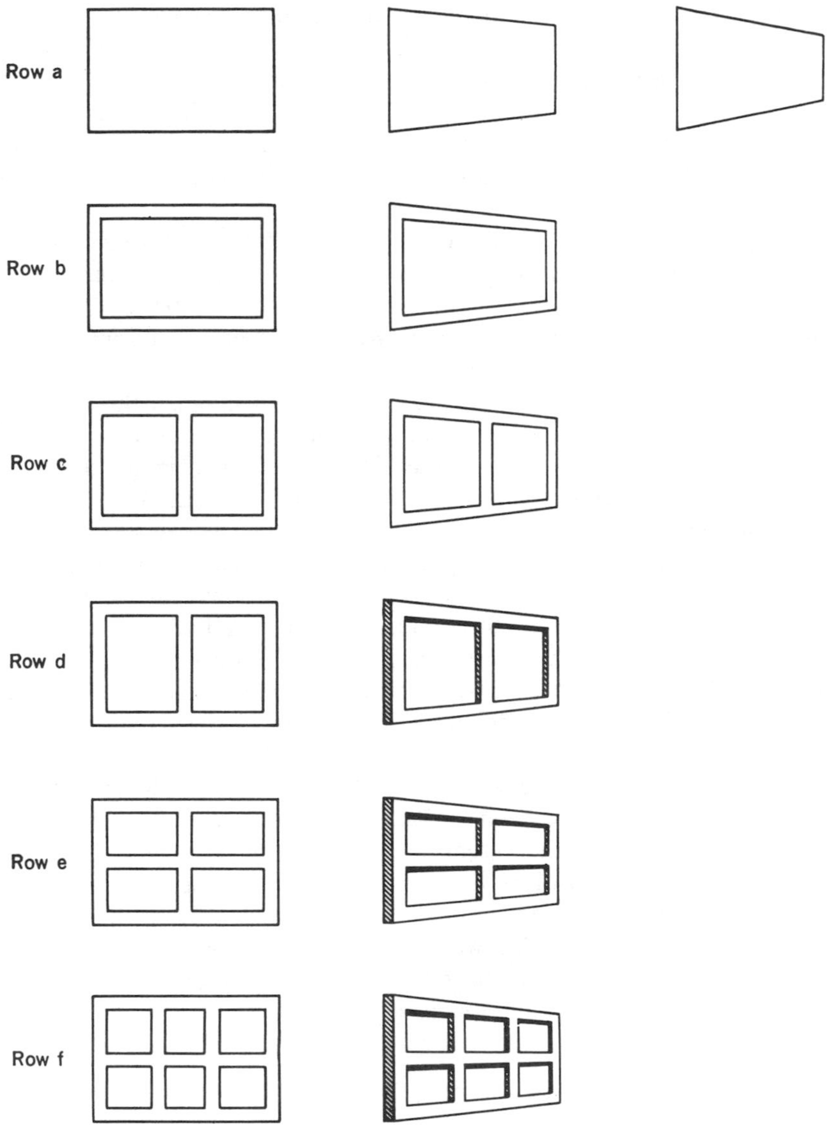

FIG. 2. *Showing various structures that were tested in determining what degree of trapezoidal variation of what type of configuration would be most effective in producing alteration of observer's perception.*

also found that larger trapezoids produced more unequivocal effects than smaller ones.

It was further determined that, with the last type of "window," if the trapezoidal variation (difference in the length of the parallel sides of the trapezoidal forms—see Row f, Figure 2) was apparent, the amount of the trapezoidal variation did not alter the general character of the visual phenomena experienced, although it did alter their degree. To ensure that an adequate degree of alteration of the visual phenomena would be experienced, it was decided to employ a considerable amount of trapezoidal variation.

As a final check a multiple-paned form (see Row f, Figure 2) without painted shadows (see Row c) was tested, and it was found that with it the same phenomena would be observed as with the trapezoidal window with the painted shadows, the only difference being that some of the phenomena were slightly more equivocal.

One more point might be mentioned. Theoretically, if a three-dimensional rectangular comparison window is used, the varied trapezoidal window should also be three dimensional; i.e., have actual thickness instead of having the appearance of thickness produced by painted shadows. However, when such a window is seen in reversed position, the sides of the mullions are apparent when they shouldn't be seen on a window in that position, and give rise to indications that conflict with those from the trapezoidal form. These conflicting indications can be obviated with a stationary form by painting the sides of the mullions black so that they cannot be distinguished from a black background. But, as this would be difficult to accomplish if the window were rotating, it was decided to use a very thin window with painted shadows.

A theoretical objection could be raised that more than the trapezoidal form of the window had been varied because the painted shadows are not quite the same as the actual shadows on the rectangular window; moreover, that the width of the shadows varies as the window turns, and also because when the trapezoidal window is edge-on it is much thinner than the rectangular window. However, it would appear that these minor variations have no effect on the alterations of perception that will be described, which apparently occur in spite of them.

DESCRIPTION OF APPARATUS

A photograph of the final apparatus is shown in Figure 3. It consists of the rectangular window (see RW) suspended by a vertical shaft S' which is driven by an electric motor M which is attached to the ceiling. The trapezoidal window TW is suspended on the vertical shaft S^2, which is rigidly fixed to the bottom of the window RW. On this shaft there is a sleeve F with two lock nuts so that the two windows can be set at any desired angle relative to each other. All the altered appearances can be

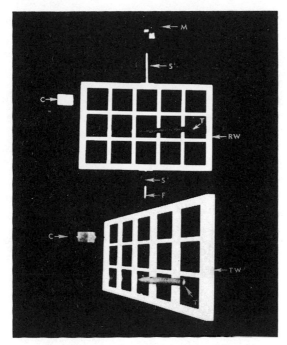

FIG. 3. *Photograph of apparatus. The photograph was taken with the surfaces of the rectangular window and the trapezoidal window in the same plane, which was perpendicular to the optical axis of the camera. The dimensions of the rectangular window are: length, 23½"; height, 16½"; thickness, ¼"; width of outside frame, ½"; width of mullions, ¼". The outside dimensions of the trapezoidal window are: length, 19½"; height of long side, 23⅝"; height of short side, 12½"; thickness, ⅛".*

seen, irrespective of the relative angles between the two windows, but comparisons of alteration in size are more easily made when they are set in the general relative position to each other as shown in Figure 4. When the motor is going, the rectangular window and the trapezoidal window rotate at the same speed about a common vertical axis. This arrangement enables the observer to compare the appearances of the two windows and note what alterations in his visual phenomena result from variation of the trapezoidal form.

The speed of the motor M can be controlled by a rheostat. A convenient speed for most observations is around 3 to 6 rpm. It is also desirable to have a switch so that the motion of the windows can be stopped at any desired position of the rotation. The direction of the rotation of the shaft S can be reversed by a reversing device on the motor controlled by a string pull.

Small cubes C and C are attached to the upper edge of the shorter side of the trapezoidal window and in corresponding position on the rectangular window, and paper tubes T and T are attached in the middle of both windows so that they extend out on both sides. (See Figure 3 and drawing in Chart I.) The role these cubes and tubes will play will become evident later.

The dimensions of the two windows are given in the legend of Figure 3. The trapezoidal window is cut out of thin aluminum. Its particular dimensions were arrived at as shown in Figure 4. A′B′ represents the

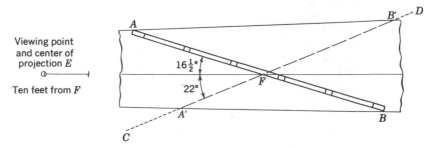

FIG. 4. *Plan showing design of the trapezoidal window. AB represents the rectangular window set at an angle of 16½° to the line of sight EF ten feet from the viewing point E. A′B′ represents the trapezoidal window which is a projection from E of the rectangular window and its mullions on a place CD tipped 22° to the line of sight EF.*

aluminum cutout of the projection of the window AB on the plane CD.

The projections of the shadows cast on the actual window by an overhead light are painted on both sides of this trapezoidal cutout. The trapezoidal window should be equally illuminated on both sides with low illumination in an otherwise dark room.

The alterations in visual phenomena that are related to the variation of the trapezoidal form of a window are empirically demonstrated by the differences between what observers with normal vision see when looking at the rotating rectangular window with its small cube and tube and when looking at the rotating trapezoidal window with its small cube and tube.

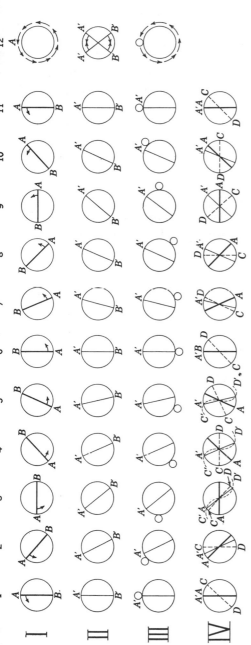

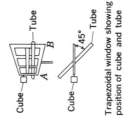

Chart I—*Rotating Trapezoidal Window:*
Explanation of Figures

Row   I Shows by the heavy solid lines a series of the actual positions of the window (A-B) as it is rotated in the direction indicated by arrows about a vertical axis through a full revolution, the last figure in the row showing the complete rotation.

Row II Shows by the light solid lines the perceived apparent localization of the window at each of the positions shown in row I, the last figure in the row showing the apparent oscillating movement.

Row III Shows by the small circles the apparent positioning and motion of the cube which corresponds to the actual movement of the end of the window (A) to which it is attached (see last figure in the row), the light solid lines showing the apparent positions of the window (A-B).

Row IV Shows the apparent positions and distortions of the tube as the window is revolved. The heavy solid lines show the actual positions of the window. The straight short dashed lines show the actual positions of the tube. The light solid lines show its apparent positions. The curved short dashed lines (see figures 3, 4, and 5) show the distortions of the tube in that phase of the rotation of the window.

Trapezoidal window showing position of cube and tube

DESCRIPTION OF WHAT OBSERVERS EXPERIENCE WHEN LOOKING AT THE ROTATING TRAPEZOIDAL WINDOW AND APPENDED CUBE AND TUBE

THE READER MUST realize that the phenomena disclosed by the demonstration can be comprehended only when they are personally experienced and that the following verbal and pictorial description of them can at best be only a secondhand communication. Moreover, the full significance of these phenomena can only be comprehended as they are related to other phenomena disclosed by the other demonstrations. However, described in general terms, all observers with normal vision, when looking at the rectangular window slowly rotating about a vertical axis, see a rectangular window of constant size and form at a constant distance rotating about a vertical axis and the small cube and tube appearing and moving with it in an expected manner, and this holds true irrespective of the distance or direction of elevation from which they look or whether they use one eye or two.

On the other hand, described in general terms, observers with normal vision, when looking (with both eyes from a distance of around 25 feet or with one eye from nearer distances) at a trapezoidal window slowly rotating about a vertical axis, see a rectangular window of constantly changing size and form oscillating at a continually varying speed through only a sector of a complete circle of revolution. They see the small cube sailing around the trapezoidal window and the tube bending at certain positions of revolution of the window. [2] However, these appearances are altered if the observer varies the distance, the direction, or the elevation from which he looks, and if he uses both eyes instead of one at near distance.

Detailed descriptions of the various appearances of the rotating trapezoidal window will be taken up now.

(1) *Description of apparent movements in both direction and speed of the rotating trapezoidal window without the cube or tube observed from a distance of about 10 feet with one eye at the level of the middle of the trapezoidal window.*

As the trapezoidal window slowly rotates about a vertical axis, instead

---

[2] The above appearances are perhaps those most commonly experienced by most observers and, for purposes of communication, it will be those appearances that will be dwelt upon. However, not only are different appearances reported by different individuals, but the appearances reported by any one individual can be altered by varying either "subjective" or "objective" factors. F. P. Kilpatrick has been investigating these phenomena and his findings are reported in Chapter 14.

of appearing to rotate completely around, it appears to oscillate back and forth through an angle of about 100°. An understanding of the nature of this movement may be obtained from a study of Chart I, "Rotating Trapezoidal Window." In the lower left-hand corner of the chart is a drawing in elevation of the trapezoidal window, the shorter side being designated by the letter A and the longer side by the letter B. In the four rows of figures in the chart, the letters A and B and the heavy solid lines show a series of the actual positions of the short and long sides of the trapezoidal window AB as it is rotated in the direction indicated by arrows about a vertical axis through a full revolution, the last figure in the row showing the complete rotation. The letters A′ and B′ and the light solid lines show the apparent position of the short and long sides of the trapezoidal window. The top row of figures shows by the heavy solid lines marked AB a series of the actual positions of the window (AB). The second row (II) shows by the light solid lines marked A′B′ the apparent localization of the window at each of the positions shown in row I, the last figure in the row showing the apparent oscillating movement.

By comparing the apparent positions shown in row II with the actual positions shown in row I, it can be seen that, as the window rotates in a counterclockwise direction, it appears to move in the same direction as it is actually moving, but lags behind, appearing to move more slowly. When the window has rotated 90° (see third figure in row I), it appears to have rotated only about 50° (see A′B′, third figure, row II). As the window rotates farther than 90° it appears very slowly to reverse its direction of rotation (see fourth figures in both rows I and II). From then on it appears to rotate in a reverse direction to its actual rotation until the window reaches a position normal to the line of sight (see ninth figures in rows I and II). From then on it appears to move in the direction of the actual rotation until it reaches its starting position (compare first and eleventh figures in both rows I and II).

The region of the apparent oscillating movement is shown in the last figure in row II. The short side of the trapezoid appears to move from A′ to A′ and the long side from B′ to B′. No part of the window ever appears to enter into the areas included between A′B′ and A′B′. The angle of apparent oscillation with the particular trapezoidal form used is about 100°. The point of actual rotation where the apparent rotation starts to reverse is when the window is normal to the line of sight and thus subtends the largest visual angle.

The apparent speed of movement varies greatly from the actual speed. As the window approaches a position normal to the line of sight, it appears to slow up gradually, come to dead stop and remain stopped for an appreciable length of time, and then slowly to reverse its direction of movement.

(2) *Description of apparent alterations of shape and size of trapezoidal window when observed with one eye from a distance of about 10 feet, eye at the same level as middle of window.*

As the trapezoidal window slowly rotates about a vertical axis, it appears as a rectangular window,[3] but it appears to be continually changing in both shape and size. These alterations are made very apparent by comparing them to the shape and size of the rectangular window just above, which remains constant. This comparison can best be made when the trapezoidal window is positioned on its supporting rod so that it is at an angle of about 38° to the rectangular window above it. When the two windows are turned so the observer's line of sight makes an angle of about 16° to the rectangular window (see Figure 4) with the shorter side of the trapezoidal window A toward the observer, the trapezoidal window appears to be in the same plane and of the same shape and size as the rectangular window as is shown in the photograph in Figure 5.

On the other hand, when the two windows are turned so the trapezoidal window is positioned so that it subtends a slightly smaller angle, although it appears in the same plane as the rectangular window, it appears much shorter and gives the impression of being smaller, as is shown in the photograph in Figure 6. When the two windows are turned so that the trapezoidal window is approximately positioned as shown in the second figure of row I of the chart, it again appears much longer than the rectangular window and gives the impression of being larger, as is shown in the photograph in Figure 7. In intermediate positions of rotation, the trapezoidal window appears of intermediate shapes and sizes.

(3) *Description of apparent alteration of distance of trapezoidal window when observed with one eye from a distance of about 10 feet, eye at same level as middle of window.*

As the two windows are observed as they slowly rotate, it is noticeable that, when the trapezoidal window appears longer and larger, it also appears nearer. However, this appearance is equivocal and seems to be counteracted by conflicting indications, such as those from the supporting rod and the rectangular window.

To test what would be observed free from other possible conflicting

[3] This is more definitely the case when the trapezoidal window is seen alone. When the rectangular window just above it is seen at the same time, although the trapezoidal window is still seen as rectangular, one is bothered by the nonparallelism of the bottom of the rectangular window and the top of the trapezoidal window.

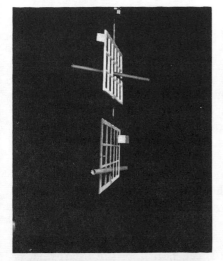

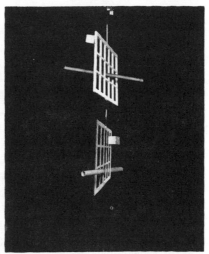

Photographs of rectangular window (above) and trapezoidal window (below), showing differences of shape and size of trapezoidal window at different positions of its rotation.

FIG. 5. *When in this position the trapezoid appears approximately the same shape and size as the rectangular window.*

FIG. 6 *(right). In this position it appears shorter than the rectangle.*

FIG. 7. *In this position it appears longer and larger.*

indications, the trapezoidal window was set up in a dark room, so that its image reflected from a half-silvered mirror could be seen uniocularly directly in front of the observer in a field in which there was a series of posts that were binocularly seen, by which the observer could judge the apparent distance of the uniocularly seen trapezoidal window. The window first was set so that it appeared longer and larger, and then so that it appeared shorter and smaller. Only preliminary observations were made, but for two observers it appeared nearer when it appeared longer and larger and farther away when it appeared shorter and smaller than the rectangular window.

(4) *Description of the apparent movement and changes in shape and size of the trapezoidal window when viewed from a distance of about 10 feet with one eye from levels above or below the middle of the trapezoidal window.*

Whether viewed from above or below the level of the middle of the trapezoidal window, the window appears to oscillate and change speed and shape and size, just as it appears to do when viewed with the eyes at the level of the middle of the window. However, instead of appearing rectangular as it revolves, it appears in trapezium form, the amount of distortion being related to the angular distance of the viewing point above or below. Its vertical axis also appears to oscillate back and forth. And further, in certain positions of revolution, it appears somewhat curved.

(5) *Description of the apparent movement and alterations in shape and size of the trapezoidal window when observed with two eyes from a distance of about 10 feet and from greater distances.*

If, at a near distance of around 10 feet, both eyes are used, what is perceived is a variable mixture of the above-described appearances and the appearances of an actual trapezoidal window rotating in the same way and at the same rates of speed as the rectangular window above it.[4]

When the observer, using both eyes, moves back from the windows to a distance of around 15 feet (the exact distance varying with the observer), the appearance of the trapezoidal window becomes less a mixture and more like what is observed monocularly. If the viewing distance is increased to around 20 or 25 feet (varying with the observer), the appearances of the trapezoidal window are almost the same as those experienced when it is viewed with one eye from a near distance.

Everything that has been said above holds true, irrespective of the elevation of the observer's eye or eyes, and irrespective of his lateral position relative to the trapezoidal window. However, when his eyes are above or below, other second-order variations also are perceived.

(6) *Description of apparent movement of small cube attached to the upper part of the short side of the rotating trapezoidal window when observed with one eye from a distance of about 10 feet, eye at same height as middle of window.*

As the trapezoidal window slowly rotates from its position as shown in figure 1, row I, of Chart I, the cube, which is attached by a wire, as shown in the drawing in the lower left-hand corner of the chart, appears to leave its point of attachment and float through the air around the front of the window, returning to its original attached position just before the trapezoidal window reaches its position as shown in figure 11, row

---

[4] One observer who had a markedly dominant eye and very poor stereoscopic vision got the same appearance with two eyes as he did with one from a near-viewing point.

I, Chart I. The apparent position of the cube relative to the apparent position of the rotating trapezoidal window is shown by the figures in row III of the chart. Throughout its course, in which it rotates once about its own vertical axis, the cube appears of relatively constant size and appears to be going at a relatively constant rate of speed.

(7) *Description of the apparent movement and distortion of the tube which is suspended through the lower middle pane of the trapezoidal window, when observed with one eye from a distance of about 10 feet, eye at the same height as the middle of the window.*

The tube is suspended, tipped at an angle of about 45° to the plane of the window, as shown in the drawing in the lower left-hand corner of Chart I. The appearances to be described can be seen with the tube at any inclination to the window, but are possibly more marked when it is at the inclination shown in the drawing.

As the trapezoidal window slowly rotates from its position as shown by the heavy solid line A in figure 1, row IV, of the chart, the tube shown by the dotted line CD appears to swing around with the trapezoidal window until the window starts to reverse its direction of rotation. When this occurs, the tube and the window appear to be rotating in opposite directions, the left side of the tube swinging toward the observer and the left-hand side of the window away from the observer. The tube then appears to swing until the left side of the tube comes up against the mullions on the left of the window and the right side of the tube comes up against the mullions on the right of the window. Up to that position the tube appears straight, but from there on, for many observers, it appears to begin to bend (see dotted lines marked C'D' in figure 3, row IV, of chart) and seems to bend more and more (see dotted lines C'D' in figures 4 and 5, row IV). When the trapezoidal window gets in the position shown in figure 6, row IV (chart), the tube suddenly snaps straight again and, for most observers, remains straight during the remaining positions of revolution shown in figures 7, 8, and 9 of row IV in Chart I.[5] The rate of movement of the tube also appears to change, as does its apparent length.

If the tube is set at right angles to the plane of the window instead of at an angle of 45°, it appears to bend and straighten out through the same sections of its rotation above described, although it starts to bend a little later and doesn't appear to bend quite so much. If the direction of rotation of the window is reversed, to many observers the tube appears bent in that section of its revolution where it appeared straight when it was revolving in its original direction and straight in that section where it appeared bent.

When both eyes are used at a near distance, variations in the appear-

[5] There are a number of variations of these appearances (cf. Chapter 14).

ances of the cube or tube are observable. These variations are related to variations in the appearances of the window. When both eyes are used at distances of around 20 to 25 feet, about the same appearances are observable as were seen at near distance with one eye.

When the window is looked at with the eye or eyes at a level slightly above or below the middle of the trapezoidal window, appearances similar to those described above are observed, but they become markedly different as the distance of observation above and below is greatly increased.

The observer sees all the above-described appearances when he looks at the trapezoidal window with the appended tube and cube. If he looks at the rectangular window with its tube and cube, the appearances are quite different. The rectangular window appears constant in form and size and movement; its cube appears at a constant relative position; its tube appears at a constant relative position, and shape and size; and none of these aspects changes when two eyes are used or when point of view changes in direction or in level. Of course, the subjective sense of the positioning of the window and its distance alters with its rotation and with the change of the point of view in either distance or direction or level.

(8) *Description of apparent movements and alterations in shape and size of the trapezoidal window and of the cube and tube when viewed from different distances and different directions.*

With variation of the distance of observation, the only marked alteration of all the above-described appearances is in respect to the apparent changes in size of the trapezoidal window. At greater viewing distances, the apparent alterations in size of the rotating trapezoidal window are greater.

With variation of the observer's tangential point of view, there is no alteration of the above-described appearances. That is, irrespective of the direction from which he looks, he will see the same oscillation, changes in shape and size of the trapezoidal window, movement of small cube, and bending of tube.

Although a given observer, looking at the rotating trapezoidal window from different tangential points of view, will perceive certain definite phenomenal happenings (i.e., the oscillating window, the flying cube and bending tube), it is important to note that the visual happening he sees from a particular viewpoint at a particular moment he would *not see* at that same moment if he were at another point of view. What he sees can be seen only at one particular moment from one particular point of view.

This also holds if the trapezoidal window is stationary and the observer is looking at it as he walks around it. As he walks around it he will see all the phenomenal happenings he would see if he stood still and the window rotated. But the visual experiences he sees from one point of view can be seen only from that point of view. No other observer walking around with him can see what he sees at the same moment when he sees it. So a number of observers standing around the rotating trapezoidal window at the same distance from its axis will all perceive the same visual happenings occurring, but *no two* of the observers will see the same visual happenings occurring at the same moment.

While it is clear that what each observer sees is determined by his viewpoint in both space and time, there are certain aspects of what each observer sees that are the same from any point of view at all times and for all other observers at other points of view and at other times. For example, the rectangular appearance of the trapezoidal window and the form and size of its small cube remain constant for all observers from all points of view at all times.

When the rectangular window is viewed from different distances and different directions, quite different phenomena occur. Irrespective of the distance or direction from which the rectangular window is looked at, the visual happenings an observer sees from a particular viewpoint at a particular moment he would see at the same moment if he were at another point of view. In other words, he would see a rectangular window of the same shape and size rotating at a constant rate of speed with the small cube in a constant relation to it and a tube of constant shape and length moving at a constant speed at the same moment, irrespective of his point of view. A number of observers standing around the rotating rectangular window, irrespective of their distance, would perceive the same visual happenings occurring, *and all* the observers would see the same visual happenings occurring at the same moment.

This concludes our attempt to communicate to the reader what he would have visually experienced if he himself had witnessed the demonstration. In the next chapter we will attempt to explain why one sees what he sees when looking at the rotating trapezoidal window, and why what he sees is so different from what he sees when he looks at the rotating rectangular window just above it. It is the same type of explanation that was formulated to account for the phenomena disclosed by the earlier, simpler demonstrations of the perception of the static aspects of the environment and of motion, and it seems adequately to account for the more complex phenomena described above. We have no illusion, however, that this account is the final word in the matter, but we present it because it seems to us the most intrinsically reasonable one that we can formulate at this time. Our hope is that its presentation will lead others to formulate still more intrinsically reasonable accounts.

13

The Rotating Trapezoid (Cont): Explanation of Phenomena

Adelbert Ames, Jr.

EXPLANATION OF THE VARIATIONS IN APPEARANCE OF THE TRAPEZODIAL WINDOW

THE APPEARANCES OF the trapezoidal window give rise to many questions, among them the following:

(a) Why does the trapezoidal window appear rectangular in shape?

(b) Why does the rotating trapezoidal window appear to oscillate instead of rotate? Why does the trapezoidal window never appear to be where it actually is?

(c) Why does the trapezoidal window, which is moving at a constant rate of speed, appear to be moving at different rates of speed?

(d) Why does the trapezoidal window, which is constant in shape, appear of changing shapes?

(e) Why does the trapezoidal window, which is constant in size, appear to be of changing size?

(f) Why does the trapezoidal window appear rectangular when the eye or eyes are at the level of the middle of the window, but of trapezium form and sometimes curved when the eye or eyes are at other levels?

(g) Why, when viewed with both eyes from a distance of around 24 feet (which is well within the distance at which stereoscopic vision is effective), does the trapezoidal window appear essentially the same as it appears with one eye?

It would seem apparent that there is no possibility of accounting for these appearances in causal terms of interactional effects between the objective phenomena and subjective appearances. The so-called "objective factor" that is varied is the shape of a window; i.e., making one side of a rectangular window longer and the other shorter. Among the many subjective appearances related to this variation is an alteration of the appearance of length and size. It in no way helps us to account for the apparent change of length and size to say that it was caused by change in the trapezoidal form of the "object." The obscurities that give rise to the above questions can be cleared up only by taking into account more particulars; i.e., other phenomenal processes that play a role in the situation, and understanding the nature of their relationships. This we will attempt to do.

In what has been said so far mention has been made of only two aspects of the situation: one, the characteristics of what the observer looks at, i.e., the so-called "objective" revolving trapezoidal window; the other, what the observer visually perceives. It is well known that there are many other phenomenal processes involved in every visual situation, among which is the physiological stimulus pattern, which plays the role of relating the "objective" window and its subjective visual awareness.

As an aid in helping the reader understand the role played by the observer's physiological stimulus processes, we will introduce the use of a large artificial eye consisting of a lens, corresponding to the dioptric system of the eye, and a ground glass which is marked off in rectangular squares, corresponding to the retina. If this is set up pointing toward the trapezoidal window, the observer can see on the ground glass stimulus patterns of the same characteristics that exist on his retina when he looks at the trapezoidal window. If this artificial eye is set up at the same level as the middle of the trapezoidal window, he will note as the window revolves:

(a) that the image on the ground glass goes through a series of varying trapezoidal forms;

(b) that the pattern on the ground glass is never rectangular;

(c) that there is no change in speed or oscillation of the trapezoidal pattern corresponding to the apparent change in speed or oscillation of the trapezoidal window;

(d) that there is no change in form or size of the trapezoidal pattern corresponding to the apparent change in form and size of the trapezoidal window.

It is apparent that a knowledge of the characteristics of these stimulus patterns in themselves does not help us in understanding why the observer sees what he does when he looks at the rotating trapezoidal window.

Let us, then, try to see if a knowledge of the characteristics of a stimulus pattern will help us in understanding what we see when we look at the rectangular window by pointing the artificial eye at the rectangular window and noting the characteristics of the images formed on the ground-glass retina by the rectangular window. It will be noted that these images have the same general characteristics as the images of the trapezoidal window, although the appearances of the rectangular window are different from those of the trapezoidal window, as has been pointed out. It is evident that a knowledge of the object viewed and our perceptual awarenesses alone do not suffice to provide us with an answer to our questions.

Where shall we turn? Apparently, a question we can ask gives us a lead; namely, "Why, when we look at the rectangular window, do we see a rectangular window, when the characteristics of its images formed on our retina are trapezoidal?" This question has extra significance, because when we look at the trapezoidal window we also see it as rectangular, which means that the perceived rectangular form does not come from either the stimulus pattern or the object. If it doesn't come from the stimulus pattern or the object, from where does it come? This same question has occurred with all our previous demonstrations. In each case the most profitable and reasonable answer lay in bringing into consideration the past experience of the observer, and that consideration appears to be equally reasonable and profitable in this instance.

In his past experience the observer, in carrying out his purposes, has on innumerable occasions had to take into account and act in respect to rectangular forms; e.g., going through doors, locating windows, etc., etc. In almost all such occasions, except in the rare case when his line of sight was normal to the door or window, the image of the rectangular configuration formed on his retina was trapezoidal. He learned to interpret the particularly characterized retinal images that exist when he looks at doors, windows, etc., into rectangular forms. Moreover, he learned to interpret the particular degree of trapezoidal distortion of his retinal images in terms of the positioning of the rectangular form to his particular viewing point. These interpretations do not occur at the conscious level; rather, they are unconscious and may be characterized as *assumptions* as to the probable significance of indications received from the environment. A person's perception thus provides him with an awareness not only of the form of the "thing" he is looking at, i.e., "what it is," but also "where it is" relative to his viewing point (1, 2, 6, 8, 9, 11, 12).

Let us now take into account past experience in explaining what the observer sees when he is looking at the revolving rectangular window. Suppose the rectangular window is in an edge-on position when it starts to revolve. When it has turned a little, the image formed by its farther side will be shorter than that formed by its nearer side. The retinal image will be trapezoidal, the particular difference in length of its sides being determined by the length of the window and the observer's distance from it. As the window revolves, the lengths of the two sides will become more and more nearly the same until the window is normal to his line of sight, when they will be equal. Then the side which was the far side will become longer and reach its greatest relative length when at its nearest to the observer; i.e., when the window is in an edge-on position. As the window turns farther, the image of the now nearer side will decrease and the image of the farther side increase until the completion of the revolution. The observer interprets these changes in trapezoidal form as changes of position and interprets the continuing changes of position as a rotation of a rectangular window.

It would seem that the above begins to provide a basis for understanding why an observer sees what he does when he looks at the rotating trapezoidal window. Suppose the trapezoidal window starts rotating from the position shown in figure 1, row I, Chart I (Chapter 12), when its shorter side A (see chart) is farther away and the longer side B nearer. When it has turned a little (see figure 2, row II, Chart I), the image formed by the farther side A will be shorter than that formed by its nearer side B. This difference in length is greater than the difference in length of the images of the far and near sides of the rectangular window above it. As it revolves, the image formed by the far side A will increase in length and that of the near side B decrease. But their relative change will not be as great as that of the images of a rectangular window at the same inclination. So the trapezoidal window will not appear to rotate so far or fast as the rectangular window above it, which is moving at a constant speed. When the trapezoidal window has rotated in a position normal to the line of sight, with the short side A to the left (see figure 3, row I, Chart I), the image of its side A will still be shorter than the image of its side B, so it appears tipped back on the left in the position shown in figure 3, row II, Chart I. This is as far forward as the short side ever appears to come. With further rotation the vertical dimension of the image of the side A will increase in length and that of the side B decrease. But the image of the short side A of the trapezoidal window can never become longer than that of the long side B, so it can never be seen as nearer. (Cf. the "line" and "balloon" demonstrations in Chapter 2.) However, this could not explain why the trapezoidal window appears to reverse its direction.

The explanation of the reversing phenomenon is apparently as follows: As the trapezoidal window starts to rotate from the position shown in figure 3, row I, Chart I, to those shown in figures 5 and 6, row I, Chart I, the total horizontal angle that the trapezoidal window subtends to the eye decreases. At the beginning of this decrease the trapezoidal window appears tipped back on the left (see figure 3, row II, Chart I). It has been learned from past experience with rectangular forms that a decrease of the total horizontal angle of our retinal images of a rectangularly perceived form which appears tipped away from us on the left could only take place if the side on the left went farther away. If it came nearer, the total horizontal angle of our retinal images would have to increase. So we interpret this decrease in the total horizontal dimension of our retinal stimulus pattern as a going away of the left side of the window. That is, the window appears to reverse its direction of rotation and, as the left side of the window keeps coming toward us (see figures 3 and 4, row I, Chart I), it appears to be going farther away (see figures 3 and 4, row II, Chart I). A similar apparent reversal is seen to take place when the trapezoidal window has revolved to a position where the short side A is to the right (see figure 9, row I, Chart I). It is due to these apparent reversals that the trapezoidal window appears to oscillate instead of rotate.

The above considerations seem to furnish a reasonable explanation as to

(a) why the rotating trapezoidal window appears rectangular in shape;

(b) why it apears to oscillate instead of rotate;

(c) why it appears to move at varying rates.[1]

But we have not yet answered the question as to why the trapezoidal window appears to change in form and size. A reasonable answer to these questions seems to be based on our making use of variations in

[1] These alterations of motion related to unaccustomed variations of the trapezoidal characteristics of the stimulus pattern are very similar to phenomena revealed by the "radial motion" demonstration, Chapter 3.

the trapezoidal characteristics of our stimulus pattern as indications to positioning of a rectangular configuration. When looking at the rotating rectangular window, the varying trapezoidal stimulus patterns have particular characteristics which give us indications of the position of the window in its rotation. For instance, when looking at the rectangular window tipped at an angle of 45° to our line of sight, the trapezoidal pattern formed on our retina will be the same shape, whether the right side or the left side of the window is nearer us, and we will relate the two patterns to rectangular configurations of the same size and shape but at different inclinations.

But when we look at the trapezoidal window what happens is quite different. When the trapezoidal window is tipped 45° to our line of sight with the longer side B nearer us (see figure 2, row I, Chart I), the shape of the trapezoidal image formed on our retina is quite different from that formed when the shorter side A is nearer us (see figure 6, row I, chart). When the longer side A is nearer there is a greater difference in the relative lengths of the sides of the trapezoid, which could only be produced either by a rectangular window of the same height at a nearer distance or by a longer rectangular window at the same distance. When the shorter side B is nearer us there is a less difference in the relative lengths of the sides of the trapezoid, which could only be produced either by a rectangular window of the same length at a greater distance or by a shorter rectangular window at the same distance.

Since there are a number of indications that the distance of the window remains constant as it rotates, we translate the difference in the trapezoidal pattern on our retinas into differences in perceived length so that when it is rotating it appears to be continually changing shape. When the indications of distance are eliminated, as was done in the preliminary experiment noted previously, we see the trapezoidal window as nearer when the longer side B is nearer, and farther away when the shorter side A is nearer (8). These considerations seem to furnish a reasonable explanation of why the rotating trapezoidal window appears to change shape (question d) and size (question e).

We will now turn to question (f): "Why does the trapezoidal window appear rectangular when the eye or eyes are at the level of the middle of the window, but of trapezium form and sometimes curved when the eye or eyes are at other levels?"

The answer to this question is apparently the following: When our eyes are the level of middle of the trapezoidal window, the trapezoidal patterns on our retinas are identical to those that could be produced by some rectangular window at some inclination at some distance. When they are above or below, our stimulus patterns for the trapezoidal window are not trapezoids but trapeziums which, although similar to, are different from the trapezium patterns that exist on our retinas when we look at a rectangular window from above or below.

A conclusive explanation of these appearances will be possible only when, by a mathematical analysis (projective geometry), it has been determined just how the two types of trapezium patterns differ. But it seems probable that the trapezium patterns from the trapezoidal window are sufficiently similar to those from the rectangular window, so that we try to translate them into rectangular configurations even to the extent of seeing the window as curved. The apparent forward and back tipping of the trapezoidal window about a horizontal axis may be explained on the basis that the trapezium patterns are similar to those that would be produced by a rectangular window tipped about a horizontal axis.[2]

This brings us to the less significant question (g) as to why the trapezoidal window appears essentially the same when we use two eyes within distances at which stereoscopic vision is effective. The apparent answer to this question is that in this situation we suppress the binocular cues and take account of the uniocular ones. We do this because the latter result in perceptions which square better with what we have learned in past experience in dealing with windows; in other words, the uniocular cues have, on the basis of past experience, greater prognostic reliability than do the binocular ones. This is confirmed by a number of our other demonstrations. It might also be well to note here that parallax indications of distances, achieved by lateral movement of the head, do give rise to secondary alterations in the appearances of the trapezoidal window. They, however, do not aid one in seeing the trapezoidal window *as* a trapezoid rotating at a constant speed.

Explanation of the Appearance of the Small Cube

The reason for using the small cube and the tube in connection with rotating trapezoidal window demonstration was to determine if and how the appearance and behavior of objects would appear to be altered when "put together" in different ways with an objective configuration whose

---

[2] In the apparatus as constructed the objective factor that is varied is the trapezoidal form. The phenomena just described make it apparent that different and interesting alterations of perception would be experienced if the window were actually made in a trapezium form. Presumably, if such a form were observed with the eye or eyes at the level of the middle of the window, its appearance would be similar to those experienced when the trapezoidal window is observed with the eye or eyes above or below the level of the window, and more exaggerated appearances would be experienced if such a window were observed from other levels. [This was verified by Kilpatrick in 1952, and is shown in the motion picture designated by item 123 of the bibliography, Appendix B. Ed.]

form was varied so that its appearance was altered. The appearances of the cube give rise to at least the following questions:

(a) Why does it appear to rotate in a circular path quite independently of the trapezoidal window to which it is attached?

(b) Why does it appear to move at a relatively constant rate when the window to which it is attached appears to oscillate at varying speeds?

(c) How is it possible for it to appear separated from the trapezoidal window to which it is attached?

An answer to the first question, which may come quickly to one's mind, is that we see the window move as it does because of the reasons given in the previous chapter, and we see the small cube rotate in a circle at a relatively constant speed because that is how it is actually moving. But this answer is not quite satisfactory, because our previous analysis has made it evident that the appearances we see are not determined by what we are looking at but by our interpretation of our stimulus patterns.

Perhaps a better answer for why the small cube appears as it does and seems to move as it does can be derived from the following considerations: To understand the appearance and movement of the trapezoidal window, it was necessary first to understand that we saw the rectangular window appear and move as it did, because we assumed it was rectangular and made use of the varying trapezoidal characteristics of our retinal images as indications of its varying positions. Our perceptions of the movement of the small cube have a similar origin and nature. Owing to the characteristics of our retinal image produced by light rays reflected from the small cube, we assume its size and other characteristics (3). In its rotation, as the cube comes toward us, its retinal image increases, and we assume it is coming nearer to us; as it goes away from us its retinal image becomes smaller and we assume it is going away. The variations in the sizes of the retinal images and the rate of their movement across our retina, although not uniform or constant in time, are nevertheless so translated, and the cube appears to be moving in a circular path at a relatively constant speed.[3]

Let us now consider the question as to how it is possible for the small cube to appear to separate itself from the trapezoidal window to which it is attached. What has been said above explains why, if the cube were not attached to the window (i.e., if the cube were just above the window), we would see them following separate paths. That the cube does

[3] Why we see objects move in a circular path at a constant speed is discussed in the "circular motion" demonstration, Chapter 3.

appear to separate itself from the trapezoidal window to which it is most evidently attached can only be explained on the basis that the indications causing the trapezoidal window to appear to move as it does and the cube to move as it does are accepted as definite and unequivocal, and cues indicating otherwise are suppressed.

Various three-dimensional objects were substituted for the cube and were attached in different ways. They all appeared to behave in the same manner. However, two-dimensional objects, such as playing cards and small sheets of paper, when attached to the upper side of the shorter end of the trapezoidal window, may or may not appear to move with the window, depending on how they are attached.[4]

Explanation of the Appearance of the Tube

The appearances of the tube give rise to at least the following questions:

(a) Why does it appear to rotate quite independently of the trapezoidal window to which it is attached?

(b) Why does it appear to move at varying speeds and at speeds different from that of the trapezoidal window?

(c) Why does it appear to bend and change length?

The answer to the question (a) has already been covered by the explanations as to why the cube appears to rotate in a circular path quite independently of the trapezoidal window to which it is attached.

The answer to the question (b) appears to be that the tube seems to move at varying speeds (which the cube did not) because it is seen "together" with the window in a way that causes the observer to take account of its motion in relation to the apparent motion of the trapezoidal window.

The answer to the question "Why does the tube appear to bend and change length?" involves the necessity of taking into account the phenomenon of overlay. Overlay is one of the numerous indications which we take into account in formulating our presumptions as to the distances of objects. If an object is so positioned that it overlays or cuts off part of another object, we presume that it is nearer and that the other object is farther away. As has been demonstrated (Chapter 2), because of its high prognostic reliability, great weight is given this indication relative to the weight given other distance indications, such as brightness, size, and parallax. With the rotating trapezoidal window and tube, this phenomenon of overlay comes into play.

As the window rotates we see the left half of the window overlaying

---

[4] Alterations of appearances related to some variations in method of attachment of objects have been investigated by Kilpatrick and are reported in (10) and in Chapter 14.

the left part of the tube, and therefore in front of the tube, and the right part of the tube overlaying the right half of the window, and therefore in front of the window. As described, the tube and the window appear to be rotating about the same axis in opposite directions. When their paths cross, the observer has to make an interpretation of the happenings that are occurring to the characteristics of his retinal stimulus pattern. There are various possible interpretations he could make. He might keep the tube straight and whole and the window straight and whole, but then we would have to stop their motion; or he might ignore his overlay indications and see gaps in the mullions of the window to let the tube pass through; or he might see the window bend. If he keeps the window and tube in motion and the window flat and whole, i.e., without gaps in it, he has to see the tube bend.[5] It is this last interpretation that is most commonly made with the particular configuration, and this is what most observers see. With this interpretation one also sees the tube increase in length when it bends because, presumably, only a longer tube could fill the length of space which the apparently bent tube fills.

All of this raises the question as to just why more weight is given to certain indications than to others or why we insist on holding to certain presumptive aspects and giving up others. Apparently, the answer is that we give weight to indications on the basis of their prognostic reliability.

Some preliminary observations were made after replacing the tube with a box (a cigarette carton) with printing on it. With this setup the appearances changed. The box did not appear to bend as the tube does or appeared to do so only very slightly; however, the window was still seen in reverse of its actual position. This apparently means that the overlay indications were given no weight, or the window would be seen in its actual position. This line of investigation should be carried further.

There remains to explain why, when the tube is set at right angles to the plane of the window, it appears bent during a certain portion of its rotation when the window is rotating in one direction, but does not appear bent during the same portion of rotation when the window is rotating in the opposite direction. The only explanation that comes to mind is that we will accept the appearance of bending when it takes place gradually, but will not accept seeing a straight tube suddenly bend. Observations have been made on this phenomenon, and they could be further checked. But if it is confirmed, it is an important disclosure and should be investigated.

[5] This phenomenon, i.e., the bending of the tube related to the apparent positionings of the trapezoidal window related to unaccustomed variations of the trapezoidal characteristics of the stimulus pattern, is very similar to the phenomenon described in the "tangential motion" demonstration, Chapter 3.

Summary

Before going on to consider further questions raised by the trapezoidal window, the material presented will be briefly summarized. The presentation up to now has been an attempt (1) to describe to the reader the aspects of his visual experiences that would be altered when observing a rotating window whose trapezoidal form had been varied and (2) to offer what appears to be a reasonable explanation of why these alterations in appearance are experienced.

The accompanying table (Table I) may be helpful in making clear just what aspects of the observer's visual perception are not altered (remain constant) and what aspects are altered.

Briefly stated, the explanation as to why the altered aspects appear altered involves the taking into account of the characteristics of the stimulus patterns, which are essentially cryptogrammic in nature, their translation in terms of the assumptions from past experience, the hypothesis that perceptions are not disclosures but essentially prognostic in nature; i.e., prognostic directives for action from the observer's point of view, in both space and time.

CONSIDERATION OF FURTHER QUESTIONS RAISED BY THE DISCLOSURES

COMMON AND UNIQUE ASPECTS OF PERCEPTION. An important additional question raised by the appearances of the trapezoidal window is: "Why do perceptions of many aspects of the trapezoidal window differ at any one time between individuals with different points of view, or at different times for the same individual from the same point of view, while the perceptions of the same aspects of the rectangular window do not differ under these conditions?" The answer apparently lies in the assumptions brought to each of these occasions by the observer.

When an observer who has had long past experience with rectangular configurations looks at the rectangular window he assumes that what he sees is a rectangular configuration of a specific size and shape at a specific distance, due to the specific characteristics of his stimulus pattern, irrespective of the particular nature of its trapezoidal characteristics. At the same time he takes account of the trapezoidal characteristics of his stimulus pattern and translates them into a specific inclination of the rectangular configuration relative to his particular spatial point of view. As the rectangular window rotates and the trapezoidal characteristics of his stimulus patterns vary, he interprets each such variation as an alteration of its inclination. Hence, he will see an assumed rectangular

TABLE I

CONSTANCY AND ALTERATION OF ASPECTS OF VISUAL
PERCEPTION EXPERIENCED BY ONE OBSERVER WHEN
LOOKING FROM ONE POINT OF VIEW AT:

RECTANGULAR WINDOW CUBE AND TUBE		TRAPEZOIDAL WINDOW CUBE AND TUBE FROM LEVEL OF WINDOW		TRAPEZOIDAL WINDOW CUBE AND TUBE FROM ABOVE OR BELOW LEVEL OF WINDOW	
CONSTANT	ALTERING	CONSTANT	ALTERING	CONSTANT	ALTERING
"Windowness"*		"Windowness"		"Windowness"	
	Inclination		Inclination		Inclination
Rectangularity		Rectangularity			Rectangularity
Size			Size		Size
Shape			Shape		Shape
Motion			Motion		Motion
Direction**		Direction		Direction	
Distance			Distance***		Distance***

* The word "windowness" is used for the observer's awareness (resulting from his interpretation of certain characteristics of his stimulus pattern) of "something out there" apart from other "things" of the nature of a window.

** "Direction" refers to the subjective sense of the direction of the window from the observer's egocentric center.

*** "Distance" will appear to alter to the degree that absence of conflicting indications permits the observer to interpret change in apparent size as change in apparent distance.

configuration of a specific size and shape at a specific distance rotating about its vertical axis. The observer has also learned from past experience just how the characteristics of these trapezoidal stimulus patterns will vary with every different point of view from which he observes the rectangular window. So, irrespective of his point of view when he looks at the rectangular window, he will see a rectangular configuration of a constant size and shape rotating at a constant speed.

The situation is quite different, as has been pointed out, when an observer, having had long experience with rectangular configurations, looks at the trapezoidal window. In the first place, because of his past experience he interprets the trapezoidal characteristics of the stimulus pattern as rectangular configurations.[6] In the second place, these varying trapezoidal characteristics are different from the varying trapezoidal characteristics that he has associated with any one particular rotating rectangular configuration. In the third place, as shown, *he keeps assuming different rectangular configurations as the trapezoidal window rotates.*

[6] Rectangular configurations are no more sacred than trapezoidal ones and, apart from his past experience, there is no more reason for the observer's assuming the window is a rectangular configuration than a trapezoidal configuration.

As a result, the significances into which he interprets the characteristics of his stimulus patterns are continually changing. They are different from moment to moment. They are also different from every different point of view.

It is believed that these phenomena are important for the light they throw on our understanding of those aspects of visual perception (1) that are similar or dissimilar from different points of view in space and time; (2) that are common; i.e., shared by two or more persons; and (3) that are unique to the individual. In Table II an attempt is made to present in easily comparable form those aspects of an observer's visual perception that would be similar and dissimilar if he could look at the windows from two points of view at the same moment. With the rectangular window, all the aspects except inclination (tipping of the window) and possibly its direction relative to the observer, are the same from any point of view at any time or at a different time. With the trapezoidal window, none of the aspects except "windowness" and rectangularity (if the observer's eyes are at the right level) are the same from a different point of view or at a different time. That is, there are many appearances when looking at the rectangular window that are the same, irrespective of the point of view in space and time which are not the same when looking at the trapezoidal window; or in other words,

TABLE II

Similarity of Aspects of Visual Perception Experienced by One Observer at Any One Moment If He Could Look at the Windows from Different Points of View from the Same Distance

Rectangular Window Cube and Tube		Trapezoidal Window Cube and Tube From Level of Window		Trapezoidal Window Cube and Tube From Above or Below Level of Window	
SIMILAR	DISSIMILAR	SIMILAR	DISSIMILAR	SIMILAR	DISSIMILAR
"Windowness"		"Windowness"		"Windowness"	
Rectangularity		Rectangularity			Rectangularity
	Inclination		Inclination		Inclination
Size			Size		Size
Shape			Shape		Shape
Motion			Motion		Motion
	Direction		Direction		Direction
Distance			Distance*		Distance*

* "Distance" will appear to alter to the degree that absence of conflicting indications permits the observer to interpret change in apparent size as change in apparent distance.

there is a "universality" of appearances of the rectangular window that is completely lacking in the appearances of the trapezoidal window.

It seems possible that the phenomenon referred to by the concept of "universality" is related to, or part of, the phenomenon referred to by the concept "common" between two or more observers (1, 3). This led to the making of Table III, which is an attempt to present in easily comparable form those aspects of two observers' visual perceptions [7] when looking at the windows that would be either common, i.e., shared, or uniquely individual. With the rectangular window, both observers experience the same common aspects of "windowness," rectangularity, size, shape, motion, and distance. To both observers the direction and inclination of the window are personally unique. With the trapezoidal window, the only shared common aspects are "windowness" and rectangularity (if both observers' eye are at the level of the window). Not only the aspects of direction, distance, and inclination relative to the individual points of view of the observers, but also the aspects of size, shape, and motion of the windows are personally unique. Thus, there is a universally common world of appearances of the rectangular window that is completely lacking in the appearances of the trapezoidal window. Maybe the important questions are "Why is this?" and "What is the relation between this phenomenon and the phenomenon of similar and dissimilar appearances for one observer assuming different points of view?"

Moreover, the whole matter becomes more involved when we consider the common and unique aspects of appearances to two observers observing the windows as they rotate throughout one or more revolutions (see Table IV). A study of this table shows that, if what is observed is a periodically repeating phenomenon, the common and uniquely individual aspects of perception (except for direction) are the same for two observers looking at the rectangular window. They are also the same for two observers looking at the trapezoidal window, but for the fact that the common aspects of perception occur at different times. The aspects that the observers see when looking at the different windows are different except for "windowness" and rectangularity. Thus, it would seem that certain aspects of the perception of periodically repeating phenomena and sequences are not related to specific points of view in either space or time.

Further, it would seem that in general every perception is by nature an integration of universals in a "milieu" more inclusive than time and space and unique individual aspects related to the observer's point of view in space and time. The universal aspects can be abstracted and can be common to two or more persons, but the unique individual as-

---

[7] No two observers have the same point of view, because their eye or eyes cannot be in the same place at the same time. A lateral shift of one's eyes of only an inch or two causes a perceptible alteration of the appearance of the trapezoidal window.

pects cannot be abstracted or shared (common), nor can the perception as a whole.

TABLE III

COMMON AND INDIVIDUALLY UNIQUE ASPECTS OF VISUAL PERCEPTION EXPERIENCED AT THE SAME MOMENT FROM THE SAME DISTANCE BY TWO OBSERVERS WITH COMMON ASSUMPTIONS BUT DIFFERENT POINTS OF VIEW

RECTANGULAR WINDOW CUBE AND TUBE FROM ANY TWO POINTS OF VIEW		TRAPEZOIDAL WINDOW CUBE AND TUBE FROM TWO POINTS OF VIEW, BOTH AT LEVEL OF WINDOW		TRAPEZOIDAL WINDOW CUBE AND TUBE FROM TWO POINTS OF VIEW, BOTH ABOVE OR BELOW LEVEL OF WINDOW	
COMMON ASPECTS	UNIQUE ASPECTS	COMMON ASPECTS	UNIQUE ASPECTS	COMMON ASPECTS	UNIQUE ASPECTS
"Windowness" Rectangularity		"Windowness" Rectangularity		"Window- ness"	
	Inclination		Inclination		Inclination
Size			Size		Size
Shape			Shape		Shape
Motion			Motion		Motion
	Direction		Direction		Direction
Distance			Distance*		Distance*

* 'Distance" will appear unique to the degree that the absence of conflicting indications permits observers to interpret unique apparent sizes as unique distances.

This apparently brings up the question, "Why are there more common aspects of appearances with periodically occurring phenomena than with nonperiodically occurring phenomena?" It would appear that any satisfactory answers to these questions can be arrived at only when we have increased our understanding of the origin and nature of our assumptions, both conscious and unconscious, and the processes that are involved in the formulation of our perceptions.

SOME ADDITIONAL CONSIDERATIONS. Another question of importance is "Why are so many significant alterations in appearance related to a variation in the trapezoidal form of a rotating rectangular window, while no comparable alterations of appearances are related to other variations in the form of rectangular windows, such as length?"

It required considerable space to describe and try to explain some of the many significant alterations of appearances related to variation in the trapezoidal form of the window. These alterations of appearances have no "correspondence" to the objective variation and are illusory in nature. The phenomena disclosed apparently throw much light on our understanding of the origin and nature of perception and of our un-

TABLE IV

COMMON AND INDIVIDUALLY UNIQUE ASPECTS OF VISUAL PERCEPTION EX-
PERIENCED FROM THE SAME DISTANCE BY TWO OBSERVERS WITH COMMON
ASSUMPTIONS BUT DIFFERENT POINTS OF VIEW WHEN LOOKING AT THE
WINDOWS THROUGHOUT ONE OR MORE REVOLUTIONS

RECTANGULAR WINDOW CUBE AND TUBE FROM ANY POINT OF VIEW		TRAPEZOIDAL WINDOW CUBE AND TUBE FROM LEVEL OF WINDOW		TRAPEZOIDAL WINDOW CUBE AND TUBE FROM ABOVE OR BELOW LEVEL OF WINDOW	
COMMON ASPECTS	UNIQUE ASPECTS	COMMON ASPECTS	UNIQUE ASPECTS	COMMON ASPECTS	UNIQUE ASPECTS
"Windowness" Rectangularity Inclinations— but at a different time		"Windowness" Rectangularity Inclinations		"Window- ness" Inclinations	
Size Shape Motion		Size Shape Motion—but at a different time		Size Shape Motion— but at a different time	
	Direction		Direction		Direction
Distance		Distance		Distance	

* If the rate of revolution of windows continually changed when looking at the windows throughout one or more revolutions, the only common visual aspects with the trapezoidal window would be "windowness" and rectangularity if eyes were at level of window.

If the assumptive worlds of the two observers differed in that one had been conditioned to rectangular configurations and the other to trapezoidal configuration, there would be no common visual aspects with any of the windows except "windowness."

If what was being looked at was emergent (not cyclical), further questions arise; but the emergent aspect could only be experienced in common to the extent that the two observers had common assumptive worlds and were experiencing the same types of stimulus excitation.

conscious assumptions and the role they play in the formulation of perceptions, besides raising many significant questions. On the other hand, the alterations of appearances related to variation in the length form of the window are relatively simple; these alterations of appearances "correspond" to the objective variation and are nonillusory. Consequently, the phenomena disclosed throw no light on our understanding of the origin and nature of perception or of assumptions and the role they play.

Why are such different consequences related to variations of such apparently similar objective factors? In trying to think out a satisfactory answer to the above question, it seems that the confusion of mind that one gets into results primarily from a failure to be clear as to the meaning of the words that have been used in the question. It may therefore be the proper place and time to try to analyze some of the terms employed. Such analysis of terminology would seem to be profitable only to the extent that we keep in mind a point made long ago by Helmholtz concerning perception; that is, that in the simplest percept there is involved a complex, integrative, judgment-like process based on experience.

> As long as the premise of the conclusion is not an injunction imposed by outside authority for our conduct and belief, but a statement related to reality, which can therefore be only the result of experience, the conclusion, as a matter of fact, does not tell us anything new or something that we did not know already before we made the statements . . . [7, pp. 24–25].
>
> Now we have exactly the same case in our sense-perceptions . . . in these cases no particular conscious conclusion may be present, yet the essential and original office of such a conclusion has been performed, and the result of it has been attained . . .
>
> These inductive conclusions leading to the formation of our sense-perceptions certainly do lack the purifying and scrutinizing work of conscious thinking. Nevertheless, in my opinion, by their peculiar nature they may be classed as conclusions, inductive conclusions unconsciously formed [7, pp. 26–27].

With this understanding of perception as a necessary basis, we may utilize the "transactional" approach set forth by Dewey and Bentley (see Chapters IV, V, VI, and X in their *Knowing and the Known* [5]) and the "operational" approach set forth by P. W. Bridgman (4) in pursuing our analysis to the extent of posing certain questions which open up what are believed to be highly significant lines of inquiry.

For example:

(1) What is referred to by the word "variation"? When we use the word "variation" (in regard to the rectangular window) we think of the "thing" that is changed as referring to something existing "objectively" as a whole apart in its own right (the rectangular configuration). We think of the "change" as referring to a modification of an aspect (i.e., the form) of the objective thing which also exists "objectively" apart in its own right. The demonstration shows that phenomenally, the rectangular configuration that is varied doesn't exist objectively apart in its own right, nor does the aspect that is varied (i.e., its form) exist objectively apart in its own right, but that they exist (are) only because they are transactionally related to innumerable other phenomenal processes

past, present and future, among them the immediate "subjective" phenomena.

(2) What is referred to by the word "alteration"? When we use the word "alteration" in regard to appearance, we think of the "thing" that is altered as something existing "subjectively" as a whole apart in its own right. We think of "alteration" as referring to a change in some aspect of "something" which also exists "subjectively" apart in its own right. The demonstration shows that phenomenally, appearances that are altered are not "somethings" that exist subjectively apart in their own right, nor are the numerous aspects of appearances that are changed "somethings" that exist subjectively apart in their own right, but that they exist (are) only because of their being transactionally related to innumerable other phenomenal processes past, present and future, among them the immediate "objective" phenomena.

(3) What is referred to by the words "varying into trapezoidal form a rectangular window"? We mean a changing of the form of a rectangular configuration and nothing else, and we think that, as a result of such localized objective changes, subjective appearances may be altered. The demonstration shows that the "objective" and "subjective" factors do not exist as entities apart in their own right but only as transactionally related, and that if one factor is varied, other factors alter only because we vary the total transactional relationship in which they are playing a role.

It seems clear, then, that each of the various aspects into which the total situation has been analyzed are not fixed or static elements but are "operations," as the word is used by Bridgman, and that the meaning of a term can only be clarified by giving an "operational" account of it. Further, no one term can have the same meaning in different operations. For example, from the "operational" point of view it is apparent that, in the demonstration when the words "trapezoidal form" are used to refer to an aspect of the "objective" operation, the phenomena they refer to are entirely different from the phenomena that are referred to when the words are used to refer to an aspect of the stimulus (physiological) operation or to an aspect of the perceptual (subjective) operation.

The above examples would seem to show that we cannot hope to formulate a satisfactory answer to many of our questions until we have become clear concerning the referents of the words used in the question. Here we are faced by the difficulty that the phenomenal transactional relationships in even the simplest percept are so multiple and involved that no abstraction or word or expression can even implicitly refer to them all. But this does not mean that abstractions and words are not indispensable. The efficacy of conceptual abstraction lies in its usefulness in inquiry when we have run up against a hitch in actual occasions of living.

Such hitches are related to particular specific aspects of the total of the transrelated phenomena that constitute the transactional relationships. It is only by abstracting the specific aspects out of the total that we are able to understand and resolve the hitches.

It appears that, in using abstractions and words, we are always in danger of forgetting that they are only abstractions that refer to but never disclose the phenomena involved in transactional occasions, and must continually endeavor as far as possible to be clear as to the "named" that is referred to by the "naming" we use.

REFERENCES—CHAPTER 13

1. Ames, A. Jr. *Nature and Origin of Perception: Preliminary laboratory manual for use with demonstrations disclosing phenomena which increase our understanding of the nature of perception.* Hanover, N. H.: Institute for Associated Research, 1946–1947. (Mimeographed.)

2. Ames, A. Jr. *Nature and Origin of Perception: Literature dealing with the significance of the phenomena disclosed by the demonstrations.* Hanover, N. H.: Institute for Associated Research. (Mimeographed.)

3. Ames, A. Jr. *"Assumptions" and the Role They Play in Perception.* Hanover, N. H.: Institute for Associated Research, 1949. (Mimeographed.)

4. Bridgman, P. W. "Some implications of recent points of view in physics." *Revue internationale de philosophie,* 1949, No. 10, 1–23.

5. Dewey, J., and Bentley, A. F. *Knowing and the Known.* Boston: Beacon Press, 1949.

6. Hastorf, A. H. "The influence of suggestion on the relationship between stimulus size and perceived distance." *J. Psychol.,* 1950, *29,* 195–217.

7. Helmholtz, H. von. *Physiological Optics.* (Ed. by J. P. S. Southall.) Optical Society of America, 1925. Vol. III.

8. Ittelson, W. H. "Size as a cue to distance." *Amer. J. Psychol.,* 1951, *64,* 54–67, 188–202.

9. Ittelson, W. H., and Ames, A. Jr. "Accommodation, convergence, and their relation to apparent distance." *J. Psychol.,* 1950, *30,* 43–62.

10. Kilpatrick, F. P. *Some Aspects of the Role of Assumptions in Perception.* Ph.D. Thesis, Princeton University, 1950.

11. Lawrence, Merle. *An Inquiry into the Nature of Perception.* Hanover, N. H.: Institute for Associated Research, 1949.

12. Lawrence, Merle. *Studies in Human Behavior.* Princeton, N. J.: Princeton Univ. Press, 1949.

14

Assumptions and Perception:

Three Experiments[1]

F. P. Kilpatrick

I. EXPERIMENT I

A. Description of the Experiment

1. PURPOSE OF THE EXPERIMENT. The purpose of this experiment was to test one specific aspect of the general proposition that under one complex of assumptions stimuli will be perceived in one way; under a different complex of assumptions they will be perceived in another way. In this instance, a regular-sized playing card was attached to the trapezoid, and experimental modification of assumptions was accomplished by altering the position of the card relative to the trapezoid. Since the change in assumptions was related to a change in a part of the total stimulus pattern, the procedure was similar to that employed by Ittelson (6).

[1] Chapters 12 and 13 should be read prior to reading this one, as they describe and discuss the visual phenomena related to the basic apparatus employed in this series of experiments.

A more specific statement of the hypothesis is that, when lateral movement and changes in width, height, trapezoidal form, and brightness are components of the total visual pattern formed by a playing card attached to a revolving trapezoid and are perceived in one way, slight alterations in other components of the total visual pattern resulting in the arousal of different assumptions will result in the perception of the unchanged components being altered in harmony with the new assumptions. The assumptions controlled in this experiment were those of "togetherness" and "apartness." Ames had previously shown that seeing objects in edge-to-edge relationship is strongly related to an assumption of "togetherness" of the objects, while seeing them with their edges apart tends to be related to an assumption of "apartness" of the objects (1). In this experiment, assumptions were altered by changes in the edge relationship of card and trapezoid.

2. APPARATUS. Essentially, the apparatus is the "rotating trapezoidal window" designed by Ames (see Chapters 12 and 13), although his conditions cannot be said to have been duplicated in every respect. Such details as the dimensions and other contents of the room in which it was located, the distance of the equipment from front and side walls, the means of concealing floodlights, etc. certainly differed. His tube and cube were not used, and, in addition, the rectangular form with its tube and cube mounted above the trapezoid was eliminated. Ames had used the rectangle and its appended equipment for purposes of making comparisons; no such comparisons were needed in this experiment. However, the trapezoid exactly duplicated his.

The accompanying photograph (Figure 1) shows the equipment as it was set up. It consists of a trapezoidal plane (TW), mullioned and with painted shadows, mounted at the center of its upper edge on a rod (R), which in turn is geared to an electric motor (M) rigidly attached to an overhead wooden platform (P). A rheostat control (RH) permits the adjustment of the motor speed so that the trapezoid rotates on its own axis in a counterclockwise direction [2] at any desired constant speed from ½ to 20 rpm. The face of the rheostat box is calibrated in rpm's to facilitate accurate settings. L_1 and L_2 are photo-floodlights mounted on 8-foot stands and so arranged as to give balanced illumination from above to the two sides of the plane from angles corresponding approximately to the angles of the painted shadows. T is a small worktable used by the experimenter, and from which the motor can be controlled. Black cloth drapes (drawn aside in Figure 1) were used to conceal from the observer the rear and left side walls of stone and cement, the overhead

[2] In this paper, motion referred to as "clockwise" or "counterclockwise" always means "when viewed from above."

FIG. 1. *Photograph of the apparatus with front drapes drawn aside. The plane of the trapezoid is normal to the optical axis of the camera and ten feet away. The lettered items are identified in the text.*

platform, and the motor. In addition, they were hung in front of the lamp stands, thus concealing the worktable, the stands, and the light sources, except for faint glows. The result of this draping was that an observer, seated 5½ feet from the drapes (10 feet from the trapezoid) saw, through a 3-foot opening in the drapes, the trapezoid and the suspending rod against a uniformly black background. Peripherally the gray cement floor, part of the ceiling, and the faint glows of the floodlights could be seen. A drape which could be drawn across the 3-foot opening was provided, thus permitting the experimenter to conceal everything behind the front drapes whenever he desired.

In addition to this basic equipment, an ordinary playing card (king of hearts, 2¼ inches by 3½ inches) was used.

3. Observers. The observers were 20 male college undergraduate volunteers, all of whom reported approximately normal vision. They had varying amounts of knowledge concerning the work in perception being done in the laboratory, but in all cases the amount of knowledge was small and none of them had ever seen or heard of the rotating trapezoid.

4. Experimental design. There were two conditions of observation, A and B. Half of the observers experienced condition A first; half of them experienced condition B first. The assignment of order to the 20 observers was randomized.

5. Procedure. The equipment was arranged so that all drapes were in place, only the two lights illuminating the trapezoid were on, and the front draw drape was closed. All observations were conducted with the trapezoid rotating at 3 rpm. The observer was seated facing the closed drapes so the center of the trapezoid was level with his eyes and 10 feet away. The small size of a playing card made a near observation point desirable, since the short distance permitted the observer to report details which would not have been seen at a greater distance. This short distance in turn necessitated monocular observation, since, for most observers, some of the illusory appearances of the trapezoid are lost when both eyes are used at less than about 25 feet (2). Consequently, a patch was placed over one of the observer's eyes so that all observations would be monocular.

Following a very brief interview in which the observer was asked his name, age, visual acuity, and whether or not he had any idea as to the nature of the experiment, a short pretest was conducted, in which the observer reported what he saw while watching just the trapezoid rotating. This was done as a means of making sure that he was perceiving unequivocal, uninterrupted oscillation. Had any observer reported otherwise, he would have been rejected.

When the pretest was completed, the front drape was closed, the motor turned off, and the experimenter attached the playing card to the trapezoid in the manner prescribed for the observer's first condition (A or B) of observation. Under condition A, the card was placed on the end of the upper edge of the short side of the trapezoid so that the bottom edge of the card was parallel with, and rested on, the edge of the trapezoid. Under condition B, the card was put in the same place, but rotated 90° on its vertical axis so that the plane of the card was at right angles to the plane of the trapezoid. After properly placing the card, the experimenter turned on the motor, opened the front drape, and secured the observer's observation of the card. These were noted on a prepared form, under the headings of *motion, height, width, shape,* and *brightness*. If the observer failed to report on some of these, the experimenter probed in a manner calculated to avoid the suggestion of any particular answer; e.g., "Please describe anything you observe concerning the height of the playing card." When a sufficiently complete report had been obtained, the experimenter closed the front drape and shut off the motor. He then placed the card on the trapezoid in the manner prescribed for the observer's second condition of observation (A or B), started the motor, opened the front drape, and secured a report in the same manner as before. At the end of the experiment, the observer was asked, "Think of how the two cards behaved in the two experimental situations. How do you think it was done?"

6. FINDINGS. Under condition A (card in edge-to-edge relationship with the trapezoid), all 20 observers reported that the card appeared to oscillate with the frame, remaining attached to it at all times. Under condition B (plane of card vertical to plane of trapezoid), the same 20 observers all reported that the card appeared to leave its point of attachment, sail at a constant speed through space around the front of part, or all, of the frame, and then reattach itself. In other words, under this latter condition the "real" motion of the card was perceived, along with the illusory oscillation of the trapezoid; under the former condition the window appeared to oscillate, speed varying, and the card was seen as remaining attached to it, swinging back and forth through an arc of about 100°, its speed of movement varying with that of the trapezoid.

An additional motion of the card on its own axis was reported by 6 observers under condition B. These 6 described the card as performing one slow, constant-speed clockwise rotation on its own axis each time it circled the axis of the trapezoid. The remaining 14 simply saw the card keep its face toward the axis of the trapezoid at all times, performing no rotation of its own.

Perception of the height of the card differed markedly between the two conditions. Table I summarizes the results. Under condition B, 3 observers reported that the height appeared to remain constant; the other 17 said that the card appeared to grow taller and shorter, but only in

TABLE I

PHENOMENAL CHANGE IN HEIGHT

	EDGE CONDITION A	NON-EDGE CONDITION B
No apparent change	5	3
Some change, but associated with changing distance		17
Changes—seems to grow and contract	15	
Total	**20**	**20**

proportion to its change in distance as it moved around in a circle. Typical of the reports of these 17 were, "The card gets somewhat taller as it comes forward and shorter when it goes back" and "It appears taller as it gets closer and *vice versa,* but anything does that and this is no more than you would expect."

Under condition A, the division between the reporting of no change in height and change in height was about the same as it was under condition B, but for all 15 who reported height change, their description of the phenomenon was markedly different than it had been under condition B. In this instance they stated that it was "peculiar," "hard to account for," that it "seemed to be a property of the card itself." Typical statements are, "There is considerable growing and contracting which seems like the card itself is doing it" and "It just seems to grow like a plant and then get shorter."

TABLE II

PHENOMENAL BRIGHTNESS CHANGE

	EDGE CONDITION A	NON-EDGE CONDITION B
No apparent change	14	11
Some change, but associated with distance		9
Changes, as though a property of the card	6	
Total	**20**	**20**

As Table II shows, the majority of the observers under both conditions reported no apparent change in the brightness of the card as it moved. In those cases where brightness change was perceived, the descriptions given under condition A again differed markedly from those given under condition B, and in much the same way as did the descriptions of height change. The 9 observers who reported seeing brightness change under condition B described it as being associated with change in distance; the 6 who saw brightness change under condition A all made such comments as "It looks as though it had a light of its own that was continually changing" and "There isn't much change, but what there is it looks like the card itself is doing."

With respect to width, all observers reported under both conditions that the card narrowed and widened as it moved, and their descriptions of this width change did not differ according to the condition of observation. In general, it was to the effect that they could see either more or less of the card as it "swung around" (condition B) or "swung back and forth" (condition A). No changes in shape other than the height and width changes noted were reported, except in two instances under condition A. These two observers reported that the card no longer appeared rectangular during part of its movement from the observer's left to his right; instead, it appeared slightly trapezoidal with the short side nearer the observer for a brief time on either side of the midpoint of the arc in which it appeared to move.

In answer to the postexperimental interview question (Table III), only 2 of the 20 observers suggested that the frame on which the card was placed actually rotated, and both of them added that it was just a guess because they didn't actually see it come all the way around. One example will serve for both. "I never saw it do it, but I think the frame turns all the way around and doesn't oscillate. But I don't know how that makes the cards act the way they do." Of the remaining 18 observers, 6 thought perhaps the answer lay in some kind of invisible mechanical device. Seven said they supposed it was some kind of illusion, and 5 simply said they didn't know and didn't want to guess.

TABLE III

ANSWERS TO THE QUESTION, "THINK OF HOW THE CARDS BEHAVED IN THE TWO EXPERIMENTAL SITUATIONS. HOW DO YOU THINK IT WAS DONE?"

ANSWERS	NO. OF OBSERVERS
Frame rotates	2
Invisible mechanical device	6
An illusion	7
Don't know	5
	—
Total	**20**

B. Discussion

None of the results of this experiment is at variance with the hypothesis which it was designed to test. In order to provide a background for showing the systematic coherence of the results, the basis for perceiving the true motion and appearance of the card will be discussed later.

Under either condition (A or B) the card does, in fact, remain attached at all times to the upper edge of the short side of the trapezoid, remains stationary on its own axis, and follows a circular path around the axis of the trapezoid. An observer using both eyes at a distance of 4 or 5 feet would perceive just that; he would see a card of constant size and shape and brightness moving at a constant speed in a circular path. An understanding of why it should be perceived in that way is basic to an understanding of the experimental results. It helps us little to refer the percept to the characteristics of the object; i.e., to say that it is seen that way because that is the way it is. If we analyze the succession of physiological stimulus patterns arising from the reflection from the card of light waves on to the retina, we can easily determine that, as far as

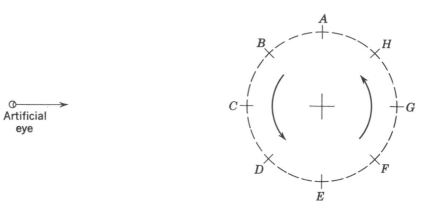

FIG. 2. *The dashed line indicates the path of the card (viewed from above); direction is indicated by arrows. The lettered cross lines represent the card in 8 different positions.*

the retinal pattern is concerned, there is no constancy of size, shape, or brightness, no constancy of speed, and no circular motion.

What does happen to the retinal pattern may be roughly determined if we take a large artificial "eye" so built that the patterns cast on a ground glass corresponding to the retina may be seen from the rear, place it in the position shown in the diagram (Figure 2), and point it at the moving card (path indicated by dashed line).

When the card is at A, the pattern on the glass is approximately rectangular; as the card moves from A to B, the pattern moves slowly but at increasing speed from left to right, becomes more and more narrow and slightly trapezoidal, and increases considerably in both height and brightness. As the card travels from B to C, the pattern moves more and more rapidly across the glass, becomes more narrow and slightly more trapezoidal, and increases only slightly in height and brightness. Finally, at C, the pattern is just a line, the edge of the card. From C to D, the movement of the pattern across the "retina" is still rapid but slowing up, height and brightness are very slowly diminishing, width is increasing, and the shape is becoming a little more rectangular. From D to E, the lateral movement of the pattern is very slow and becoming slower, the reduction in height and brightness is much more rapid, and the shape continues to widen and become more rectangular, until at E it is finally at its widest and almost rectangular. Through the rear half of the circle (E to A), the same changes in the pattern that have been described for the forward half occur in reverse and in diminished amount.

Even with this simple analysis it becomes obvious that what one sees is not the succession of patterns described. In the case of the human observer, the situation is incredibly more complex and variable. For example, it is certain that a large part of the effective physiological stimulus pattern is nonretinal. The movement across the ground-glass "retina" has no real counterpart on the human retina; instead, both sweep and saccadic eye movements may take place. In addition, the observer may move his head or entire body up or down, forward or backward, or from side to side, without altering his perception of the "true" appearance and movement of the card. Somehow, this complex of stimuli from a variety of sense departments is integrated into visual perception. If we follow the theory outlined in this book, this integration is based on assumptions built up through past experience; that is, through acting with respect to the same or similar stimulus patterns. It follows that the perception is an interpretation, a "bet" as to what is occurring "out there."

Thus, changes in height and brightness are perceived as radial motion as long as it is assumed that the card is of constant size and free to make such motion; changes in width and trapezoidal form are perceived as changes in inclination in space as long as the card is assumed to be of constant size and shape; and movements across the retina, eye movements and body movements, are integrated into the perception of lateral movement as long as the observer's assumptions as to his egocentric localization relative to the card are not altered sufficiently to cancel these factors.[3]

We will now turn to a discussion of the experimental results. Any indication of attachment of the card and trapezoid arouses an assumption of "togetherness" of the two. Such an assumption is incompatible with the assumptive complex that is otherwise involved. The resulting conflict may be resolved in at least the following ways:

1. The assumption of "togetherness" of the card and frame may be abandoned, and the cues related to it repressed.

2. The assumption that the trapezoid is a rectangle may be abandoned, and the true rotary motion of the frame perceived.

3. The assumption of constancy of the properties of the card may be dropped. This may occur with respect to height, width, brightness, or shape, or any combination of the four.

4. Changes in height, width, brightness, or shape of the card, which are at variance with "togetherness" of the card and frame and "constancy" of the properties of the card, may be repressed.

Under condition B, the manner of attachment of the card and frame was such that the indications of "togetherness" of the two were given less weight than were the conflicting indications, and alternative 1 was

---

[3] The "train" illusion is a good example of the perception of illusory lateral movement of an object due to false assumptions as to egocentric localization relative to the object.

"chosen" as the "best bet." Apparently, the true movement of the card and the illusory oscillation of the trapezoid were both accepted as unequivocal, necessitating the repression for a part of each revolution of those cues indicating the attachment of the two. Thus, the card was seen by all 20 observers to break away, float around through space, and then reattach itself. Height change was interpreted as radial motion by all 20 observers, so completely in 3 cases that no height change at all was perceived. Change in brightness also was interpreted as radial motion by all the observers. Since the actual change in brightness was relatively small, more than half (11) of the observers reported brightness constancy; the other 9 saw some change, which they described as being associated with difference in distance. Also, under condition B, the only alteration in shape perceived (other than change in height) was that of width, and this was unanimously associated with seeing more or less of the card as it "swung around." Width, then, was assumed to be constant, and the widening and narrowing (changes in horizontal visual angle subtended to the eye) were interpreted as changes in the inclination of the card relative to the observer.

It would seem that the shifts from the rectangular form to trapezoidal forms were either at or below the limen for many observers. The difference between the vertical visual angles subtended to the eye by the two vertical edges of an object assumed to be a rectangle (as the card is) ordinarily is utilized in perceiving which edge is near and which is far. (Cf. Ames's discussion in Chapter 13.) In this case, 6 observers reversed the location of the near and far edges of the card, suggesting that perhaps the trapezoidal form cues were not available to them. This mislocalization of the card edges resulted in the perception of one slow, constant clockwise revolution of the card on its own axis each time it circled the axis of the trapezoid. Apparently they utilized only the systematic variations in width as cues to inclination, and these variations in width would be the same, whether the card performed such a rotation or remained stationary on its own axis. There is also a possibility that the variations in trapezoidal form were available as cues to the 6 observers, but were repressed in favor of an assumption of rotation. The fact that the card touches the trapezoid only at the card's center of balance—a familiar position for rotating objects—lends some support to such an hypothesis.

The actual variability in the speed of lateral movement was not reported by any of the observers; instead, it was integrated with the perceived radial motion in such a way that the card was seen as moving in a circle at a constant speed. (Cf. the "Circular Motion Demonstration," Chapter 3.)

Now we may turn to a discussion of the results obtained under condition A. In this case, the edge-to-edge relationship of the card and trapezoid is one which, in our past experience, has been associated almost without exception with "togetherness." Seeing the card as being firmly attached to the frame thus becomes a "better bet" than it was under condition B. Thus it is more likely to be maintained in case of conflict with other assumptions. Apparently this is what happened for all 20 observers under condition A. The "togetherness" of the card and frame was maintained at all times, the illusory oscillation of the trapezoid continued to be perceived, and indications not in harmony with this over-all perception were either perceived differently than under condition B (alternative 3) or were repressed (alternative 4).

For example, interpreting changes in height as radial motion conflicts with seeing the card oscillate with the frame. Five subjects simply repressed this cue; the other 15 abandoned their assumption of size constancy of the card and perceived it as growing and contracting "like the card itself is doing it" (Table I). The same thing was true of the brightness change, except that the variation in brightness was sufficiently small that repression was more common than in the case of height changes (Table II).

The maintenance of an assumption of width constancy and the perception of the changing width of the card (horizontal visual angle) as changing inclination relative to the observer does not conflict to any great extent with seeing the card oscillate with the trapezoid. This is true because the changes in horizontal visual angle of a card describing a circle in space are substantially the same as those of a card oscillating through an arc of about 100°. There are minor differences, of course. The retinal image of the card is wider than it should be at each end of its arc because the card has actually turned 90°, but is seen as being turned only about 50°. Also, during the apparent left-right swing, the card is seen farther away than its real position; consequently, the horizontal visual angle of the card is always proportionately greater during the apparent left-right swing than during the right-left swing. However, these differences are not great, due to the small size of the card and the distance from which it was observed. The result was that all 20 observers perceived the width changes simply as changes in inclination as the card "swung back and forth."

Substantially the same thing holds true of changes in trapezoidal form. To the extent that they were above threshold (not determined by this experiment) they apparently were completely integrated into the perception of the position of the card relative to the observer. But there still remains to be explained the two instances in which the card was seen as a trapezoid with the *short edge near* during portions of the illusory left-right swing of the card and frame. The answer would appear to involve at least two considerations. The first is that the difference between the visual angles related to the two vertical edges of the card must have been above threshold for the two observers. The second is that the card was perceived as being farther away than its real position. It is well known that under these conditions a tipped-back rectangle will be seen as a trapezoid with its short edge near.[4] The reason for this, apparently, is that the retinal pattern given by the rectangle at the real distance is that which would be given by a trapezoid, short edge near, at the false distance at which the object is perceived. Consequently, it is perceived as just such a trapezoid.

The variability in the rate of lateral movement of the card was perceived by all 20 observers, since the card was seen as remaining attached to the trapezoid, which appeared to oscillate at a variable speed. No particular conflict was involved in this, since the radial movement with which the lateral movement had been integrated under condition B was no longer present perceptually, allowing the observers to see the lateral movement "by itself."

Answers to the postexperimental interview question indicate that the differences in appearance and motion of the cards under the two experimental conditions were real as far as the observers were concerned. Only two of them suspected that the frame actually rotated and thus, that the two cards actually moved in the same way. Even these two added that it was just a guess. Six observers were so convinced of the differences that they postulated hidden mechanical devices, such as black wires, transparent rods, and even a concealed battery of motion-picture projectors.

We may summarize the results of this experiment by stating that all the findings were in line with the predictions stated in the hypothesis form at the beginning of this section. Lateral movement, changes in width, height, trapezoidal form, and brightness of a playing card were components of the total physiological stimulus pattern related to a revolving trapezoid and attached playing card. The assumptions of "togetherness" and "apartness" were experimentally altered by minor alterations of other components of the total pattern, with the result that the perception of the unchanged components was altered in harmony with the assumptions.

II. EXPERIMENT II

A. Description of the Experiment

1. PURPOSE OF THE EXPERIMENT. The general purpose of this experiment is the same as that of Experiment I; i.e., to test one specific aspect

---

[4] Donders reported this fact in 1864 (4, pp. 158–61).

of the general proposition that under one complex of assumptions stimuli will be perceived in one way and that under a different complex of assumptions they will be perceived in another way. As in Experiment I, the modification of assumptions was accomplished by making alterations in a small part of the total visual pattern. Ames had previously shown in a number of demonstrations that one extremely generalized unconscious perceptual assumption is that similar things are identical (1). In this instance a regular-sized playing card was attached to the rotating trapezoid, and experimental modification of assumptions (from "nonidentity" to "identity" and vice versa) was attempted simply by altering the pattern on the back of the card.

Specifically, it was hypothesized that, if the front-back patterns of the card differ, the observer will assume he is seeing first one side and then the other side of the card ("nonidentity"); that if the front-back patterns of the card are the same, he will assume he is seeing the same side of the card all the time ("identity"); and that perception of the motion of the card will be different under these two conditions, even though it is actually exactly the same.

2. APPARATUS. The apparatus is that described in Experiment I. In addition, three identical playing cards (king of hearts, 2¼ inches by 3½ inches) were used. Two of them were pasted back to back, making one card with the same "king of hearts" pattern on both sides.

3. OBSERVERS. The observers were 20 male college undergraduate volunteers, all of whom reported approximately normal vision. As in the previous experiment, the observers had some small knowledge of the work being done in the laboratory, but none at all concerning the rotating trapezoid.

4. EXPERIMENTAL DESIGN. There were again two conditions of observation, A and B. Half of the observers experienced condition A first, half of them condition B, and the assignment of order to the 20 observers was randomized.

5. PROCEDURE. The arrangement of the apparatus (with the exception of the playing cards), the placement of the observer for monocular observation, the pre-experimental interview, and the pretest with just the rotating trapezoid were exactly the same as in Experiment I.

When the pretest had been completed the front drape was closed and the motor turned off. The experimenter then placed on the trapezoid the card which was proper for the condition of observation (A or B) which came first for the particular observer. The placement of the card was exactly the same in either case; it was attached about one inch from the end of the upper edge of the short side of the trapezoid, the bottom edge of the card resting on the edge of the trapezoid, the plane of the card at right angles to the plane of the trapezoid. (This placement of the card is the same as that used in Experiment I, condition B.) In condition A, the card with a face on only one side was used, placed so that the face was toward the middle of the trapezoid. In condition B, the card with the same face on both sides was used.

After the proper card had been installed, the trapezoid was set in motion, the front drapes opened, and the observer was told, "Please describe as completely as you can the motion of the playing card." The experimenter probed in as nonleading a fashion as possible ("Do you see any other motion?") until he was sure that all aspects of perceived motion had been described, being particularly careful to determine what motion, if any, the card seemed to make on its own vertical axis. Responses were summarized on a prepared form. The front drapes were then closed, the trapezoid stopped, the proper card for the observer's second condition of observation installed, and the procedure just described was repeated.

At the end of the experiment the observer was asked, "Were the cards used in the two experimental situations indentical?" If he said, "No," then he was asked, "In what way did they differ?"

6. FINDINGS. Under both conditions A and B all 20 observers reported seeing the card detach itself from the trapezoid when the trapezoid began its illusory reversal of motion with the card at the observer's left, sail forward and around part or all of what appeared to be the near edge of the frame, and on the right side attach itself once again to the frame, and continue with the frame until the two again appeared to be separate. This is the motion found under condition B, Experiment I. It will be referred to as the *orbital* movement of the card.

With respect to another type of motion of the card, however, there were marked differences between conditions A and B (see Table IV). Under condition A, 12 observers perceived no movement of the card other than the orbital movement; in other words, for them the card moved around in its orbit, keeping its face toward the center of the trapezoid at all times; and by 8 observers the A card was seen as making a slow, constant, clockwise rotation on its own vertical axis (axial motion), once for each orbital revolution. This is in sharp contrast to condition B, in which the nonrotation was seen by only one observer and the slow, constant clockwise rotation by two others. Instead, two entirely different types of motion of the card on its vertical axis were perceived, one of them by 11 observers, and the other by 6 observers. The one reported by the 11 observers consisted of two definite clockwise quarter-turns for each orbital revolution, one of these quarter-turns occurring when the card was farthest to the observer's left as it emerged from the position in which its plane was parallel to the observer's line of sight; the other occurring in a corresponding position on the other side of the card's orbit. This reported motion is shown in Figure 3.

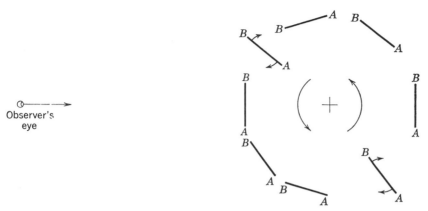

FIG. 3. *Type of apparent motion reported by 11 observers under Condition B (viewed from above). Quarter-turns are at observer's near left and far right.*

The other type of motion which was reported by 6 observers also consisted of two clockwise quarter-turns, but the turns were seen to occur in different regions of the card's orbit than was the case with the 11 observers. This motion is shown in Figure 4.

There is a definite relationship between the type of motion seen in condition A and that seen in condition B (Table IV). Of the 12 observers who saw no rotation of the A card, 1 of them saw the B card perform in the same way, and 11 saw it do clockwise quarter-turns in

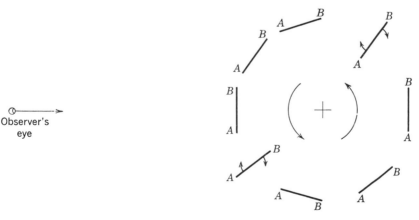

FIG. 4. *Type of apparent motion reported by 6 observers under Condition B (viewed from above). Quarter-turns are at observer's far left and near right.*

TABLE IV

TYPE OF MOTION REPORTED FOR CONDITION A ACCORDING
TO TYPE OF MOTION REPORTED FOR CONDITION B

| | CONDITION A | | |
CONDITION B	NO ROTATION	ORBITAL	SLOW, CONSTANT CLOCKWISE ROTATION, ONCE FOR EACH REVOLUTION	TOTAL
No rotation	1			1
Slow, constant clockwise rotation, once for each orbital revolution			2	2
Two clockwise quarter-turns—near left and far right positions	11			11
Two clockwise quarter-turns—far left and near right positions			6	6
Total	12		8	20

the near-left and far-right positions, but none saw any axial motion in the far-left and near-right positions. On the other hand, for the 8 observers who saw the A card rotate slowly in a clockwise direction, 2 saw the B card behave the same way, 6 saw it perform the clockwise quarter-turns in the far-left and near-right positions. In other words, if one excludes those cases in which the A and B cards were seen as performing the same, there is a perfect correlation between the type of motion perceived under condition A and that perceived under condition B.

The order in which conditions A and B were experienced apparently had no effect on the type of motion perceived under either of the conditions.

TABLE V

ANSWERS TO THE QUESTION "WERE THE CARDS USED IN
THE TWO EXPERIMENTAL SITUATIONS IDENTICAL?"

ANSWER	NO. OF OBSERVERS
Yes, they were identical	5
Don't know, because I never saw the back of one of them	2
One of them seemed to have face on both sides, but not sure	4
One of them had face on both sides	9
Total	20

Answers to the postexperimental question "Were the cards used in the two experimental situations identical?" (Table V) indicated that 7 of the 20 observers never suspected at all that the B card had a face on both sides. Four of them thought it might be two-faced, but were not sure, giving answers such as "Maybe one of them had a face on both sides, but I don't really think so." The remaining 9 observers were sure that one of the cards had a face on both sides. It is worth noting that the only 3 observers whose perceptions of the motion of the cards were the same under conditions A and B were among the 9 who saw the B card as two-faced.

B. Discussion

The orbital movement of the card reported by all observers under both conditions A and B has already been discussed in connection with Experiment I. It was not expected that the perception of this orbital movement would differ according to conditions in this second experiment. Since this expectation was borne out, we may confine our discussion to the apparent *axial* motion of the card; that is, the apparent rotation of the card on its own vertical axis.

Under condition A, 12 of the 20 subjects perceived no axial rotation. Instead, the observers saw the card move in its orbit, keeping its face toward the center of that orbit at all times. The other 8 saw the card perform a slow, constant clockwise rotation on its own axis, once for each orbital revolution. These two types of motion are exactly those reported under condition B, Experiment I, for which the experimental conditions were exactly the same as for condition A of this experiment. At the risk of being repetitious, the explanation of this axial movement given in the discussion of the preceding experiment will be reviewed because it is basic to an understanding of the results of this one. As an aid in presentation, the diagram (Figure 5) has been drawn.

As the diagram shows, a card may be seen either as rotating or not rotating on its own axis as it moves in a circle if no indications other than horizontal visual angle (width) are integrated into this aspect of perception. Ordinarily, the difference between the vertical angles subtended by the two vertical edges of the card (trapezoidal form) is utilized in perceiving which edge of the card is near and which is far.

However, it would seem that this difference between angles is either at or below threshold for most observers viewing the card from the distance (10 feet) prescribed for this experiment, with the result that seeing or not seeing axial movement is almost a chance affair (14 to 6 in Experiment I, 12 to 8 in this experiment) or perhaps is influenced by the way in which the card is "balanced" on the frame. It follows from

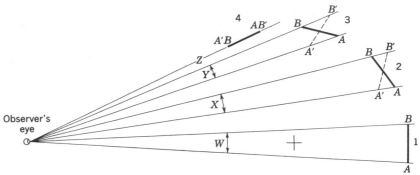

FIG. 5. *Horizontal angles (w, x, y, and z) subtended to the eye by the playing card in 4 different positions in its orbital path. Direction is from 1 to 4. A-B is the real position of the card; A'-B' is the illusory position seen by some observers.*

this that one should be able to induce, with proper manipulation of assumptions, any series of axial movements which are not incompatible with the changing horizontal angles subtended to the eye.

Such manipulation was performed successfully with 17 out of 20 observers. The two-faced B card was calculated to arouse in the observer the assumption that he was seeing the same side of the card at all times. The 12 observers who perceived no axial rotation under condition A apparently perceived the same thing under condition B, except that two clockwise quarter-turns were superimposed on this motion by 11 of them, presumably due to their assumption that they were seeing the same side of the card all the time. Since these 11 observers perceivd no rotation between positions 1 and 2 in Figure 6, the "front" of the card was

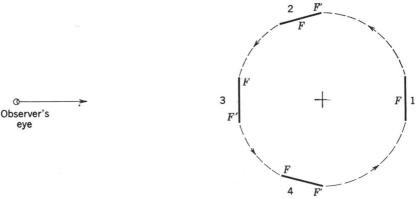

FIG. 6. *Real and illusory positions of the two sides of the card. F in positions 2, 3, and 4 is the real position of the side of the card designated F in position 1. F' is the illusory position of the same side.*

assumed (correctly) to be at F in position 2. In line with the assumption that the same side of the card continued to face them, an illusory clockwise quarter-turn was perceived between 2 and 3. No axial rotation was perceived between 3 and 4, thus the "front" of the card was assumed (incorrectly) to be at F′ in position 4, and another clockwise quarter-turn was necessary between positions 4 and 1.

Six of the 8 observers who perceived a slow, constant clockwise axial rotation of the A card suspended this rotation during two portions of the B card's orbit, presumably because they assumed they were seeing the same side of the card at all times. For them the card appeared to perform a quarter-turn clockwise between positions 1 and 2 (Figure 6), and they assumed (incorrectly) that the "front" of the card was at F′ in position 2. In order to keep this "front" of the card toward them, axial rotation was "stopped" by the observers between positions 2 and 3. From positions 3 to 4, the continuation of the clockwise rotation perceived under condition A by these 6 observers could be perceived under condition B without conflicting with any assumptions as to the side of the card being viewed. Thus, they reported seeing the card perform a clockwise quarter-turn from 3 to 4, with the result that the "front" of the card was assumed (correctly) to be at F in position 4. To see it continue to rotate from positions 4 to 1 would have conflicted with their assumption that they were seeing the same side of the card at all times; consequently, they perceived no axial movement between positions 4 and 1.

It will be noted that the foregoing interpretation supposes that, in spite of the differences in perception between observers, each observer saw the A card and the B card perform in the same way, and that the differences between conditions are due to the imposition of either rotation or nonrotation on to the basic perception peculiar to the individual. This would certainly be reasonable if all observers had experienced condition A first, but that was not the case. However, such an interpretation appears to be necessary in view of the high correlation between perceptions under the two conditions. It would seem that the observer saw the A card do, if it were experienced first, established a basic pattern which carried over to the B condition; and what the observer saw the B card do, if it were experienced first, weighted the odds in favor of one of the two basic patterns reported under the A condition. This would also account in part for the lack of experimental order effect in the type of motion perceived.

One further aspect of lack of order effect should also be accounted for, however. One might expect that experiencing condition A first would be necessary to the success of the B part of the experiment; i.e., that seeing both the back and the front of the card would be a necessary forerunner to establishing with a two-faced card the assumption that one is seeing the same side at all times. Undoubtedly, such would have been the case had a more unfamiliar object than a card been chosen, but in our culture almost everyone is so familiar with the front-back patterns of playing cards that any little additional experience offered by condition A would be gratuitous.

Apparently success in establishing the expected assumption was achieved in 17 out of 20 cases, if we base this conclusion on the perceptual differences. But how is this to be reconciled with the fact that 6 of the 17 were sure that the B card had a face on both sides? Here we must bring into consideration the fact that intellectual awareness and an unconscious assumption are not the same thing. For example, an individual may be thoroughly aware that what he is looking at is a rotating trapezoid; nevertheless, at the proper viewing distance, he will still perceive it as an oscillating rectangle. It is probable, then, that these 6 observers, on the basis of their past experience with playing cards, unconsciously assumed that they were seeing the same side of the card all the time, even though they established an intellectual knowledge of the true state of affairs by taking account of other indications as they continued to watch the card.

We may summarize the results of this experiment by stating that the original hypothesis was borne out in 17 of the 20 cases. For the 17 observers, the perceived motion of a playing card was altered simply by altering the pattern on the back of the card and making it the same as that on the front. The theoretical explanation offered is that an assumption of "identity" was thus aroused; i.e., an assumption that the same side of the card was being seen at all times.

III. EXPERIMENT III

A. Description of the Experiment

1. PURPOSE OF THE EXPERIMENT. Experiments I and II were designed to show that minor modifications in a stimulus pattern resulting in the modification of the assumptive complex will alter the perception of the entire stimulus pattern. One may criticize these experiments by stating that the introduction of assumptions as an explanatory concept is purely gratuitous—the stimulus changed and so did perception, and hypothetical constructs relating the two are superfluous. Even though such an evaluation seems inadequate to account for the results of the first and second experiments, it still would seem necessary to have *exactly the same* dynamic and complex stimulus pattern perceived in different ways by the same individual, these differences being related in a predictable

fashion to experimentally induced differences in assumptions. That is the purpose of this third experiment.

A generalized formulation of the hypothesis to be tested is as follows: The assumptions of "rigidity" and "flexibility" will, under certain conditions, arouse different perceptions whose nature can be predicted from the nature of the assumptions, even though the visual patterns under the two assumptions are identical.

Stated in a form which is specific to this experiment, the hypothesis is as follows: Experimentally induced assumptions of "rigidity" and "flexibility" will have a significant effect on the perception of a plastic cylinder placed through a pane of the rotating trapezoid; when the cylinder is assumed to be flexible, significantly more distortion of the cylinder (lengthening and/or bending) will be perceived during a certain portion of its rotation than when it is assumed to be rigid.

2. APPARATUS. The apparatus is that described in Experiment I. In addition, three cylinders 18 inches long and 1½ inches outside diameter were prepared, one of them of plastic tubing, one of steel tubing, and one of flexible rubber tubing. In order to make them visually indistinguishable from over 5 feet in moderate illumination, their open ends had to be plugged because their inside diameters differed; also, they were painted the same light-green color with ordinary water paint. Each of

FIG. 7. *Photograph of the trapezoid with the plastic cylinder in place.*

the cylinders had a ⅛ inch hole through it, 9 inches from either end, through which could be placed the clamp rod used to hold the cylinder to the trapezoid. Figure 7 is a photograph of the apparatus with the plastic rod in place.

3. OBSERVERS. In this experiment, also, 20 observers were used. They were again male college undergraduates who differed in no pertinent way from those used in the previous two experiments.

4. EXPERIMENTAL DESIGN. As in Experiments I and II, there were two conditions of observation, A and B; half of the observers experienced condition A first, half of them experienced condition B first, and the assignment of order to the 20 observers was randomized.

5. PROCEDURE. The arrangement of the observer for monocular observation at 10 feet, the pre-experimental interview, and the pretest using the rotating trapezoid without attachments proceeded in the same manner as in the preceding experiments. None of the observers was rejected.

Following the pretest, the experimenter followed the procedure prescribed for the experimental condition (A or B) which came first for the particular observer. If condition A came first, the experimenter picked up the rubber cylinder from the concealed worktable behind the drapes, walked around in front of the drapes, and handed it to the observer. The observer was permitted to handle the cylinder for about 10 seconds; the experimenter then took it and, holding it in both hands while talking, stated, "I am going to place this in motion with the object you saw a few moments ago." While stating this, he lightly flexed the cylinder so that the observer saw it bend. The experimenter tried to perform this so that it appeared to be an unconscious act and not staged for the observer's benefit. The experimenter then stepped behind the drapes, silently laid the rubber cylinder on the worktable, picked up the plastic cylinder, and installed it in the center pane of the trapezoid at an angle of 45° to the plane of the trapezoid (see Figure 8), and started

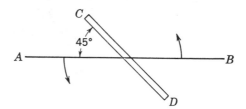

FIG. 8. *Position of the cylinder relative to the plane of the trapezoid, viewed from above. A-B is the plane of the trapezoid with A the large and B the small. C-D is the cylinder. The arrows indicate the direction of rotation.*

the trapezoid rotating at the 3 rpm speed used at all times in the experiments. After opening the front drape, the experimenter told the observer, "Please observe the cylinder and describe its appearance and behavior." This description was summarized on a prepared form. Any probing necessary was restricted to the questions, "Can you describe anything else with respect to the appearance and behavior of the cylinder?" and simply, "Anything else?" The front drape was then closed, the motor turned off, and the presentation of condition B begun.

Under condition B, the experimenter picked up the steel cylinder from the concealed worktable and handed it to the observer, who was allowed to hold it and examine it for about 10 seconds. The experimenter then took the cylinder, and while stating, "Now I am going to put this in motion with the frame," casually slapped the end of it into the palm of his hand twice so that it made an audible metallic click against a ring which he wore on his finger. Then the experimenter stepped behind the drapes and pretended to install the steel cylinder, but actually left the plastic one in place. When the motor had been started and the front drape opened, the observer was asked to report his observations as before. After completing this, the drape was again closed and the trapezoid stopped.

If the order of conditions for the observer was B-A, the steel cylinder was presented first and the rubber one second and the details of procedure appropriately modified.

Following the presentation of the two cylinders, the experimenter went behind the closed drapes and made some noises of the kind which occurred whenever a cylinder was installed in the trapezoid, but actually left the plastic cylinder in place. After starting the motor, he stated, "I have put one of the two cyinders in motion with the frame. When I open the drape please tell me, if you can, which one of the two cylinders it is and why you think so." When these answers had been recorded, the drape closed, and the motor turned off, the experimenter conducted the postexperimental interview, which consisted of the following questions:

(1) "How many cylinders were used in the experiment?"

(2) "What were they made of?"

(3) "How was each one used?"

(4) "Did you feel at any time during the experiment that I tricked you; that is, that I said I would do something and didn't do it?"

6. FINDINGS. All 20 of the observers under both conditions A and B and in the trial in which they were asked to identify the cylinder reported that they saw the frame oscillating on its vertical axis while the cylinder continued to rotate in a counterclockwise direction. Thus, for a part of one revolution, the frame and the cylinder were seen as moving

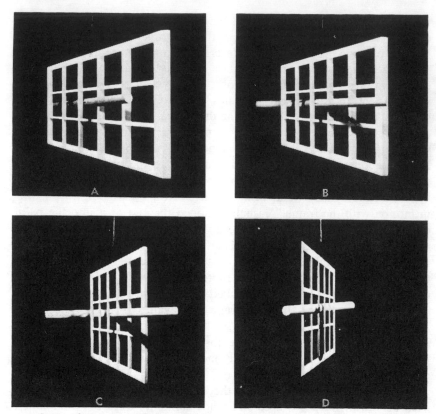

FIG. 9. *In this series of pictures, from A through D the short side of the trapezoid is moving nearer the camera; however, it appears to be moving away. The real motion of the cylinder continues to be perceived, so it apparently comes nearer and nearer the plane of the trapezoid (A through C), until finally at D it has "somehow" reached the other side.*

in opposite directions, the cylinder gradually coming against the frame, somehow getting to the other side of the frame, and continuing its rotation. This phenomenon occurred during the portion of the trapezoid's rotation when the false clockwise motion was perceived. In Figure 9 a series of photographs illustrates these conditions.

We are concerned in this experiment with what happens, perceptually, to the cylinder, as it comes against the frame and "somehow" gets to the other side. The reported perceptual experiences fell, naturally, into four categories. The four categories, arranged in order from most to least distortion of the shape of the cylinder, are:

(1) "Bends into S shape, lengthens; does not cut through frame."

This category includes those cases who reported that, as the frame and cylinder began to come together, the cylinder began to lengthen and bend, continued this until it become much longer and bent into an S shape, then suddenly snapped straight again and shortened. When this was completed, the cylinder was seen to have reached somehow the other side of the frame, even though it was never seen passing through the frame.

(2) "Bends and lengthens; also cuts through frame." These observers reported the same bending and lengthening as those in category 1, but they also reported that, before the cylinder snapped back to its former shape, it cut through the frame, leaving gaps in it which did not close immediately.

(3) "Lengthens and cuts through frame; does not bend." These observers reported that they saw the cylinder lengthen and cut right through the frame, leaving gaps in it which remained for a moment even after the cylinder had passed through.

(4) "Cuts through frame; does not lengthen or bend." In this category fall those observations in which no distortion at all of the cylinder was reported; instead, it was seen as remaining straight and of a constant length as it sliced through the frame, leaving gaps in it.

In Table VI these categories are used in plotting the observations reported by the 20 observers under condition A against those reported by the same 20 observers under condition B. For 7 of the 20 observers (those falling on the diagonal from upper left to lower right, Table VI), perception of the rotating trapezoid and plastic cylinder was unrelated to the experimental conditions; i.e., they first saw it behave in one of the four ways, and the subsequent experience with either the rubber or the steel cylinder did not result in any reported change in perception. The 12 cases above this diagonal, however, reported marked differences in perception which were related in the predicted fashion to the differences between experimental conditions, 5 of them to the extent of seeing bending, lengthening, and no cutting through under condition A, and cutting through with no lengthening or bending under condition B. Only one observer (the single case below the diagonal) reported observations which were the opposite of those predicted.

In the third trial, in which the observer was asked to state which of the two tubes had been placed in the frame and his reasons for thinking so, all the observers who had perceived the plastic cylinder as behaving differently under the two conditions felt that they could tell, on the basis of the amount of distortion perceived in the third trial, which of the two cylinders had been installed even though they were, unknowingly, still looking at the plastic one (see Table VII). This was true even in the

TABLE VI

REPORTED PERCEPTIONS OF PLASTIC CYLINDER ACCORDING TO
CONDITIONS A AND B

	CONDITION B				
CONDITION A	BENDS INTO S SHAPE, LENGTHENS; DOES NOT CUT THROUGH FRAME	BENDS AND LENGTHENS; ALSO CUTS THROUGH FRAME	LENGTHENS AND CUTS THROUGH FRAME; DOES NOT BEND	CUTS THROUGH FRAME; DOES NOT LENGTHEN OR BEND	Total
1. Bends into S shape, lengthens; does not cut through frame	1		3	5	9
2. Bends and lengthens; also cuts through frame	1	2	2	2	7
3. Lengthens and cuts through frame; does not bend			3		3
4. Cuts through frame; does not lengthen or bend				1	1
Total	2	2	8	8	20

* Under condition A, the observer was shown the rubber cylinder prior to observing the plastic cylinder in motion; under condition B, he was shown the steel one.

case of the one observer who fell outside the predicted pattern in Table VI; he identified the cylinder as metal because "it bends more than the rubber one." The 7 observers for whom there was no difference in perception between A and B either said they couldn't tell which cylinder it was (3 cases) or said it was the rubber one, adding that they couldn't really tell and were just guessing (4 cases). Among those who felt that

TABLE VII
IDENTIFICATION OF PLASTIC CYLINDER ACCORDING TO
DIFFERENCE BETWEEN PERCEPTIONS UNDER CONDITIONS A AND B

IDENTIFICATION OF PLASTIC CYLINDER	DIFFERENCE IN PERCEPTIONS UNDER A AND B			
	DIFFERED IN PREDICTED WAY	NO DIFFER-ENCE	DIFFERED IN REVERSE OF PREDICTED WAY	Total
Rubber, because it bends (or bends *more* than metal one)	5			5
Metal, because it does not bend (or bends *less* than rubber one)	7			7
Rubber, but just a guess—no way of telling		4		4
Unable to identify		3		3
Metal, becuase it bends more than rubber one			1	1
Total	**12**	**7**	**1**	**20**

they could identify the cylinder, there was a sight preference for identifying it as metal (8 cases) rather than rubber (5 cases), but the difference could easily be due to chance. In addition, this identification of the cylinder as either rubber or metal appears to be unrelated to the order of the experimental conditions.

The effect of the order of experimental conditions was analyzed in connection with the difference between perceptions under conditions A and B, the kind of perception reported under condition A, and the kind of perception reported under condition B. In no case was there enough difference between the two orders to warrant notice.

The series of questions employed in the postexperimental interview was designed to determine the extent to which the observer had been deceived into believing that there were only two cylinders, one of rubber and one of metal, and that both were installed in the rotating trapezoid in the order stated. Judging by the answers to the questions, all but three observers accepted this and suspected no deception. One observer said he thought the experimenter might have switched cylinders, installing them in reverse of the stated order. He reported no difference in perception between the A and B conditions. Two observers suspectd that three cylinders had actually been used, two of them being just shown to them, and the third one being left in the frame; they added, however, that they had no evidence for their suspicions. To one of these two, the thought that he might have been tricked occurred to him only after the experiment was over; his reported perceptions under conditions A and B differed in the predicted fashion. The other observer, though, said he thought all through the experiment that he probably was seeing the same cylinder; his reported perceptions were the same under the A and B conditions.

B. Discussion

The assumptive complex involved in perceiving the rotating trapezoid as a straight, whole rectangle oscillating on its own axis and the assumptive complex involved in perceiving the cylinder as a straight, whole, constant-length object rotating on its own axis come into conflict during a portion of each revolution. This conflict begins when the trapezoid starts its illusory clockwise swing and ends as it passes the edge-on position (plane parallel to the observer's line of sight). In order to make the discussion which follows somewhat clearer, Figure 10 has been prepared showing four stages in the perception of the illusory clockwise swing of the trapezoid and the real counterclockwise movement of the cylinder.

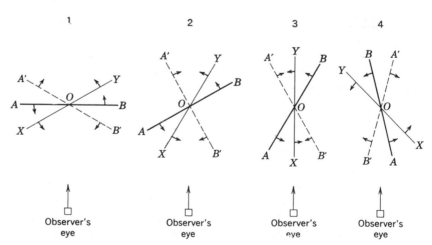

FIG. 10. *Four stages in the perception of the trapezoid and the cylinder.*

As the diagram shows, when the trapezoid begins its illusory clockwise swing (position 1), the cylinder (X–Y) and the perceived frame (A′–B′) are perceived as moving in opposite directions about a common axis; consequently, they appear to come closer and closer together (positions 2 and 3) until somewhere between positions 3 and 4 they pass one another. Beginning at 3, X–O is seen as overlaying B′–O and therefore in front of it, and A′–O is seen as overlaying Y–O and therefore in front of it. As the perceived movement of the frame and cylinder continue, more and more of such overlay is seen. Finally, the observer is faced with the perceptual problem either of seeing two solid bodies occupy the same space or of altering his interpretations of his visual stimulus patterns.

The possible means of resolving such a perceptual conflict are many. For example, the observer might cease to perceive the illusory position and motion of the frame or he might stop the movement of the frame and cylinder. However, in this experiment neither of these alternatives was chosen; instead, perceptions of the characteristics of the frame or of the cylinder or of both were modified. The resolution of the perceptual conflict was confined to the alteration of assumptions as to the characteristics of those two objects.

It should be made clear at this point that it is not considered that any given assumption was altered in the sense that "the weighted average of experience" was changed. Instead, it is believed that the *assumptive complex* was modified in the sense that the observer replaced certain assumptions with others. The components of an assumptive complex are determined both by the immediate stimulus configuration as it is related to past experience and by the "state of the organism" as it is influenced by purposes, expectancies, prior perceptions, etc. Thus one might expect intellectual knowledge, suggestion, persuasion, etc. to alter perception through altering the assumptive complex, but nothing new will have been added unless assumptions themselves are modified through action.

It seems clear that the experiment was successful in modifying the assumptive complex in the predicted fashion for 12 out of 20 observers, 5 of them to the extent that they perceived extreme distortion of the cylinder and no distortion of the frame when the cylinder was assumed to be flexible; no distortion of the cylinder and gaps in the frame when the cylinder was assumed to be rigid. That 7 observers reported that their perceptions were the same for both conditions is not surprising, in spite of the fact that all but 2 of them apparently accepted the suggestion that under one condition they were viewing a rigid cylinder and under the other condition a flexible one. It seems quite reasonable to suppose that the assumptive complex was not altered by suggestions as to the nature of the object they were viewing, but was determined instead by the immediate stimulus configuration as it was related to their past experience.

The case of the single observer whose reported perceptions differed in the reverse of the predicted fashion is somewhat more difficult to explain, but may be fitted comfortably to theory through a bit of *post hoc* reasoning. This observer was hostile and negative in his reactions from the beginning of the experiment. His first words when he entered the room were (approximately), "I only signed up for this experiment because I think I know as much about this stuff as you do. If you think you can fool me, go ahead and try, but I know things are arranged here to make you see things the opposite of what they are supposed to be." He experienced condition A first (supposedly the rubber cylinder) and reported that he saw it bend and lengthen slightly and cut through the frame. When he was handed the steel cylinder under condition B, he volunteered, "This one is steel, so you must be going to make it *really* bend. I guess you can see I'm an awfully suspicious guy." He then perceived the cylinder as lengthening and bending a great deal and not cutting through the frame at all. This contrariness even carried over to the third observation. He identified the cylinder as metal because, para-doxically, "it bends more than the rubber one did." It seems clear that the differences between the cylinders shown to the observer suggested to him just the opposite of what the experimenter intended due to an underlying assumption that perceptions would be "the opposite of what they are supposed to be." Thus the assumptive complex was altered, but in the reverse of the predicted manner.

The results of the third trial, in which the observers were asked which of the two tubes had been placed in the frame and their reasons for thinking so, provides excellent verification of the main results. The fact that all the observers who reported perceptual differences between conditions A and B felt that they could definitely identify the cylinder in the third trial on the basis of its appearance indicates that they ac-cepted the perceptual differences between the first and second trials as being real and associated with particular kinds of objects. This is further substantiated by the fact that the only observers who said they couldn't tell which cylinder it was, or qualified their identification by stating that it was "just a guess," were the seven who reported no differ-ence in perception between the A and B conditions.

The lack of relationship between the order of experimental conditions and the third trial identification of the cylinder as either rubber or metal requires some discussion. Theoretically, either recency or primacy might have some significant effect. In the former case, one would expect the observer's second perception to carry over to the third trial, resulting in a greater number of "rubber" identifications for order B-A, and a greater number of metal identifications for order A-B. In the latter case, just the reverse would be expected. Perhaps primacy and recency merely canceled one another, but it appears much more likely that the observers, *when told that one of the two cylinders was to be put back in the frame, immediately began to guess which one it would be, with the result that their assumptive complexes and therefore their perceptions were determined by the guess they made. If this occurred, the process apparently was unconscious, as the observers who had experienced perceptual differences between the A and B conditions all felt that they had made the third trial identification on the basis of perceptions rather than vice versa.*

In summary it may be stated that the experiment was successful in 13 out of 20 cases in modifying the assumptive complex of the observer so that exactly the same dynamic stimulus configuration was perceived differently under one set of assumptions than it was under another. In only one of the 12 cases was the modification of perception different than that predicted and, due to special factors involved, that case would not appear to be necessarily at variance with the original hypothesis.

IV. CONCLUSIONS

SINCE THE IMPLICATIONS of these experiments for perceptual theory were discussed at the beginning and end of each experiment, the closing remarks on this subject are brief. The experiments show quite clearly that the role of assumptions in perception is a crucial one, and that any perceptual theory which is restricted to object-to-percept relationships must of necessity be limited in the adequacy of its explanations of perceptual phenomena. The fact that these experiments placed fewer restrictions on the observer and utilized a more dynamic and complex perceptual situation than had any previous experiments designed with similar hypotheses in mind increased substantially the generality for perceptual theory of these findings compared to earlier ones. The gap between extended theory and experimental evidence has been lessened.

The results of these experiments also raise an important question in the area of learning theory. What do the experimenters mean when they talk about the "stimulus" or "stimulus pattern" in any particular learning situation? The experiments, particularly the third one, would seem to show that the "stimulus pattern" does not exist objectively apart from the assumptive complex and other aspects of the transactional process to which it is related. It should be relatively easy to perform a learning experiment in which the "objective" stimulus pattern is left constant, but the percepts to which responses are related are varied by altering the assumptive complex. For example, an observer under the assumption that the cylinder in the trapezoid is rubber might learn one sort of response to a rotating bending tube; under the assumption that the cylinder is steel he might learn a different response to a rotating non-bending tube, and either or both of these discriminatory responses might carry over to "really" rotating bending or nonbending tubes.

Probably there is no necessary relationship between "objective" stimulus patterns (situations) and what behavior is learned or later displayed in those situations as long as the present behavior does not result in the modification of the assumptive complex. This means that modification of the objective environment would be effective in modifying behavior only in so far as it impinged on that behavior in such a way as to modify the assumptive complex. If, as this analysis suggests, the important relationship in learning is between percept and response, it would seem to behoove learning theorists to take seriously Leeper's (7) suggestion that study be undertaken of that "neglected portion of the field of learning—the development of sensory organization." We may be justified in going even further and stating that an understanding of the principles involved in the modification of old assumptions, the development of new ones, and the organization of the assumptive complex is basic to any adequate theory of learning.

The experimental findings also have some important implications for social psychological theory, provided one is willing tentatively to accept the hypothesis that, apart from complexity, the roles of assumptions in visual and social perception are approximately the same. To the extent that such extrapolation is sound, they suggest that much of the conflict and misunderstanding found in almost any social situation is due, not to different conscious interpretations or judgments of a situation or set of facts which the participants perceive in the same way but to actual differences in perception. For example, it would have been possible to have made the third experiment much more dramatic by having two people seated side by side looking at the "same objective situation," but seeing different things. If our theoretical approach is sound, argument and persuasion could be effective in bringing their perceptions into agreement only to the extent that the participants have available common assumptions to be integrated into their assumptive complexes. If the common assumptions are not available, the only possibility for perceptual agreement lies in making them available through common experience.

Perhaps here lies the key to the problem posed by the relative ease with which we reach agreement about physical objects and the extreme difficulty we experience in reaching agreement about social occurrences. The properties of physical objects tend to be relatively common and constant; therefore, experience with them tends to be relatively common for different individuals and from time to time for the same individual. For social occurrences, on the other hand, quite the opposite tends to be true. More detailed developments of these lines of thought concerning assumptions, including the related functions of other variables, are contained in the writings of Cantril (3) and Hastorf and Knutson (5), as well as in subsequent chapters of this volume, especially Chapter 21.

These experiments also suggest a starting point for understanding percepts which are labeled "false" or "abnormal" because there is no obvious cause-and-effect relationship between object and percept. It is extremely likely that much of the "abnormal" behavior of psychiatric patients is a reflection of "abnormal" perceptions, and that these in turn are related to assumptions or integrations of assumptions peculiar to the individual. If this is true, learning research of the kind proposed above is basic to the development of adequate psychotherapeutic measures.

REFERENCES—CHAPTER 14

1. Ames, A. Jr. *Some Demonstrations Concerned with the Origin and Nature of Our Sensations (what we experience). A laboratory manual (preliminary draft)*. Hanover, N. H.: Institute for Associated Research, 1946. (Mimeographed.)

2. Ames, A. Jr. "Visual perception and the rotating trapezoidal window." *Psychol. Monogr.*, 1951, *65*, No. 7 (whole No. 324).

3. Cantril, Hadley. *The "Why" of Man's Experience*. New York: Macmillan, 1950.

4. Donders, F. C. *Accommodation and Refraction of the Eye*. (Trans. from the author's manuscript by W. D. Moore.) London: New Sydenham Society, 1864.

5. Hastorf, A. H., and Knutson, A. L. "Motivation, perception, and attitude change." *Psychol. Rev.*, 1949, *56*, 88–94.

6. Ittelson, W. H. "Size as a cue to distance." *Amer. J. Psychol.*, 1951, *64*, 54–67, 188–292.

7. Leeper, R. "A study of a neglected portion of the field of learning: the development of sensory organizations." *J. Genet. Psychol.*, 1935, *46*, 41–74.

C H A P T E R

15

Binocular Methods in Psychological Research [1]

Edward Engel

I T IS SOMETIMES THE case that trivial phenomena offer special opportunities for investigative work. *Binocular rivalry,* as an aspect of everyday visual perception, hardly merits a great deal of attention. However,
as a methodoligical tool it has interesting properties. In binocular rivalry
something akin to a competition between two different processes obtains,
and what is perceived represents the outcome of this competition. An
analysis of the perceptual report allows one to determine the relative
effectiveness of the processes initiated separately in the two eyes. In this
chapter we shall examine some of the uses to which the binocular rivalry
situation has been and can be applied.

In designating the experimental conditions to be discussed as binocular rivalry situations, we are simply alluding to a single common element
in all these situations, that is, the fact that different targets simultaneously

[1] This review and some of the work reported was supported by a research
grant (M-2528) from the National Institute of Mental Health, U. S. Public
Health Service.

[*290*]

stimulate the two eyes. This condition may or may not arouse the experience of an alternation between the two "monocular" patterns.
Unfortunately, the traditional use of the term "binocular rivalry" has
been ambiguous since it has been employed to designate both the situation of presenting different targets and the experience of alternation
obtained from them. It is also useful to indicate at this point that the
target differences with which we are concerned and which define our
situation do not include those that occur as a function of the lateral separation of the eyes in the head, i.e., binocular disparities. Also excluded
are those slight differences between the two images due to aniseikonic
errors, prismatic distortion, etc.

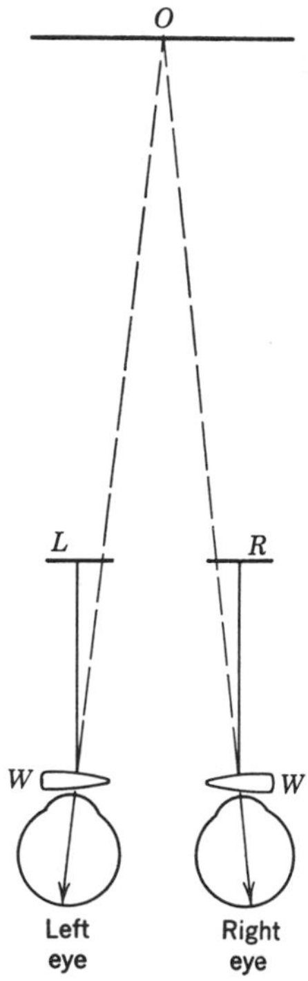

FIG. 1. *A Brewster prism stereoscope. L and R are the separate sources of stimulation to the left and right eyes, respectively. WW are wedge-shaped lenses which provide plus dioptric power and prismatic effect. As a result of passing through the lenses, the light received from L and R has the same properties as would be provided by a single larger, more distant object and is so perceived. O represents the apparent object.*

A prism stereoscope, as shown in Figure 1, is a convenient device
for presenting different targets simultaneously to the two eyes. If the left
and right halves of a stereoscopic slide contain different visual material,
the left and right eyes will correspondingly form different images when
viewing through the prism eyepieces. An observer looking at such a
slide will usually be aware of two distinct visual objects or scenes, one
superimposed upon and conflicting with the other. One can easily

establish that the two figures or scenes are contributed separately by the right and left eye by merely closing and opening a given eye, in which case the scene imaged upon that eye will disappear and reappear.

In most cases and depending upon the nature of the targets presented, two diverse monocular components will not be represented equally in the perceptual field. Instead, one of the components is likely to stand out more definitely than the other. In fact, the relative strengths of the two components may be such that only one is reported as represented in the field. The greater representation of one component relative to the other is labeled *monocular dominance*.

Following the initial response to two discrepant targets, there is often the appearance of alternations between sectors or between the two monocular components as a whole. The two components or their parts may supplant each other in a more or less rhythmical manner. This is referred to as *binocular alternation*. In this phase, one of the two components ordinarily will dominate. However, here the dominance is manifested in time, in that one component remains longer than the other in the sequence of alternation.

A good bit of evidence can be marshaled to indicate that monocular dominance reflects the differential effectiveness of the two targets as stimuli to visual perception. Panum (17), in the first systematic investigation of binocular rivalry, found that a simple line target presented to one eye remained in view practically all the time when the other eye was stimulated by a plainly illuminated surface. When one eye was presented with a vertical and the other with a horizontal line, alternation occurred at their point of crossing, with neither component having any particular advantage. Another early investigator, Breese (4), carried out a careful investigation of binocular rivalry in which he determined the proportion of time each target was represented during the successive phases of alternation. He found that a target containing simple lines prevailed over a plain target about 70 per cent of the time, while a target containing a letter of the alphabet prevailed almost continuously. He also determined that the more intensely illuminated of two targets would have an advantage and this advantage would increase with greater disparities in intensity. One further finding of Breese was that target movement enhanced dominance.

More recent studies using binocular rivalry situations tell essentially the same story: factors known to influence a target's effectiveness as a stimulus to perception appear to be identical to those that influence monocular dominance. In 1952, Vernon summarized the findings of rivalry studies stating that "the field of greater brightness, color saturation, color contrast with background, clearness, movingness, etc., tends to dominate over the field possessing less of these qualities" (19, p. 204).

What seems indicated in all these findings is that dominance increases as perceptually relevant differences between targets increase. *Implied herein is the fact that perceptually relevant differences between targets may be detected and measured by determining the degree to which either target dominates in a binocular rivalry situation.*

I. BINOCULAR RESOLUTION:
STRUCTURALLY DISSIMILAR FIGURES

CONSIDER THE FOLLOWING experiment in which monocular dominance was used to determine the residual effects of previous experience on perception (8). A stereoscopic arrangement was used to present a photograph of a man's face in its usual upright orientation to one eye of an observer and an inverted photograph of a face to the other eye. The two monocularly exposed faces were made to stimulate corresponding areas of the two retinas and, therefore, to overlap each other in the binocular field of vision. The hypothesis tested was that the upright face, recapitulating as it does the overwhelmingly more frequent conditions of previous stimulation, would have a reliable advantage with regard to dominance in the binocular field.

APPARATUS. The basic apparatus was a modified stereoscope enclosed in a light-tight box. The interior of the apparatus contained the shaft of a conventional stereoscope suspended 1 inch from the floor of the box. A stereogram-holder was attached to the shaft, and a pin which allowed the holder to be moved along the shaft was fastened to the bottom of the holder. The floor of the box had a narrow opening, ⅓ inch in width, which ran the length of the shaft and directly below it. The holder-pin protruded through this opening 2 inches below the floor of the box, enabling the subject to adjust the stereogram.

Running along the shaft, and above it, was a length of opaque black cloth equivalent in height to the stereogram. This arrangement so separated the field of the left and right eyes that neither eye could view any portion of the inappropriate field. In the front right- and left-hand corners of the interior, two 7-watt lamps were suspended which illuminated the stereogram. Two variacs outside the box regulated the voltage.

Two stereograms were employed. They were constructed by stapling together two squares of cardboard, one of which served as the front of the stereogram, the other as the back. Two squares, each measuring 1¾ inches, were cut out of the front board, and the photo of a man's face was inserted into each square, one of the faces inverted. The stereograms were of standard size, measuring 7 inches by 3⅝ inches.

FIG. 2. *Two faces as they appeared on Stereogram A.*

The faces of Stereogram A are shown in Figure 2. Stereogram B was the same as A except that the faces were, in the orientation shown, interchanged. The two stereograms were used also in the inverted position, thus reversing the orientation of the faces of each and giving a total of four presentations.

OBSERVERS. Twelve men aged 18–65 years. They had no history of visual defects of any kind, never having worn corrective glasses nor ever having been advised to do so. In general, the Os had 20/20 vision or better. The only exceptions were the two oldest, whose vision was equivalent for the two eyes but below 20/20.

PROCEDURE. A stereogram having a small circle as one monocular component and a large circle as the other was inserted in the stereoscope. The observer was then instructed to manipulate the adjusting pin until the small circle was centered within the larger circle. When he reported that the circle was centered, he was informed that it would no longer be necessary to make any further adjustments in subsequent observations. He then observed Stereograms A and B, each in two orientations, upright and inverted. The order of presentation was random. For each condition, the observer was instructed, "Place your head in the viewing position and close your eyes." The light switch was then turned on and the subject instructed, "Open your eyes and describe what you see." If, after one minute, the observer's report did not clearly contain information as to the relative dominance of the two faces, the following question or its equivalent was asked: "Does either face predominate or are they equally predominant?"

RESULTS. Of the 48 responses given by the group as a whole, the upright face dominated in 41, the inverted in 3, and there was no clear dominance in the remaining 4 (Table I). Each of the subjects reported more upright than inverted pictures as predominant, an outcome which is significant at a level of confidence well beyond 1 per cent ($P = 0.5^{12}$). The pattern presented to the left eye dominated 22 times, the pattern presented to the right eye dominated 22 times, and there was no difference in the remaining 4 cases. One of the two faces dominated 21 times (the left face of Figure 2), the other dominated 23 times, and there was no difference in the remaining 4 cases.

The following verbatim transcript of the report of one of the subjects is representative:

First presentation. I see a boy—a boy's face, but there is something else there that I can't see at the moment. Something interfering with this. Ah—now wait a minute. There's something upside-down. I can't see it too well. I would guess it was somebody's face upside-down but I can't see it. I can see the nose at the top of the boy's face. It comes and goes, but I can't see much of it. I can see his hair; oh wait a minute —he's coming in now. No, he went again. I can see his hair if I look down and it looks like a beard on the young man's face. He goes away again. If I look up I can see his mouth and his nose a bit. The eyes must correspond. That must be the secret of this. But the eyes of the two if I look up, no I can't really, the best I can get in the way of seeing two is to look up and then I can see them both with beards as it were. (E: Which one dominated in the picture?) The upright one. All the time or 99.9 per cent of the time I could see him completely.

Second presentation. Another boy, but there is something definitely behind there, but I can see him pretty well clear at the moment. Now the other one is coming through. Oh—now I can see it upside-down, just for a fleeting instant—yes, it's always the same boy, i.e., the photograph upside-down. I get the fleeting impression of a gorilla in the middle of this. Now I can see the one right-way-up with just a few bits of the other. The other boy is coming back—not really though. Ah, yes, he's there now, just for a second though. Maybe I can get him back if I work hard on him. Yeh, there he is. It's not the same boy though, is it? (E: Which one was dominant?) The vertical one; the right-way-up, but not as much this time as last time.

Third presentation. The same boy is back. Again there's somebody else there. And ah—oh I can see him this time—nearly. I got him for a second and he went away a second after. Now there is a strange sort of a mixture there—yes, I can get—I got the second boy now, the upside-down face. Why, you get a horrible view when they both come—when they clash. There's the vertical, the straight-up-and-down man again. Yes, I can get the upside-down man. I'm getting better at this. It's mainly the vertical man, but if I work very hard I can get the upside-down man on his own.

Fourth presentation. I can see the—oh, the upside-down man has

TABLE I

RESPONSE DISTRIBUTIONS FOR EACH OBSERVER

0	UPRIGHT DOMINANT	EQUAL	INVERTED DOMINANT
1	4	0	0
2	4	0	0
3	2	1	1
4	4	0	0
5	4	0	0
6	2	2	0
7	4	0	0
8	2	1	1
9	4	0	0
10	4	0	0
11	3	0	1
12	4	0	0
Total	41	4	3

(From E. Engel. "The role of content in binocular resolution." *Amer. J. Psychol.*, 1956, *69*, 87–91. By permission of the publisher.)

come, and almost first this time and I can see the other man on his own now. Now the upside-down man is pretty clear but those eyes are bothering me this time more than they did last. Yeh, the upside-down man is there in toto now. The other man has come back. I can't (pause) the right-way-up chap is spoiling it. Most of the time I can see him in the background. I don't seem to get this clearing away that happened last. I can see the (pause) never does the right-way-up man fade out of the picture entirely. His hair is always there. His eyes particularly are always there. The upside-down (pause) I could see practically all of him. I could almost describe him but the other fellow is always there. He's dominant all right—he tends to be there. In fact, I can't get rid of him—not entirely.

An examination of the transcripts indicated that the dominance of the upright figure is exhibited in two distinguishable ways. There is, first of all, a tendency for the upright face to dominate when the two figures are simultaneously perceived. In this case, the tendency is for the upright face to emerge as an organized figure whose appearance is marred somewhat by isolated and partial details and contours of the inverted face. These details are perceived as conflicting with, and extraneous to, the dominant impression. To a lesser extent, the reverse occurs with the inverted face emerging as figure and the upright as contributing extraneous detail. Secondly, there is a tendency for the upright figure to predominate where the two figures are perceived alternately in the field. In this case, the upright figure tends to remain longer in awareness during the successive phases of alternation.

The experiment just described differs from previous rivalry experiments in at least one important respect. Whereas, in previous work, differences in physical stimulus attributes accounted for the dominance effects, in this case, dominance was attributable to an internal condition, presumably a function of the residual effects of previous stimulation. It is to be noted that the latter condition affects binocular rivalry in the same way as does a difference in physical stimulus value. One might reasonably say, for example, that the influence of target orientation in this experiment was functionally equivalent to that of a three- or four-fold difference in the intensities of two otherwise equal targets. Of course, this does not mean that the neural events which underlie dominance are equivalent in the case of differentially illuminated targets. In fact, it would be surprising if this were the case.[2]

It might be argued that a drawback of the experiment described is the fact that observers were required to compress a minute's work of observing into a single determination of dominance, particularly since alternations between the two figures were commonly reported. This point was raised by Hastorf and Myro (14) in a recent article in which they reported data obtained using exposures of one-tenth and two-tenths of a second. In the Hastorf-Myro study, three series of targets were exposed in a stereoscopic apparatus of 12 observers. In Series I and II, three stamps, each depicting a face in profile, were paired in upright and inverted orientations. In Series III, two pairs of photographs of men's faces were used, each pair being identical but mounted in inverse orientation. Table II summarizes their main findings. Hastorf and Myro concluded that "the shorter period of presentation seems to insure that the relative predominance of right-side-up figures is not a function of mere estimation of the balance between two alternating stimuli" (14, p. 400).

Thus far we have considered the use of the binocular rivalry situation as a means of determining the relative effects of two targets which differ in a simple and prescribed manner. Moreover, the analysis of the data obtained was limited to a test of whether a difference was actually present. According to our analysis of the binocular rivalry situation, however, it should be possible to compare any two targets differing

---

[2] Whereas intensity differences would instigate differential retinal gradients of excitation that would be maintained throughout, the effects attributable to learning would probably originate at a more central locus. However, it is entirely possible that these effects are peripherally exercised although centrally initiated. At the present time we can do little more than guess about the mechanisms involved.

TABLE II
RELATIVE FREQUENCY OF PERCEIVING THE STIMULI

		RIGHT-SIDE-UP			UPSIDE-DOWN		
SERIES	EXPO-SURE	EXCLU-SIVE	PRE-DOMINANT	EQUALS	NO-FACE	EXCLU-SIVE	PRE-DOMINANT	**Total**
I	0.1 sec.	65	15	15	33	36	4	**168**
II	0.2 sec.	56	24	27	16	39	6	**168**
III	0.2 sec.	11	7	3	0	1	2	**34**

(From A. H. Hastorf and G. Myro. "The Effect of Meaning on Binocular Rivalry." *Amer. J. Psychol.*, 1959, *72*, 393–400. By permission of the authors and the publisher.)

simultaneously in any number of dimensions and obtain the same type of dominance determination. Moreover, we need not be limited either to only two targets or to a difference or no-difference analysis.

As an illustration, consider the following preliminary study that was carried out when the writer served as a consultant to the National Analysts Perception Laboratory. Ten magazine covers were chosen to comprise a series of targets to be measured. A specially constructed apparatus was employed to simultaneously present pairs of covers, one to each eye.[3]

The apparatus was basically a Wheatstone Stereoscope enclosed in a large cabinet and suitable for presenting large-scale displays. Two pairs of highly polished front surface mirrors within the cabinet served to alter the path of light so that two displays mounted appropriately were imaged on corresponding parts of the two eyes. Diffuse lighting in the cabinet permitted uniform illumination of the targets and an automatic timer governed the interval of exposure.

The procedure was to expose pairs of covers, one to each eye, for five seconds of observation. By means of a second viewing aperture, after each presentation observers viewed the two covers separately, with instructions to state which of the covers predominated in the previous exposure. The pairing of covers was determined according to the Method of Paired Comparisons, modified so as to permit fewer presentations per subject (13, p. 235). The proportion of times each target was judged as dominant over every other target for the group as a whole was determined. These proportions were then treated analytically according to Thurstone's Law of Comparative Judgment and scale values were derived for each cover. These values were taken as

[3] The apparatus was given the name STEREORATER by National Analysts.

an index of the relative "strengths" of the covers in the series. Following this, a check on the reliability of the scale values was made by splitting the data in half and deriving two sets of scale values which were then correlated with each other. A correlation of approximately .90 was obtained in this instance.

The use of the dominance report as a form of comparative judgment is novel in two respects: (1) the comparison is made without the observer being aware that a decision is being reached and (2) the decision is immediately registered in perception. Neither of these factors could be assumed to detract from the reliability of the data as compared with data obtained in the usual form of comparative judgment experiments and may, in fact, act to enhance reliability.

II. BINOCULAR RESOLUTION: STRUCTURALLY SIMILAR FIGURES

IN THE COURSE of our investigation of rivalry, using complex and familiar objects as targets (9), a rather remarkable phenomenon was uncovered. If structurally similar yet discriminally different targets are used as stimuli to the two eyes, a most surprising fusion occurs. Stereograms made up with similarly posed faces as paired monocular targets can be used to obtain the effect. One such set of stereograms was constructed from photographs that appeared in a Princeton football program. The photos chosen as pairs depicted faces that were similar in size and position of head and facial parts. Otherwise the two faces were clearly different and could easily be discriminated from one another. Figure 3 shows one of the stereograms.

FIG. 3.

A great many persons have viewed these stereograms and have described their observations while viewing. A small proportion of their descriptions was recorded verbatim and analyzed in detail. Almost invariably an observer will simply report that he sees a man's face. Rarely is there any intimation that dissimilar figures are being viewed in combination, unless the binocular efficiency of the observer is poor or impaired.

Further information is obtained from the subject by having him compare the "binocular face" with that of the two "monocular faces." This is done by extinguishing one target, having the person respond to the other alone, and then reversing the procedure. The same thing can be achieved by having the observer close one eye and then the other while continuing to view the stereogram. When asked to compare the "monocular" and "binocular" faces, very often the first reaction of the subject is that the "binocular face" is a composite of specific features borrowed from each "monocular face." Further inspection usually reveals that what at first appears to be simply a combination of dominant features is, in large part, a blending of features. Also, the "binocular face" is very often reported as more attractive than either of the "monocular faces." Observers are struck by this and, in many instances, report the effect spontaneously. If the observer is allowed to switch back and forth between monocular and binocular appraisal, changes are sometimes reported as having occurred in the binocular impression. Sometimes a breakdown of "fusion" occurs and alternation and doubling of the two images is reported. The latter also is sometimes reported after prolonged observation of a stereogram.

Differences occur between observers in the matter of which face dominates in the binocular combination. This is to some extent explained by differential acuities in the two eyes of observers as well as "eye dominance." However, other factors are clearly operative, since in most cases the same observer viewing different stereograms will sometimes report the left-eye face to dominate, sometimes the right and sometimes neither. There is every reason to believe that the same influences as were found in the previously discussed rivalry experiments also obtain in this situation, these influences being retinal image gradients and learning effects. Apropos of the latter, in a few cases, one of the photos presented for viewing chanced to be that of a person with whom the observer was well acquainted. Each time this happened, the familiar face was noted to dominate over the nonfamiliar face, i.e., the characteristics of the "binocular face" were reported as being mainly or wholly those of the familiar component.

Some time after having found what was believed to be a new phenomenon, the author read the appendix of Francis Galton's *Inquiries into Human Faculty* which clearly showed that Galton was aware of the possibility of fusing dissimilar photographs in a stereoscope. Galton, in fact, considered using this technique to obtain his "typical facial types." He rejected the technique, however, reasoning that the stereoscope "cannot of itself combine two images; it can only place them so that the office of attempting to combine them may be undertaken by the brain" (12, p. 227). He therefore preferred his method of composite portraiture which provided "true optical combination."

It would seem that Galton discarded this technique for the very reason that it is of interest to us. To obtain true optical combinations Galton required an unbiased instrument. The brain, having characteristics of its own, could not serve in this capacity. It would be apt to impose its characteristics upon the act of combination, thus biasing the product. In utilizing the "fusion" experiment as a method, we attempt to measure and interpret what was for Galton an unwelcome bias.

As an illustration of the fusion method, consider the rather ingenious study recently reported by Drs. Halla and John Beloff of the Queens University at Belfast (3). These investigators obtained the photographs of 52 elementary psychology students who participated as subjects in the experiment. The students were not aware that their photos had been obtained. In the experimental session, each subject viewed a "binocular face" made up of two strangers of the same age and sex as the observer and a second "binocular face" made up of another stranger and the observer's own photo. The three stranger photos were chosen from among ten which the observer had previously been asked to rate for attractiveness and which he had rated as being equal to himself in attractiveness.

The main concern of the investigation was to determine whether individuals would respond differently to a composite that incorporated their own image than they would to a composite made up of two strangers. More specifically, the experimenters were testing whether the self-composite would be rated as more attractive than the stranger composite when the individuals did not recognize themselves in the self-composite.

About one third of the subjects recognized themselves in the selfcomposite and were therefore not considered in the analysis of results. The remaining group of 34 subjects who did not recognize themselves gave significantly higher ratings to the self-stranger composite than to the stranger-stranger composite. Table III summarizes the findings.

The stereoscopic devices used in our binocular fusion studies, and those of other investigators, were constructed to accommodate small photographs as targets. It is possible, however, to construct a stereoscope which will accommodate live human faces as stimuli rather than photographs. Such a device was designed by Dr. Arthur Adlerstein

TABLE III

| | ATTRACTIVENESS RATING | | | | | | |
	—3	—2	—1	0	+1	+2	+3
Control Composite	0	1	3	13	12	5	0
Self Composite	0	0	2	8	11	12	1

(From H. Beloff and J. Beloff. "Unconscious self evaluation using a stereo-scope." *J. Abnorm. Soc. Psychol.,* 1959, *59,* 275–78. By permission of the authors and the publisher.)

and named the *Humascope* (1). Two people sitting behind the apparatus, each with his head on a chin rest, are viewed by an observer in front, as shown in Figure 4. What typically appears to the observer

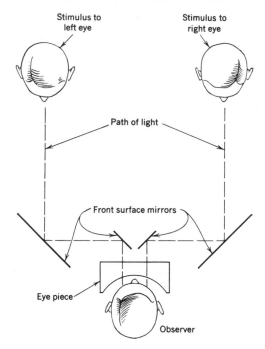

FIG. 4. *Schematic diagram of "fusion" situation with an observer viewing two live faces as stimuli.*

is a single composite head resting on a single chin rest. The appearance of a live composite head made up of two heads that are familiar to the observer is truly an extraordinary sight. Dr. Hadley Cantril, who had much to do with the development of this device, gives a vivid account of the impact of viewing members of his family in the Humascope (5).

Recently we obtained an interesting effect by means of a variant of the fusion experiment. The effect as it occurs in the typical case is as follows: A pair of photos depicting two different faces serve as the two monocular targets in a stereoscopic device. The faces are similar in size and position of facial parts and, by means of a previous adjustment of the apparatus, stimulate corresponding places on the two eyes of an observer. At the outset of the presentation only one of the monocular targets is illuminated. The observer, viewing binocularly, is asked to describe what he sees. The illumination is then extinguished and a second presentation given, but this time the second monocular target is also illuminated but to a very slight degree. The observer is then asked to state whether any change has taken place in what he sees. Following this report, the illumination is again extinguished and the procedure repeated, but again adding a slight increment of illumination to the second target while keeping the first at the same level. The entire procedure is repeated until the second target reaches the illumination level of the first. The remarkable thing is that, although the second target is raised in illumination, at each step the observer reports that he sees the same face as before. This continues to be his report even after the second target reaches the same degree of illumination as the first.[4]

The reverse procedure is then begun. The second target is kept at the same level of illumination while the illumination of the first is brought down in small decrements on each trial. On the last trial only the second target is illuminated. What is most striking is that the observer will continue to report seeing the same face to the bitter end. This occurs despite the fact that on the last trial a clearly different face is shown than on the first. Needless to say, there is a good deal of perplexity and, in fact, doubt when the observer is again shown the original target and told that this is the face he was first shown.

A study just completed by Ittelson and Seidenburg (15) clearly establishes the generality of the effect and also adds a great deal to our knowledge of it. A number of problems were dealt with. One was simply the question of how frequently individuals obtain the effect. Thirty-six males whose ages ranged between 25 and 40 were shown

---

[4] Minor changes are sometimes reported in shading, emphasis, aspects of certain features, etc., even though a face of constant identity is perceived. Some of these changes seem to be due to the fact that the illumination level is being altered throughout the sequence of presentations. It would be preferable to arrange conditions so that each eye receives a constant level of illumination with changes being made only in the articulation of the two targets. A further improvement would be to have a constantly exposed frame presented to each eye. This would aid the subject in maintaining symmetric convergence.

three pairs of "fusion" faces using a precedure similar to that outlined in the preceding paragraphs. Thus 108 sets of responses were obtained. In 97 instances, the same face was still being reported at the point of equal intensity, i.e., when both faces were exposed at the same level of illumination. In 67 cases, the same face was still being reported on the final exposure when the second face alone was being exposed.

Another facet of the Ittelson-Seidenburg study involved the use of "disparate content" figures. The figures used were a Negro-white and a male-female pair of faces. In this case, the investigators sought to determine the point at which a change of identity would be reported, raising the question of whether the attitudes of the observers were related to this point of change. An attitude measure was obtained by means of the California "F" scale and a masculinity-femininity inventory. Thirty-six subjects were shown a "disparate" pair after having been exposed to three "similar" pairs. Twelve subjects were shown a disparate pair first. For the 36 subjects, the correlation between attitude and point of change was essentially zero. For the 12 subjects, a definite trend was obtained relating attitude and point of change. The investigators were cautious in interpreting this finding and are pursuing the matter further.

In the preceding pages an attempt has been made to acquaint the reader with the rationale and application of the binocular rivalry technique to problems in psychological research. In approaching the task from the point of view of methodology, some of the studies utilizing this technique were omitted. The interested reader is referred to studies of social perception (2, 18), visual learning (10), personality (7), market research (11, 6), and to discussions by Cantril (5) and by Ittelson and Slack (16).

REFERENCES—CHAPTER 15

1. Adlerstein, A. "The humascope: A modified stereoscope." *J. Psychol.,* 1958, *45,* 109–13.

2. Bagby, J. "A cross cultural study of perceptual predominance in binocular rivalry." *J. Abnorm. Soc. Psychol.,* 1957, *54,* 331–34.

3. Beloff, H., and Beloff, J. Unconscious self evaluation using a stereoscope. *J. Abnorm. Soc. Psychol.,* 1959, *59,* 275–78.

4. Breese, B. B. "On inhibition." *Psychol. Rev. Mon. Sup.,* 1899, *3,* No. 1.

5. Cantril, H. "Perception and interpersonal relations." *Amer. J. Psychiat.,* 1957, *114,* 119–26.

6. Daniels, H. "A visual perception laboratory in commercial research." *Percept. mot. Skills,* 1958, *8,* 331–38.

7. Davis, J. M. "Personality, perceptual defense, and stereoscopic perception." *J. Abnorm. Soc. Psychol.,* 1959, *58,* 398–402.

8. Engel, E. "The role of content in binocular resolution." *Amer. J. Psychol.,* 1956, *69,* 87–91.

9. Engel, E. "Binocular fusion of dissimilar figures." *J. Psychol.* 1958, *46,* 53–57.

10. Engel, E. "Perceptual effects of retinal orientation." In preparation.

11. Engel, E. *"A Binocular Method for Measuring the Effectiveness of Visual Displays."* Unpublished manuscript.

12. Galton, F. *Inquiries into Human Faculty.* London: Macmillan, 1883.

13. Guilford, J. P. *Psychometric Methods.* New York: McGraw-Hill, 1936.

14. Hastorf, A. H., and Myro, G. "The effect of meaning on binocular rivalry." *Amer. J. Psychol.,* 1959, *72,* 393–400.

15. Ittelson, W., and Seidenburg, B. Personal communication to the author.

16. Ittelson, W., and Slack, C. "The perception of persons as visual objects." In *Person Perception and Interpersonal Behavior,* Tagiuri, R., and Petrullo, L. (Eds.). Stanford Univ. Press, 1958.

17. Panum, P. L. "Physiologische untersuchungen über das sehen mit zwei augen." *Dubois, Reymond's Archiv,* 1867, p. 63.

18. Pettigrew, T.; Allport, G.; and Barnett, E. "Binocular resolution and perception of race in South Africa." *Brit. J. Psychol.,* 1958, *49,* 265–78.

19. Vernon, M. D. *A Further Study of Visual Perception.* Cambridge: Cambridge Univ. Press, 1952.

16

Ultra-Stimulus Perception[1]

Adelbert Ames, Jr.

[In previous chapters we have been at pains to analyze the transactional relationships of "impingements," or patterns of stimulation, to assumptions, purposes, and other variables abstracted from the transactional process called "perception." In this paper, Ames calls attention to the limited nature of such analysis and offers clues for extending our understanding and research.—Ed.]

A S I SIT HERE in my office facing my desk, the wastepaper basket on the floor behind my chair and the dictionary on a small table behind me within reaching distance are in the ultra-stimulus-perceptual field behind me. Repeatedly throughout the day I drop wastepaper into the basket without looking around, and not so often I reach back and get my dictionary without looking around. And I carry out these purposeful actions with my swivel chair and my body in it at constantly varying angles to the basket and dictionary. That is, I have an awareness of the "thatness" of the basket and the dictionary and their "therenesses" to me

---

[1] From "Reconsideration of the Origin and Nature of Perception in Situations Involving Only Inorganic Phenomena" appearing in Ratner, S. (Ed.) *Vision and Action* Essays in Honor of Horace M. Kallen on his 70th Birthday (Rutgers University Press, New Brunswick, N. J., 1953). Printed here with the permission of the author and the publisher.

without seeing them, and this awareness provides me with prognostic directives for carrying out my purpose.

Similarly, in regard to my ultra-stimulus perception of the "thatnesses" and their "therenesses" beyond my range of vision in front of me, I have very definite awareness of the "thatnesses"—"objects"—and where they are in our little building, as I also have of those parts of the layout of the town of Hanover where I have been, and these awarenesses provide me with prognostic directives for carrying out particular purposes as they arise.

I am as convinced of the "reality," so to speak, of the "thatness-thereness" I am aware of through my ultra-stimulus perception as I am of the "reality" of the "thatness-thereness" I am aware of through my stimulus perception. We have no sense of a transition in "reality" where stimulus perception merges into ultra-stimulus perception.

We will now go on to consider the similarities and differences between stimulus perception and ultra-stimulus perception.

SIMILARITIES

(1) AS TO NATURE AND ORIGIN. The "thatness-thereness" significances of which we are aware in stimulus and ultra-stimulus perception are of the same origin and nature. They have their origin in past experience. They are registered in our higher mental processes and continue to exist on the subconscious-subawareness level. The significances in both cases are subject to being reactivated—brought to the awareness level. They differ primarily only in that the phenomena involved in their reactivation differs. In stimulus perception they are reactivated by impingements and stimulus patterns. In ultra-stimulus perception they are reactivated by attention directed by purpose and value. This difference will be gone into later when we consider differences between stimulus and ultra-stimulus perception.

(2) AS TO UNIQUENESS AND CONCRETENESS. The "thatness-thereness" significances of which we are aware in both stimulus and ultra-stimulus perception are similar in that they are unique, concrete, and specific as differentiated from abstracted universals, either universalized assumptions or conceptualized forms. For example, my awareness of the "thatness" and "thereness" of the wastepaper basket behind me or of my home is as unique and concrete and specific as is my awareness of the "thatness" and thereness" of the chair at which I am directly looking.[2]

---

[2] I have the capacity to imagine "thatness-thereness" significances as existing in my ultra-stimulus perceptual fields that do not exist. Such imaginings are unique and specific; however, in my saner moments at least I know they are not "real" in that they are not reliable prognostic directives for effective action.

(3) AS PROGNOSTIC DIRECTIVES. The significances of which we are aware in stimulus and ultra-stimulus perception have the same operational function, namely, they both provide prognostic directives for valueful, purposeful action.

(4) AS TO "REALITY." The significances of which we are aware in both cases are equally "real" and "important" to us, i.e., the wastepaper basket behind my chair is as "real" and "important" to me as the chair at which I am looking. Together these two types of "thatness-thereness" significances of which we are actually aware, which have the potentiality of being brought into awareness, constitute what we conceptually think of as the "objective world in space." They can also be thought of as the "thatness-thereness" aspect of our Form Worlds.

DISSIMILARITIES

(1) AS TO THE PRESENCE AND LACK OF IMPINGEMENTS AND STIMULUS EXCITATION. What appears offhand to be the greatest difference between stimulus and ultra-stimulus perception is that in the former our awareness is of "thatness-thereness" significances of "environmental phenomena" from which light rays are impinging on our retinas, while in the latter our awareness is of "thatness-thereness" significances of "environmental phenomena" from which no light rays are impinging on our retinas. .

However, when it is recognized, for reasons that have been presented, that even in stimulus perception perceptual awareness is *post* impingement and stimulation, it becomes apparent that this difference is only one of degree and, as has been pointed out, that in respect to the efficacy of our awareness of environmental significances that remain constant, the length of the time lag between the instant of impingement stimulation and perceptual awareness makes no difference.

Bearing importantly on this conclusion is the fact that the differentia- . tion of our retinal stimulus patterns decreases so markedly from the fovea to the extreme periphery. That is, there is a continual decrease of stimulus effectivity from the fovea peripheryward to almost no effectivity at the extreme periphery. That our retinas have evolved in this way, when they might have evolved with equally highly differentiated receptors over the whole retinal field,[3] indicates that stimulus excitation is not the only controlling factor in perception.

(2) AS TO REACTIVATING PHENOMENA. Another more marked difference between stimulus and ultra-stimulus perception is the above-

---

[3] Certain birds have supplementary highly differentiated receptor areas on the lower parts of their retinas.

mentioned difference in the phenomena that reactivate registered significances—aspects of the Form World—and bring them up to the awareness
level. In stimulus perception the reactivating phenomena that play the
dominant role are impingements from our environment and stimulus
excitations. In ultra-stimulus perception, although earlier experienced
impingements and stimulus excitation have played a role, the dominant
role is played by higher psychical factors involving purpose, values,
importance to the individual, which in ways not yet understood, by
directing our attention to those registered significances that are immediately of importance to the individual, bring them into his awareness.

For example, as I sit here in my office, I can't help being aware of
the chair from which rays are impinging on my retinas and are giving
rise to stimulus excitations. However, my awareness of the wastepaper
basket behind me only takes place when I want to accomplish the purpose of getting rid of some wastepaper, for I hope proper reasons.

These considerations lead to another difference between stimulus and
ultra-stimulus perception.

(3) As TO VIVIDNESS. Another universally experienced difference
might be referred to by the word "vividness." In general, stimulus perception is vivid, definite, manifest, while ultra-stimulus perception is
hazy, indefinite, obscure. But apparently this difference is only one of
degree. Under many situations the vividness of awareness reactivated
by ultra-stimulus excitations can be as pronounced as that reactivated
by impingements and stimulus excitations. For example, the other night
I took an upholstered stool outdoors to hang up a bird-feeding box and
forgot to bring it in. That night it rained, and my wife asked me if I had
brought in the stool. With complete vividness, I could see that rain-
soaked stool just where I had left it. That awareness of significances
reactivated by ultra-stimulus excitations can be as vivid as that reactivated by stimulus excitations seems to be conclusively confirmed by
the vividness of the perceptual awareness experienced in dreams, hal-
lucinations, by those who have eidetic images or are under mesmeric
influence.

(4) As TO MULTIPLICITY OF SIGNIFICANCES IN AWARENESS. Ordinarily in stimulus perception of "thatness-thereness" significances, we are
simultaneously aware of a multiplicity of significances, i.e., "thatnesses"
("objects") at their "therenesses." When we give our attention to the
sequential significances, our awareness becomes limited to one or two
"objective" significances. On the other hand, in ultra-stimulus perception, ordinarily we are aware of only single "thatness-thereness" significances at any one time. If I am aware of the wastepaper basket
behind me, I am not simultaneously aware of the dictionary, or the

telephone in the next office, or my home. That is, while I can be simultaneously aware of all the "thatness-thereness" significances and their interrelation within the field of stimulus perception, I cannot be simultaneously aware of all the "thatness-thereness" significances and their interrelation in the field of ultra-stimulus perception. Apparently this is not simply because it is impossible for me to be aware of the multitude of "thatness-thereness" significances in my ultra-stimulus field at the same time,[4] but because if I were I would not be able to give my attention to those particular "thatness-thereness" significances that would be effective as prognostic directives for action in carrying out my immediate specific purposes.

As has been pointed out, in stimulus perception when we give our attention to some particular "object" in our field of view, because of some purpose we wish to carry out, in so doing we cease to be aware of it simply as an "object" and become aware of its sequential significances, and when we do that we cease to remain aware of the other "objects" in the field of view. That is, when we give our attention to prehending sequential significances in relation to our purposes, we automatically limit the fields of our awareness.

Apparently, in general, we only become aware of registered "thatness-thereness" significances of aspects of our ultra-stimulus fields because such awareness will help us carry out purposes; e.g., I become aware of the wastepaper basket behind me only when I want to drop waste-paper into it. I can, of course, in contemplation give my attention to my wastepaper basket or my home or what not as "thatness" ("objects") at "therenesses" without any prehensive awareness of their sequential significances, but in general in carrying on my life's activities, when I give attention to significances that are not being activated by stimuli, my awareness has to do with prehension of the sequential significances of what I give my attention to.

In other words, with stimulus perception we are constantly aware of a total field of multiple "thatness-thereness" significances that are re-activated by the differentiated stimulus excitations. With ultra-stimulus perception we are never aware of the vast total field of "thatness-thereness" significances that are registered. We are usually aware only

---

[4] Although we like to imagine an all-knowing mind that has the capacity of being simultaneously aware not only of all our own "thatness-thereness" significances and all the "thatness-thereness" significances of everyone else, but also of all the "thatness-thereness" significances that man *might* possibly become aware of, from the "thatness" and "thereness" of the infinity of all the heavenly bodies to the "thatness" and "thereness" of all the grains of sand to that of all the atoms. The belief in such an all-knowing mind has affected both our educational methodology and our concepts of God.

of detailed aspects, when and in so far as such particular significances are relative to our valueful purposes.

CONCLUSIONS

FROM THE ABOVE IT appears that to a great extent stimulus and ultra-stimulus perceptions are of the same origin and nature and play similar operational roles, yet in some respects they play different roles which supplement each other and are indispensable for effective human behavior. But for our ultra-stimulus perception, our stimulus perception would be worse than "half a loaf." Consider the condition we are in when we are lost, for example, in the woods. Being lost is that situation in which we find ourselves when we no longer have or can bring to awareness the "therenesses" of "thatnesses" that are ultra (beyond in space) the field of our stimulus perception.

Under such situations we become panicky and abandon all other purposes except that of finding out where we are, i.e., re-establishing our ultra-stimulus perception.

The relative importance of ultra-stimulus perception is evidenced by the fact that, with our eyes open and with complete stimulus perception, if we don't know where we are we are panicky. On the other hand, if we do know where we are, the complete lack of stimulus perception which takes place whenever we voluntarily close our eyes in no way disturbs us.

The importance to us of knowing where we are is not due to a desire to know our egocentric localization in an abstracted spatial field, but has to do with our continued well-being or the necessity of carrying out of purposes; e.g., I am less panicky if I am lost in the wood in the morning than I am if I am lost at dusk. The difference is that when I am lost at dusk my well-being is in much greater jeopardy.

As a further example: If, when I was lost at dusk and in panic, by chance I came across a well-stocked cabin, which I did not know was there, I would no longer feel panicky, although I would not know *where* I was any more than I did before.

Through ultra-stimulus perception we are aware only of "thatness-thereness" significances of constantly continuing form, i.e., determined aspects of past "thatness-thereness" significances only. Through stimulus perception we are aware of "thatness-thereness" significances in the "now," so to speak. It is in the "now" that "the determined meets the undetermined" and "form" is altered, i.e., "flows." It is in the "now" that the validity of the constantly continuing form aspects that we are aware of through stimulus perception are being questioned by awarenesses that are in conflict with them. The determined is altered by the undetermined, flow takes place when the "thatness-thereness" significances of which we become aware through stimulus perception surprise us, are not what we expected.

For example, as an aspect of our Form Worlds of ultra-stimulus perception we can all bring to awareness the "thatness-thereness" significances derived from long-past experiences at certain places. When we go back to such places we are surprised, maybe shocked. Maybe we can't even recognize them because of the extent to which they have changed. Our ultra-stimulus perception has ceased to have any operational efficacy, i.e., any prognostic reliability for valueful purposeful action.

If the cosmos were totally determined, stimulus perception would have no operational function beyond that of ultra-stimulus perception. We could all live in ivory towers.

If the cosmos were totally undetermined, ultra-stimulus perception would have no operational function. We would have no responsibility.

Our stimulus perception, if we have the faith to accept it ("Allah's will be done"), brings us up to date, so to speak.

We will end with some collateral considerations of apparent interest.

Together with stimulus perceptual awareness, our ultra-stimulus perceptual awareness provides us with our extended "thatness-thereness" potential operational field. The "thatness-thereness" significances in this field are primarily related to the particular egocentric position of the observer. When we change our position, the "thatness-thereness" significances change. That is, our "thatness-thereness" potential operational fields exist only from a first-person point of view. It is this characteristic of our perceptual operational fields that basically differentiates them from abstractly conceived space which we think of as being referred to by maps of all kinds. We think of such "map space" existing independent of the significance of the "thatnesses" in its various parts to a behaving person at any particular point, i.e., as from a nonpersonal point of view.[5]

---

[5] The first person's point of view is a *sensed* awareness of the significances to that person of the "thatness-therenesses" in his operational field. The nonpersonal point of view is a thought conceptual awareness. For example, as I sit here at my desk I perceptually sense the "thatness-thereness" of my fountain pen on the desk before me. *Without* thought I can pick it up. If the reader were sitting beside me to my right, he would also have his first-person point of view as to the "thatness-thereness" of my pen, but a different one from mine. The nonpersonal point of view is that, with regard to me, my pen is 2½ feet away in a due east direction, etc., etc., ending up in relativity; in regard to the reader, my pen is three feet away in a northeast direction, etc., etc., ending up in relativity. The important thing to note is that the nonpersonal point of view would not only in no way help either of us pick up my pen, but if we were thinking about it, it would interfere with our picking it up.

Our perceptual "thatness-thereness" operational field also differs from "map space" in that in some respects it includes only a "part," sometimes a very small "part," of what may be included in map space. For instance, my perceptual "thatness-thereness" operational field of the very small town of Hanover is limited to the streets I have been on, and there are many streets and alleys on the map of Hanover where I have never been.

On the other hand, our perceptual "thatness-thereness" operational fields include ever so much more than could be included on any map or series of maps. I am perceptually aware not only of roads and buildings, but also of the "thatness-thereness" of many other kinds of "things," such as the layout of the rooms in many houses and the furniture in them, not to mention where particular trees and flowers, etc., are. And this will be true, although more and more space maps are being made and will forever be made of more and more different kinds of things. Moreover, a person can never get from maps the integrated "thatness-thereness" significances he gets from experience.

Space maps are most useful, indispensable, when we are lost or go into inquiry, but when used on such occasions we look at only that part of them that has to do with our particular position, and from the point on the map where we think we are, i.e., from our own egocentric first-person point of view, for the purpose of reorienting ourselves in our own particular unique perceptual "thatness-thereness" potential operational field.

Our stimulus and ultra-stimulus perception of the "therenesses" of "thatnesses," as described above, can be thought of as a spatial field in reference to which we translate immediate stimulus patterns. The word "geographic" cannot be used to refer to this spatial field, because it implies an isometric space field only, not involving a polar field, as viewed from an egocentric first-person point of view.

In our abstract thinking we conceive of a combination of all possible space maps as referring to space existing in its own right, filled with innumerable kinds of static objects existing in their own right, which together constitute the foundation of reality in which unfortunate organisms, including human beings, have to find their way. Maybe such thinking is the first step toward a bifurcated reality.[6]

If the above considerations are correct, they would seem to throw light on the problem of the bifurcation of "reality" into the "objective"

[6] The roles played by such modern mechanistic developments as the telescope, microscope, and radar are very different from the roles played by "space maps." They extend the individual's "thatness-thereness" potential operational fields from his first-person point of view.

and "subjective." We will digress to this apparently collateral matter, as it may be significant when we come to considering the differences between social and nonsocial perception.

At one time or another we all seem to continue to be haunted by the question as to whether or not the "objective" is the reality and the "subjective" is the shadow, or vice versa, and these hauntings give rise to questions that every individual seems unable to answer in a satisfactory and permanent way.

Apparently, the nearest an individual can come to resolving this dilemma is (1) to formulate an intellectual philosophical structure that denies the reality of the "objective" (matter) and confirms the reality of the "subjective" (values), or vice versa, or (2) through conditioning to develop an emotional faith that blinds him to the role of the "objective" and confirms the reality of the "subjective," or vice versa, or (3) to assume an agnostic position.

In fact, few individuals apparently are really successful in solving this dilemma. If a man professes to be a philosophical materialist, he prays at times in spite of his beliefs. If he professes to be a philosophical "subjectivist," he backslides at times into a materialistic point of view. If he has an emotional faith that either the "subjective" or the "objective" alone is reality, his intellectual processes will give rise to conclusions that will shake his faith. If he is an agnostic, half the time he half prays and half the time he half backslides.

If the above observations as to the nature of our perceptions are sound, are they in any way helpful in solving any of the above dilemmas?

In my own case it seems to me that they are helpful. I think my greatest help comes from the light that is thrown on the nature of "objects." Notwithstanding the apparently sound intellectual conclusion we arrived at from our earlier investigations into the origin and nature of perception, i.e., that perceptions were not disclosures of objects existing in their own right apart from us but only prognoses of the significances to us of "what" we perceive and serve as potential prognostic directives for valueful purposeful action, experientially I was continually aware of objects existing as objects without any other significances and having nothing to do with myself. And I had no grasp of any explanation of why this should be so.

However, all this seems to be altered if the above observations as to the nature of stimulus perception are correct, namely, that for the greater behavioral advantages to be gained from the simultaneous perceptual awareness of multiple significances we ourselves have developed the capacity to be aware of lower order significances—the "thereness of thatness"—of what we perceive, without taking into account the actually inherent higher order significances such as sequential, purposeful, and valueful significances. That is, we ourselves have created the objective aspects of reality in order that we can behave more effectively.

Further, the above observations (1) of the difference between awareness of environmental significances from the first-person point of view and awareness of environmental significances from the nonpersonal point of view, (2) of the much greater reliability of the prognostic directives of awarenesses from the first-person point of view, and (3) that although awareness of environmental significances from a nonpersonal point of view plays an indispensable role, it supplements the awareness of the first-person point of view and not vice versa—provide me with intellectual confirmation of the importance of the personal subjective role and that neither the objective nor the subjective alone is the reality.

And, finally, the clarification of my understanding of how we can be aware of "objects" in two entirely different ways, one experientially, as sensed, the other conceptually, as thought of, and that although both ways play indispensable roles in effective behavior, the latter way supplements the former and not vice versa, enables me to recognize that neither alone is the reality.

Perception in Critical

Situations[1]

F. P. Kilpatrick

PERCEPTION IS THAT complex process whereby we transform the code of our nervous impulses into the world as we know it; the world of space, objects, sounds, colors, people, and of dangers and disasters. Each of us acts in terms of the world he thus creates. Consequently, knowledge of the perceptual process should be useful in our effort to understand human behavior in disaster.

A review of the disaster literature indicates that this fact is not always fully appreciated. Disaster victims are often described as "notoriously inaccurate reporters" or as "giving completely different accounts of the same event." Then the effort is made to piece together all the "fragmentary" accounts into the story of "what actually happened." Once a composite reconstruction of events is obtained, the researcher then attempts to relate large categories of behavior found with certain

[1] Originally published under the title "Problems of Perception in Extreme Situations," *Human Organization*, Vol. 16, No. 2. Printed here in shortened form by permission of the publisher, The Society for Applied Anthropology.

frequencies in the population to the "objectively determined" series of events. This is a legitimate approach for many purposes, but from the point of view of the student of perception the key to understanding why people act as they do is in understanding what they are reacting to. Why is one man calm and collected, while another is stunned and bewildered? Why do some people flee while others remain? Perhaps part of the answer lies in age differences, sex differences, personality differences, or other such factors. But an equally good possibility is that the answer lies mostly in the individual's unique perception of the situation from his own unique point of view as it relates to his past experience, his purposes, and his experientially based estimate of his own capacities to act effectively.

A complex predictive equation is involved in any instance of behavior. Included in this equation is the person's assessment of "what is out there," and the assessment of "what is out there" depends in large degree on where the person is, what he is attending to, and his experience in decoding patterns of nervous impulses of that kind. Included also in this equation is the person's perception of himself; including, among other things, his purposes, his ability to act in certain ways, and his relationships with others. Somehow these perceived attributes of "other" and "self" are brought into relationship in the perceptual process. Emerging from this relational process is a prognosis or "best bet," unique for the individual, as to the probable consequences of the total situation as perceived (see Chapters 20 & 21).

Such a highly individualistic approach to human behavior does not rule out the possibility of generalization. . . . The principles which follow are, for the most part, extrapolated from basic laboratory research and should be regarded as hypotheses.

(1) *There is an initial tendency to assimilate all happenings to an established perceptual structure, and this generally is a familiar structure.* This tendency emerges very clearly in a great many of the Ames perceptual illusions. . . . It was the tendency to assimilate all happenings to a familiar perceptual structure which was noted by the National Opinion Research Corporation investigators in several of their studies, including one of a destructive tornado. It was reported that many of the victims interpreted the roar of the approaching tornado as the sound of a train (4). Similarly, in Cantril's analysis of the effects of the *Invasion from Mars* broadcast, it was found that among people who attempted to check by looking outdoors, many interpreted the empty street as "everybody has fled," while by others a street full of traffic was interpreted as "everybody is fleeing" (2).

The practical implications of this assimilative tendency for problems of disaster are many. For example, it suggests that, during an emergency, presenting just the facts, or the "truth," is simply not enough. The facts must also be interpreted. Fact alone, or truth alone, is apt to be assimilated by the hearers to their dominant percepts; and thus may actually facilitate the very actions which the communicator desires to prevent or modify.

(2) *Actions tend to be appropriate to the situation as perceived, even though they may seem illogical or inappropriate to others.* Appropriateness of action becomes even more a matter of individuality when we consider the role of purpose. For example, you as a responsible authority (let us say) not only have your own unique perceptions of the disaster from your own point of view, but have the purpose, say, of minimizing danger to the group. To you my action may appear illogical and come under the heading of panic, not only because you do not perceive the same situation I do, but because *my* purpose may be to save my life, or some particular person's life, or to secure attention which I have always lacked, or any number of other things.

A quotation from the National Opinion Research Center's disaster studies is much in point here. The authors say: "Our data indicate that the immediate problem in a disaster situation is neither uncontrolled behavior nor intense emotional reaction, but deficiencies of co-ordination and organization, complicated by people acting upon individual (and, often conflicting) definitions of the situation. It is this aspect of disaster behavior which is frequently identified erroneously as 'panic' " (4, p. 33).

(3) *Under stress there is a tendency to isolate oneself from immediate ongoing events, and hold on to a familiar stable perceptual organization. Concurrent with this perceptual restriction, there is a tendency to act in familiar ways that have proved reliable in the past, even though they are no longer appropriate to the immediate occasion.* This generalization stems from a number of studies conducted by Slack and Wittreich (5). They induced stresslike physiological reactions through the use of amyl-nitrite and cold-pressor in a great variety of perceptual and perceptual-motor situations including one-dimensional tracking, induced perceptual distortion, and size constancy in the laboratory and out of doors. The unmistakable tendency in each of these cases was for the subject to isolate himself from immediate input and to perceive and act in terms of a stable perceptual construct or constancy which had proved reliable in the past. Feedback of evidence that the ways of perceiving and acting were inappropriate not only failed to correct this restrictive tendency, but in many instances even aggravated it. Fatal jamming of exits in a fire and much other behavior common in extreme situations might reasonably be ascribed to these basic perceptual tendencies.

These findings suggest, among other things, that if people are to be drilled in actions to be taken during an emergency, the actions should be ones which will in no case be inappropriate. They also suggest that any tension-reducing mechanism, such as humor or expressive action, will help to relieve this tendency toward perceptual restriction and inflexibility.

(4) *In the absence of reliable guides from past experience for perceiving or acting, suggestibility is high.* There is little point in a lengthy discussion of this generalization as it is a familiar one to students of social psychology, first clearly formulated in Cantril's *Psychology of Social Movements* (3). Much of our experimental work in which we systematically place perceptual cues in conflict has not only demonstrated its validity, but has added some qualifications of interest. During the period of perceptual conflict, cues which would otherwise be extraneous are often seized upon and utilized as a means of resolving the conflict, and ordinarily the conflict will not be tolerated for long if there is any means of avoiding it. Once a dominant percept and action pattern is established, there is a tendency to suppress inharmonious cues and to enhance harmonious cues. One practical implication of these findings is that if suggestions in an emergency are to reach the audience when it is in a state of maximum receptivity timing is of great importance. The suggestions must be given early in the period of perceptual conflict.

(5) *Prolonged subjection to conflicting perceptual cues induces emotional depression, followed by elation when the conflict is resolved.* Slack's study of induced emotional reactions to the perceptual conflict involved in prolonged wearing of aniseikonic glasses is an excellent example of the perceptual research on which this generalization is based. He used himself as a subject, wearing aniseikonic glasses for one week. Results of wearing the glasses were marked emotional depression, followed by some degree of adaptation. Removal of the glasses resulted in feelings of elation so great that Slack felt that he had to put the glasses back on and gradually adapt himself to not wearing them.

The leads in such studies for understanding the emotional reactions of disaster victims are numerous. Also they suggest that, in an emergency, immediate structuring of the situation is important in avoiding psychological aftereffects. Perhaps this is true even if the structure which must be given to the situation is unpleasant.

(6) *The most effective way of accomplishing perceptual reorganization is through action by the perceiver.* This point is demonstrated most clearly in the studies of perceptual learning reported earlier which made use of action in the small monocular room. There we saw that perceptual learning occurs very slowly if an individual merely sits passive and observes while events, such as the bouncing of a ball in the room or

the movements of a wand, yield him clues as to the inappropriateness of his original percept. Perceptual learning occurs much more swiftly if the observer himself tosses the balls and feels around the room with the wand.

Strangely enough, advance intellectual knowledge about the true shape of the room has no helpful effect on perceptual reorganization through action. Bagby's experiment showed that it has an initial inhibiting effect (1). Apparently, the clues being generated through action are initially checked against a set of abstract concepts if they are available, and only some time later does the observer actually get down to the business of attempting to correlate them with what is actually being seen. Some later experiments have indicated, however, that when the abstract information is given *after* instead of *before* some testing out through action has taken place, perceptual learning is speeded up.

The results of these experiments merely underline the importance of securing common action and common experience if people are to perceive the situation in similar ways. They also leave us with the tentative suggestion that if the period of perceptual conflict in an emergency has passed and undesirable perceptual sructuring has taken place, attempts at verbally restructuring the situation for the participants should not come *before* the initiation of some common action, but should follow shortly thereafter.

REFERENCES—CHAPTER 17

1. Bagby, James. *The Relative Roles of Information and Action in the Genesis of a Perception.* Ph.D. Thesis, Columbia University, 1955.

2. Cantril, Hadley. *The Invasion from Mars.* Princeton, N. J.: Princeton Univ. Press, 1947.

3. Cantril, Hadley. *The Psychology of Social Movements.* New York: Wiley, 1941.

4. Fritz, Charles E., and Marks, Eli S. "The NORC studies of human behavior in disaster," *J. Soc. Issues,* 1954, *10,* No. 3, 26–41.

5. Kilpatrick, F. P. *Final Report, Contract N6onr-27014 with Princeton University.* Princeton, N. J.: Psychology Research Center, 1955. (Mimeographed.)

18

The Learning of Values:
An Experimental Inquiry [1]

Hans H. Toch & Hadley Cantril

I T HAS BECOME almost a truism that education is not a dissemination of facts but a preparation for life. The success of the process is gauged by the degree to which a child is able to cope with emergent situations and obstacles, as well as by the extent to which he has achieved maturity and intellectual depth.

If psychology is to aid in the enterprise it must take cognizance of its objectives. Rather than providing rules for effective memorization or laws of habit formation, the psychologist has to begin to concern himself more with principles that might aid in deepening the learner's sensitivities, expanding his value horizons, and preparing him to meet contingencies and crises that call for value judgments rather than facts or logic.

[1] Originally published under the title "A Preliminary Inquiry into the Learning of Values," *The Journal of Educational Psychology,* Vol. 48, No. 3, March, 1957 (printed in U. S. A.). Printed here by permission of the authors and the publisher, Warwick and York, Inc.

Conventional problem-solving studies begin to approach what is needed, but far from fill the gap. They deal with situations of what we might call the "how to do" kind. What is generally involved is the practical task of collecting and evaluating factual information and bringing it to bear on difficulties in achieving a goal. They provide few suggestions on how to approach *choices of goals,* deciding *what aims* to pursue. The processes involved here are qualitatively very different from the rational evaluation in the "how to do" problem. They comprise the intuitive, unconscious weighing of feelings and purposes. They bring into play the value standards acquired through acculturation. It is this process with which we shall be concerned here.

In the conventional problem-solving experiment the subject has to learn to disregard pat solutions and ready-made formulae in his repertoire, in order to arrive at a synthesis of past experiences appropriate to the situation. Analogously, every occasion involving choices of goal demands a creative revaluation of purposes and values, an active "inquiry" into one's value system.

Effectiveness is here also related to the readiness with which old solutions are abandoned in the face of new needs. Unfortunately, there are many ways of disguising the inadequacy of values, such as self-involvement in the mechanics of living, seeking out distractions, adopting ready-made values, or referring value questions to "authorities" in such matters.

The challenge to learning theory is evident. Is it possible to devise ways to break into routine? Are there ways of promoting the transcendence of instrumental considerations in favor of purposive "inquiry"? What techniques could be used to promote it? What is this process like? What forms does it take? These are questions that should be subject to experimental investigation. The present paper represents a preliminary effort at this task.

LOWERING THE "HITCH" THRESHOLD

WHEN WE SPEAK of active inquiry into values and goals we imply an interruption in routine. Only by pausing in one's tracks does one open the possibility of changing course. Why pause? The most obvious reason would be a hitch or obstacle which prevented one from proceeding. As Dewey put it, "Only a signal flag of distress recalls consciousness to the task of carrying on." Obstacles, however, have to be recognized. Some of us hoist "signal flags" more readily than others. A question of individual thresholds arises.

History provides illustrations of individuals who do not even seem to require an isolable obstacle to become conscious of "the task of carrying on." Gandhi perpetually meditated on the wisdom and rightness of his aims and ideals. Lincoln questioned and requestioned himself at every turn. In cases like these the hitches that are perceived seem to the outside observer to be self-generated. It would appear that this is not a capacity shared by most of us. To illustrate this point we placed 12 college students twice in a bare, soundproof room and told them to occupy their minds with whatever they liked for fifteen minutes. After each session we asked them to record "anything that you may have mulled over or any worries or feelings you may have had."

Only 9 responses were obtained in the area of introspection and self-examination. These responses were largely situational (e.g., worries about reactions to the experiment or trying to decide what to think about). In general, the subjects' thoughts centered mainly around the experimental room and the purpose of the experiment. Other recurrent categories were schoolwork (which was mentioned 17 times), dates (9 times) and reminiscences (7 times). Miscellaneous responses ranged from hockey, tennis, and basketball to worries about a lapel pin and gurgling of the subject's stomach.

A similar picture is provided by 40 affirmative responses to the question "What, if anything, do you think about before going to sleep at night?" The most frequently mentioned topics were events of the following day (7), current annoyances and problems were mentioned 6 times and "girls" were recorded by 5 respondents. Four subjects referred to prayer or religion; 3 indicated worrying about getting up the next morning. Only 2 subjects mentioned thinking about their life in general, about questions of purposes.

The above suggests that it is not the lack of opportunity or conditions for meditation that is primarily responsible for its absence. Given silence and solitude, most of us tend to continue concerning ourselves with purely "how to do" matters. Value inquiry seems usually to be aroused only in crisis situations which jolt us into self-awareness.

THE HYPOTHETICAL CRISIS SITUATION

SINCE PRACTICAL and ethical considerations make it difficult to experiment with actual crises, we explored the possibility of using hypothetical situations. The purpose of the experiment was to ascertain whether hypothetical "crises" could provide a useful and effective didactic tool.

Three experimental groups, each consisting of four male undergraduates, were used. In one of these groups, each subject was administered the material separately. In the other two situations, all four subjects were taken as a group, with silence imposed in one case and discussion permitted in the other. A control was provided by three comparable groups instructed to work on crossword puzzles. Each of the 24 subjects filled out a questionnaire after his session in which he was asked for general and specific impressions about the situation.

The "stimulus material" consisted of the following mimeographed "letter":

Dear Mike:

Forgive me for not letting you know long before this how much I appreciated your kind note wishing me a speedy recovery. I was released from the hospital only yesterday, but unfortunately there is no question of a recovery. Their half-dozen lung men all agree that I have *at the most six weeks* left, although there is no danger for the next twenty days or so. They wouldn't tell me this at first and I had to pry it painfully out of the doctor. Now I almost wish I hadn't.

It is very, very difficult to get used to the idea, and I don't think I am quite convinced of it yet. Unfortunately, there is no way of getting around it, and I have to sit down and do some very serious thinking as to what to do with the infinitesimal time left me.

The one consolation I have is that my wife and children are provided for. With the insurance, the social security, and what I have managed to save, they should be able to get along. If things go well, John might even get through college. I took care of the will this morning, so there is no worry on that score.

Ironically enough, I don't feel too badly. I will not be confined to bed and the doc says to do anything I feel like doing.

But what am I to do, Mike? Somehow I don't think I can just proceed as usual and pretend nothing is going to happen. Put yourself in my shoes, Mike. What would you do? Yours, Steve.

After the subjects had read the material the experimenter instructed them as follows:

"The problem is, what would *you* do? Imagine yourself in this situation. Try seriously to commune with yourself and honestly indicate what you think you would do or feel in these circumstances. Jot down anything that comes to your mind. Do not try for style, sentence structure, or anything else in the way of form. Key phrases will do. Above all, be sure you tell us what you *really* think you'd do. I'll be back in half an hour."

The questionnaire asked the subjects to indicate their feelings "about doing what you were asked to do," and to specify concretely these feelings by means of ranking. The subject was asked to check a square on each of the three modified scalometers.[2] One of these ranged from "worthwhile" to "pointless." The other two dimensions were "satisfying-annoying" and "fun-hard."

Another item on the questionnaire was "Do you think you learned anything? If so, about what (psychology, yourself, etc.)?" A section headed *Comments, if any* permitted elaboration on this question.

The averages of the scalometer rankings are provided by Table I.

TABLE I

AVERAGE SCALOMETER RANKINGS

	FUN-HARD	SATISFYING-ANNOYING	WORTHWHILE-POINTLESS
Experimental group (letter)			
Single subjects	3.3	4.0	4.3
Silent group	0.5	3.0	3.8
Discussion group	1.5	3.8	4.5
Total average	**1.8**	**3.6**	**4.2**
Control group (puzzle)			
Single subject	2.0	—0.8	1.8
Silent group	2.5	2.3	0.3
Discussion group	1.8	0.8	0.4
Total average	**2.1**	**0.8**	**0.8**

The figures show a consistent tendency for the "letter" problem to be ranked as considerably more worthwhile and satisfying than the crossword puzzle. In the case of the letter, the subjects who worked on it by themselves and those who discussed the situation in a group found it easier and more pleasant and worthwhile than did the group which was prevented from discussion. The subjects who faced the problem *alone* found it much easier than those in both group situations. In the case of the puzzle, the "satisfaction" rankings were highest for the silent group. The puzzle was found most worthwhile by the subjects who worked on it alone.

In response to the question as to whether anything had been learned, five of the subjects who had worked on the puzzle replied in the negative. Out of the other seven, four indicated they had noted weaknesses in their vocabulary, and the other three mentioned deficient working habits or inadequate knowledge.

[2] The scalometer consists of a vertical series of ten squares, five of which are positive and five negative. The scale is scored +5 (top square) through —5 (bottom square). The instrument has been found to yield high reliability and validity measures.

Only two of the experimental subjects claimed that they had *not* learned anything from the session, and one of them added "but I thought it a very valuable experience." A third subject replied that he didn't know. Following are some of the responses of the other nine subjects:

> Mostly about myself.
>
> Brought out opinions which were in my mind but had never surfaced.
>
> Formulating things which had been present in me but never expressed.

Some replies were more specific:

> It would be a good idea to lead your life as though it might end tomorrow.
>
> Maybe I could start on what I suggested I do.

Some of the elaborations in the section provided for comments were:

> Something which never occurred to me before and which appeals to me more and more as a philosophy of life.
>
> This is an excellent way of making people delve into their own thoughts concerning values and metaphysics.
>
> A situation such as the one imposed is one which touches most deeply into the core of feelings not too easily reached in the abstract.
>
> I am very glad to have been forced to think of the possibility of such a situation. It is amazing how many shortcomings I have.

In their discussion of the actual problem most subjects agreed that it would be impossible to go on living as usual. Besides preparing the family and completing financial and other arrangements, there was general agreement that it would be necessary to re-examine one's life and, if possible, concentrate some manner of improvement in the last weeks. Here are a few of the statements falling into this category:

> I think my life has been directed through a basically selfish motivation thus far. To finish off in such a way would not leave me with peace of mind which I must have. . . . How to use myself at a maximum for the benefit of others in a minimum of time is a problem—but I must go on from there. . . . Why hasn't this been my way of life always? I guess because of that selfishness previously mentioned.
>
> These six weeks are actually the only time in your life that you

know and can find out what life means to you. It is a time in which you definitely consider everything from a new point of view.

This is essentially a personal time. It is limited in terms of time, but has an element of freedom and infinite scope in the thoughts, feelings, and actions potentially to be realized.

Complete lifelong desires: Visit hospitals, etc.

I would . . . decide what my mistakes are and why I made them —decide whether [my] life was a success or failure—would undoubtedly arrive at latter conclusion—would probably be thinking to the effect "if only I had more time."

Many regrets about things I could have done or done better— haven't lived up to my ideals.

There was only one subject who indicated "I would continue in my normal life pattern." This was the subject who replied "no" to the question as to whether or not he had learned anything.

In all other cases the evidence indicates that learning of the predicted type had taken place. This learning consisted of (1) sensing the inadequacy of current routine and (2) formulating conclusions as to the direction of desirable change. The situation itself, of course, provided no suggestion as to the direction of this change. The possibility of specific directional suggestion remained to be explored next.

THE INDUCEMENT OF SPECIFIC INQUIRIES

THE "STIMULUS MATERIAL" consisted of seven quotations chosen because they appeared potentially conducive to inquiry into deficiencies or shortcomings in current behavior patterns:

Men will often say that they have "found themselves" when they have really been worn down into a groove by brutal and compulsive force of circumstance.—THOMAS WOLFE

A foolish consistency is the hobgoblin of little minds. . . . With consistency a great soul has simply nothing to do. He may as well concern himself with his shadow on the wall. Speak what you think now in hard words and tomorrow speak what tomorrow thinks in hard words again, though it contradict everything you said today. —EMERSON

Only blockheads are incapable of improvement.—GOETHE

Try to expand. Remember, the only sign of life is motion and growth.—VIVEKENANDA

And above all: to thine own self be true, And it must follow, as the night the day, Thou canst not then be false to any man. —SHAKESPEARE

Tell him time as a stuff can be wasted.—SANDBURG

At no time in the world will a man who is sane over-reach himself, over-spend himself, over-rate himself.—LAOTZU

Subjects were instructed to read the quotations carefully and mull them over "especially as they may bear on your own life and activities— that is, as they may be relevant to you." In order to gain an idea of the manner in which the material was responded to, the subjects were instructed to try to keep running notes of anything that occurred to them.

Another experimental task was used to gain an indication of whether learning had, in fact, taken place. The subjects, and an equal number of controls (who had not been given quotations), were told: "Imagine that today is January 1 and write a set of New Year's resolutions." These instructions were elaborated as follows: "Don't just write any old resolutions. Instead, cover things which you feel actually need to be changed or done, which you think you would actually do something about. Write as many or as few resolutions as you like."

The rationale behind the choice of a learning measure was the fact that a resolution denotes desired change. As such, it implies the realization of a deficiency or gap, of a shortcoming or weakness in the area it covers. This is what the quotations were designed to produce.

Fifty subjects were used—25 in each group. The groups were selected by splitting two advanced psychology courses. In each session a group of four to six subjects participated.

All resolutions were analyzed for content by means of a comprehen-

TABLE II

COMPARATIVE FREQUENCIES OF RESOLUTIONS
FOR EXPERIMENTAL AND CONTROL GROUP

	GROUPS	
	EXPERIMENTAL	CONTROL
Scholastic or working habits	11	23
Other personal habits	17	39
Social relations	7	18
Activities, participation	20	16
Attitude toward others	13	13
Specific action	5	4
Self-improvement	69	33
Total	142	146

sive code. The figures obtained from this analysis, covering the experimental and control groups, are summarized in Table II. Since totals are almost identical, the relative frequencies may be compared without percentaging.

The table indicates clear differences between groups. Whereas the control group has a relatively large number of resolutions concerning personal and working habits and social relations, the experimental group has almost double the number of control group resolutions dealing with self-improvement.

Table III presents the subcategories of self-improvement resolutions derived from the quotes which show clear differences in favor of the experimental group.

In order to evaluate these differences, we have to examine the written responses elicited by the quotations.

TABLE III

SELECTIVE BREAKDOWN OF SELF-IMPROVEMENT RESOLUTIONS

	GROUPS	
	EXPERIMENTAL	CONTROL
Be true to self—realize own limitations	9	2
Be creative—fulfill own potentialities	8	1
Expand, grow, become more mature	7	0
Stop wasting time	4	0
Total	28	3

THE PROCESS OF SENSITIZATION

THE RESPONSES TO THE quotations varied widely in nature and content. Most (57 per cent) consisted of general statements, amplifications, comments, expressions of agreement and commentary. Also frequently (19 per cent) were disagreements and critical remarks about the quote or the author. There were some generalizations about people (7 per cent) and a moderate number of references to the self, mostly favorable or autobiographical (11.5 per cent). Only a few expressions of self-criticism (5.5 per cent) were found. This small number of self-criticisms could not account for the differences in the resolutions. In fact, half of these overt statements (four out of eight) were made by a subject whose resolutions did not significantly differ from the pattern of the control resolutions.

The realization of the deficiency in the self was clearly an unconscious process, in so far as it occurred. Subjects did not state "I am deficient in X" and then "I resolve to concentrate on X." They did, however, deal with the material in ways which culminated in an unconscious dissatisfaction manifest in a conscious resolve.

In order to derive indications as to the kinds of processes which could result in revaluation it seemed desirable to examine the protocols of those subjects whose resolutions showed the most marked effect of the quotations. Accordingly, a subsample of eleven protocols was selected on the basis of resolutions falling into the subcategories listed in Table III. These protocols were examined with the purpose of gaining an idea of how the resolutions were arrived at.

The analysis yielded a listing of possible operations involved. Given the impressionistic character of the analysis, this list is very tentative. It does, however, appear to point to directions for more systematic research into characteristics of effective stimulus material and the "why" of its effectiveness.

The following seven factors seem to emerge from the data:

(1) MAKING IMPLICATIONS FOR ACTION EXPLICIT. An alternative characterization of this operation is "translation into imperatives." It covers restatements of general ideas in terms which permit something to be done about them. Thus, for example, the idea "be true to self" was restated as "have the courage to do what you feel is right."

(2) REFORMULATION IN MORE CONCRETE TERMS. This is a related category, consisting of providing definitions more specific in scope. The following are illustrations of this process: "Mental growth . . . is an awareness of the reality of things." "It just occurred to me, and belatedly too, after three years at Princeton, that the term 'finding themselves' requires some clarification. My interpretation: The personal knowledge that a person now knows what he wants in life to enable him to enjoy existence . . . and also that he knows how he can arrive at this objective. External circumstance does not provide this."

(3) THE DISCOVERY OF CONNECTIONS WITH RELEVANT EXPERIENCE. This heading refers to explicit identification of material with an idea previously encountered; e.g., "this statement is similar to the idea in social psychology that . . ." "Something which I just read in John Dewey." Such recognized familarity might very well enhance plausibility.

(4) EXPRESSIONS OF APPEAL. Possibly related to the above are positive affective responses to material, as revealed by phrases such as "a particularly perceptive statement," "impresses me tremendously," "the most delightful in these two pages."

(5) CREATIVE SYNTHESIS. There were several attempts to integrate and even systematize the ideas of various quotes. Following is an illus-

tration in which self-improvement has been related to the desirability of being true to oneself: "Life can be wasted by simply neglecting to improve yourself each day, by neglecting at least to try to create or be creative each day, by ceasing to grow. Yet . . . there is a point beyond which we cannot go. If there is a final answer, it is to strive to become all that we are capable of becoming, in honesty with ourselves . . . improve to the limit of our capacities."

(6) SELF-EXAMINATION. The sample contained questions such as "Can my consistency be the equivalent of pride?" "Have I found myself . . . or have I just begun to adapt self to circumstance?" Such queries appear to constitute attempts to inquire actively into one's value system.

(7) RECOGNITION OF OWN WEAKNESS. Some protocols went a step further, with statements like "perhaps I am a blockhead" or " I rarely let my introspections influence my actions." If taken seriously, realizations of inadequacy of this sort might well result in reformulation of values.

The above suggest the possibility of experimenting with material that

(1) clearly implies concrete inferences for behavior;

(2) contains simple and specific definitions;

(3) rcfcrs to things in the subject's past experience;

(4) Makes a satisfying impact through its presentation;

(5) allows for integration of component ideas, and perhaps even suggests them in various degrees;

(6) explicitly or implicitly poses the possibility of relevance to the subject himself.

These are not rules for effectiveness of learning material. They are modest hunches as to possible first steps leading to active inquiry and possible revaluation. A more intimate acquaintance with processes of this order may well open the door to the experimental investigation into the unconscious weighing of values and their consequent rejection, strengthening, or modification.

C H A P T E R

19

A Note Concerning
Homeostasis[1]

Hans H. Toch & Albert H. Hastorf

[This chapter omits the excellent analyses of representative homeostatic psychological theories contained in the original paper. It is presented as an introduction to the two "constancy" chapters which follow (Chapters 20 and 21) in order to make clear an understanding that "constancies" are regarded in transactional theory, not as ends in themselves but as "conditions" for assessment, prediction, and action—a set of relationships basic to emergence.—Ed.]

I N THE DEVELOPMENT of any theoretic concept or group of related concepts, an occasional stocktaking is useful. This paper is an attempt to perform such a service for the term "homeostasis" in the various connotations it has acquired in contemporary psychological theorizing.

[1] Part of "Homeostasis in Psychology," *Psychiatry: J. for the Study of Interpersonal Processes,* 1955, *18,* 81–91. These portions reprinted by permission of the of The William Alanson White Psychiatric Foundation, Inc. Copyright by The William Alanson White Psychiatric Foundation, Inc.

In tracing the history of this concept, we shall be primarily concerned with locating common denominators among the various specific adaptive connotations it has acquired in line with the points of view and purposes of particular theorists. Focusing on these common denominators and distinguishing among connotations is essential for clear definition and for critical and methodological purposes.

THE ADVENT OF HOMEOSTASIS

THE TERM "HOMEOSTASIS" was first used by W. B. Cannon in 1926 (2) and was formally brought into the academic world in 1932 in Cannon's biological classic, *The Wisdom of the Body* (3). Somewhat allied concepts, however, have been traced to other writers, notably to C. P. Richter, whose paper appeared in 1927 (10), and to the nineteenth-century biologist, Claude Bernard (1).

As defined by Cannon, homeostasis consists of "the co-ordinated physiological processes which maintain most of the steady states in the organism." Cannon called these states *equilibria*. These processes, peculiar to living organisms, were described as complex in nature, "involving, as they may, the brain and nerves, the heart, lungs, kidneys and spleen, all working co-operatively." "The word," added Cannon, "does not imply something set and immobile, a stagnation. It means a condition—which may vary, but which is relatively constant" (3, p. 24).

Cannon elaborated the concept with a set of tentative propositions, three of which may be relevant here. According to the first, "in an open system [such as the human body] . . . constancy is in itself evidence that agencies are acting, or ready to act, to maintain this constancy." The second affirms that "if a state remains steady it does so because any tendency toward change is automatically met by increased effectiveness of the factor or factors which resist the change." According to the third, "the regulating system which determines a homeostatic state may comprise a number of co-operating factors brought into action at the same time or successively" (3, pp. 281–82).

Biologists following Cannon greatly expanded the scope of homeostasis until, as indicated by E. W. Dempsey, "it now cannot be restricted to any single mechanism or activity," and comprises all sorts of somatic functioning (6, p. 229). Many aspects of this expansion have bordered on the realm of the psychological.

Among the first systematic attempts to apply homeostasis as a covering concept to strictly psychological problems is that of J. M. Fletcher (8). Beginning with the premise of "the current concept of body-mind as an organic whole," Fletcher indicated that "there is ground for assuming that Cannon's findings have quite as important an implication for psychology as they do for physiology." This statement was to be considered "not mere analogy" but as empirically verified (8, p. 81). As potential areas of application for this biologically derived explanatory concept, Fletcher discussed theories of color vision, afterimage of motion, and visual constancy, as well as performance levels and "personality adjustments" comprising mechanisms of defense.

Two differences were explicitly noted by Fletcher between homeostasis as defined by Cannon and his own application of the concept: First, instead of the original restriction to "normal body states," homeostasis was now to be extended to acquired states. Second, consciousness was envisioned as permitting the *anticipation* of the disturbance originally seen as the agent automatically arousing homeostatic mechanisms. . . . A third difference between the original concept and that utilized by Fletcher was not mentioned by Fletcher himself, but has been isolated by J. R. Maze in his excellent critical paper on the subject. He pointed out that Fletcher, like others after him, dealt with homeostasis as a restoring force rather than "simply the fact of restoration." Homeostasis thus acquired a causal connotation in lieu of its original role "as the effect of various specific qualitative processes in the organism" (9, p. 406).

Homeostasis, as seen by Fletcher, has become an equilibrium-restoring force operating when any state of the organism, innate or acquired, finds itself disturbed or threatened. It can hardly be argued that the evidence compiled by Cannon of such tendencies as that of re-establishing depleted blood substances through the intake of food or water is susceptible to invocation in support of this modified concept. Thus Cannon cannot be cited as in any way offering an explanation of Fletcher's homeostasis. The latter is a new concept, not an application of an established one.

It may be useful to speculate briefly as to the reasons for the popularity and widespread adoption of the term. The first reason that suggests itself for the importation of homeostasis into the psychological vocabulary is the evolutionary implications, both of the original mechanism [2] and of the various psychological constructs derived from it. One can regard homeostatic theorizing as a specific manifestation of the genetic reasoning in psychology which was stimulated by Darwin. The investigator who follows this type of reasoning attempts to isolate mechanisms common to the species, to show their adaptive significance—with the explicit or implicit premise that adaptiveness has causal efficacy—and

[2] See Dempsey (6) for a discussion of evolutionary aspects of homeostasis.

to trace the changes in the operation of these mechanisms brought about in the course of ontogenetic or phylogenetic development. Since evolution is a biological process, constant referral to it may perhaps fall under the heading of *biologism.*

An allied reason for the popularity of the term "homeostasis" may be that the utilization of biological concepts, suitably modified, in psychological systems constitutes a metaphysical act of faith. Few, if any, contemporary investigators would subscribe to the contention that psychology should deal with, or even acknowledge the existence of, forces of a nonmaterial variety. This materialistic bias is such that the psychologist has a greater feeling of security when he talks of body balances or neural physiology data.

An additional factor in the adoption of homeostatic theories is the desire for concepts unifying several—and eventually all—scientific disciplines, which has long been cherished by philosophers of science, as well as by workers in the various fields themselves. Many theorists show, in fact, a sort of allergy toward the use of different levels of conceptualization for different kinds of phenomena. Unfortunately, the result is that unifying concepts are frequently established prematurely, without being justified by the data at hand. The categorization of a multiplicity of events of any sort under the heading of some inclusive process or mechanism not only obscures the functional relationships among these events but also precludes their investigation: it provides a closed system for the universe it covers.

Extreme care must be exercised in defining homeostasis. If, for example, one were to define homeostasis as a physiological state, only reductionist theories would find such a definition useful. Similarly, characterizations in terms of specific equilibria or general organismic stability, automatic readjustment versus cognitive control, or comfort as against constant change, would apply to some specific frameworks but not to others. *In dealing with homeostasis one is concerned not with a single concept but with many concepts having a common origin.*

One can, however, point to two denominators shared by all these concepts. The first of these is the formal sequence—that is, the following of a state of disturbance by a state of relative quiescence; the other is the premise that the achievement of the second state is somehow the direct or indirect object or cause of behavior initiated in connection with the first state. In other words, behavior is seen as ultimately aimed at a state categorized as "equilibrium." These two common denominators may perhaps be characterized as *phenotypic homeostatic sequence* and *equilibration dynamics,* respectively. They constitute the descriptive and explanatory aspects of homeostasis. The explanatory use of homeostasis calls for a number of cautions and comments, mostly applicable to specific frameworks.

John Dewey has very aptly indicated that "if we follow an infantile logic we shall reduplicate the unity of result in an assumption of unity of force behind it" (7, p. 111). This, it has been pointed out by Maze, is a major fallacy in homeostatic thinking, in so far as he has examined it. Thus, for instance, "the rough stability of a society over a period of time . . . is [in fact] just a by-product of the many-sided clash of sectional interest" (9, p. 412). After discussing this clash of specific impulses, Maze concludes his paper as follows: "The doctrine of homeostasis at best only points to the facts of opposition and co-operation without advancing knowledge of the impulses whose activities these are; at worst, it hinders that inquiry by ignoring those impulses and concentrating on their resultant (or even on their mere equilibrium) and by offering a pseudosolution of how the more or less stable resultants are maintained" (9, p. 412).

The danger of a pseudosolution is a matter of special concern in view of its effect on research. There is a tendency on the part of busy investigators to accept plausible formulae as explanatory of what would otherwise require research for its elucidation. To avoid this pitfall one must demand that concepts to be utilized be abstracted from the concrete process containing the event to be explained, and not elaborated as abstractions, in analogy to the *deus ex machina* on the stage. The tendency to work toward the evidence instead of from it is dramatically apparent in approaches which postulate a tendency to equilibrium and then proceed to explain why behavior that does not seem to obey this law actually does do so. Such an approach, starting with an explanation —based on evidence for a statement similar to it in form but on another level entirely—and ending up with the data to be explained away, is hardly science at all.

Thus the main general criticism of homeostatic theory is the assumption implicit in much of this theory of a general principle or force accounting for the result observed, which causes one to overlook the multiplicity of determinants actually involved in every concrete psychological event. The principal corollary of this criticism is that the "equilibrating force" assumption precludes further investigation, since it leaves no remaining questions.

Another problem is whether, in some instances, the proposed explanation does not pose more questions than it answers. The acquisition of a complex piece of machinery without instructions as to its operation is a futile step. Similarly, the postulation of a mechanism for some hypothetical psychological function carries with it the obligation of explicitly indicating how, in given concrete situations, the proposed mechanism operates. One is thus justified—when faced with hierarchies of values, cognitively controlled reactions to anticipated disturbances, or achievements of stability in perception—in asking the question "How?" and in waiting self-righteously for an answer.

But even though we consider many—or even all—of the psychological applications of the concept of homeostasis to be open to one or more methodological reservations, we do not question the legitimacy of the general attempt to conceptualize a tendency toward stability in many aspects of mental life. The validity of this tendency is certainly not to be regarded as contingent on the validity of its particular embodiments. Effective behavior requires reliability in the prognosis of its results; hence at least a minimum of stability is required in the experienced world and the experienced self. It stands to reason, therefore, that the person will strive to minimize unpredictability, lack of surety, ambiguity, or low reliability. Cantril has commented on the necessity of creating subjective certainties out of empirical probabilities if one is to act effectively in concrete situations. "Things," symbols, ideologies, and personal and institutional characteristics all tend to be made into absolutes, and to be experienced as such (5). In the area of social movements, a need for meaning seems to operate in crisis situations which favors movements holding out solutions for problems the individual himself cannot interpret (4). Rigidity studies in perception have shown a tendency variously interpreted as intolerance of ambiguity, schematization, or inability to accept novelty. In the cognitive area, efficient functioning certainly requires reasonably high prognostic reliabilities, and hence conditions of stability.

Similarly, in other aspects of behavior, experience—that is, past solutions—will tend to be relied upon until it is perceived as no longer functional. As Dewey has pointed out, "it is the essence of routine to insist upon its own continuation. Breach of it is a violation of right. Deviation from it is transgression" (7, pp. 75–76). It is only when past solutions are perceived as inapplicable to present problems (and the ease with which this is perceived varies widely with individuals) that new solutions are sought.

All this suggests that the operation toward achieving high reliability is a general tendency in human functioning. It does not imply mechanisms for attaining high reliability, nor does it suggest that the general tendency toward reliability can validly be used as an explanation for any given piece of behavior. The ideal of high reliability has to be reconciled with other tendencies which appear to manifest themselves in human behavior, such as the tendency toward seeking new or more valuable experiences, which can be done only if old and tried paths are departed from. Whether the general tendency toward some degree of constancy in human living can fruitfully be categorized under the heading of homeostasis is a moot question. When a term cumulatively acquires a series of undesirable connotations, a point is reached at which it becomes more of a liability than an asset. This point may well have been arrived at with Cannon's homeostasis as an item in the psychological lexicon.

REFERENCES—CHAPTER 19

1. Bernard, C. *Leçons sur les propriétés physiologiques et les alterations pathologiques des liquides de l'organisme.* Paris: Balliere, 1859.

2. Cannon, Walter B. "Some general features of endocrine influence on metabolism." *Amer. J. Med. Sci.,* 1926, *171,* 1–20.

3. Cannon, Walter B. *The Wisdom of the Body.* New York: Norton, 1932.

4. Cantril, Hadley. *The Psychology of Social Movements.* New York: Wiley, 1941.

5. Cantril, Hadley. "The qualities of being human." *Amer. Quart.,* 1954, 3–18.

6. Dempsey, E. W. "Homeostasis," in *Handbook of Experimental Psychology,* ed. by S. S. Stevens. New York: Wiley, 1951, pp. 209–35.

7. Dewey, John. *Human Nature and Conduct.* New York: Modern Library, 1930.

8. Fletcher, John M. "Homeostasis as an explanatory principle in psychology." *Psychol. Rev.* 1942, *49,* 80–87.

9. Maze, J. R. "On some corruptions of the doctrine of homeostasis." *Psychol. Rev.,* 1953, *60,* 405–12.

10. Richter, C. P. "Animal behavior and internal drives." *Quart. Rev. Biol.* 1927, *2,* 307–43.

The Constancies in Visual

Perception[1]

William H. Ittelson

I

W E LIVE AND ACT in a world which we perceive as relatively stable in spite of the ever-changing impingements on our sense organs. This fact becomes a problem to those interested in evolving simplified conceptual explanatory systems. It has interested philosophers of
all times and has troubled psychologists ever since that discipline was
born. It has helped to form the foundation of one psychological system
and to work the downfall of another. Whatever may be the ultimate
evaluation of psychological theorists, on one statement all can agree:
it is this simple fact of perceptual constancy that makes effective actions
possible, from the simplest to the most complex, from walking across

[1] Originally published under the title "The Constancies in Perceptual Theory,"
Psychol. Rev., 1951, 58, 285–94. Printed here by permission of the author and
publisher, The American Psychological Association.

the street to striving for a sane social order. Without it mere survival would be impossible.

As most commonly used in psychological literature, constancy refers to the similarity between specific apparent properties (such as the size, shape, or color) of two or more objects producing different "proximal" stimuli, with emphasis on the correspondence between these perceived properties and the "actual" properties of the objects. The objects need not be viewed simultaneously and indeed may be the same object viewed at different times. This leads directly to the continuous viewing of the same object, which is related to effects which can be termed "continuity" as opposed to constancy (26, p. 304). In actual experience, however, continuity is the rule, and constancy, as traditionally investigated, merely represents a "sample" picked out for study from the more general experienced continuity. In this paper, therefore, any behavior which tends to preserve the continuity and stability of the perceived world in the face of ever-changing relationships between observer and environment will be labeled "constancy."

The perceptual constancies are studied experimentally by comparing the relevant characteristics of the "percept" with those of the "object" (4, 39). Such studies are neither the discovery nor the exclusive property of the Gestalt psychologists who have brilliantly extended them as a means of demolishing their archenemy, the constancy hypothesis (26, 27). If perception remains constant as stimulation changes, then clearly there can be no constant relationship between stimulation and perception. The substitution of perceptual constancy for the rejected constancy hypothesis introduces a confusion of terms which, although deplored by some, may eventually be judged quite apposite. For Gestalt theory remains primarily concerned with stimulation to percept relationships and, in a sense, merely hypothesizes a constant geometrical distortion in place of the constancy hypothesis, of which the law of Pragnanz can be seen as an elaboration. While such geometrical constancy is becoming seriously challenged by recent work on the role of subjective determinants in perception (cf. for example, 6), more functionally oriented psychologists, taking a cue from behaviorism, have shifted the focus of interest from "perceptual" constancy to "object" or "thing" constancy with all that this implies in terms of conceptual and experimental reorientation.

The study of constancy by comparisons of object with percept has not escaped without methodological criticism. The frequently used constancy ratio (10, 32) offers the paradox of ratios greater than one; i.e., overconstancy, which clearly must be considered as much an "error" as underconstancy. This objection has been met by the substitution of correlations (7), which will give a more meaningful measure of the extent to which the organism is in functional rapport with its environment. The most serious limitation of such measures of correspondence is that they channel interest away from the means by which the organism achieves constancy toward a description of the final achievement. Far from being viewed as a limitation, however, this one-sided emphasis is hailed as crucial by those who would adhere strictly to the narrow definition of constancy in terms of percept and object comparisons, and who would, for example, rule out the Gestalt studies in constancy on the grounds that they are "not properly concerned with 'distal' object relationships" (6, p. 58). It will be one of the primary arguments of this paper that such an artificial dichotomizing of the problem makes the attainment of an adequate solution impossible. Constancy is functional only in so far as "veridical distal relationships" are established. (We shall return to this statement later in an effort to pluck the verbal plumage and reveal the behavioral meat beneath.) It is dangerous, however, to forget that such relationships are achievements of an acting organism, and the means by which they are achieved are as much a part of the problem as are the relationships themselves. Constancy mechanisms and constancy achievements are inseparable. Any complete theory of perceptual constancy must encompass all its aspects.

II

A SIMPLE LABORATORY demonstration may serve to illustrate this point.[2] Let us photograph an ordinary playing card and reproduce it in three different sizes: one "double size," one "normal size," and one "half size." If we now view the double-size card with one eye from a distance of, for example, eight feet, the card alone being illuminated in an otherwise dark room, it will appear to be only four feet from us and of normal size. Similarly, the half-size card placed at four feet distance will appear normal size and at eight feet, while the normal-size card placed at six feet will indeed appear to be a normal card at six feet. We are thus confronted with three cards physically spaced from the observer in the order *small-normal-large* but seen in the reverse order, *large-normal-small;* and of physical sizes *small-normal-large* but seen in size as *normal-normal-normal*. Clearly by any definition of constancy

2 What follows is a description of one of a series of perceptual demonstrations designed by Adelbert Ames, Jr. The author is grateful to Mr. Ames for permission to report this demonstration.

calling for correspondence between perceived and objective properties, this performance is the very antithesis of constancy behavior.

If we now make two slight changes in the above-described configuration, the performance becomes quite different. In place of the half-size card let us substitute a wrist watch in a rectangular case the same size and shape as the small card, and in place of the double-size card we substitute the cover of a pocket magazine which is the same size and shape as the large card. This new arrangement, when viewed with one eye as described above, presents us with three objects in both physical and apparent order *watch-card-magazine,* and both physical and apparent sizes *watch-card-magazine.* This performance, therefore, is typical of perceptual constancy. These relationships are summarized in Table I.[3] Figure 1 shows both the *card-card-card* and the *watch-card-magazine* combined into a single demonstration.

TABLE I

APPARENT SIZES AND DISTANCES IN
TWO MONOCULARLY VIEWED CONFIGURATIONS
(SIZE AND DISTANCE OF NORMAL PLAYING
CARD TAKEN AS UNITY)

CONDITION I SHOWS DEVIATION FROM, AND
CONDITION II AGREEMENT WITH,
CONVENTIONALLY DEFINED "CONSTANCY"

TEST OBJECT	VISUAL ANGLE	ACTUAL SIZE	APPARENT SIZE	ACTUAL DISTANCE	APPARENT DISTANCE
			CONDITION I		
Half card	¾	½	1	⅔	1⅓
Normal card	1	1	1	1	1
Double card	1½	2	1	1⅓	⅔
			CONDITION II		
Wrist watch	¾	½	½	⅔	⅔
Normal card	1	1	1	1	1
Magazine	1½	2	2	1⅓	1⅓

[3] The description in the text, and as summarized in the table, is of the "ideal" performance. Careful records have been taken for a group of observers. The typical performance closely approximates that indicated in the table, and even extreme deviations from this typical performance are closer to it than to any of the other possibilities.

FIG. 1. *The watch-card-magazine demonstration photographed from the viewing point.*

This demonstration raises many questions of relevance to perceptual theory (1, 19, 22, 23, 28, 31). We are here concerned only with its relationship to the problem of problemization in the study of perceptual constancy. With reference to a narrow definition of constancy, in terms of percept to object correlations, we must view the performances under the two conditions as different: in the one case we have "constancy"; in the other we do not. Similarly, as isolated responses to isolated stimuli from which behavior in the isolated situations may be predicted, they are different. Behavior in the one case will be "successful," and in the other "unsuccessful." On the other hand, the two cases are certainly identical in terms of the perceptual processes involved. One cannot maintain that a "constancy mechanism" was operating in the one instance and not in the other. In order to avoid labeling the same performance both constancy and nonconstancy, we must seek a conceptualization which will encompass both aspects, the intra-organism constancy mechanism as well as the functional relationship between organism and environment. Such a conceptualization can be reached only by recognizing that "object-to-percept" and "response-to-goal" are not one-way roads, nor are they completely isolated from each other, but rather represent two abstracted aspects of the same continuing process in which they are mutually affecting and being affected by each other.

III

THERE HAVE, OF COURSE, been many attempts to link these two aspects conceptually. Every investigator, no matter which isolated aspect may initially dominate his thinking, has eventually found it impossible completely to ignore the other. Two major lines of thought may be traced, fully recognizing that such an oversimplified presentation does violence to many views which cannot so neatly be classified. One line of approach is primarily concerned with perceptual mechanisms. It may call upon the generalized configurational or field effects introduced by the Gestalt psychologists, or upon specific mutually canceling processes which leave the resultant perception unchanged. This latter type of explanation has been of recurring popularity since its early statement by Wheatstone, who noted that in his mirror stereoscope "the perceived magnitude of an object . . . diminishes as the inclination of the (optic) axes becomes greater, while the distance remains the same; and it increases, when the inclination of the axes remains the same, while the distance diminishes. When both these conditions vary inversely, as they do in ordinary vision when the distance of an object changes, the perceived magnitude remains the same" (36). This quotation may be compared with more recent statements of the same type of explanation by, for example, Wallach (35), Schlosberg (30), and Gibson (17), as well as with the general Gestalt treatment of invariance (26). This approach has sought fixed "laws" of perception, usually natively or innately determined, and has considered the high degree of functional validity shown by perceptions to be fortuitous and fortunate. For example, to say that "luckily we are so made, and the world is so made, *that under the normal conditions of life* there exists in general a definite correspondence between our perceptions and the objects of the physical events which give rise to them" (29, p. 217) is but to state in its most extreme form a view which is representative of this approach (26, p. 305). The emphasis on the uniqueness of "normal" conditions holds throughout. Truth is to be had for the looking, seeing is believing, provided the conditions are auspicious.

The other major tradition specifically concerned with the constancies has followed a diametrically opposed orientation. It has consistently been impressed with the very obvious need for, and attainment of, functionally useful responses. It has concentrated on the observation of such responses and the specification of the conditions which arouse them (5, 9). When questioned as to the intra-organism processes which mediate effective response to extra-organism factors, it either is not interested or is content to accept functional effectiveness as itself a sufficient explanatory principle. An unspecified evolutionary theory is implied here, and the "fortuitous and fortunate" implications are not missing.[4]

Attempts to account for the perceptual constancies along one or the other of these two general approaches have not been completely successful, nor have they met with universal acceptance, simply because neither approach deals with the whole problem. Attempts to pick and choose various parts from each, in an effort to fit together the parts thus selected into some sort of jigsaw pattern, as advocates of eclecticism would have us do, can be adequate only if the initial artificial separation of the problem has not distorted it beyond recognition.

> "Indeed!" said Mr. Pickwick, "I was not aware that that valuable work contained any information respecting Chinese metaphysics."
>
> "He read, sir," rejoined Pott, laying his hand on Mr. Pickwick's knee, and looking around with a smile of intellectual superiority, "he read for metaphysics under the letter M, and for China under the letter C, and combined his information, sir!" (15, p. 789).

If, instead, all phases of constancy behavior are treated as merely different aspects abstracted out of a unitary whole, no aspect of which would exist except for the whole, an adequate conceptualization seems possible (12). In this view, functional effectiveness is mediated by the perceptual constancies, and constancy is in turn mediated by functional behavior. The stimulus-to-response phase of behavior has long been studied in psychology. This must now be supplemented by the parallel study of the effect of the response on the receptor system; i.e., the response-to-stimulus sequence. Such a study may well lead to a reconsideration of the meaning of "stimulus" in psychological theory.

IV

ACTION AND PERCEPTION are inseparably related. An evaluation of the many theoretical attempts to link perception and action is a major study

---

[4] This common point of view, which sees one or another aspect of constancy phenomena as a more or less chance occurrence, is carried to a *reductio ad absurdum* in much recent work in which the attempt seems to be made to prove that perceptual constancy is achieved *in spite of* the organism's best efforts to avoid it. By superimposing motivational or personality factors on unspecified perceptual processes, which are then removed from consideration after being mollified with some such high-sounding title as "autochthonous," this approach has concentrated on displaying distortions of perception. The resulting contradiction in terms which finds motivational factors called upon to account for essentially nonfunctional behavior, is still further emphasized when perceptual distortion is used as an explanatory principle to account for the functional nature of perceiving.

in itself and cannot be pursued in detail at this time. Suffice it to say that we are here referring neither to the mental "acts" of the act psychologists, nor to the kinesthetic cues which interested many of the early empiricists and functionalists, nor to the incipient motor responses of the motor theorists, nor to the overt, observable motor responses so dear to the behaviorists, although all these may properly be seen as among the historical antecedents of the position presented in this paper.

Rather, "action" as used here is more adequately defined in the homely words of the dictionary, "the doing of something." The "perceiving of something" and the "doing of something" are treated as two abstracted aspects of a continuing process of living, no one aspect of which can be understood without reference to all. Dewey and Bentley have noted that the "differences between perception and manipulation seemed striking to the earlier stages of the development of psychology, but today's specialization of inquiry should not lose sight of their common behavioral status" (14, p. 299). It is only in terms of this common behavioral status that such currently popular phrases as the "distal focusing of perception" take on any meaning. Reference to "veridical distal relationships" means nothing, unless it means that perception and manipulation have been mutually consistent.

A clear recognition of the unity of perception and action enables us to achieve a conceptualization which does not rest on a meaningless apriorism, and at the same time avoids what Whitehead has termed the "Berkeleyan dilemma," from which one readily descends to "a complete scepticism which was not in Berkeley's own thought."

There are two types of answer to this sceptical descent. One is Dr. Johnson's. He stamped his foot on a paving stone, and went on his way satisfied with its reality. . . . The other type of answer was first given by Kant. We must distinguish between the general way he set about constructing his answer to Hume, and the details of his system, which in many respects are highly disputable. The essential point of his method is the assumption that "significance" is an essential element in concrete experience. The Berkeleyan dilemma starts with tacitly ignoring this aspect of experience, and thus with putting forward, as expressing experience, conceptions of it which have no relevance to fact. In the light of Kant's procedure, Johnson's answer falls into its place; it is the assertion that Berkeley has not correctly expounded what experience in fact is.

Berkeley himself insists that experience is significant; indeed, three-quarters of his writings are devoted to enforcing this position. But Kant's position is the converse of Berkeley's; namely, that significance

is experience. . . . For Berkeley the significance is detachable from
the experience (37, p. 11–12).[5]

"What is significance?" Whitehead then asks. "Significance is the
relatedness of things. To say that significance is experience, is to affirm
that perceptual knowledge is nothing else than an apprehension of the
relatedness of things." This relatedness of things, in the view presented
in this paper, is revealed through action, or, more precisely, action
provides the concrete, "operational" definition of the relatedness of
things, with reference to a particular space and time framework. Perception, then, is the product of the continual recording of the relatedness
of things as defined by action. Perception is the apprehension of significance.

The psychological consequence of action, then, is a change of significance. Change, because the "relatedness of things" is ever-changing; the
perceiver himself operates within the process and his very perceiving
and acting constitute part of the relatedness of things. However, change
is relative, and some significances are relatively stable and enduring;
i.e., have a high probability of recurring (8, 20, 33). Perceiving is,
therefore, the apprehending of *probable* significances. It is predictive in
function, or, as Ames has expressed it, perceptions are prognostic
directives for action (1).

Out of the relatively stable significances, as determined from the
relative effectiveness of actions, a pattern of unconscious "assumptions"
is built. These assumptions may be conceptualized variously as relatively
stable ways of reacting, as patterns of probable significances, as value
systems, or as concepts as to the nature of the objective world, which
have been constructed through active participation in living, and may
be considered as "weighted averages" of past experiences.[6] The sum
total of assumptions which the individual makes as to the nature and
significances of the external world constitutes his assumptive world
(11, 12, 22, 24). The assumptive world of any particular individual
at any particular time determines his perceptions; i.e., provides him
with predictions of probable significances. His assumptive world is,
therefore, in a very real sense, the only world which he knows; and
since the assumptive world of each individual is to a certain extent
unique, to that extent each one of us resembles Thurber's spy, who

[5] We might add that for most psychologists who have sought an empiricistic
explanation the most extreme example of detaching significance from experience
is undoubtedly to be found in Titchener's context theory of meaning, which sets
a fashion from which much of psychology has yet to emancipate itself.

[6] Since these "weights" are a function of the situation, no fixed "hierarchy"
can ever hope to be established independent of the specific conditions.

reported that what he had seen was "something very much like nothing anyone had seen before."

V

SUCH AN APPROACH makes possible a more adequate understanding of the perceptual constancies. Consider, for example, the constancies which are encountered in the study of depth perception. The most commonly cited case undoubtedly is size constancy, which, it is universally agreed, is dependent on the proper estimation of distance (4, 13, 17, 26, 34). Apparent size equals objective size only when apparent distance equals objective distance, or, in other words, "size constancy" and "distance constancy" are inseparably related, and both are essential for functional effectiveness.[7]

But apparent size is only one of the constancies dependent on apparent distance. Changes in many other important aspects of the perceived properties of objects are related to deviations from distance constancy; i.e., to cases in which apparent distance does not correspond to actual distance. At least apparent size, shape, orientation in space, and possibly brightness (1, 3, 17, 21, 32, 34) can be shown to be dependent on apparent distance. Apparent distance, however, is in turn dependent on size, shape, orientation in space, and brightness (1, 3, 16, 17, 22, 24), so that analogous statements can be made reversing the direction of the effect. If the apparent size, shape, orientation, and brightness of an object deviate from the objective size, shape, etc., then both the apparent absolute distance of the object and the apparent relative distances of various parts of the object will deviate from the corresponding objective distances (1, 2, 19, 22, 24). Apparent "thingness" and the apparent distance of the "thing" are complexly interdependent. There seems to be no reason for asserting the invariable primacy of one over the other.

There is, in fact, no aspect of depth perception which cannot be shown to be interdependent on all other aspects. There is no basis for asserting that some aspects are independent and some dependent, that some serve as cause and others as effect. Any apparent property can be altered in many ways: by varying impingements directly related to

---

[7] It is interesting to speculate as to why "distance constancy" is not included among the constancies commonly studied. Certainly the relative independence from specific proximal stimulation shown by apparent distance is at least as striking as that shown by size, for example. Size constancy, however, of all the constancies, has provoked the most interest simply because it astounds the most people. This astonishment can probably be traced to an unacknowledged but binding conceptual link to the Lockian primary qualities.

that aspect, by changing impingements related to other aspects which in turn are related to that aspect, or by keeping impingements constant and altering significances attributed to the impingements (19, 22, 24, 25, 31). The individual makes sense out of the intrinsically meaningless impingements by assessing their significance in terms of his assumptive world. He endeavors to create in the "now" a world which as closely as possible resembles his world of the "past" and which, therefore, gives him a feeling of surety that he can act effectively in the "future." He does so not only because he "wants" to, but because he has no other alternative; this is the only world which he can know (cf. 2, 11).

It should be further pointed out that the effects described above, which apply to the perception of static objects, become immensely more complicated when movement is introduced. For example, the factor of relative movement (parallax) becomes important. Everything said above with respect to the static constancies applies in this case. Relative apparent distance is very strongly dependent on parallax indications (18). However, if relative apparent distances deviate from objective relative distances, parallax indications become perceptually related to the apparent movements which deviate markedly from the corresponding objective movements (1, 2, 24). The number of apparent properties (in terms of which constancies can be specified) also increases to include such aspects as the speed and direction of movement. In addition, the relative importance of the static constancies changes. For example, static apparent size and shape can readily be altered by varying either apparent distance or objective size and shape, but when movement is introduced there is a strong tendency to see the moving object as constant in shape and size (19, 22, 24, 25, 31). It may well be, therefore, as suggested earlier, that the static constancies are special cases derived from the more commonly experienced movement and continuity.

VI

A CONCEPTUALIZATION OF the perceptual constancies, such as that outlined in the preceding sections, can be extended into other areas of human behavior. We are able, thereby, to resolve the paradox which has found those psychologists most concerned with studying the functional effectiveness of man in his total environmental surroundings; i.e., social, personality, and clinical psychologists, frequently neglecting the role of such supremely functional behavior as that represented by the constancies, although they are actively concerned with analogous problems variously conceptualized in terms of prejudice, stereotype, frame of reference, suppression, etc. The probable reason that these psychologists have not found the conventional treatment of perceptual constancy to be of value in their disciplines lies in the definition of constancy in terms of correspondence between objective and apparent properties. Much of what might properly be labeled constancy behavior in social and personality studies lies outside this definition, and indeed consists of maintaining a stable perceptual world which in one or more ways deviates markedly from the "objective" world. This contradiction disappears (and incidentally, leaves room for a more adequate definition of the "reality" to which we are often told we must all adjust) when we define constancy behavior as the attempt of the individual to create and maintain a world which deviates as little as possible from the world which he has experienced in the past, which is the only world he knows, and which offers him the best possible chance of acting effectively and continuing to experience the particular satisfactions which he seeks out of living.

This view, incidentally, enables us to account for the maladaptive behavior evidenced by individuals whose perceptions quite grossly disagree with the "objective" situation. Such conditions are readily established in the perceptual laboratory; for example, one may cite the distorted room of Ames (see Chapters 2, 8, 9, 10), or the tilting-room-and-tilting-chair of Witkin (38). Some writers profess to see an element of stupidity in behavior in such situations (6, p. 59; 38, pp. 40 f). However, in the conceptualization presented in this paper, such "errors," far from being stupid, represent the best possible, and hence "wisest," attempt to interpret the perceptual situation in terms of the individual's assumptive world, with its host of weightings and probabilities relating the results of past actions to similar situations. To go contrary to the dictates of this accumulated experience, even though in any particular instance it may be wrong, would indeed be stupid.

VII

IT MAY BE FITTING, in a paper devoted to constancy, to close with a few remarks on change. The conceptualization presented here has stressed the functional importance of constancy as well as the psychological mechanism by which constancy is achieved. Behavior will be random and ineffective unless it takes off from some relatively stable and determined foundation. Once the situation changes, however, in such a way that this foundation ceases to be the best possible one on which to base action, preserving it (i.e., constancy) ceases to be of functional value. As outlined above, the consequence of action is a change in the individual's assumptive world, either reinforcing or modifying it. The consequence of consistently ineffective action will therefore be an alteration of the assumptive world in the direction of a relatively stable, but changed, pattern of assumptions with resulting new constancies appropriate for effective action in the new situation. Paradoxical as it may seem, change is the midwife at the birth of constancy. As the world changes, so must we.

[The next chapter, on *the constancies in social perception,* continues the discussion of the functional role of constancies in the area of social behavior.—Ed.]

REFERENCES—CHAPTER 20

1. Ames, A. Jr. *Some Demonstrations Concerned with the Origin and Nature of Our Sensations* (what we experience). *A laboratory manual (preliminary draft).* Hanover, N. H.: Institute for Associated Research, 1946. (Mimeographed.)

2. Ames, A. Jr. "Visual perception and the rotating trapezoidal window." *Psychol. Monogr.,* 1951, *65,* No. 7 (whole No. 324).

3. Bartley, S. H. *Beginning Experimental Psychology.* New York: McGraw-Hill, 1950.

4. Boring, E. G. *Sensation and Perception in the History of Experimental Psychology.* New York: Appleton-Century, 1942.

5. Boring, E. G. "The Perception of objects." *Amer. J. Phys.,* 1946, *14,* 99–107.

6. Bruner, J. S., and Krech, D. (Ed.). *Perception and Personality.* Duke Univ. Press, 1950.

7. Brunswik, E. "Thing constancy as measured by correlation coefficients." *Psychol. Rev.,* 1940, *47,* 69–78.

8. Brunswik, E. "Organismic achievement and environmental probability." *Psychol. Rev.,* 1943, *50,* 255–72.

9. Brunswik, E. "Distal focussing of perception: Size constancy in a representative sample of situations." *Psychol. Monogr.,* 1944, No. 254.

10. Brunswik, E. "Systematic and representative design of psychological experiments." *Proc. Berkeley Symp. Math. Statistics and Probability.* Univ. of California Press, 1949.

11. Cantril, H. *The "Why" of Man's Experience.* New York: Macmillan, 1950.

12. Cantril, H.; Ames, A. Jr.; Hastorf, A. H.; and Ittelson, W. H. "Psychology and scientific research." *Science,* 1949, *110,* 461–64, 491–97, 512–22.

13. Carr, H. *An Introduction to Space Perception.* New York: Longmans, 1935.

14. Dewey, J., and Bentley, A. F. *Knowing and the Known.* Boston: Beacon, 1949.

15. Dickens, C. *The Posthumous Papers of the Pickwick Club.* Philadelphia: Macrae Smith, 1927.

16. Donders, F. C. *Accommodation and Refraction of the Eye.* (Trans. from the author's manuscript by W. D. Moore.) London: New Sydenham Society, 1864.

17. Gibson, J. *The Perception of the Visual World.* Boston: Houghton Mifflin, 1950.

18. Graham, C. H.; Baker, K. E.; Hecht, M.; and Lloyd, V. V. "Factors influencing thresholds of monocular movement parallax. *J. Exper. Psychol.,* 1948, *38,* 205–23.

19. Hastorf, A. H. "The influence of suggestion on the relationship between stimulus size and perceived distance." *J. Psychol.,* 1950, *29,* 195–217.

20. Helmholtz, H. *Physiological Optics* (1866 trans. by J. P. C. Southall) Optical Society of Amer., 1925, Vol. 3.

21. Holway, A. H., and Boring, E. G. "Determinants of apparent visual size with distance variant." *Amer. J. Psychol.,* 1941, *54,* 21–37.

22. Ittelson, W. H. "Size as a cue to distance." *Amer. J. Psychol.,* 1951, *64,* 54–67, 188–202.

23. Ittelson, W. H., and Ames, A. Jr. "Accommodation, convergence, and their relation to apparent distance." *J. Psychol.,* 1950, *30,* 43–62.

24. Kilpatrick, F. P. *The Role of Assumptions in Perception.* Unpublished Ph.D. Dissertation, Princeton University, 1950.

25. Kilpatrick, F. P., and Ittelson, W. H. "Three demonstrations involving the visual perception of movement." *J. Exper. Psychol.* (to be published).

26. Koffka, K. *Principles of Gestalt Psychology.* New York: Harcourt, Brace, 1935.

27. Kohler, W. *Gestalt Psychology.* New York: Liveright, 1947.

28. Lawrence, M. *Studies in Human Behavior.* Princeton: Princeton Univ. Press, 1949.

29. Michotte, A. *La Perception de la Causalité.* Paris: Vrin, 1946.

30. Schlosbreg, H. "A note on depth perception, size constancy, and related topics." *Psychol. Rev.,* 1950, *57,* 314–17.

31. Smith, W. M. *A Study of the Influence of Past Experience on Apparent Size and Distance.* Unpublished dissertation, Princeton University, 1950.

32. Thouless, R. S. "Phenomenal regression to the real object." *Brit. J. Psychol.,* 1931, *21,* 339–59; *22,* 1–30.

33. Tolman, E. C., and Brunswik, E. "The organism and the causal texture of the environment." *Psychol. Rev.,* 1935, *42,* 43–77.

34. Vernon, M. D. *Visual Perception.* Cambridge Univ. Press., 1937.

35. Wallach, H. "Brightness constancy and the nature of the achromatic colors." *J. Exper. Psychol.*, 1948, *38*, 310–24.

36. Wheatstone, C. "Contributions to the physiology of vision. Part the second." *Philos. Mag.*, 1852, Ser. 4, *3*, 504–23.

37. Whitehead, A. N. *The Principles of Natural Knowledge.* Cambridge Univ. Press, 1925.

38. Witkin, H. A. "Perception of body position and of the position of the visual field." *Psychol. Monogr.*, 1949, No. 302.

39. Woodworth, R. *Experimental Psychology.* New York: Holt, 1938.

21

The Constancies in Social

Perception

F. P. Kilpatrick & Hadley Cantril

INTRODUCTORY ANALYSIS

ALTHOUGH THERE IS AN enormous amount of literature available on the constancies, a surprisingly small amount of it has anything to say about what the constancies *do* for the organism. Most of the studies in size constancy, for example, concern themselves with such matters as relationships between size constancy and distance, size constancy and visual angle, size constancy and number of cues available, methods of measuring degrees of size constancy, and so forth. Symptomatic of this general structural approach is the way in which the visual constancies are often treated in the literature: one section will consider size constancy, another shape constancy, another color constancy, etc. It is a rare work indeed that considers the constancies as a general phenomenon in vision and tries to find the principles running through them all, as Ittelson did in the previous chapter.

Here we will simply indicate how certain general functional principles are common to the constancies in our perception, particularly those we build up and make use of in our social behavior.

We can begin our analysis with object constancies [1] in visual perception. Let us return to the object—a chair—with which we began our analysis in Chapter 2. Across the desk from me is a chair which I perceive as being upright, three-dimensional, as having a rectangular seat, etc. Now, as I move my head back and forth, I continue to perceive the chair as upright, three-dimensional, with a rectangular seat, in spite of the fact that with each movement of my head or body or eyes the impingements on my organism related to that "object" have gone through a bewildering variety of changes. Clearly, there is no constancy here as far as sensory input is concerned, and our demonstrations (especially Chapter 2) have already shown that I cannot attribute this constancy simply to the fact that there "is" a chair there. The constancy of the chair is an abstraction based on past experience with similar impingements.

But why abstract in this particular way; in fact, why abstract at all? Previous chapters have already suggested the answer: the abstraction "chair" is, functionally speaking, a prognostic directive for action. But we can carry this analysis just a little bit further. It is true that the attributed chairness of the object does give us a generalized prognosis as to the probable consequences of dealing with it in any particular way. Yet we must not forget that the constancy of the chair also functions in other ways. This hinges on the fact that without the constancy of the chair I am unable to relate myself to it satisfactorily in time or space. For example, when I move my head back and forth, the difference between the impingements which are "constant chair" at one point in time and the impingements which were "constant chair" at another point in time are interpreted as *alterations of the relative positions of me and the chair in space over time.* This happens even in any instance of static perception of an object. That is, the particular organization of impingements which are abstracted as a constant chair are "compared" with the patterns of previous impingements similarly interpreted as constant chair in order to permit me to interpret this difference as a reliable spatial relationship between the chair and me.

So far this analysis presents nothing particularly new. Other demon-

---

[1] The term "constancy" as used in psychology is itself an abstraction. While this point is obvious, it should constantly be borne in mind because of the tendency of investigators to forget that we are dealing with a process in time, and that when we take a cross section of this and call it a constancy we are merely cutting a slice out of what may be more aptly called continuity.

strations have already shown that such is the case. Some of them verify the accuracy of this analysis by reversing the circumstances; that is, by changing the position of the "object" but leaving the pattern of impingements on the organism constant, with the result that no perceived alteration in space relationship between object and organism occurs.

This, it is true, is functional analysis. But we must go further and it will help us to do this if we consider another aspect of human behavior brought out by some of the demonstrations. We refer to the fact that *we act not in terms of what "is" but in terms of a prognosis of what "will be"* at the projected point in time at which we expect our act to take effect on whatever it is we are dealing with, whether an object, a person, or a long-range aspiration we are trying to achieve. This is shown in a simple situation when we catch a baseball. Things are constantly changing and our acts cannot be instantaneous, with the result that successful action can only occur in terms of a projection in time, that is, a prognosis of what will be. This is equally true for quite stable situations. A prognosis of no change or of little change is just as much of a prognosis as one of great change.

Object constancy, then, appears to be a dual function in prognosis. The first function is that of providing a generalized prognosis as to the probable consequences of a general class of ways of dealing with the object as we abstract it out of its surroundings. In older psychological terminology one might say that constancy provides the organism with a general set, that is, a range or class of possibilities. For example, even in a completely static situation, the general range or class of possibilities based on past experience, which are related to a table as compared to a pencil, are quite different. However, we never act in a uniform and generalized way simply because we cannot act on all these possibilities at the same time. While we can take into account the general nature of the prognosis, the fact remains that what emerges is a particular prognosis related to a particular act to achieve a particular purpose. Here the second function of the constancies comes in.

The second function of a constancy is to provide a basis for assessing the probable consequences of a particular act. Without the constancy as a reference it is impossible for the individual to assess his unique position in relation to the object in order to make the particular prognosis that would be effective at the projected instant in time at which the act is to occur. For example, in looking at the chair across from my desk I can specify certain things about the effect on my behavior of its constancy; that is, the function in my behavior of its constancy. In the first place its constancy gives me a certain generalized prognosis or class of possibilities. For example, because of its abstracted characteristic as an object of a particular kind, there is implicit in my perception the prognosis that I can lift it, sit on it, push it, turn it over, break it, etc. But the fact remains that I cannot do any of these things without further prognoses in a sequence of acts as to where I will be in relation to the chair at each successive instant in time and what my purposes are at the moment. Thus my unique acts became possible only by virtue of my particular prognoses as to where I am in relation to the chair and what function it can serve. These in turn are only possible in terms of differences in impingements on my organism which can be attributed to a change in the spatial relationships between me and the chair, together with the nature of my intentions. My action is not due to any changes in the chair itself or to any changes in myself alone: my action is a functional relationship.

And so it is that in order to have any prognosis for a unique act one must have not only constancy in whatever one is acting toward, but *self-constancy as well.* It follows that constancies, both of the externality and of the self, provide the basis for the unique assessment of unique relationships necessary for an act which is itself always unique.

Thus there are no concrete absolutes in perception: instead, what is perceived may roughly be described as a series of functional probabilities. These functional probabilities, despite their abstract and non-absolute nature, must be treated as absolutes in everyday behavior.

If this analysis is correct, then any instance of behavior involves:

(a) A generalized prognosis with respect to the externalities; that is, a general class of probable consequences, a general class of acts. This may be summarized as attributed "other" constancy.

(b) A generalized prognosis concerning the self; that is, a generalized class of possibilities of acting. This may be summarized as "self" constancy.

(c) A unique relationship between these two, projected forward in time. This should not be understood as a single projection but rather as a projection in sequential form—as a process, a continuance.

Self-constancy, as the term is used here, should not be confused with the more traditional concept of "self-image." From our point of view it would appear that the self-image concept is but a single aspect of self constancy. Both "self" constancy and "other" constancy are to some degree necessary if differences are to be assessed for purposes of action. To the extent that either of these constancies breaks down, differences may be referred to alteration in the "other" or to changes in the "self."

It seems likely that constancy of the self is primary and may roughly be defined as the sum total of the estimates one has, based on past experience, of one's own capacities to deal with particular sets of impingements. "Other constancy" would seem to consist primarily of the referral of a class of these capacities to the externality as related to a particular set of impingements.

We further need to discriminate between what one might call the constancies in the "object" realm and the constancies in the "social" realm, simply because additional factors come into play when we start dealing with other people which tend to reduce the reliability of prediction. Constancies of self and others then become extremely more complex. One no longer is concerned with one's capacities alone, but also with one's capacities in relation to the purposes and capacities of others.

When self-constancy consists of a class of probable or estimated capacities in relation to particular social situations or groups of people at hand, then it cannot be referred solely to the individual but must include the individual and his dealings with others. When the individual in his dealings with others has his predictions upset, this is reflected in an alteration of the personal estimate he has of his own capacities and the reliability of these estimates. In this sense, then, we can say that deviant individuals, or deviant groups in a society, upset the self-constancy of all other members in society who participate with them, and thereby may lower the capacity of these individuals for assessing the differences which are necessary for unique and effective action.

To the degree that constancy of the self is upset, it becomes more and more difficult for us to assess change adequately. It would also seem that our social form—that is, constancies of the self in relation to other people and our own capacities for dealing with other people in particular ways—is a product of socialization. That is, we learn it from the evaluations of other people, the responses of other people to our acts, etc. It was pointed out above that deviant individuals or deviant groups are upsetting to our self-constancy. They in a sense violate the self. This is also the case when an individual departs from his own culture or subculture and moves into a situation where socialization has undergone a different development. For example, whenever a person travels in a foreign country he must deal with individuals who are "deviant" from his own point of view, thus running the risk of upsetting his own self-constancy. Thus, it is important—for most people, anyway—to have available supports for their own self-constancy; perhaps in the form of a companion from their own culture and preferably someone from their own small in-group.

SOME BRIEF EXAMPLES

IN ORDER TO HELP clarify some of the implications for social psychology of this conceptual framework, and to illustrate the sorts of results it yields as an analytic tool, we shall treat briefly a number of concepts and problems.

CULTURE. If we are to establish functionally effective constancies of self and the social externality, we must deal with the purposes of other people, the prehension of sequential events they are following in order to achieve certain purposes, the constant change and flexibility in both of these, together with the fact that as we react to others and as they interact with us we are affecting each other's purposive behavior and modifying the sequential events leading to goals, etc. Social living is never static, it is always a flow.

The process of socialization seems to be aimed at increasing the probability of securing these constancies of self and others in order to increase predictability. This is true for both the person being socialized and the individuals doing it.

From this point of view, "culture" is essentially a common pattern of learned significances and constancies. Among the welter of constancies that make up a culture it may be useful to differentiate two different varieties.

First are those comprising the rules and regulations devised in order to give a greater degree of constancy to social life: the mores, customs, standards, and laws of a society. These range all the way from the rules for playing a certain game and the niceties of social etiquette to the violations of moral ends which mean death or life imprisonment. Such regulations concern both the aims and values handed down as guides to experience, that is, that honesty is the best policy, to the means or methods of conducting ourselves in order to achieve goals and values.

A second variety of constancy man utilizes that becomes part of "culture" are the artifacts he devises in order to extend the range of his sensory motor apparatus and bring greater standardization and predictability to a wide variety of behavior as well as to provide some people with common significances, that is, radio, television, microscopes, tools, motors, etc.

It should be emphasized, however, that these cultural forms— whether they are standards for behavior or artifacts used to give reliable performance—are essentially forms society provides in order to enable a person to get along more effectively with his own being. In democratically oriented societies, where the individual welfare is the measure of a society's functioning, "culture" serves as a consensually agreed-upon matrix and form for personal development and flow.

If a person "overlearns" social values and prescriptions, if he becomes overorganized, so that all of his behavior is completely predictable, then, of course, he loses his individuality, becomes a social bore or the automaton that may be sought in those societies or organizations that separate "society" and "organization" as ends in themselves.

THE STIMULUS. How does it happen that so much of learning theory and so many learning experiments have so long been able to talk about static stimuli and situations in-the-now as the stimuli to which the organisms in their experiments respond?

If it is true, as we suggest, that what the organism utilizes in making predictions for purposive action is *differentiation* which depends upon self-constancy and other constancy, then it does seem peculiar that learning experiments and theories do not more often run head on into this fact.

The answer would seem to be that practically all of them take advantage of a prediction of *no change*. They use physical objects (or symbolic representations) which change so slowly, if at all, that the most efficient prediction to make on the basis of past experience is that of no change. One can easily see that it is possible to treat a prediction of "no change" as though it were not a prediction at all but merely a "response" to an "object." However, when one moves over into learning situations involving social processes where successful action almost always depends upon the assessment of changing differences projected forward in time —that is, upon predictions of change—then much of classical learning theory breaks down and loses its explanatory power. It would seem that the rigid stimulus-response oriented way of looking at the behavior of the organism is probably a blind alley for much of social psychology.

ATTITUDES. Employing this theoretical approach, we would say that an attitude is an attributed constancy consisting of a class of possibilities related to the capacities of the self for dealing with certain objects, persons, institutions, ideologies, or situations. Since the constancy is comprised of a *class* of possibilities, it does not give a *unique* prediction for any given situation, but functions roughly as a base line for assessing the relationship between the person, object, situation, institution, or what not and the unique position, capacities, and purposes of the self. The relationship in time and space of these two constancies permits the assessment of difference and the relation of this difference to the probable consequences of the unique act which is to take effect at a unique point in time and space.

Thus one would not be surprised that people who are most highly prejudiced again the Jews would, in a party situation at which Jews were present, be the ones who are most solicitous of the Jewish people present. In addition, one would expect the most highly prejudiced people to be most sensitive to the presence of Jewish people in any group, etc.

In terms of attitude measurement, this would mean that traditional measurements would only discern a *class* of possibilities and that further specification would have to be obtained in order to get any idea of what might occur in a unique situation. The additional information one would have to get would include at least something about the individual's purposes, as well as other constancies that are brought into functional effectiveness in the particular situation, and that determine how the individual sees the situation from his particular reality world.

WORDS, SYMBOLS, ABSTRACTIONS. What happens when a functional constancy principle is brought into awareness for purposes of communication?

It would seem that when a functioning principle is brought into awareness and labeled, it is thus given a rigid structure which makes it far less amenable to change than would have been the case if it had been left purely at the operating level. This familiar observation is of interest here because there is often slippage between the abstraction as it *functions* in behavior and the abstraction as it is *named*. There is a basic tendency to treat whatever is perceived as both concrete and absolute, despite its abstract and nonabsolute nature. To do otherwise is to inhibit the rapid and effective action necessary to the process of living. And so we use words as concrete and absolute. This may be true because we do not have sufficiently refined or inclusive namings available to handle all our operating principles. An abstraction such as that represented by a word or other symbol thus becomes indispensable for much of human experience which would not be what it is except for man's capacity to hang on to some fixed reference as experience goes on and happenings in the environment swirl around him. Abstractions serve us in social life as the "melting pot" serves the country. It also seems to be true that previous namings or naming habits cause us to misname these operating principles. Whenever tension or stress is aroused, for example, the individual tends to resist the change in perceptual organization called for by new impingements from the environment and to hold on to a stable perceptual absolute or constancy. This resistance occurs also in language behavior.

FAITH.[2] The experience of "faith" is one of the most real, yet one of the most ineffable, that characterizes human living. Without this capacity,

[2] For a more detailed discussion, see the article from which this portion was abstracted with permission of the publishers: Cantril, H. "Faith and value constancies." *J. Indiv. Psychol.*, May, 1959, *13*, No. 1, 26–37.

"human nature" would be far different than it is. And so would all man's social and political organizations.

For the process we call "faith" plays the crucial role of holding our values together and of integrating our purposes. Without faith, living would be a much more hit-and-miss affair. It would be much less directed. And it would be empty of many of the value overtones that we lump together as those that make living "worth while."

In spite of the importance of faith in the process of living, contemporary psychology has rarely met the problem of faith head on. In fact, psychological mention of the subject is even hard to find in the literature.

We would have no need for faith at all if the world were static with everything neatly determined and predictable. For in such an ordered world our lives would be characterized by certainties and repeatabilities. And they would, of course, be deadly monotonous, even worse than the life of a prison inmate confined for the rest of his days.

But as everyone knows, we are not living in a static world. Change and flow are the rule. And change and flow are accompanied by the unforeseen and the unexpected.

Since our experience is so much a matter of probability, of the bets we are constantly making in a changing world as to the characteristics of things, of people, of events, we *must* do something to put order and repeatability into the world in which we carry on our living. We are more comfortable if we think we can predict with a fair degree of accuracy the chain of events that will occur if we undertake a certain action. We crave certainty rather than doubt. We want enough form and pattern in our thoughts and feelings to give direction to flow.

So we *create constancies* concerning things, people, and events. We attribute certain consistent characteristics to them, so that we shall be provided with enough interpretation to guess with fair accuracy what the significances and meanings are of the variety of signals that reach our sense organs, without having to make fresh guesses at every turn.

Equally important is constancy of the "self." If the constancy of the self is upset, it becomes difficult to assess change and accommodate to it. We lose the compass that keeps us going in a direction. We don't know what significances to take into account. "We" are lost.

When we say that self-constancy must be maintained, we do not imply that there can be no growth or development. On the contrary, self-development is itself an aspect of self-constancy. But development must flow from form if it is to be recognized. Without such flow from form there is no standard for comparison, no sure sense of continuity.

This means that our sense of self and our faith in that self must constantly be reaffirmed through our participation with others. For our feeling of self, and our own self-constancy and self-significance are determined to a large extent by our significance to other people and the way they behave toward us.

All these significances that we build up about the self and about objects, people, events, symbols, or ideas fuse and orchestrate together to give us our own unique reality world. Everything that has significance for us takes on its significance from our own personal behavior center —in terms of *our own* purposes and *our own* actions.

These significances become more or less common depending upon the experiences and purposes we share with other people.

But in addition to these personal significances which we take into account as we participate in one occasion after another, we also utilize in our living the significances conveyed by the abstractions man has created through the ages. Man has devised these abstractions in his perpetual attempt to bring order into disorder, to explain to himself various types of phenomena, or to find universal principles and guides for more ordered living, no matter what the unique purposes or circumstances of any one individual may be.

Among such abstractions are our scientific formulations, our maps, our legal, ethical, political, and religious systems. They can be recalled or referred to at will. They can be experienced by anyone at any time, since they are repeatable, fixed, spelled out, and formulated. They can become universal.

And there are other abstractions man uses: abstractions represented by symbolic forms in art, in music, and in religion which are hard to conceptualize or put into words.

All these abstractions are by their very nature fixed and static. Hence they can never become true substitutes for the personal meanings and significances assigned to events. For the abstraction cannot take into account the unique contingency any unique individual is likely to meet in life any more than a scientific formulation concerning the behavior of atoms can predict the behavior of a single atom.

Nevertheless, these abstracted conceptions of reality can and do play an indispensable role in helping us through our periods of frustration and doubt if and when our personal reality systems prove strained or inadequate.

When the tangibles of our personal reality worlds break down, we can turn to the intangibles. We can recall those abstractions that have been created by others and that have proved useful to others. We can apply them to the particular problem we face. We can make ourselves aware of creeds, beliefs, parables, maxims, aesthetic representations of moods. We can recall as a symbol for ourselves the courageous or appropriate behavior of others who have faced similar crises.

If we can put the abstraction to work for us, *if* we can use it as a basis for *our* choice and action in the undetermined situation *we* face here and now, then we can transform the abstraction into a personal reality. But the abstraction becomes real *only* if it becomes functional in our *own* behavior. *For when it becomes functional, we can experience what the abstraction refers to.* Then we may get the exciting or profound sense of a fleeting identity with something more universal—a sense of identity with abstract "truth," "love," "mankind," "nature," or "God."

Men thus have the capacity to sense the experience of the imminent becoming transcendent, of the particular becoming universal, as some abstraction, not bounded by intervals of time or units of space, becomes relevant and operational in the concreteness of the here and now of a person's own behavioral center.

It is this capacity of man to *recall* and to utilize relevant abstractions that makes it possible for him to have an abiding faith, a faith which transcends time and space. It is this capacity to *create* and to utilize relevant abstractions that makes it possible for men to share their faith with people in all ages and places and to communicate their faith to others.

As pointed out earlier, social forms serve the function of improving the degree of correspondence between what is in our awareness and what is potentially in the social environment to be aware of. And the reason for attempting to increase this correspondence is, of course, to provide purposeful action of a more predictable direction and with a greater chance to repeat itself in satisfying ways with more certain value constancies.

The process is—and always will be—a never-ending one. For correspondence where people are involved can never be perfect. Increased correspondence in our social perceptions of each other will inevitably be accompanied by increased satisfactions which themselves will point to new potential satisfactions.

In this ceaseless process, the individual searching for faith gets support for his value standards from others who seem to share them—his family, his friends, and the various groups he identifies himself with. As long as they help him carry out his purposes by their actions, help him maintain and develop his own self-constancy, he will find them fortifying his faith and deserving of it. But it is only in times of personal crisis and emergency that this faith in people is manifested and filters into awareness. At other times it is part of the relatively normal "neutral" world: it is *potentially* with us and we may take it into account in our behavior even though we are not aware of it.

A person will be able to become more aware of faith and to gain faith when he is able to see the *potential* values in living which he has not sensed before, *and* when he feels there is a good chance that he will be be able to participate effectively in bringing about these potential value satisfactions in his own experience.

But if his doubts and frustrations are continually unresolved through action, he is likely to find himself in a psychiatric condition where he lacks surety concerning the present, where he refuses to accept the past, or where he is unduly apprehensive about the future. In each case, faith and hope are abandoned and can only be re-established by painstaking relearning and reconditioning. Such reconditioning will require above all else a therapy which simplifies goals so that their accomplishment will be assured through the individual's own action, thereby rebuilding his confidence in himself. Once self-confidence is regained on a simple level, goals can gradually be raised.

And what holds for a single individual also holds for members of a group or culture.

Appendices

APPENDIX A

SOME SUGGESTIONS FOR EXPERIMENTATION
STEMMING FROM A TRANSACTIONAL POINT OF VIEW

F. P. Kilpatrick

Contributors of research suggestions:
Hadley Cantril
W. H. Ittelson
F. P. Kilpatrick

I. INTRODUCTION

A PARTICULAR METHOD or theoretical approach can be said to be valuable, in spite of any defects of logic or inclusiveness, if it stimulates fruitful hypotheses and experiments relevant to the main questions with which it is concerned. We who have worked with transactional perceptual theory feel that it meets this pragmatic test in admirable fashion. In fact, the theory has been so productive of research ideas that our major job has been that of selecting from numerous possibilities the few investigations that limited time and personnel make it possible to carry out. We have not always felt sure that the selections we made were the best

[*367*]

ones; much of the completed research may contribute less to an under-standing of perception than would some of the research thought of but not done. Aware of this likelihood, each of us has kept a file of research ideas in the hope that one day we would find the means of getting them done. It has become increasingly apparent that this hope is unrealistic; in the process of doing one experiment and thinking through its im-plications for perceptual theory, a half dozen new experiments or lines of investigation are thought of and added to the files. The result has been an ever-increasing backlog of research plans.

Our purpose in gathering a number of them together in this memo-randum is twofold. First, there is the hope that other researchers working in this area will find some of the suggestions of value for their own pro-grams of investigation. Second, such a memorandum helps to reveal the relationships of the lines of investigation and their over-all direction. However, no brief is held for the system of classification used here. All the proposed experiments are obviously interrelated, and any classifi-catory scheme is therefore arbitrary. Many of the experiments could be placed in several categories.

Attention should be called to the fact that the use of the term "experi-ments" to designate the items that follow is not very accurate. Some of them are experiments, but many of them might better be called "prob-lems for investigation" or "areas of interest and some ideas on how one might investigate them."

Finally, it should be mentioned that in what follows discussions of theory and concepts have been kept to a bare minimum, and demonstra-tional and experimental apparatus have been named, but not described. Complete apparatus descriptions are available elsewhere (2).

II. THE CHARACTERISTICS, DEVELOPMENT AND MODIFICATION OF ASSUMPTIONS

THE IMPORTANCE OF the concept "assumption" to the transactional view of perception can hardly be overemphasized. This abstraction from the total perceptual process has been described with respect to characteristics and function as follows:

> By assumption is meant that generally unconscious aspect of the transactional process which may be described as a weighted average of past experience in dealing with those portions of the impingements from the environment to which it is related. Assumptions function as as probabilities which are built up by action, checked by action, and modified by action as the consequences of these actions are registered in relation to purposes. Taken altogether, our assumptions form our

"assumptive world" which we bring to every occasion and on which our perceptions are based; therefore, the only world we know is determined by our assumptions. The assumptive world is conceptualized as that complex set of internalized, interrelated generalizations or standards which are not dependent for their effectiveness on any given reference point in space or in time. It thus provides whatever constancy there is in our environment, and whatever continuity there is in our experience.

It will be noted that this characterization is quite general. It lacks specificity as to the sort of "weighted average" of experience that is meant, how the consequences of action are registered in relation to purposes, exactly what is meant by action, the functions of intellectualization and knowledge, the factors involved in the implied temporal integration, etc. Thus several lines of research are suggested by the need for further specification in this area.

(a) WEIGHTED AVERAGE. Several of the demonstrations lend themselves to a study of the factors involved in the averaging process, but the "thereness-thatness" table probably offers the most convenient starting point. It provides an indirect measure of assumed size by requiring the subject to make a distance setting in the absence of distance indications other than assumed size.

For example, one might choose an unfamiliar or non-sense object, and copy it in a number of sizes ranging from very small to very large. Through having the subject manipulate the objects as a part of some task, and systematically varying such factors as size, frequency, or recency, and obtaining frequent measures of assumed size on the thereness-thatness table, one could plot the "averaging" curves resulting under these different conditions. In this way, one should be able to learn a great deal about the "averaging" process. The effects of other factors such as degree of motivation, stress, etc. could be studied in a similar manner.

One interesting variation of this kind would be to check the effects on the averaging curve of experiences of success or failure in accomplishing a task with particular sizes of the object. For example, one could ask the subjects to toss the objects at a mark or through a slot, and let them be successful with certain sizes and not with others.

Another experiment could be set up along this line to check our notion that similarity and dissimilarity are not inherent properties of objects, but depend upon the differential consequences of purposeful action. First, a group of subjects would be required to perform a task with mixed sizes of an object until each subject had attained a stable assumed size as measured by the thereness-thatness table. Then a new object of a size much different than any of the "norms" would be introduced and the subjects divided into two groups. One group would utilize the new object in the same task as before, the other would employ it in an entirely different task. The hypothesis would be that for the former group the norm for the "old" object would shift in the direction of the size of the new object; but that the "old" object norm of the latter group would not be significantly affected.

Also, in this general area, one might ask "How are assumptions modified when two or more assumptions are put into conflict?" There would be no single answer to this question, but the distorted rooms, aniseikonic glasses, and the surety demonstration would seem to be admirably suited to such investigation. A logical extension of the research would be to see if and how assumptions are differentially modified when two or more are put into conflict and (a) withdrawal is permitted or (b) choice action is demanded.

(b) THE GENESIS OF ASSUMPTIONS. This area of inquiry is not clearly distinguishable from the preceding one. Here, however, the emphasis is on the study of assumptions as they develop outside the laboratory.

We feel that systematic studies are needed which are concerned with when and under what conditions assumptions are established in relation to various kinds of impingements, both social and nonsocial, in the course of daily living. The logical starting point would be with children of different age levels and backgrounds as a means of determining when and how common significances for various objects, events, and people emerge and, in turn, what these mean for communication, effectiveness of action, feelings of security or insecurity, etc. If the work proved sufficiently informative and enough understanding were gained, it might be reasonable to extend the same sort of analysis to adults in rather complex situations.

Practically all of the demonstrations could be adapted to the initial, simpler stages of such an investigation. For example, aniseikonic lenses might be utilized in studying the degree to which children at different age levels experience different objects or persons as distorted. Also, a modified thereness-thatness table would be especially useful with children. From children of different ages, distance settings of a wide variety of objects could be obtained. Comparisons of the distances at which they were set and the stability of the settings would be extremely revealing concerning the developmental aspects of assumed size.[1]

(c) TEMPORAL ORDER AND TEMPORAL DURATION. In all the proposals discussed so far temporal aspects have been implicit. However, it would seem a good idea to deal with them more explicitly because without in-

[1] Pilot studies using this method have been completed.

tegration of processes in time there would be no assumptions, no perception. Objects and events are static abstractions from constant change, and the characteristics assigned to these static abstractions certainly are in large part a function of their duration and relationship in time.

Several diverse kinds of inquiries fall logically under this heading, and we will simply list a few of them.

1. Ames (see Chapters 12 and 13) has pointed out that the tube in the trapezoidal window appears to bend or cut through the window during one portion of its revolution when rotated in one direction, but does not appear to do so during the same portion of its revolution when rotated in the opposite direction. An investigation and analysis of this phenomenon should be helpful.

2. A similar effect using a Jim Davis or a Heider-Simmel type of movie occurs when the movie is run first forward and then backward. This is especially worth analyzing, because what the observer "sees," the significances he assigns, generally have quite obvious personal and social reference.

3. Binocular viewing of a single moving object should also provide some worthwhile clues. Each static position gives no binocular disparity, but as the object moves through a succession of positions, docs this provide binocular disparity? If so, the implications for the temporal summation of information are important.

4. The problem of time delay in conflict situations enters here. The leaf room with aniseikonic glasses seems to be the best way of studying this, as there is generally a· measurable and variable delay between the moment of putting on the glasses and the time when distortion first appears. In addition, the distortion does not appear full-blown, but gradually increases to a fairly stable maximum. The same technique offers a possible means of getting temporal order perceived in the reverse of its occurrence, as well as distortions in duration. For example, if monocular indications are of one configuration, while binocular indications are of another, it is possible that the temporal order of presentation of these two can be reversed in perception, particularly if conflicts are introduced. Possible variations of this would be to have two events occur at the same time, one indicated binocularly and the other monocularly. Perhaps they would appear to start at different times. Also, if a binocularly perceived event started before a monocularly perceived event finished, the antecedent event might be seen as starting subsequently.

III. ASSUMPTIONS, PERCEPTION AND
THEIR INTERRELATIONSHIPS

A CONSIDERABLE NUMBER of experiments have already been performed in this area; enough, at least, to show the usefulness of the concept "assumption" in setting new problems in perception and in explaining certain perceptual phenomena. Also, they have provided rather precise verification and extension of demonstrational findings. What is needed now is a routine, systematic series of such studies aimed at quantifying the variables such as size, brightness, overlay, etc. employed in the demonstrations and at the establishment of norms. Such a series of studies would provide the groundwork for further experimentation and extensions of theory.

Three less routine experiments are as follows:

1. It may be hypothesized that, when the rotating trapezoid is observed with both eyes and seen as oscillating instead of rotating, binocular cues to rotation are available to the observer, but repressed; and further, that through the effects of differential experience these binocular cues may be either (a) utilized or (b) further repressed. The experimental procedure would be to first find the minimum distances for binocular perception of unequivocal oscillation of the trapezoid for each of a fairly large group of subjects. The subjects would then be split into three groups. Each Group A subject would be placed slightly closer than his previously established minimum distance and required to perform a task in which success depends on observing not oscillation but rotation. Group B subjects would be placed slightly farther away than their minimum distances and required to perform a task in which success depends on seeing not rotation but oscillation. Group C, the control group, would receive no training. If the hypothesis is borne out, on retest the minimum distances for binocular perception of unequivocal oscillation will have increased for Group A, decreased for Group B, and will not differ significantly for Group C.

2. Some observations made while working with rotating trapezoids and rectangles probably should be followed through systematically and analyzed. A plane surface with panes cut in it and shadows painted on it like the rotating trapezoid, but rectangular in shape, is required for the first experiment. If such a rectangle is rotated in illumination from one side only from a completely concealed light source and observed from about ten feet or more in an otherwise dark room, it will appear to oscillate instead of rotate. In addition, the light source will phenomenally

move from left to right and back again in phase with the apparent oscillation. Reveal the light source and the rectangle will be seen as rotating and the light source fixed in position.

Another effect on perception of assumptions concerning the directionality of light source may be illustrated with the rotating trapezoid. The trapezoid should be rotated while illuminated on one side only by a small amount of daylight coming from a concealed source. Observed thus from ten feet or more in an otherwise dark room, the usual illusion of oscillation occurs, but in addition the trapezoid appears luminous part of the time. It is not perceived as *being* lighted, but as generating its own light.

3. Emmert's law is generally stated in verbal form approximately as follows: The apparent size of the after-image is directly proportional to its apparent distance from the observer. It also may be stated,

$$O : A :: d : D$$

in which

O is the linear size of the stimulus object,

A is the apparent linear size of the afterimage,

d is the linear distance of the stimulus object from the observer,

D is the apparent distance at which the afterimage is projected.

Analysis suggests that recent controversies over Emmert's law stem from the common implicit assumption that "stimuli" and "backgrounds" exist objectively apart from the perceiving organism. The result is that the above formula has been altered by many without the realization that it has been altered. D in the formula has been defined as the real or measured distance from the observer of the background onto which the afterimage is projected. Apparent and linear distances have been treated as the same thing, and Emmert's law has been successfully "verified" in that form, probably because (1) the experimental apparatus gave the observer quite reliable cues as to the distance of the background with the result that linear and apparent distances coincided so well that deviant findings were small and could easily be ascribed to "error" and (2) the measuring devices used were seen "with" the background.

Apparatus has been designed, built, and checked out in preliminary fashion which shows that D in the formula must be the apparent distance of the afterimage. When, as with this apparatus, a projection background is employed, but so arranged that its real distance and apparent distance are not the same, Emmert's law holds for the apparent distance and not for the real distance of the background. Further, by using part of the afterimage apparatus in conjunction with the thereness-thatness table, it can be shown that no background is necessary. This means that, under such conditions, the apparent size will be the assumed size, and that the image will be localized in space at a distance consonant with its assumed size.

These matters, and several other afterimage problems treatable in similar fashion with the same apparatus, are in need of precise experimental treatment and further analysis.

IV. PERCEPTUAL CUES

IN THIS GENERAL area of what might more strictly be called "cues in visual perception," there are a number of unanswered questions that should be worked on, particularly the whole problem of the specific cues to distance and the necessity of demonstrating that each of these cues is ambiguous and must be supplemented by some specific assumption. We have done this mathematically only for size, illumination, movement parallax, and binocular disparity and in adequate experimental fashion only for size.

The general details of the experiment would all be the same. The hypothesis is that any specific case of any of the visual cues to distance is ambiguous, that with cue constant different perceptions can be obtained by different assumptions, and that specification of the conditions necessarily involves both the cue and the assumptions brought to bear. The outlining of a single series of experiments dealing with parallax will serve to illustrate the basic point and the general procedure.

Our general hypothesis is that parallax, like all other cues to depth perception, is dependent on some subjective factor in the form of assumptions built up from past experience. In the case of parallax, the specific assumption involved is that of the appropriate "correction" factor to be applied to the movement pattern, including motion across the retina, eye movements, and head and body movements. When this correction factor is made inappropriate by any means, such as forcing a discrepancy between the linear and the apparent distance of the object, not all of the eye, head, etc. movement will be corrected for and perceived as apparent distance; and the portion uncorrected for will be seen as apparent motion of what is being viewed.

The sequence of procedures which would serve to explore this matter from extremely simple to very complex cases is as follows:

1. Show that, with head movement, a single object correctly localized will appear stationary, while an incorrectly localized object will appear to move as the head is moved.

2. Show that, with head movement, two objects incorrectly localized will either appear to move or to take different apparent positions,

depending on the strength of other assumptions involved (e.g., two playing cards versus two plain rectangles).

3. Extend 2 into more complex configurations such as the static trapezoidal window.

4. Show that apparent movement introduced by parallax is not dependent on any actual relative angular movement. This is already touched in 1 above, but probably can be extended by the use of apparent parallactic movement in a stereoscope and perhaps by means of two monocularly viewed objects such as playing cards actually at the same distance but apparently at different distances.

5. Extend to a complex laboratory situation in which different correction factors are continuously being applied to different parts of the field. This can be done quite easily with the rotating trapezoid for both monocular and binocular observation.

6. Generalize to everyday environments.

Here is a very different experiment which, nevertheless, probably belongs here under the general heading of "perceptual cues" because it is concerned with fixation disparity. The question is, "How would fixation disparity be modified if the linear distance of the target were left constant, but its apparent distance altered through the use of monocular cues?" This involves a theoretical issue of great interest to those people dealing with binocular problems, and is analogous to the work done by Ittelson and Ames on accommodation and convergence and their relation to apparent distance (see Chapter 5).

V. SOCIAL PROCESSES

ONE OF THE MAIN values of this work in visual perception has been the way in which it has increased our understanding of social psychology. The individual acts in terms of the world as he perceives it, and this includes the way he perceives people. There is continuity of both principles and processes from the perception of the simplest pinpoint of light to the perception of the complex social factors weighed and integrated by leaders of men. Basic to an understanding of any of this is an understanding of the perceptual process. Some of our experiments have been quite directly concerned with social aspects, and it is anticipated that a progressively greater proportion of our time will be devoted to that area in the future.

Several examples of social research problems which have developed directly out of our consideration of visual perception are given in this section.

It has been noted in our earlier experimental work that an important variable which must be taken into account in many problems of visual perception is that of inclusiveness; that is, the number of cues which are taken into account by the individual in making a judgment or choice. In extending this to experimental social situations, it would be necessary to design a series of experiments aimed at determining under varying conditions how many purposes and value reactions of other people we can take into account at once as single individuals. A series of studies such as this, properly done, could have important consequences in an understanding of such matters as leadership, effective group size, communion versus argument, sense of frustration in participation in groups, and so forth.

As an example of a particular problem which might be attacked under this heading we shall consider the question "What is the ideal number for a small group in terms of effective action and participation?" Many empirical studies indicate that this number lies somewhere in the order of eight, but, as far as we know, no reason for this is offered. An approach to the reason might be to try to find out what the sequential events are which a person must take into account in order to deal effectively with the other members of the group. Once this is determined, it may turn out that one can only take account of the sequential significances of a limited number of people if one is to deal with them as individuals. With greater numbers it may turn out to be necessary to lump them together and to take account of them as small groups or subgroups. Another aspect to be studied would be the feelings of participation on the part of the individuals, which would certainly be greatest if they were treated as individuals by the other members and less if they were treated as part of a larger group.

It appears from our work in the visual area that each man's perceptions are his own, unique and personal, simply because he is a unique organism and because the past experience which he brings to any occasion is to some degree unique. Common perceptions, therefore, become possible only in so far as common experiences, common strivings are shared among individuals. These conclusions would seem to provide a key to many problems in interpersonal communications and understanding.

Specifically an experiment which could be done with apparatus already available is to have two or more people wearing different aniseikonic glasses, but not knowing this, look at the leaf room and have to arrive at some mutual agreement or solution of a problem. Another possible experimental setup would be the trapezoid with two people viewing from two different directions, and having to agree on some aspect which is different from these two directions. Also it would contribute to our understanding of interpersonal relationships in these two situations if the relationships between the individuals used were systematically varied. For example, one might expect different processes and results for strangers, good friends, people who dislike each other, parents and children, married couples, and so forth. The use of exploratory observations here should point to more systematic follow-up in terms of personality background and interpersonal relations.

Just as a note here we might guess that the important part of the process involved in this series of experiments would simply be the recognition that it is possible to have two different worlds; in other words, the loss of the assumption that the objective world is the same to the other person. Once this is recognized, the problem solution or agreement might be fairly quickly arrived at.

In transactional psychological theory, the concepts of purpose and of value attributes play an important role in the explanation of how and why people act as they do in relation to other people. The most complete exposition of the nature and function of these abstractions is to be found in Cantril's book, *The "Why" of Man's Experience* (1).

A helpful experiment would be to devise a situation with two small groups in which each person in each group would be given a specific task to perform. The tasks for Group A would be arranged in such a way that each person in the group could accomplish his own task only by taking into account the purposes of every other person in the group; thus co-operative behavior will be discovered necessary for a resolution of individual tasks. The Group B setting, on the other hand, would be so arranged that each person could accomplish his own task only by disregarding completely the purposes of others, even though he is still physically in a group situation. Of interest here would be the ways in which the tasks were accomplished, the degree of organization present in each of the groups, the development of hierarchal arrangements and the emergence of leadership, and the value attributes experienced by the individuals in the different situations. An extension of this experiment which would have implications for leadership would be to vary the instructions for people in the A and B groups concerning the ways in which their own purposes can best be accomplished; that is, by taking into account the purposes of others or by ignoring the purposes of others.

It is our impression that the speed with which a person learns to see the distorted room differently while he acts in it is somehow related to the number and intensity of his prejudices. Again, impressionistically, this seems also to hold for the rate of change and the amount of change in the appearance of the leaf room when aniseikonic glasses are worn.

The meaning of this relationship, if it exists, is not entirely clear, but merits investigation.

As a corollary to this it might be worth inquiring as to why some people so resist some of our demonstrations, refusing to see what most observers see, intellectualizing the situation (sometimes correctly, sometimes quite incorrectly), cheating themselves, etc. Perhaps careful examination of the life histories of such individuals, particularly their relationships with other people, is called for.

VI. PSYCHIATRIC PROBLEMS

(a) CONFLICT. The problem of perceptual conflict is a large area of study, some aspects of which are the conditions under which one has conflicts, the type of reaction to conflicts, the state of surety or lack of surety associated with conflicts, and the relation of perceptual conflicts to other types of conflicts such as those encountered in social situations. In addition, the area of conflicting sequential assumptions, although not dealt with at all as yet in an experimental fashion, should be as possible to study as the perceptual area. The general methodology that might be followed in both the perceptual and sequential conflicts is as follows:

First, present a situation to the observer which offers him conflicting indications of two or more cues, and then evaluate his response to the conflict in terms of his resolution of the cues. The kinds of responses or reactions to conflicts in the perceptual area which have already been identified are compromise, suppression, temporal delay, temporal alternation, and combinations of these. The conditions of presentation which were studied include static presentation of static cues; one cue static, the other dynamic; and both cues dynamic. In addition, the role of expectancy plays an important part here. Specific examples from the demonstrations include the balloons, which provide cue conflicts; the leaf room with aniseikonic glasses, which provide primarily expectancy conflicts; and the distorted room, which provides both of these plus sequential conflicts.

The bearings of such studies on psychiatric problems would be diverse. For example, they would undoubtedly aid in understanding the problems of rigidity and anxiety and the extent to which individuals of different clinical and psychiatric symptoms can tolerate different degrees of uncertainty, and how uncertainty is handled. In addition, they might help in understanding the relationship between certain varieties of mental illness and the extent to which the patient will give up certain standards under the stress of uncertainty or conflict. For a more specific illustration it might be suggested that such things as the suppression of vision in one eye or the alteration of threshold acuity under the stress of asymmetrical stimuli might lead to clearer understanding of the mechanism and process of hysterical loss of bodily functions. Also a study of the factors which change such suppression of functions might throw light on therapy.

At a somewhat more complex level of analysis of conflicts, our thinking has led us to the conclusion that every conflict situation, every what-to-do situation, may profitably be considered as having two essential components in varying proportions. The first of these components involves a decision as to the mechanics of carrying out a particular course of action; a how-to-do decision which necessitates inquiry as to means. The second component involves a decision as to the aim of the activity, a what-for decision which necessitates a quite different type of inquiry characterized by self-analysis as to goals or ends. Most of the hitches we meet in daily life are mainly how-to-do but a few are heavy on the what-for side. It is our guess that very often the basic what-for aspects of problems are unresolved and are anxiety-producing, that unresolved what-fors interrupt how-to-do decisions, and that very often people retreat from what-fors into how-to-do's. Three proposals are offered here as examples of what might be done research-wise.

1. The initial step in this experiment would be to devise a series of situations in which what-for hitches may be perceived as how-to-do hitches. Thus it would be possible to compare the hitch-resolving processes when (a) it is perceived as a how-to-do hitch and (b) it is perceived as a what-for hitch. The hypothesis would be that under (a) condition as compared to (b) condition, the process of resolution will be slower, more anxiety-producing, and even when the course of action is decided upon there will be residual anxiety unless the what-for aspect has been recognized and resolved.

2. The same set of what-to-do situations which may be interpreted either as what-fors or how-to-do's could be used in another investigation. The procedure would be to present them to a number of people of known interests, abilities, etc. and determine how each of them perceives the problem, that is, as what-fors or how-to-do's. Decisions as to how they have perceived the problems should be made on the basis of the methods of inquiry chosen by the individuals as means for solving the problems. A comparison of the characteristics of the people who tend to refer such problems to value systems with people who tend to refer them to mechanisms should then follow.

3. It is our feeling that a certain basic level of personal security is a prerequisite for an individual's choosing what-fors as opposed to how-to-do's. From this we may deduce, and test experimentally, that given a

choice of a number of problems to work on, composed about half and half of what-fors and how-to-do's, the subjects will tend to choose what-fors after an experience of success, and how-to-do's after an experience of failure in a prearranged problem situation.

(b) ASSUMPTIONS. In our brief discussion of assumptions in Section II, it was suggested that probably any aspects of object form, distance from the observer, movement, angle from the observer, etc. can be replaced in whole or in part by assumptions without altering the perception. This, it seems to us, suggests a starting point for understanding percepts which are labeled false or abnormal because there is no obvious cause-and-effect relationship between object and percept. All the lines of research, therefore, outlined in Sections II and III of this memorandum should be of value in this respect.

Also, it would be helpful to conduct research into the extent to which normal individuals and clinical patients are willing or unwilling to test out their assumptions. This would help to get at some of the devices used by those who are mentally ill to avoid testing their assumptions. It is even possible that we will be able to work out eventually a method of showing people in concreteness how assumptions may be tested and how the successful testing brings satisfaction and a sense of well-being.

(c) DIAGNOSTIC TEST. The use of our demonstrations with psychiatric patients at the naval medical centers and elsewhere shows that some of them may have potential usefulness as diagnostic tests. Included in this category are the surety demonstrations, the rotating trapezoid, the distorted room, the aniseikonic glasses, and the thereness-thatness table. Preliminary results are not sufficiently definitive to permit any positive statements in this regard, but the research is promising and is being continued.

In addition, we should be able to devise demonstrations and experiments concerning sequential significances for particular use as potential diagnostic tools. In this connection the sequential situations used probably should start with simple inorganic sequences and work up through sequences involving lower organisms, then animals, then persons as objects used, then persons as objects to help, etc. Probably we should include not only the comprehension of sequential events but also action in relation to sequential events. Among other things to look for would be the following:

1. Degree of tolerance of the wrong prehension of sequential significance.
2. What happens when a person is out of phase with other sequential events?
3. What happens if the chain of sequential events, normally in phase with others, is temporarily out of phase, that is, not concurrent?

4. The problem of a person's attaching sequential significances to following events that others do not attach to them.
5. The problem of apprehension; that is, the problem of how to get a comprehension of consequences that would make for more reliable prognosis.
6. Failing to comprehend an immediate event as related to the whole milieu; that is, failure to relate current change of events with preceding events, with the result that the immediate event thus becomes inconsequential.

REFERENCES IN APPENDIX A

1. Cantril, Hadley. *The "Why" of Man's Experience.* New York: The Macmillan Co., 1950.

2. Ittelson, W. H. *The Ames Demonstration's in Perception.* Princeton: Princeton University Press, 1952.

APPENDIX B

BIBLIOGRAPHY

of

Book and Articles Referring to
Research in Human Behavior
From the Transactional Point of View

Fourth Revision—June, 1959

Prepared by Hadley Cantril and Pauline R. Smith

PRIMARY REFERENCES

1. Adlerstein, Arthur M. "The Humascope: A modified stereoscope." *J. Psychol.,* 1958, *45,* 109–113.

2. Allport, Gordon W., and Pettigrew, Thomas F. "Cultural influence on the perception of movement: The trapezoidal illusion among Zulus." *J. Abnorm. Soc. Psychol.,* July, 1957, *55,* No. 1, 104–113.

3. Ames, A. Jr. "Binocular vision as affected by relations between uniocular stimulus patterns in commonplace environments." *Amer. J. Psychol.,* 1946, *59,* 333–57.

4. Ames, A. Jr. "Transaction of living." Chart I: *Analysis of sub-phenomena involved in and involving perception, 1949.*
The chart with brief accompanying textual material was designed to help in gaining a grasp of the interrelation of the phenomena experienced in the perception demonstrations.

5. Ames, A. Jr. "Sensations, their nature and origin." *trans/formation, 1950, 1,* 11–12.

6. Ames, A. Jr. "Visual perception and the rotating trapezoidal window." *Psychological Monographs,* September, 1951, *65,* (7), Whole No. 324.
A description of the apparatus and detailed theoretical analysis of phenomena observed.

7. Ames, A. Jr. "Reconsideration of the origin and nature of perception," in *Vision and Action* (Ratner, S., ed.). New Brunswick, N. J.: Rutgers Univ. Press, 1953, pp. 251 ff.

8. Ames, A. Jr. *An Interpretative Manual.* Princeton: Princeton University Press, 1955. $1.00.
The nature of our perceptions, prehensions and behavior. For the Demonstrations in Perception. May be ordered.

9. Bagby, James. "A cross cultural study of perceptual predominance in binocular rivalry." *J. Abnorm. Soc. Psychol.,* May, 1957, *54,* No. 3, 331–34.

10. Buchanan, William, and Cantril, Hadley. *How Nations See Each Other.* Urbana: University of Illinois Press, 1953. Chapter 9.

11. Cantril, Hadley. *Understanding Man's Social Behavior. Preliminary Notes.* Princeton: Office of Public Opinion Research, 1947.
Discussion of perception, social perception, action, expectancies, etc. and their interdependence.

12. Cantril, Hadley. "The nature of social perception." *Trans. N. Y. Acad. Sci.,* 1948, *10,* 142–53.

13. Cantril, Hadley. "Toward a scientific morality." *J. Psychol.* 1949, *27,* 363–76.

14. Cantril, H.; Ames, A. Jr.; Hastorf, A. H.; and Ittelson, W. H. "Psychology and scientific research." *Science,* 1949, *110,* 461–64, 491–97, 517–22.
Considers the nature of scientific inquiry and points out the distinction between scientific inquiry and scientific method. Specific implications are derived for psychology from an orientation described as "transactional."

15. Cantril, Hadley. "An inquiry concerning the characteristics of man." *J. Abnorm. Soc. Psychol.,* 1950, *45,* 490–503.

16. Cantril, Hadley. *The "Why" of Man's Experience.* New York: Macmillan, 1950.
Outline of a systematic psychology including the implications of the Institute's perceptual demonstrations especially in the area of social psychology.

17. Cantril, Hadley, and Ames, A. Jr. *Further Notes toward an Understanding of Human Behavior: Values, Choice and Action.* (Interoffice memo.) Lithoprinted, 1951.

18. Cantril, Hadley. "The Qualities of Being Human." *Amer. Quart.* Spring, 1954, *6,* No. 1, 3–18.

19. Cantril, Hadley, and Hastorf, Albert H. "They saw a game: A case study." *J. Abnorm. Soc. Psychol.,* 1954, *29,* 129–34.

20. Cantril, Hadley. "Toward a humanistic psychology." *ETC: A Review of General Semantics,* 1955, *12,* No. 4, 278–98.

21. Cantril, Hadley. "Ethical relativity from the transactional point of view." *J. Phil.* November, 1955, *52,* No. 23, 677–87.

22. Cantril, Hadley. "Concerning the nature of inquiry." *Sociologica* (Frankfurter Beiträge zur Soziologie) Frankfurt am Main, Europäische Verlagsantalt, 1955, pp. 293–304.

23. Cantril, Hadley. "The nature of faith." *J. Indiv. Psychol.,* May, 1957, *13,* No. 1, 24–37.

24. Cantril, Hadley. "Perception and interpersonal relations." *Amer. J. Psychiat.,* August, 1957, *114,* No. 2, 119–26.

25. Cantril, Hadley. "The nature of our reality worlds." *Indian J. Psychol.,* 1957, *32,* Parts I and II, 51–63.

26. Cantril, Hadley. "Effective democratic leadership: A psychological interpretation." *J. Indiv. Psychol.,* November, 1958, *14,* 128–38.

27. Cantril, Hadley. *The Politics of Despair.* New York: Basic Books, Inc., 1958.

28. Engel, Edward. *Meaningful Content in the Study of Rivalry and Fusion—Preliminary Observations.* Progress memorandum, March, 1955. (Mimeographed.)

29. Engel, Edward. "The role of content in binocular resolution." *Amer. J. Psychol.,* March, 1956, *69,* No. 1, 87–91.

30. Engel, Edward. "Binocular fusion of dissimilar figures." *J. Psychol.,* 1958, *46,* 53–57.

31. Hastorf, A. H., and Knutson, A. L. "Motivation, perception and attitude change." *Psychol. Rev.,* 1949, *56,* 88–94.

32. Hastorf, A. H. "The influence of suggestion on the relationship between stimulus size and perceived distance." *J. Psychol.,* 1950, *29,* 195–217.

33. Hastorf, A. H., and Way, K. S. "Apparent size with and without distance cues." *J. Gen. Psychol.,* 1952, *47,* 181–88.

34. Hunt, David E., and Schroder, Harold M. "Failure-avoidance in situational interpretation and problem solving." *Psychological Monographs,* 1957, *71,* No. 3, Whole No. 432.

35. Ittelson, W. H., and Ames, A. Jr. "Accommodation, convergence, and their relation to apparent distance." *J. Psychol.,* 1950, *30,* 43–62.

36. Ittelson, W. H., and Ames, A. Jr. "Accommodation, convergence, and their relation to apparent distance." *Optical Developments,* 1950, *20,* No. 8; slightly abridged reprint of No. 35.

37. Ittelson, W. H. "Size as a cue to distance: static localization." *Amer. J. Psychol.,* January, 1951, *64,* 54–67.

38. Ittelson, W. H. "Size as a cue to distance: radial motion." *Amer. J. Psychol.,* April, 1951, *64,* 188–202.

39. Ittelson, W. H. "The constancies in perceptual theory." *Psychol. Rev.,* 1951, *58,* 285–94.

40. Ittelson, W. H., and Kilpatrick, F. P. "Experiments in perception." *Scientific American,* 1951, *185,* 50–55. Contained in *Scientific American Reader,* New York: Simon and Schuster, 1953, pp. 576–96.

41. Ittelson, W. H. "The effect of viewing objects at illusory distances: A reply to Pollack." *Amer. J. Psychol.,* 1952, *65,* 294–97.

42. Ittelson, W. H. *The Ames Demonstrations in Perception.* Princeton: Princeton Univ. Press, 1952. Out of print.
This volume contains for each of the Ames demonstrations a brief introductory note, photograph, description of the equipment and its operation, outline of typical phenomena observed, illustrated where possible, and a reduced-size construction drawing.

43. Ittelson, W. H. "A note on 'Familiar Size and the Perception of Depth.' " *J. Psychol.,* 1953, *35,* 235–40.

44. Ittelson, W. H., and Cantril, Hadley. *Perception.* Doubleday Papers in Psychology (Hartley, Eugene L., ed.). May, 1954. College Department of Doubleday & Co., 575 Madison Ave., New York, N. Y. 85¢.

45. Ittelson, W. H., and Slack, C. W. "The perception of persons as visual objects," in *Person Perception and Interpersonal Behavior.* (R. Taguiri and L. Petrullo, eds.) Stanford: Stanford Univ. Press, 1958. Chapter 14.

46. Kallen, Horace M. *Human Beings and Psychological Systems.* Remarks at dedication of the Perception Demonstration Center, Princeton University, March 6, 1954. Foreword by Hadley Cantril.

47. Kilpatrick, F. P. *Some Aspects of the Role of Assumptions in Perception.* Ph.D. Thesis, Princeton University, 1950.
Three experiments using the "rotating trapezoidal window" and a theoretical discussion stemming from these experiments and other Institute demonstrations.

48. Kilpatrick, F. P., and Ittelson, W. H. "Three demonstrations involving the visual perception of movement." *J Exper. Psychol.,* 1951, *42,* 394–402.

49. Kilpatrick, F. P. (ed.). *Human Behavior from the Transactional Point of View.* Hanover, N. H.: Institute for Associated Research, 1952. Out of print.

50. Kilpatrick, F. P. *Motivation, Perception and Action.* 1953. Mimeographed.

51. Kilpatrick, F. P. (ed.) (contributors: Hadley Cantril, W. H. Ittelson, F. P. Kilpatrick). *Some Suggestions for Experimentation Stemming from a Transactional Point of View.* 1953. Mimeographed.

52. Kilpatrick, F. P. "The Ames oscillatory effect: A reply to Pastore." *Psychol. Rev.,* 1953, *60,* 76–79.

53. Kilpatrick, F. P., and Ittelson, W. H. "The size-distance invariance hypothesis." *Psychol. Rev.* 1953, *60,* 223–31.

54. Kilpatrick, F. P. "Two processes in perceptual learning." *J. Exper. Psychol.,* May, 1954, *47,* No. 5, 362–70.

55. Kilpatrick, F. P. "Recent experiments in perception." *Trans. N. Y. Acad. Sci.,* June, 1954, Ser. II, *16,* No. 8, 420–25.

56. Kilpatrick, F. P. "Perception theory and general semantics." *ETC: A Review of General Semantics,* 1955, *12,* No. 4, 257–64.

57. Kilpatrick, F. P. "Problems of Perception in Extreme Situations." *Human Organization,* 1955, *16,* No. 2, 20–22.

58. Pettigrew, Thomas F.; Allport, Gordon W.; and Barnett, Eric O. "Binocular resolution and perception of race in South Africa." *Brit. J. Psychol.,* November, 1958, *49,* Part IV, 265–78.

59. Slack, Charles W. "Learning in simple one dimensional tracking." *Amer. J. Psychol.,* 1953, *66,* 33–44.

60. Slack, Charles W. "Some characteristics of the range effect." *J. Exper. Psychol.,* 1953, *46,* 76–80.

61. Slack, Charles W. "Familiar size as a cue to size in the presence of conflicting cues." *J. Exper. Psychol.,* September, 1956, *52,* No. 3.

62. Slack, Charles W. "Critique on the interpretation of cultural differences in the Ames trapezoid." 1959. (To be published in *Amer. J. Psychol.)*

63. Smith, George Horsley. "Size-distance judgments of human faces (projected images)." *J. Gen. Psychol.,* 1953, *49,* 45–64.

64. Smith, George Horsley. "Size-distance settings as indicative of personal adjustment." *J. Soc. Psychol.,* 1954, *40,* 165–72.

65. Smith, William M. *Past Experience and Perception: a study of the influence of past experience on apparent size and distance.* Ph.D. Thesis, Princeton University, 1950.

66. Toch, Hans H., and Hastorf, Albert H. "Homeostasis in psychology." *Psychiatry: Journal for the Study of Interpersonal Processes,* February, 1955, *18,* No. 1, 81–91.

67. Toch, Hans H. "How are data interpreted? A transactional view." *ETC: A Review of General Semantics,* 1955, *12,* No. 4, 309–14.

68. Toch, Hans H. "The perceptual elaboration of stroboscopic presentations." *Amer. J. Psychol.,* September, 1956, *69,* No. 3, 345–58.

69. Toch, Hans H., and Ittelson, W. H. "The role of past experience in apparent movement: A revaluation." *Brit. J. Psychol.,* August, 1956, *67,* Part III, 195–207.

70. Toch, Hans H., and Cantril, Hadley. "A preliminary inquiry into the learning of values." *J. Educ. Psychol.,* March, 1957, *48,* No. 3, 145–56.

71. Toch, Hans H. "The psychology of heresy." *ETC: A Review of General Semantics,* Fall, 1957, *15,* No. 1, 9–20.

72. Toch, Hans H. "The perception of future events: Case studies in social prediction." *Public Opinion Quart.*, Spring, 1958, *22*, No. 1.

73. Wittreich, Warren J. "The Honi phenomenon: A case of selective perceptual distortion." *J. Abnorm. Soc. Psychol.*, 1952, *47*, 705–12.

74. Wittreich, Warren J. *Aniseikonia and Distortion of the Self Image*. Progress memorandum mimeographed, 1953.

75. Wittreich, Warren J. "The influence of simulated mutilation upon the perception of the human figure." *J. Abnorm. Soc. Psychol.*, 1955, *51*, 493–95.

76. Wittreich, Warren J., and Grace, Marea. *Body Image Development*. Progress memorandum mimeographed, 1955.

77. Wittreich, Warren J., and Radcliffe, Keith B. Jr. "Differences in the perception of an authority figure and a non-authority figure by navy recruits." *J. Abnorm. Soc. Psychol.*, November, 1956, *53*, No. 3.

78. Wittreich, Warren J. "Visual perception and personality." *Scientific American*, April, 1959, *200*, No. 4, 56–60.

OTHER REFERENCES ARRANGED
ACCORDING TO AREAS OF INTEREST

Art and Architecture

79. Ames, A. Jr. "Statement about paintings of Alexander James." *Hanover Gazette*, July 19, 1951. (Comments on art stemming from Institute Research.)

80. Creighton, Thomas H. (ed.). *Building for Modern Man*. Princeton: Princeton Univ. Press, 1949. (Contains chapter on "architextural form and visual sensations" by A. Ames, Jr., pp. 82–91.)

81. Gropius, Walter. Design Topics. *Magazine of Art*, 1947, *40*, 299–304.

82. "Notes on the Ames demonstrations: Art and perception." *trans/formation*, 1950, *1*, 8–10. (Sigfried Giedion discusses "chair" demonstration; Alfred Barr, Jr., discusses the broad implications of Institute demonstrations.)

83. Newton, Norman T. *An Approach to Design*. Cambridge: Addison-Wesley Press, 1951.

84. "Progress Report: Form still follows function." *Progressive Architecture*, 1947, p. 20. (Contains a tentative summation of architectural implications of the Institute visual experiments.)

85. Sherman, Hoyt L. *The Visual Demonstration Center at the Ohio State University: A manual of operation with an emphasis on the arts*. Columbus, Ohio: University Book Store.

Education

86. Bode, Boyd H., and Morse, William C. Manual to accompany *Education for What Is Real* (by Earl C. Kelley). Minneapolis: Professional Books, Inc., 1948. (Analysis of main values of Kelley's book.)

87. Bristow, William. "Curriculum: Foundations (Chapter 1)." *Rev. Educ. Res.*, 1948, *18*, 221–230.

88. Gordon, Leonard V. *Instructor's Manual for the Visual Demonstration Center.* Columbus: Bureau of Educational Research, Ohio State University, 1950.

89. Kelley, Earl C. *Education for What Is Real.* New York: Harper, 1947. (Theory of education based in part on formulations stemming from the Institute demonstrations.)

90. Mooney, Ross L. *Teacher's Manual on the Distorted Room Demonstration.* Columbus: Bureau of Educational Research, Ohio State University, 1950.

91. Mooney, Ross L. *Student's Manual on the Distorted Room Demonstration.* Columbus: Bureau of Educational Research, Ohio State University, 1950.

92. Mooney, Ross L. "Problems in the development of research men." *Educ. Res. Bull.*, 1951, *30*, No. 6, 141–50.

93. Mooney, Ross L. *Lecture-Demonstrations on Perception as a Transaction.* Columbus: Bureau of Educational Research, Ohio State University, 1951.

94. Mooney, Ross L. *Perception, Language, and the Part-Whole Problem.* Columbus: Bureau of Educational Research, Ohio State University, 1951.

95. Price, Mary Alice. *Teaching Mental Hygiene with Visual Demonstrations.* Columbus: Bureau of Educational Research, Ohio State University, 1950.

96. Price, Mary Alice. *Notes on the Presentation of the Demonstrations to Groups of Widely Different Interests and Backgrounds.* Columbus: Bureau of Educational Research, Ohio State University, 1950.

Mathematics

97. Luneburg, R. K. *Mathematical Analysis of Binocular Vision.* Princeton: Princeton Univ. Press, 1947.

98. Luneburg, R. K. Chapter entitled "Metric methods of binocular visual perception" in *Courant Anniversary Volume.* New York University, 1948.

99. Luneburg, R. K. "The metric of binocular space." *J. Opt. Soc. Amer.*, 1950, *40*, 627–42.

100. Stein, Anna. "A certain class of binocularly equivalent configurations." *J. Opt. Soc. Amer.*, 1947, *37*, 944–62. (A mathematical

study of a series of binocular visual phenomena experienced in certain of the Institute demonstrations.)

Philosophy

101. Bentley, Arthur F. "Kennetic inquiry." *Science,* 1950, *112,* 775–83.
102. Cantril, Hadley. "Ethical relativity from the transactional point of view." *J. Phil.,* 1955, *52,* No. 23, 677–87.
103. Freeman, Eugene. "Veridical perception." *Amer. J. Optom. and Arch. Amer. Acad. Optom.,* 1951, *28,* 213–20.
104. Fries, Horace S. "Perception and value inquiry." *Amer. J. Econ. and Soc.,* 1951, *2,* 19–32.
105. Fries, Horace S. "Five suggestions for research and action." *transformation,* 1951, *1,* No. 2, 107–09.
106. Fries, Horace S. "To sail beyond the sunset." *Educ. Theory,* 1951, *1,* 23–24. (Some research and practical uses of the Institute demonstrations.)
107. Hildum, Donald C. *Thoughts on Transactional Psychology and Its Relation to Language.* Mimeographed, 1953.
108. Hildum, Donald C. *Preliminary Investigation of Some Relations between Language and Personality.* Mimeographed, 1953.

General

109. Allport, F. H. *Theories of Perception and the Concept of Structure.* New York: Wiley, 1955. Chapter 11.
110. Barnett, Lincoln. "Discoveries of the illusion lab." *Think,* May, 1959, *25,* No. 5, 2–6.
111. Cantril, Hadley. *Final Report, Navy Contract Nonr 496(01).* Hanover, N. H.: Institute for Associated Research, July, 1954.
112. Dempewolff, R. F. "You think you're going crazy." *Popular Mechanics,* April, 1950, *88–93,* 266.
113. Editorial. "A plastic and fluid world." *Christian Science Monitor,* Oct. 17, 1949.
114. Hilgard, Ernest R. "The role of learning in perception." Chapter 4, pp. 95–120, in the symposium *Perception, an Approach to Personality,* by Robert R. Blake and Glenn V. Ramsey. New York: Ronald Press Co., 1951.
115. Ittelson, W. H. "The involuntary bet." *Vogue,* March 15, 1952, p. 76.
116. Kaempffert, W. "Seeing is really far from believing." *New York Times,* Sunday, Dec. 4, 1949, p. E 13.
117. Kilpatrick, F. P. *Recent Transactional Perceptual Research, a Summary.* Final Report, Navy Contract N6onr 27014. Mimeographed, Princeton: May, 1955.

118. Laurence, William L. "Unique topsy-turvy laboratory may give key to human behavior." *New York Times*, Sept. 26, 1949, p. 27.

119. Lawrence, Merle. *Studies in Human Behavior*. Princeton: Princeton Univ. Press, 1949. Illustrated.

120. U.S. Department of State, Office of International Information Magazine, *Amerika*, October, 1949, No. 35, pp. 40–47. "Perception" (Russian text).

121. "Vision-perception." *Ohio State University Monthly*, April 15, 1950, Vol. 41, pp. 3–6.

122. "Your eyes do deceive you." *Life*, Jan. 16, 1950, pp. 57–62.

123. Motion Picture: *Demonstrations in Perception*, produced by U.S. Naval Photographic Center, Department of Navy. A 25-min. 16-mm. film with sound track and silent interludes for instructor discussion. Permits presentation of phenomena of six of the perception demonstrations.

To borrow film, write:
> Audio-Visual Training Section
> Bureau of Medicine and Surgery
> U.S. Navy Department
> Washington, D.C.

124. *Motion Picture:* A 20-min. film in color, with narrative, showing some of the perception demonstrations.

For detailed information, write to:
> Alfred Butterfield, Executive Producer
> Horizons of Science
> 5 East 57th Street
> New York 22, N. Y.

INDEX